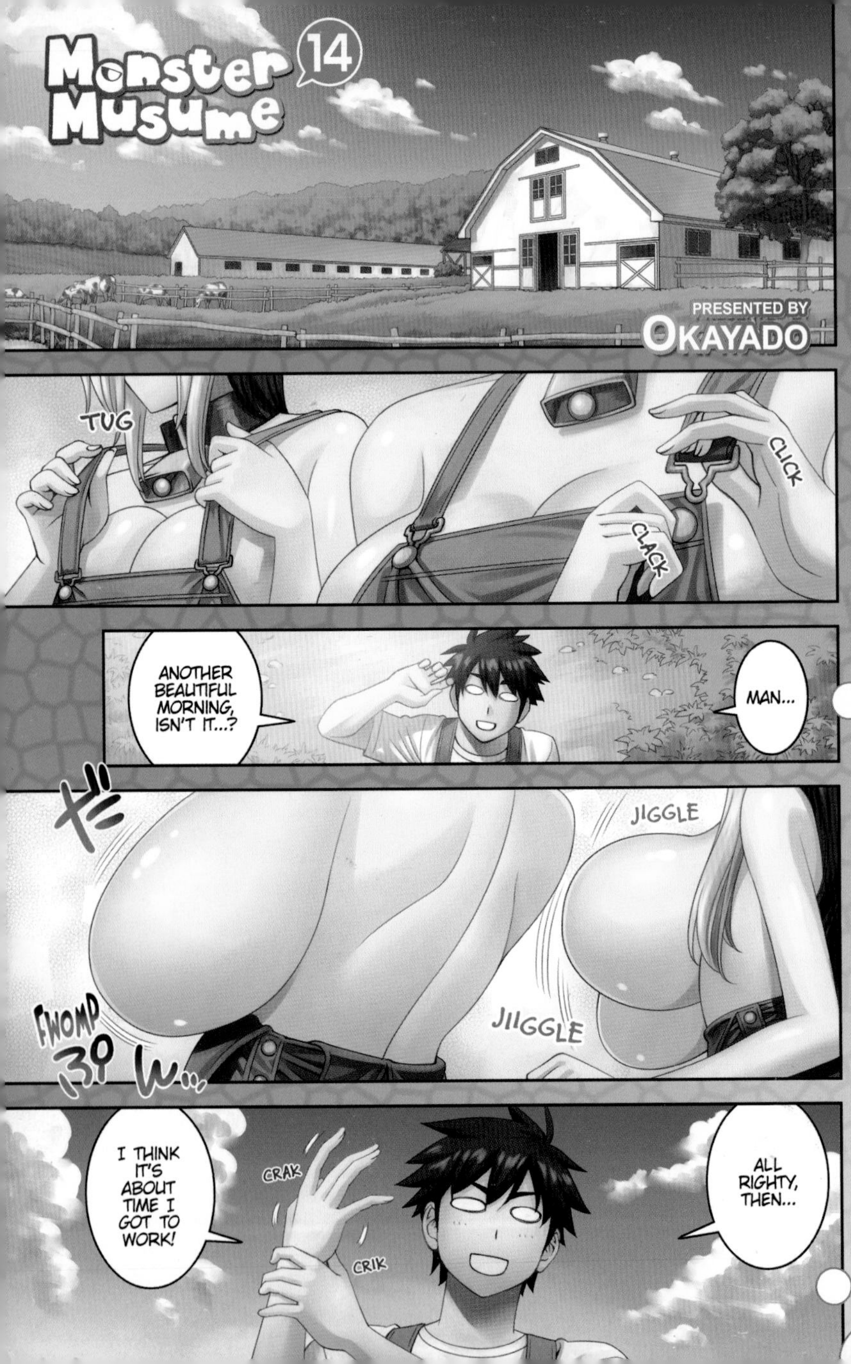

Monster Musume 14
PRESENTED BY
OKAYADO
CLICK
CLACK
TUG
MAN...
ANOTHER BEAUTIFUL MORNING, ISN'T IT...?
JIGGLE
JIIGGLE
FWOMP
ALL RIGHTY, THEN...
CRAK
CRIK
I THINK IT'S ABOUT TIME I GOT TO WORK!

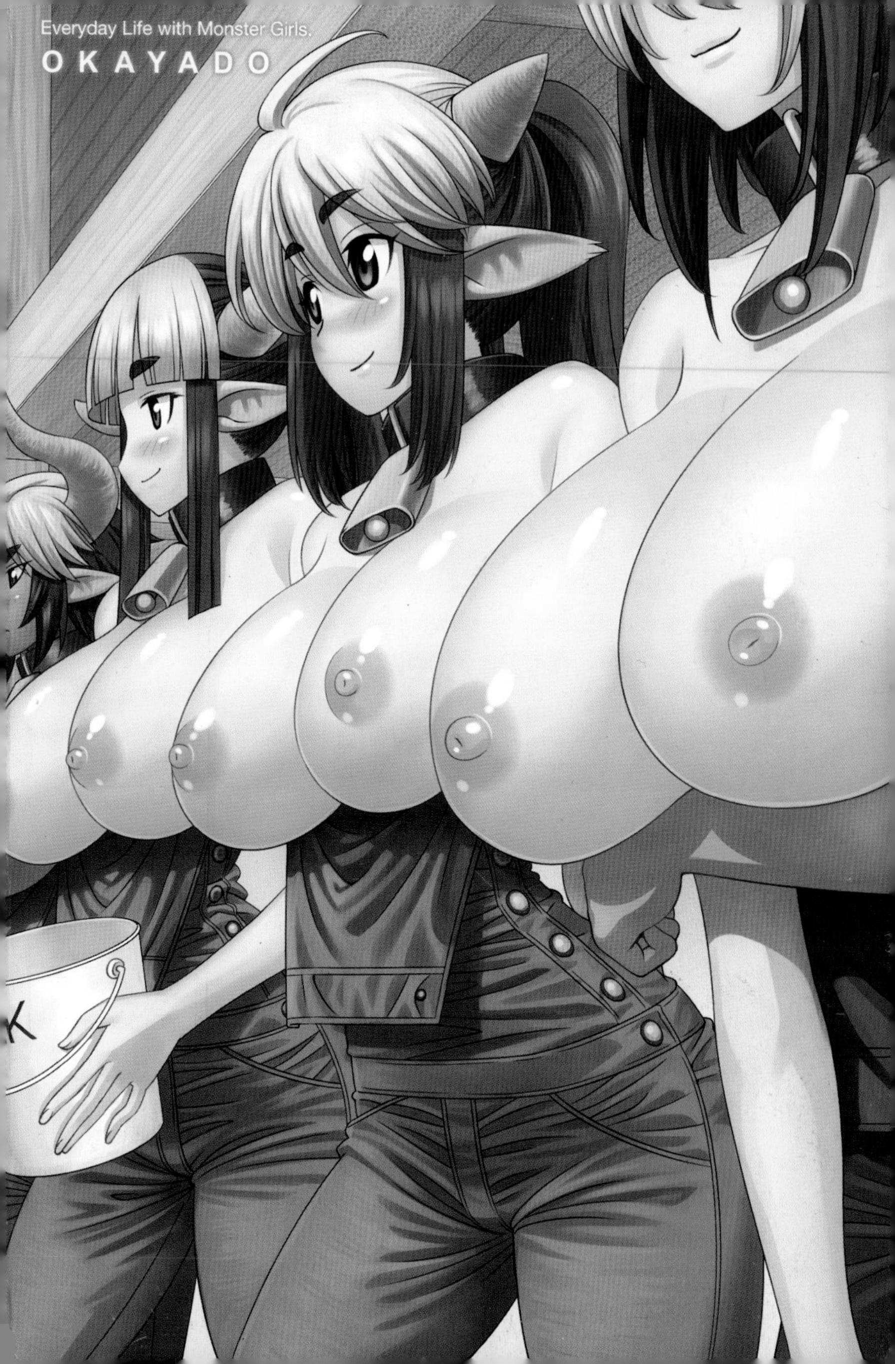
Everyday Life with Monster Girls.
O K A Y A D O

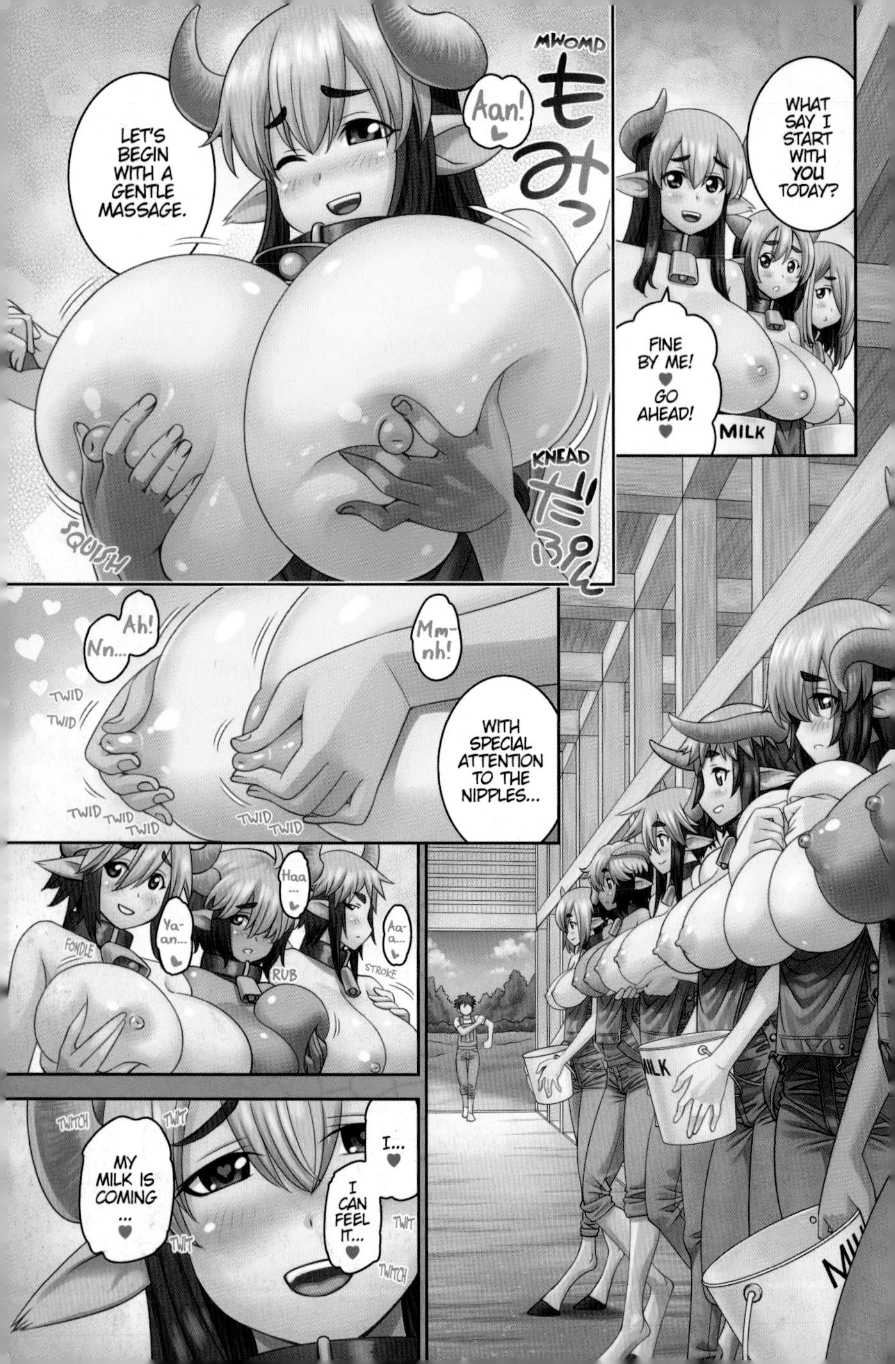
WHAT SAY I START WITH YOU TODAY?
FINE BY ME! ♥ GO AHEAD! ♥
MILK
MWOMP
もみっ
Aan! ♥
LET'S BEGIN WITH A GENTLE MASSAGE.
KNEAD
だぷん
SQUISH
MILK
MILK
Mm-nh!
Ah! Nn...
WITH SPECIAL ATTENTION TO THE NIPPLES...
TWID TWID
TWID TWID TWID
TWID TWID
Aa-a... ♥
Haa... ♥
Ya-an... ♥
STROKE
RUB
FONDLE
I... ♥
I CAN FEEL IT... ♥
MY MILK IS COMING ... ♥
TWITCH TWIT
TWIT TWIT TWITCH

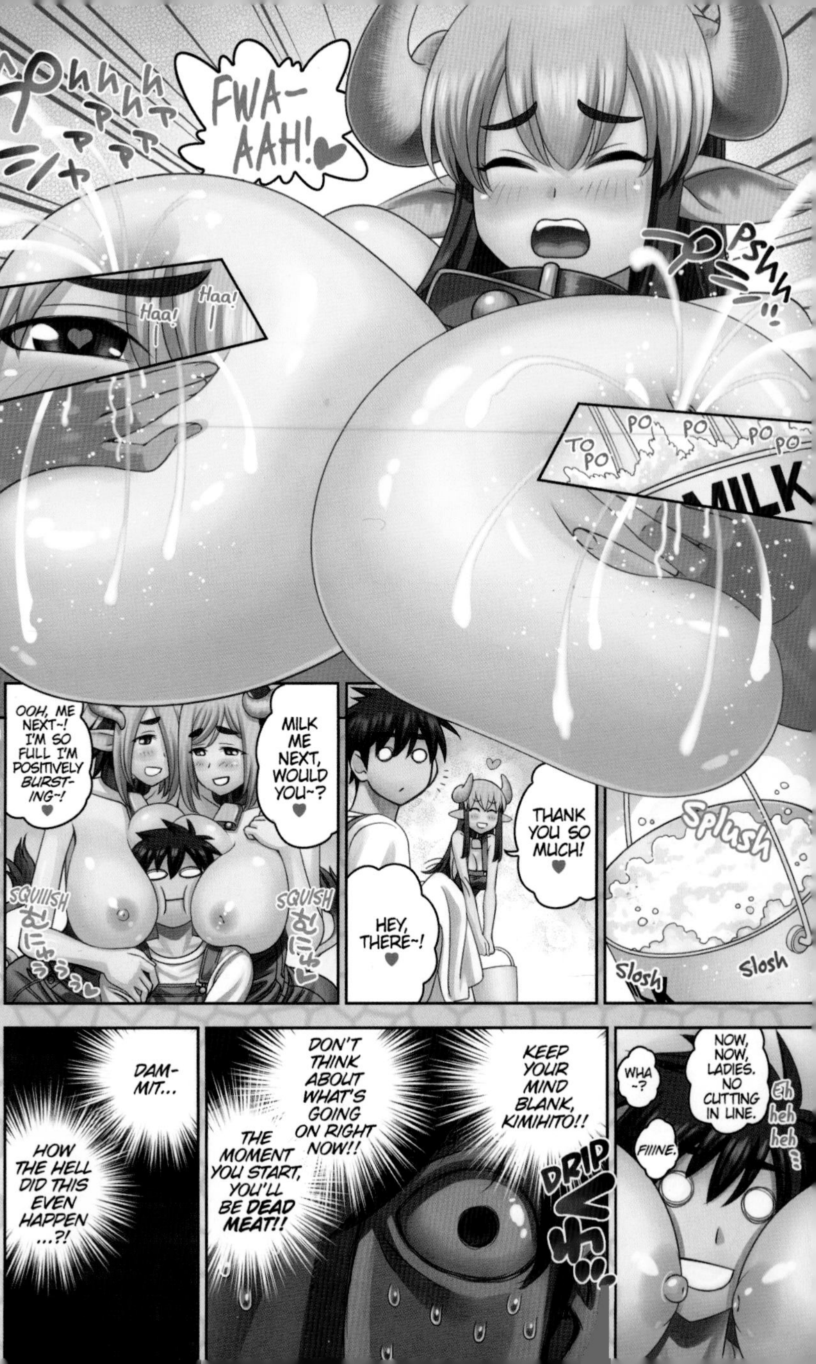
FWA-AAH!♥
Pshhhhhh
Pshhh
Haa! Haa! Haa! Haa!
TOPO PO PO PO PO
MILK
Splush
Slosh
Slosh
THANK YOU SO MUCH! ♥
HEY, THERE~! ♥
MILK ME NEXT, WOULD YOU~? ♥
OOH, ME NEXT~! I'M SO FULL I'M POSITIVELY BURST-ING~! ♥
SQUISH
SQUIISH
NOW, NOW, LADIES. NO CUTTING IN LINE.
WHA ~?
Eh heh heh...
FIIINE.
KEEP YOUR MIND BLANK, KIMIHITO!!
DON'T THINK ABOUT WHAT'S GOING ON RIGHT NOW!!
THE MOMENT YOU START, YOU'LL BE DEAD MEAT!!
DRIP
DAM-MIT...
HOW THE HELL DID THIS EVEN HAPPEN ...?!

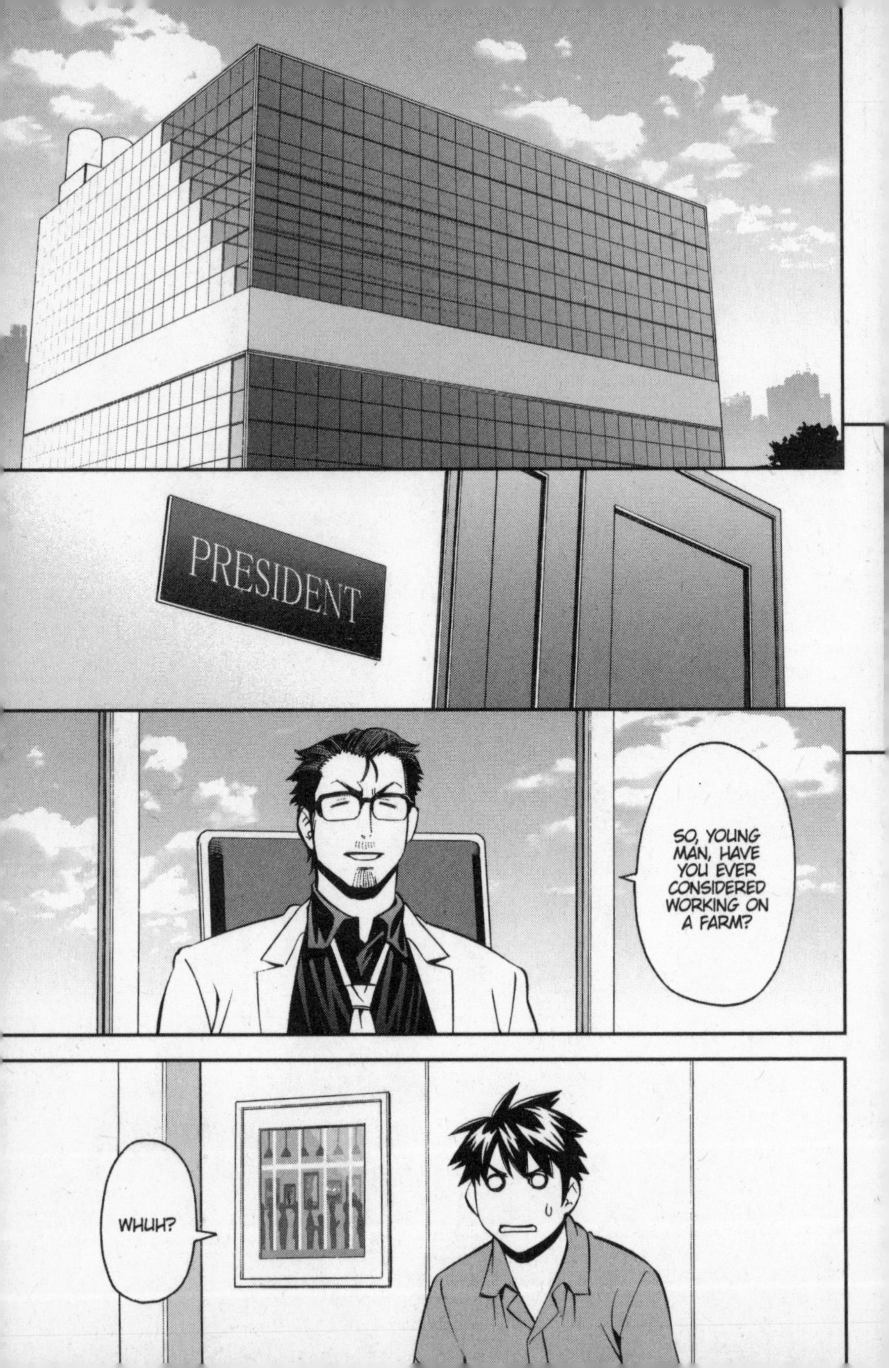
PRESIDENT
SO, YOUNG MAN, HAVE YOU EVER CONSIDERED WORKING ON A FARM?
WHUH?

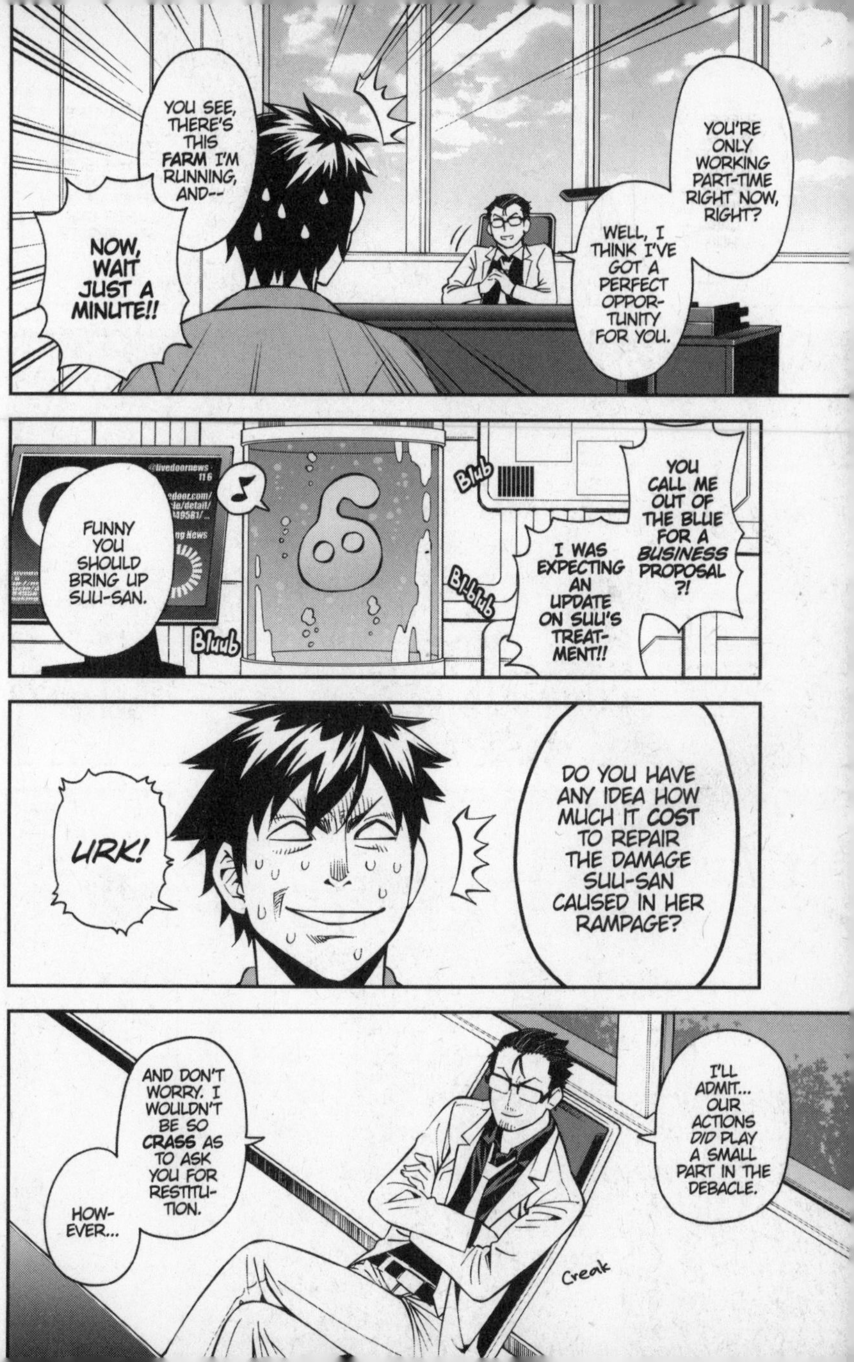
YOU'RE ONLY WORKING PART-TIME RIGHT NOW, RIGHT?
WELL, I THINK I'VE GOT A PERFECT OPPOR-TUNITY FOR YOU.
YOU SEE, THERE'S THIS FARM I'M RUNNING, AND--
NOW, WAIT JUST A MINUTE!!
YOU CALL ME OUT OF THE BLUE FOR A BUSINESS PROPOSAL?!
I WAS EXPECTING AN UPDATE ON SUU'S TREAT-MENT!!
Blub
Bl-blub
FUNNY YOU SHOULD BRING UP SUU-SAN.
Bluub
DO YOU HAVE ANY IDEA HOW MUCH IT COST TO REPAIR THE DAMAGE SUU-SAN CAUSED IN HER RAMPAGE?
URK!
I'LL ADMIT... OUR ACTIONS DID PLAY A SMALL PART IN THE DEBACLE.
AND DON'T WORRY. I WOULDN'T BE SO CRASS AS TO ASK YOU FOR RESTITU-TION.
HOW-EVER...
Creak

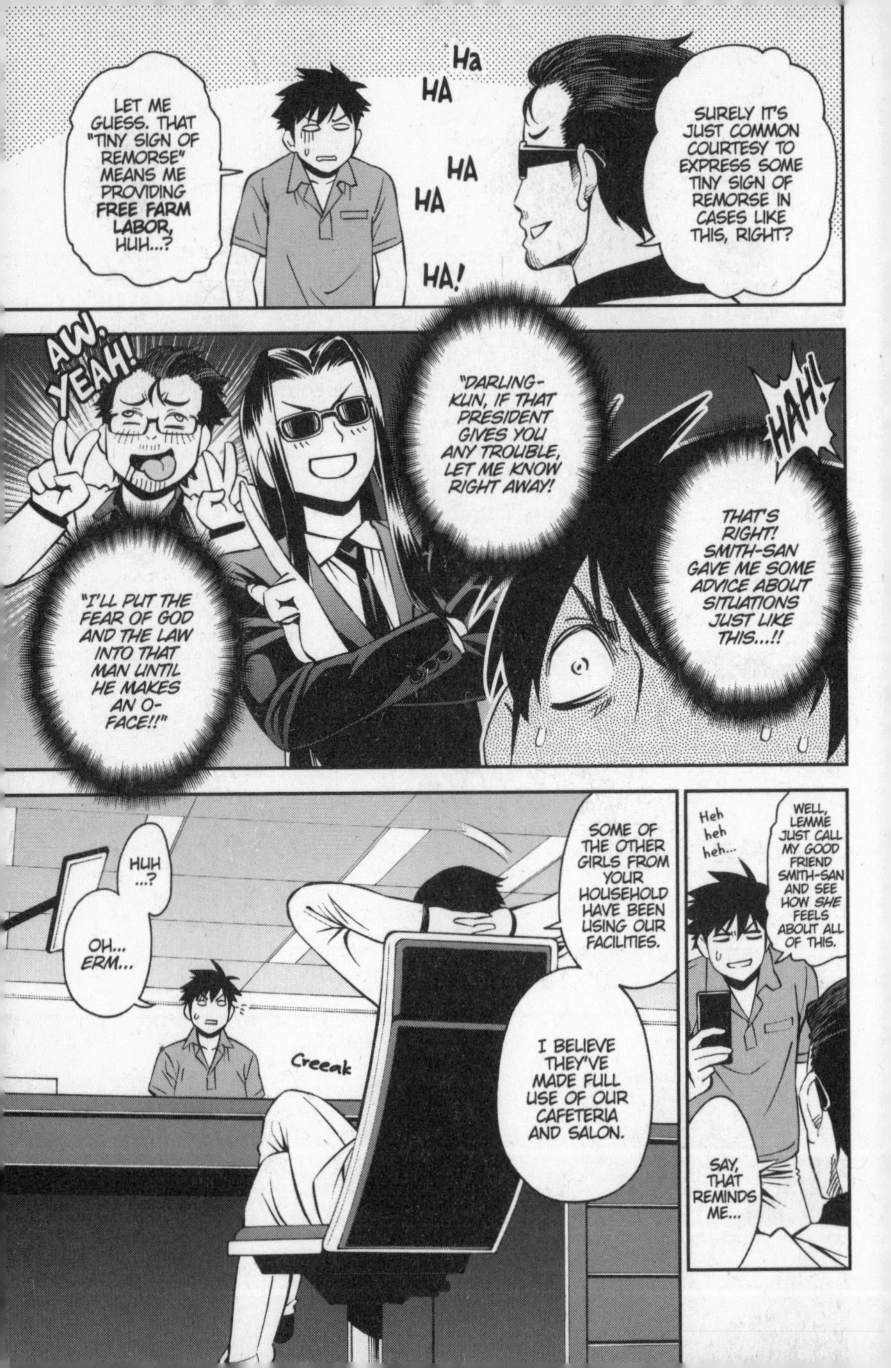
SURELY IT'S JUST COMMON COURTESY TO EXPRESS SOME TINY SIGN OF REMORSE IN CASES LIKE THIS, RIGHT?
Ha HA HA HA HA!
LET ME GUESS. THAT "TINY SIGN OF REMORSE" MEANS ME PROVIDING FREE FARM LABOR, HUH...?
HAH!
THAT'S RIGHT! SMITH-SAN GAVE ME SOME ADVICE ABOUT SITUATIONS JUST LIKE THIS...!!
"DARLING-KUN, IF THAT PRESIDENT GIVES YOU ANY TROUBLE, LET ME KNOW RIGHT AWAY!
AW, YEAH!
"I'LL PUT THE FEAR OF GOD AND THE LAW INTO THAT MAN UNTIL HE MAKES AN O-FACE!!"
WELL, LEMME JUST CALL MY GOOD FRIEND SMITH-SAN AND SEE HOW SHE FEELS ABOUT ALL OF THIS.
Heh heh heh...
SAY, THAT REMINDS ME...
SOME OF THE OTHER GIRLS FROM YOUR HOUSEHOLD HAVE BEEN USING OUR FACILITIES.
HUH ...?
OH... ERM...
I BELIEVE THEY'VE MADE FULL USE OF OUR CAFETERIA AND SALON.
Creeak

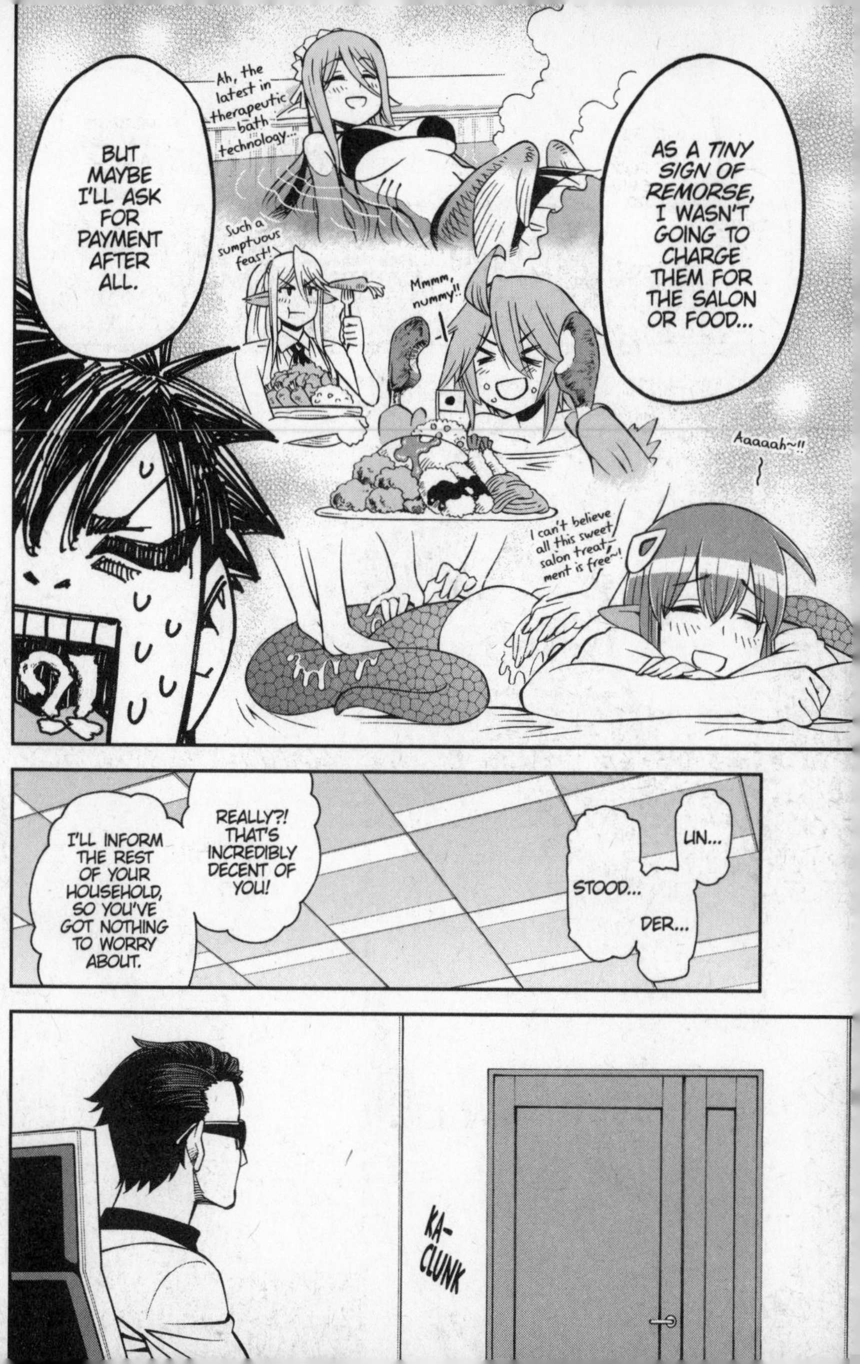
AS A TINY SIGN OF REMORSE, I WASN'T GOING TO CHARGE THEM FOR THE SALON OR FOOD...
Ah, the latest in therapeutic bath technology...
Mmmm, nummy!!
Such a sumptuous feast!
Aaaaah~!!
I can't believe all this sweet salon treatment is free~!
BUT MAYBE I'LL ASK FOR PAYMENT AFTER ALL.
UN...
STOOD...
DER...
REALLY?! THAT'S INCREDIBLY DECENT OF YOU!
I'LL INFORM THE REST OF YOUR HOUSEHOLD, SO YOU'VE GOT NOTHING TO WORRY ABOUT.
KA-CLUNK

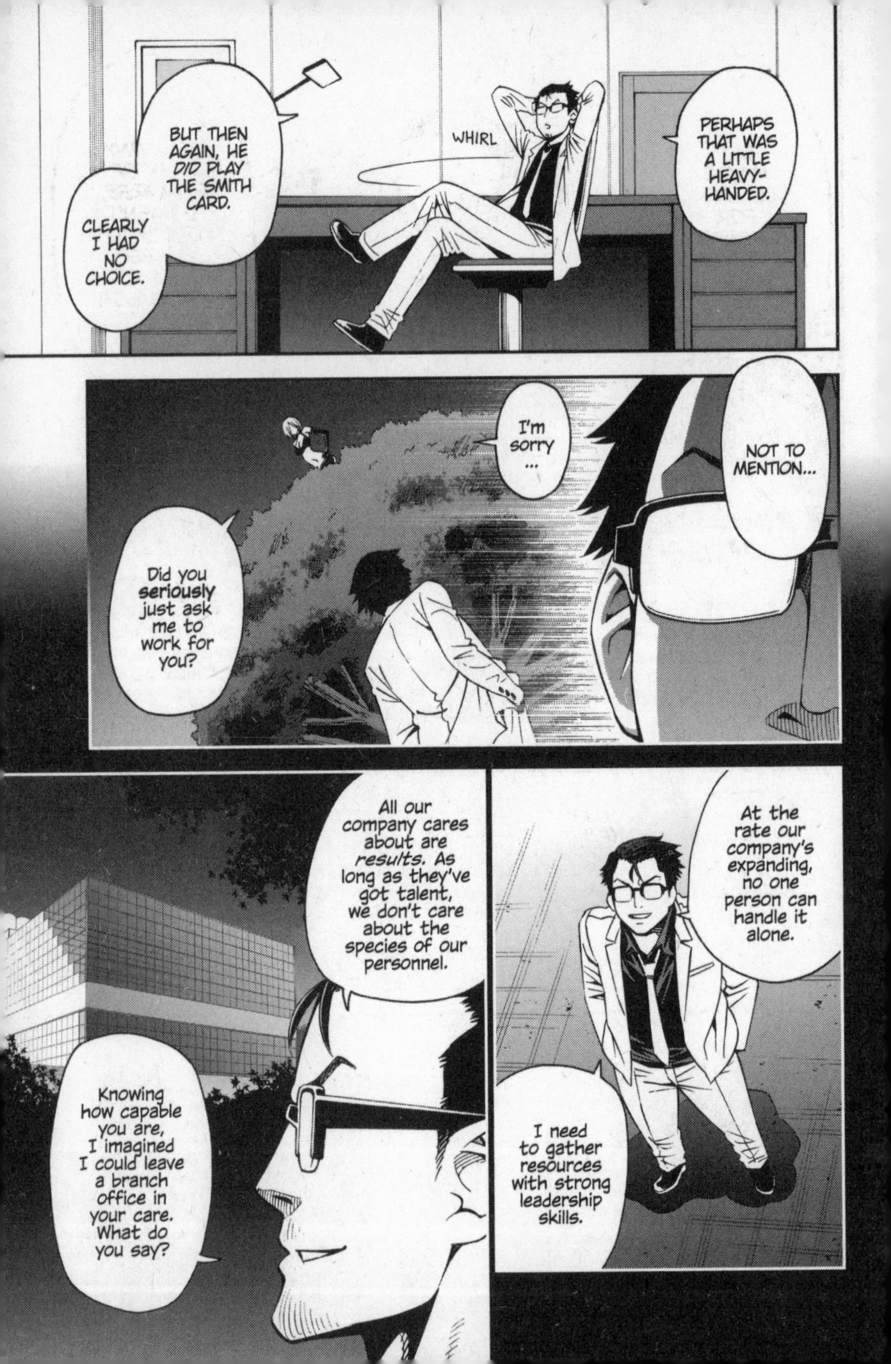
PERHAPS THAT WAS A LITTLE HEAVY-HANDED.
WHIRL
BUT THEN AGAIN, HE *DID* PLAY THE SMITH CARD.
CLEARLY I HAD NO CHOICE.
NOT TO MENTION...
I'm sorry ...
Did you **seriously** just ask me to work for you?
At the rate our company's expanding, no one person can handle it alone.
I need to gather resources with strong leadership skills.
All our company cares about are *results.* As long as they've got talent, we don't care about the species of our personnel.
Knowing how capable you are, I imagined I could leave a branch office in your care. What do you say?

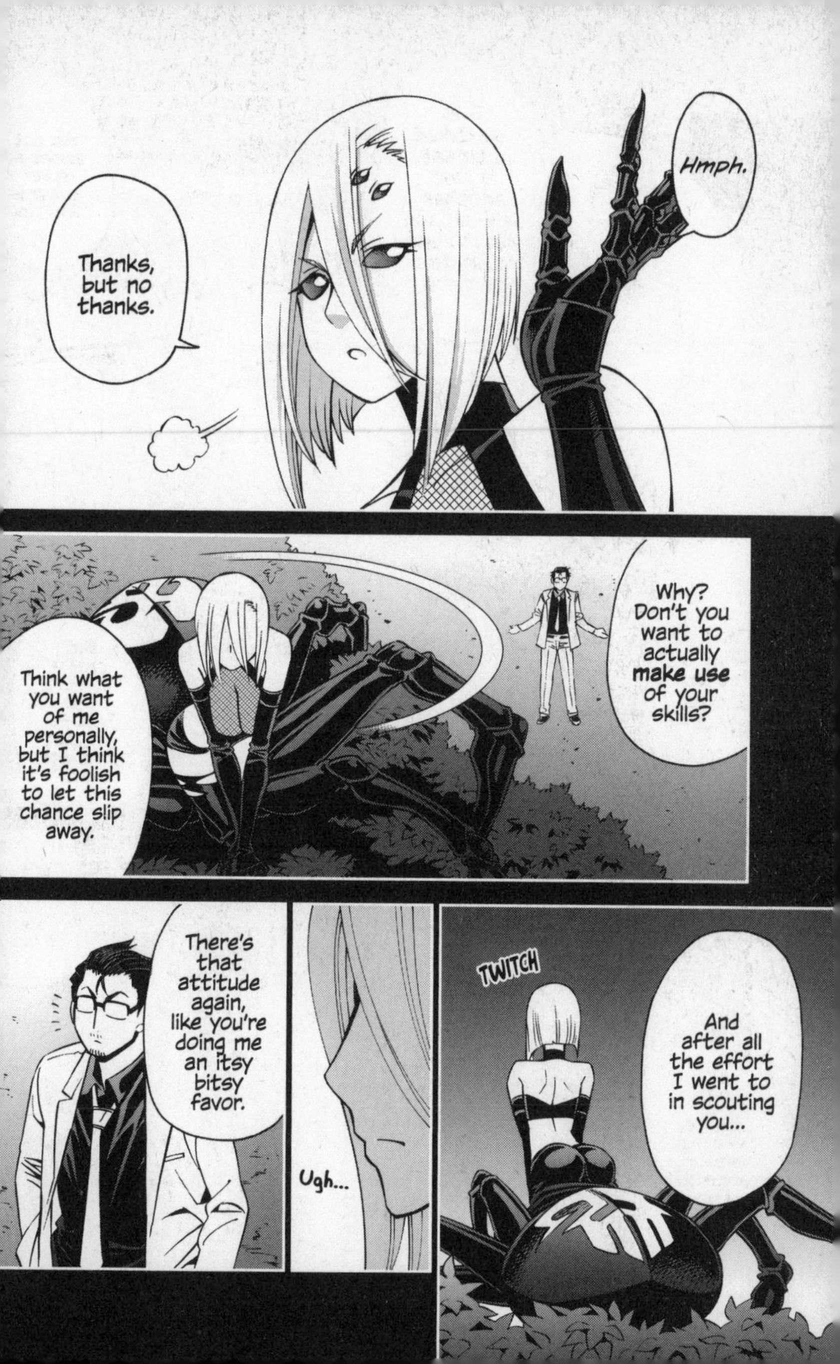
Hmph.
Thanks, but no thanks.
Why? Don't you want to actually make use of your skills?
Think what you want of me personally, but I think it's foolish to let this chance slip away.
TWITCH
And after all the effort I went to in scouting you...
Ugh...
There's that attitude again, like you're doing me an itsy bitsy favor.

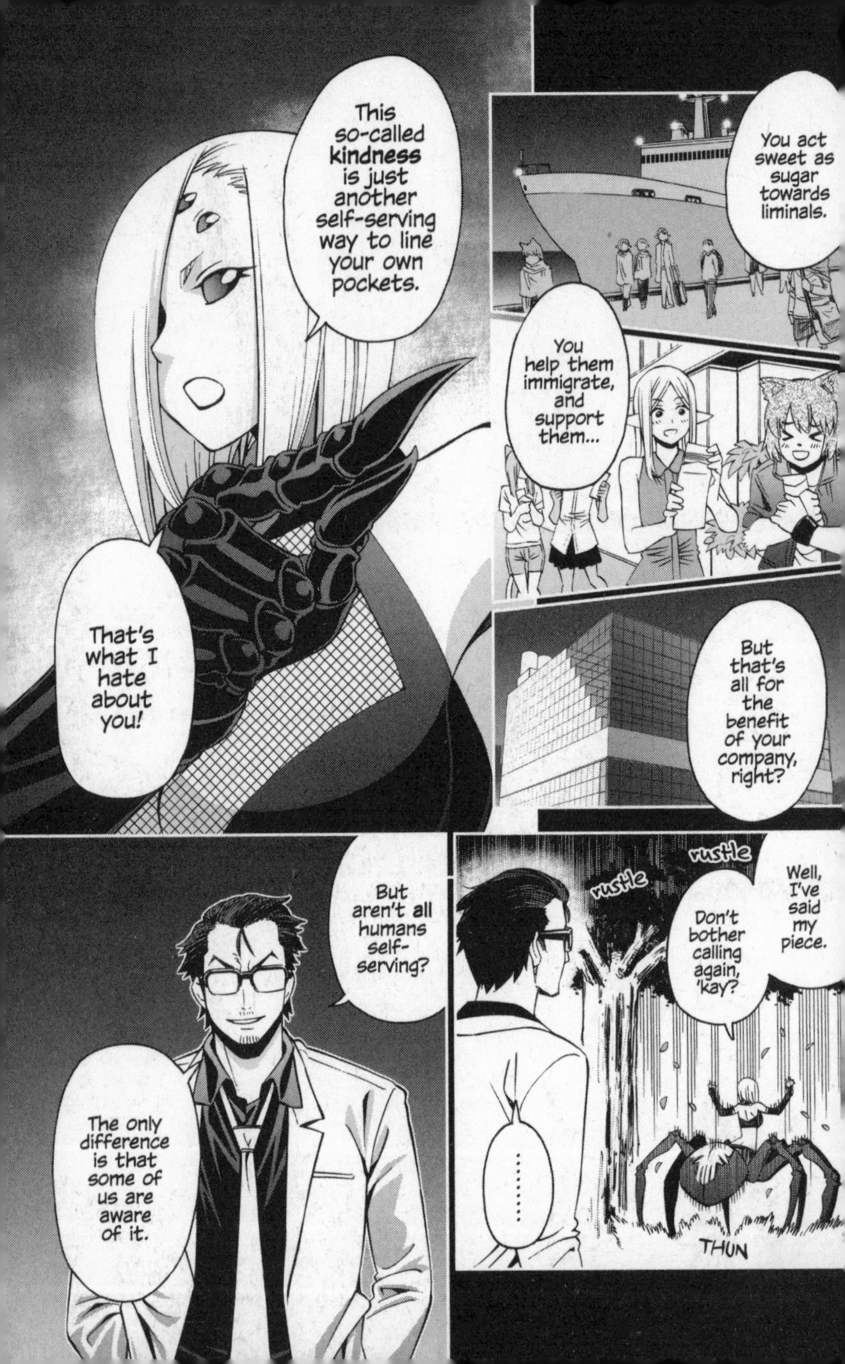
You act sweet as sugar towards liminals.
You help them immigrate, and support them...
But that's all for the benefit of your company, right?
This so-called **kindness** is just another self-serving way to line your own pockets.
That's what I hate about you!
Well, I've said my piece.
Don't bother calling again, 'kay?
rustle
rustle
......
THUN
But aren't all humans self-serving?
The only difference is that some of us are aware of it.

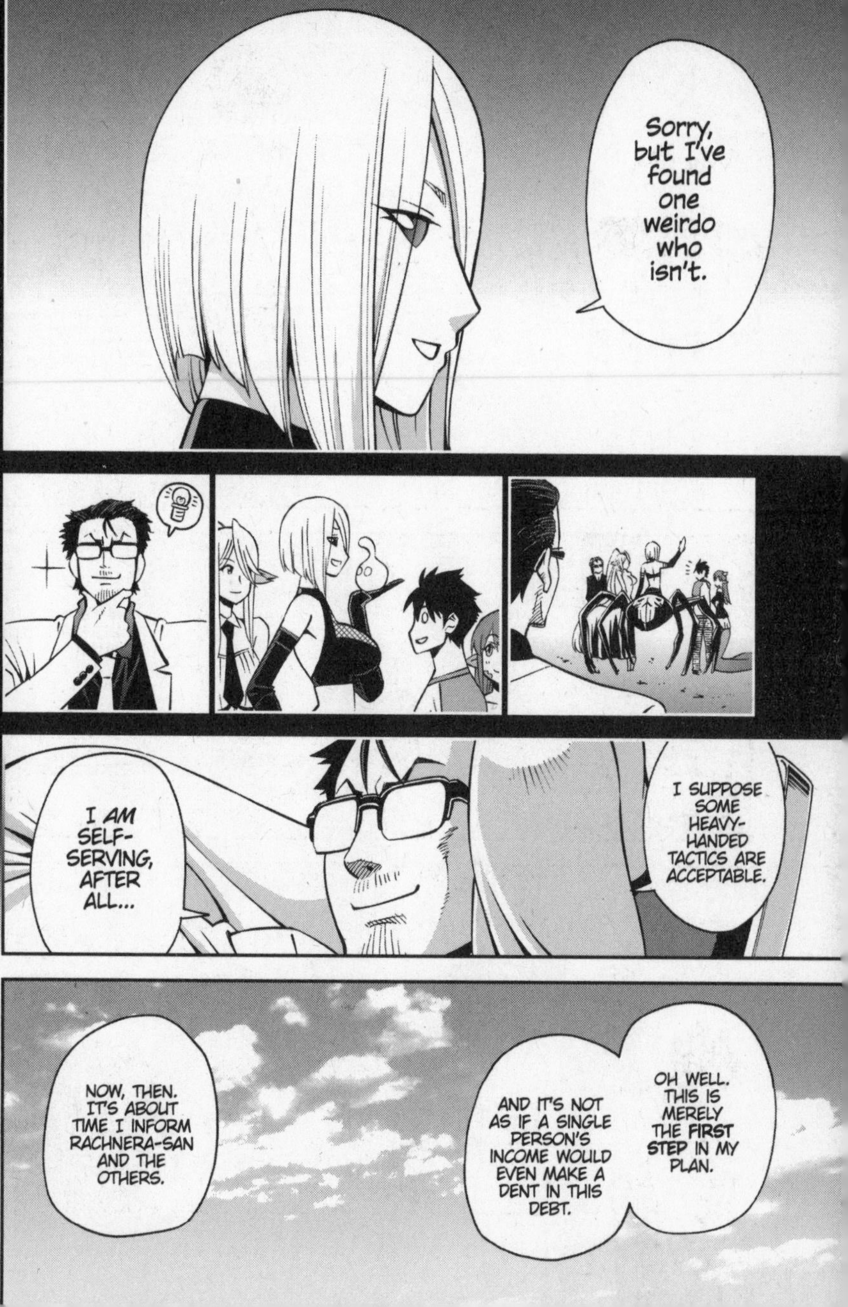
Sorry, but I've found one weirdo who isn't.
I SUPPOSE SOME HEAVY-HANDED TACTICS ARE ACCEPTABLE.
I *AM* SELF-SERVING, AFTER ALL...
OH WELL. THIS IS MERELY THE **FIRST** STEP IN MY PLAN.
AND IT'S NOT AS IF A SINGLE PERSON'S INCOME WOULD EVEN MAKE A DENT IN THIS DEBT.
NOW, THEN. IT'S ABOUT TIME I INFORM RACHNERA-SAN AND THE OTHERS.

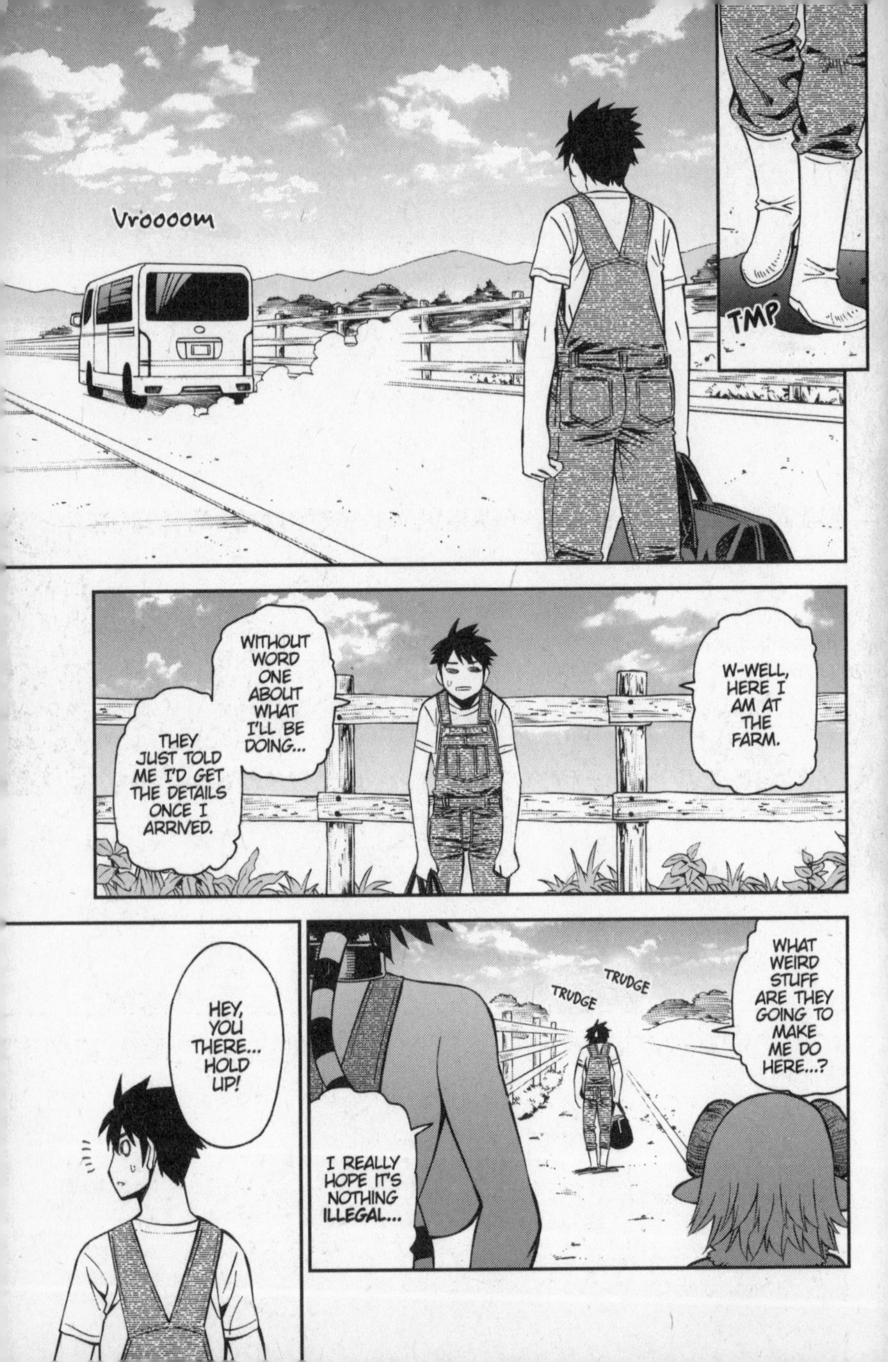
TMP
Vroooom
W-WELL, HERE I AM AT THE FARM.
WITHOUT WORD ONE ABOUT WHAT I'LL BE DOING...
THEY JUST TOLD ME I'D GET THE DETAILS ONCE I ARRIVED.
WHAT WEIRD STUFF ARE THEY GOING TO MAKE ME DO HERE...?
TRUDGE
TRUDGE
I REALLY HOPE IT'S NOTHING ILLEGAL...
HEY, YOU THERE... HOLD UP!

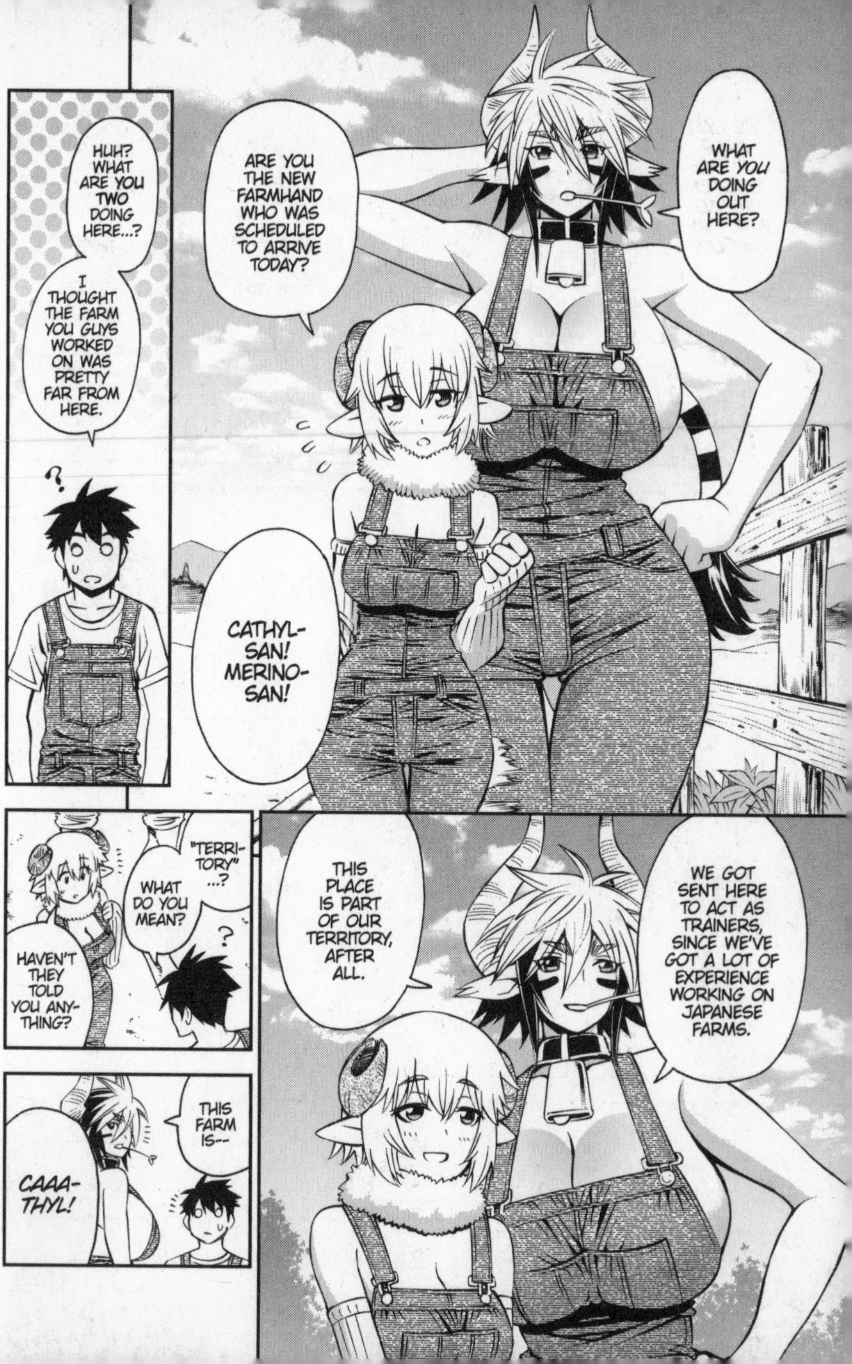
WHAT ARE YOU DOING OUT HERE?
ARE YOU THE NEW FARMHAND WHO WAS SCHEDULED TO ARRIVE TODAY?
CATHYL-SAN! MERINO-SAN!
HUH? WHAT ARE YOU TWO DOING HERE...?
I THOUGHT THE FARM YOU GUYS WORKED ON WAS PRETTY FAR FROM HERE.
WE GOT SENT HERE TO ACT AS TRAINERS, SINCE WE'VE GOT A LOT OF EXPERIENCE WORKING ON JAPANESE FARMS.
THIS PLACE IS PART OF OUR TERRITORY, AFTER ALL.
"TERRITORY" ...?
WHAT DO YOU MEAN?
HAVEN'T THEY TOLD YOU ANYTHING?
THIS FARM IS--
CAAATHYL!

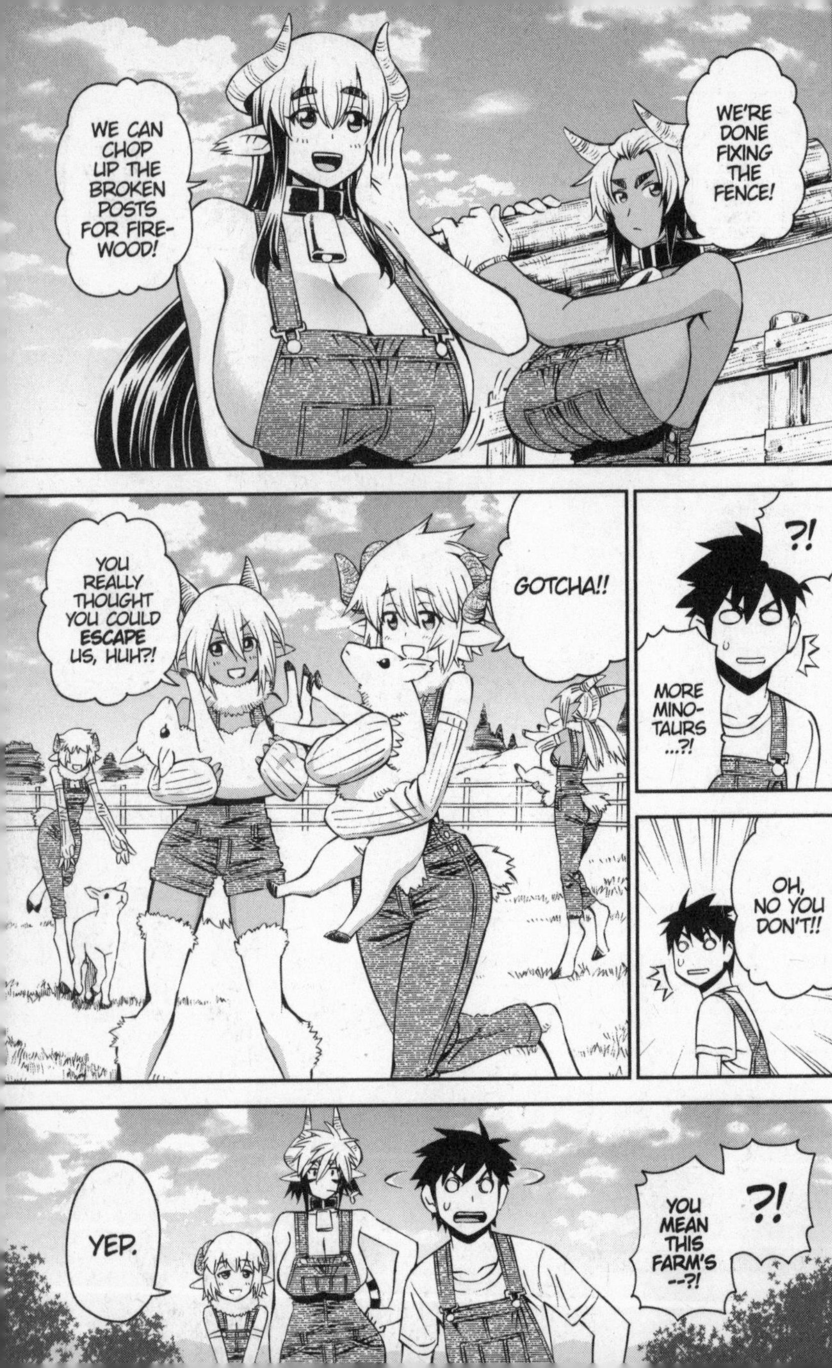
WE'RE DONE FIXING THE FENCE!
WE CAN CHOP UP THE BROKEN POSTS FOR FIRE-WOOD!
?!
MORE MINOTAURS ...?!
OH, NO YOU DON'T!!
GOTCHA!!
YOU REALLY THOUGHT YOU COULD ESCAPE US, HUH?!
?!
YOU MEAN THIS FARM'S --?!
YEP.

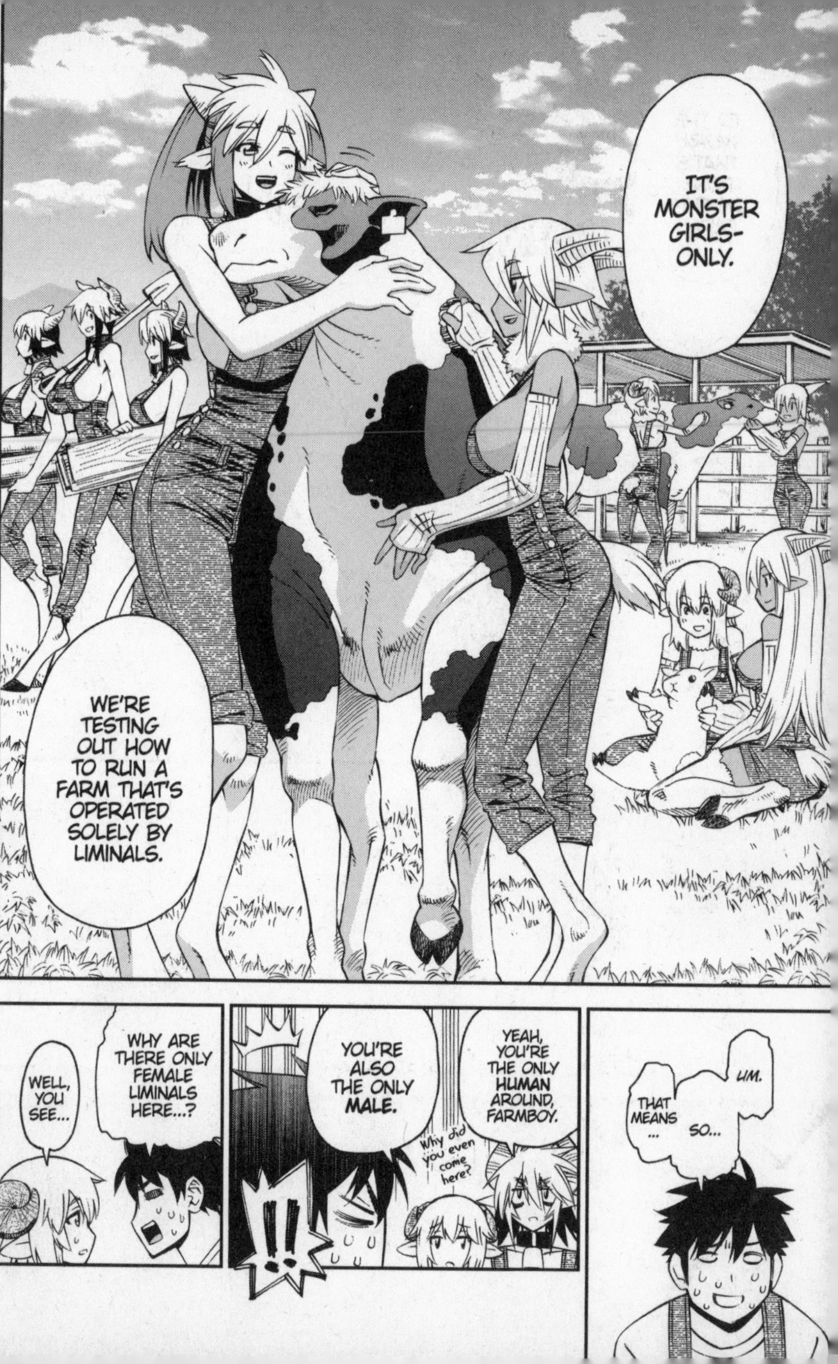
IT'S MONSTER GIRLS-ONLY.
WE'RE TESTING OUT HOW TO RUN A FARM THAT'S OPERATED SOLELY BY LIMINALS.
UM.
SO...
THAT MEANS ...
YEAH, YOU'RE THE ONLY HUMAN AROUND, FARMBOY.
YOU'RE ALSO THE ONLY MALE.
...Why did you even come here?
WHY ARE THERE ONLY FEMALE LIMINALS HERE...?
WELL, YOU SEE...

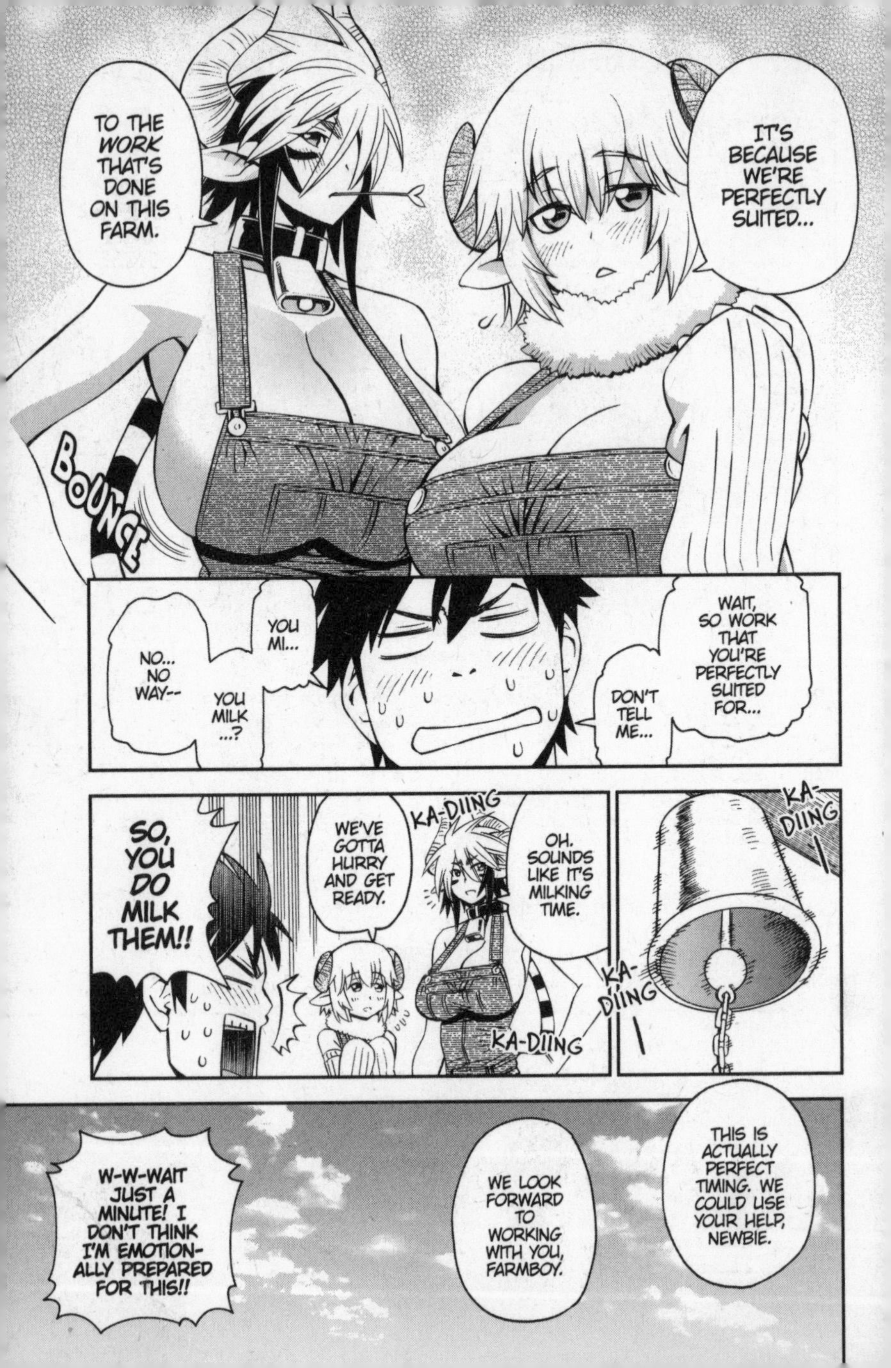
IT'S BECAUSE WE'RE PERFECTLY SUITED...
TO THE *WORK* THAT'S DONE ON THIS FARM.
BOUNCE
WAIT, SO WORK THAT YOU'RE PERFECTLY SUITED FOR...
DON'T TELL ME...
YOU MI...
YOU MILK ...?
NO... NO WAY--
KA-DIING
KA-DIING
OH. SOUNDS LIKE IT'S MILKING TIME.
KA-DIING
WE'VE GOTTA HURRY AND GET READY.
KA-DIING
SO, YOU *DO* MILK THEM!!
THIS IS ACTUALLY PERFECT TIMING. WE COULD USE YOUR HELP, NEWBIE.
WE LOOK FORWARD TO WORKING WITH YOU, FARMBOY.
W-W-WAIT JUST A MINUTE! I DON'T THINK I'M EMOTION-ALLY PREPARED FOR THIS!!

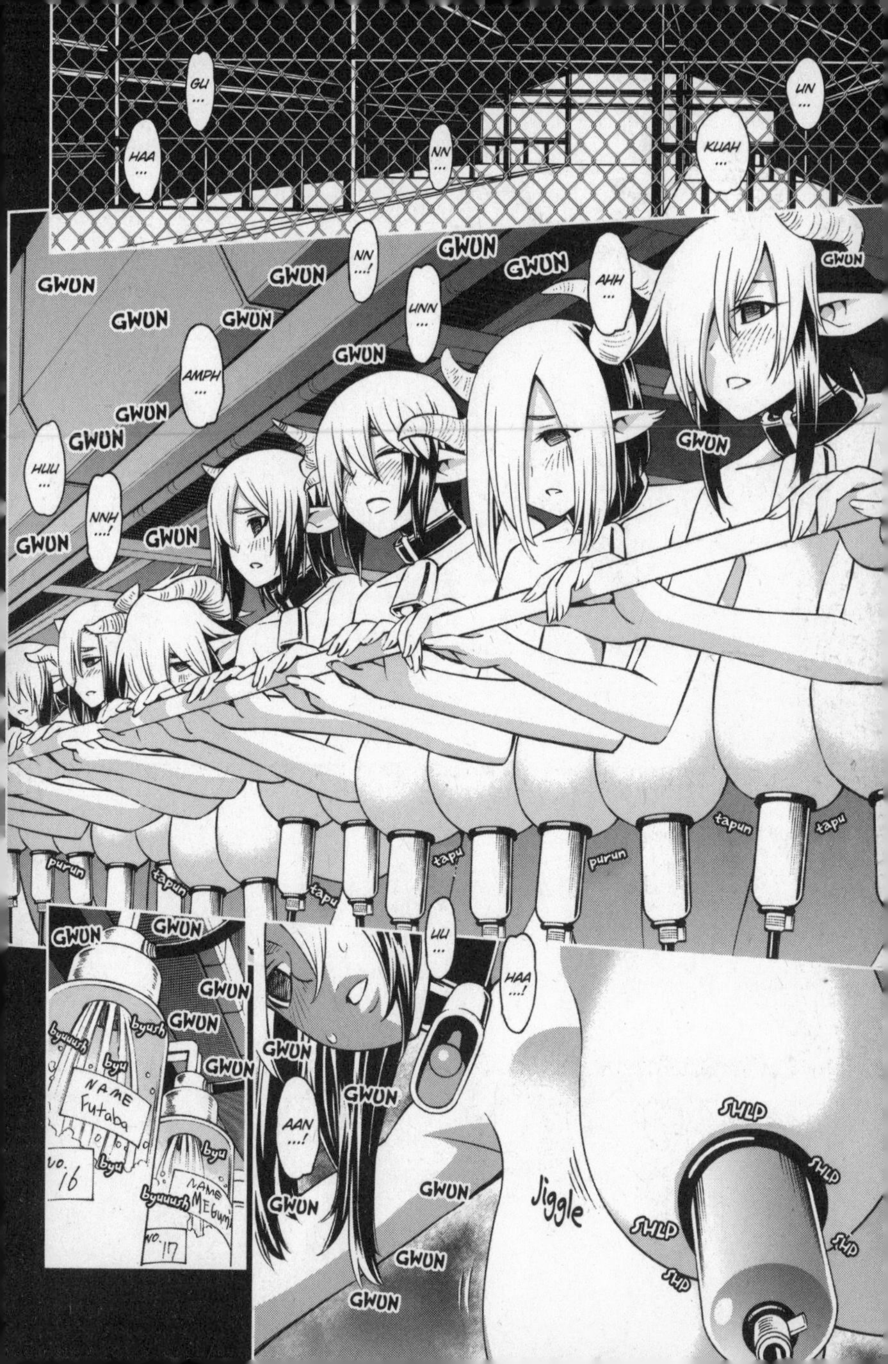
UN...
KUAH...
NN...
GU...
HAA...
GWUN
AHH...
GWUN
GWUN
NN...!
UNN...
GWUN
GWUN
GWUN
GWUN
AMPH...
GWUN
GWUN
HUU...
NNH...!
GWUN
GWUN
GWUN
GWUN
tapu
tapun
purun
tapu
tapu
tapun
purun
SHLP
SHLP
SHLP
SHLP
SHLP
Jiggle
UU...
HAA...!
GWUN
GWUN
AAN...!
GWUN
GWUN
GWUN
GWUN
GWUN
GWUN
GWUN
GWUN
GWUN
byush
byuush
byu
NAME Futaba
byu
No. 16
byu
byuuush
NAME MEGUMI
No. 17

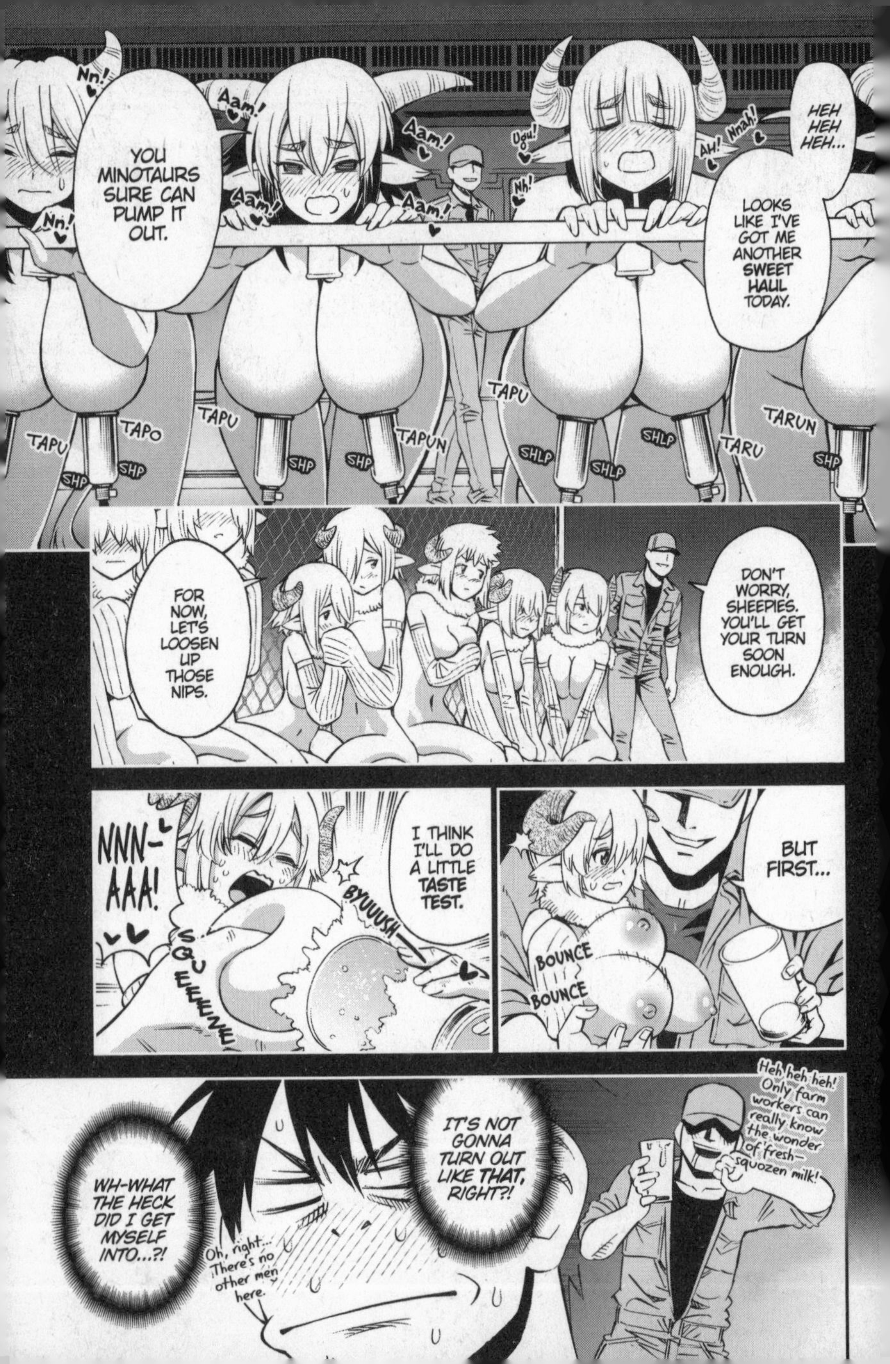
HEH HEH HEH...
LOOKS LIKE I'VE GOT ME ANOTHER SWEET HAUL TODAY.
Nnah!
AH!
Nh!
Ugu!
Aam!
Aam!
Aam!
Aam!
Nn!
YOU MINOTAURS SURE CAN PUMP IT OUT.
Nn!
TARUN
SHP
TARU
SHLP
SHLP
TAPU
TAPUN
SHP
TAPU
SHP
TAPO
SHP
TAPU
SHP
DON'T WORRY, SHEEPIES. YOU'LL GET YOUR TURN SOON ENOUGH.
FOR NOW, LET'S LOOSEN UP THOSE NIPS.
BUT FIRST...
BOUNCE
BOUNCE
I THINK I'LL DO A LITTLE TASTE TEST.
BYUUUSH
NNN-AAA!
SQUEEEEZE
Heh heh heh! Only farm workers can really know the wonder of fresh-squozen milk!
IT'S NOT GONNA TURN OUT LIKE THAT, RIGHT?!
WH-WHAT THE HECK DID I GET MYSELF INTO...?!
Oh, right... There's no other men here.

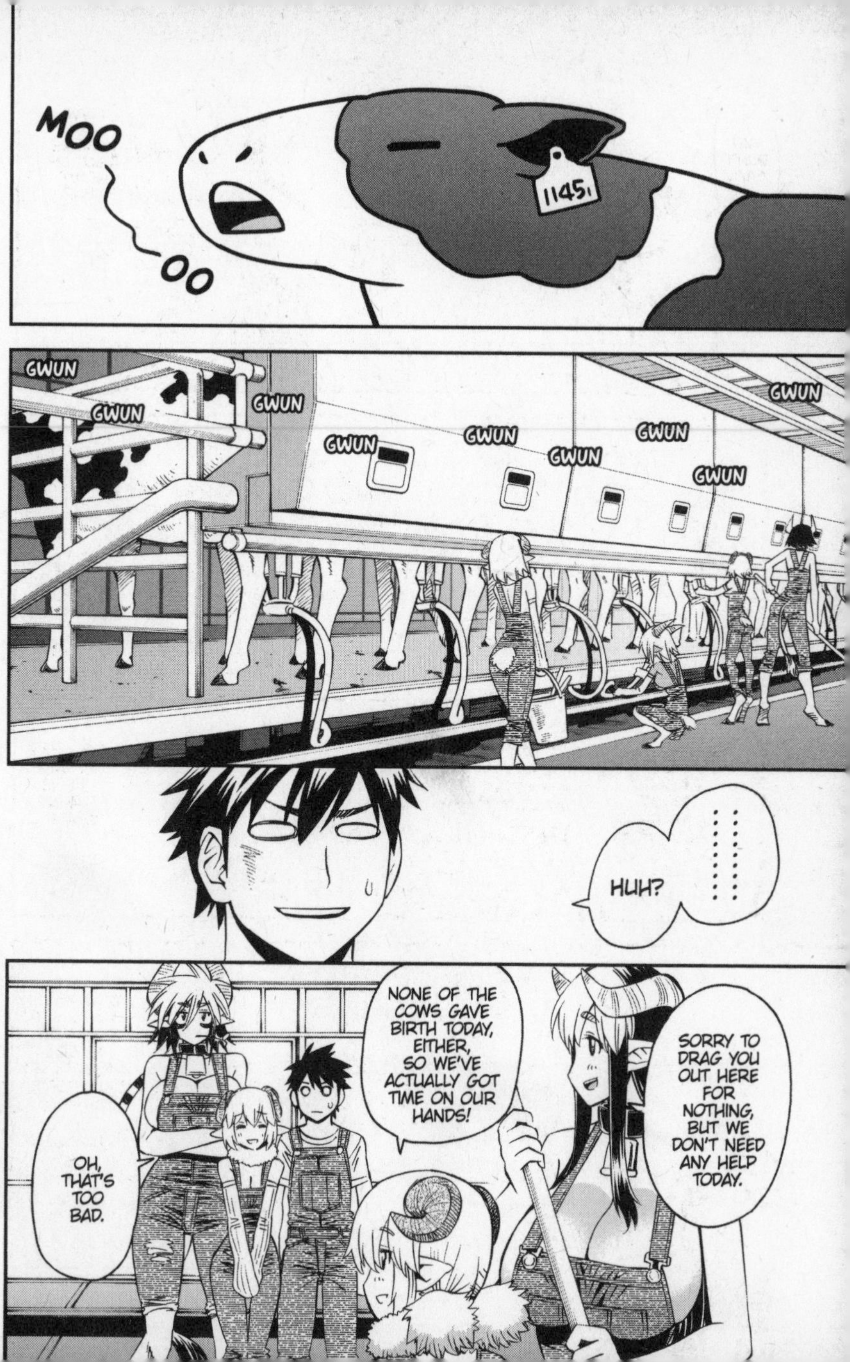
1145
MOO
-OO
GWUN
GWUN
GWUN
GWUN
GWUN
GWUN
GWUN
GWUN
GWUN
......
HUH?
SORRY TO DRAG YOU OUT HERE FOR NOTHING, BUT WE DON'T NEED ANY HELP TODAY.
NONE OF THE COWS GAVE BIRTH TODAY, EITHER, SO WE'VE ACTUALLY GOT TIME ON OUR HANDS!
OH, THAT'S TOO BAD.

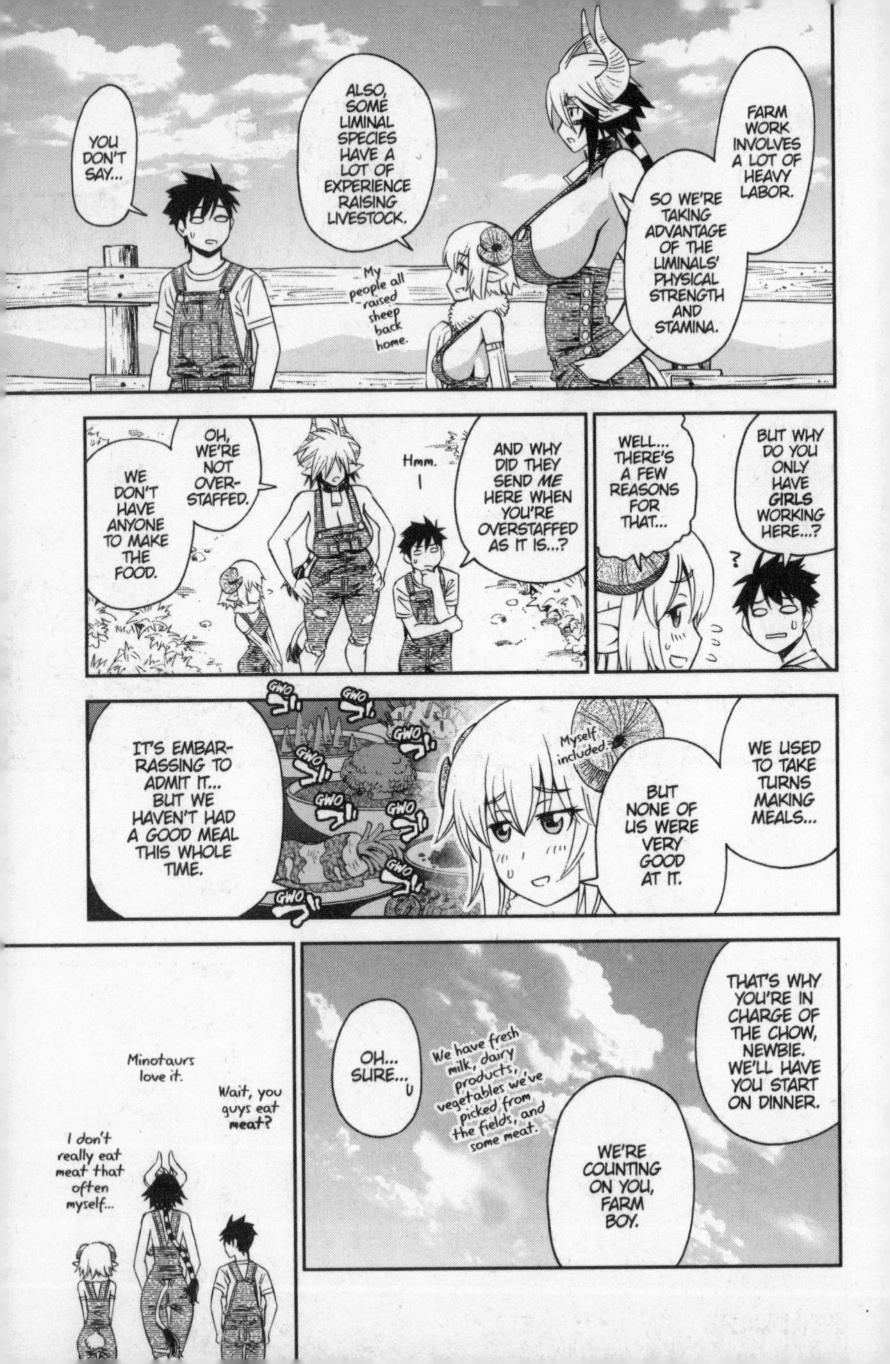
FARM WORK INVOLVES A LOT OF HEAVY LABOR.
SO WE'RE TAKING ADVANTAGE OF THE LIMINALS' PHYSICAL STRENGTH AND STAMINA.
ALSO, SOME LIMINAL SPECIES HAVE A LOT OF EXPERIENCE RAISING LIVESTOCK.
My people all raised sheep back home.
YOU DON'T SAY...
BUT WHY DO YOU ONLY HAVE GIRLS WORKING HERE...?
?
WELL... THERE'S A FEW REASONS FOR THAT...
AND WHY DID THEY SEND *ME* HERE WHEN YOU'RE OVERSTAFFED AS IT IS...?
Hmm.
OH, WE'RE NOT OVER-STAFFED.
WE DON'T HAVE ANYONE TO MAKE THE FOOD.
WE USED TO TAKE TURNS MAKING MEALS...
Myself included.
BUT NONE OF US WERE VERY GOOD AT IT.
IT'S EMBAR-RASSING TO ADMIT IT... BUT WE HAVEN'T HAD A GOOD MEAL THIS WHOLE TIME.
GWO GWO GWO GWO GWO GWO GWO GWO
THAT'S WHY YOU'RE IN CHARGE OF THE CHOW, NEWBIE. WE'LL HAVE YOU START ON DINNER.
WE'RE COUNTING ON YOU, FARM BOY.
OH... SURE...
We have fresh milk, dairy products, vegetables we've picked from the fields, and some meat.
Wait, you guys eat **meat**?
Minotaurs love it.
I don't really eat meat that often myself...

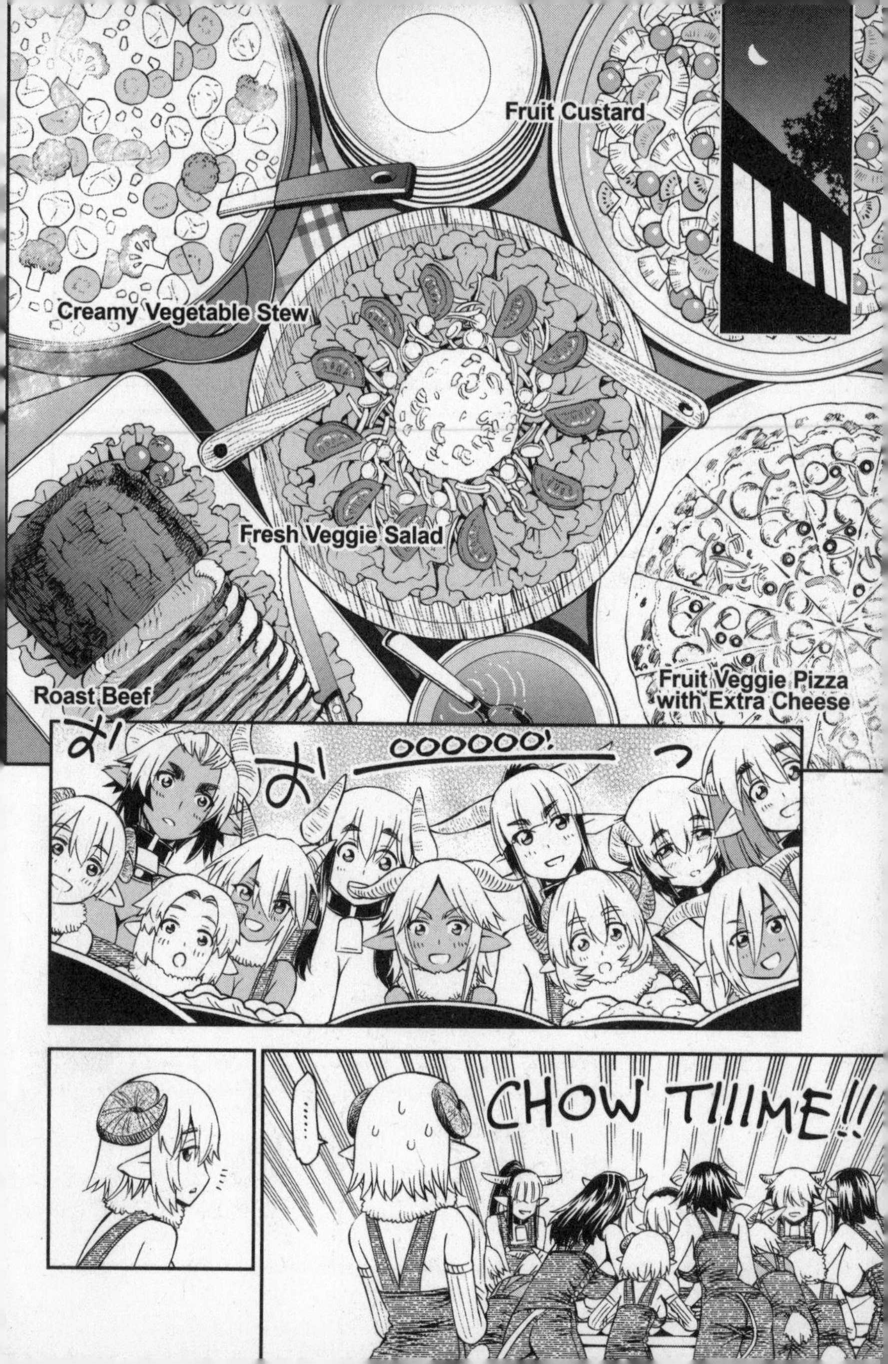
Fruit Custard
Creamy Vegetable Stew
Fresh Veggie Salad
Fruit Veggie Pizza with Extra Cheese
Roast Beef
おお
OOOOOO!
っ
......
CHOW TIIIME!!

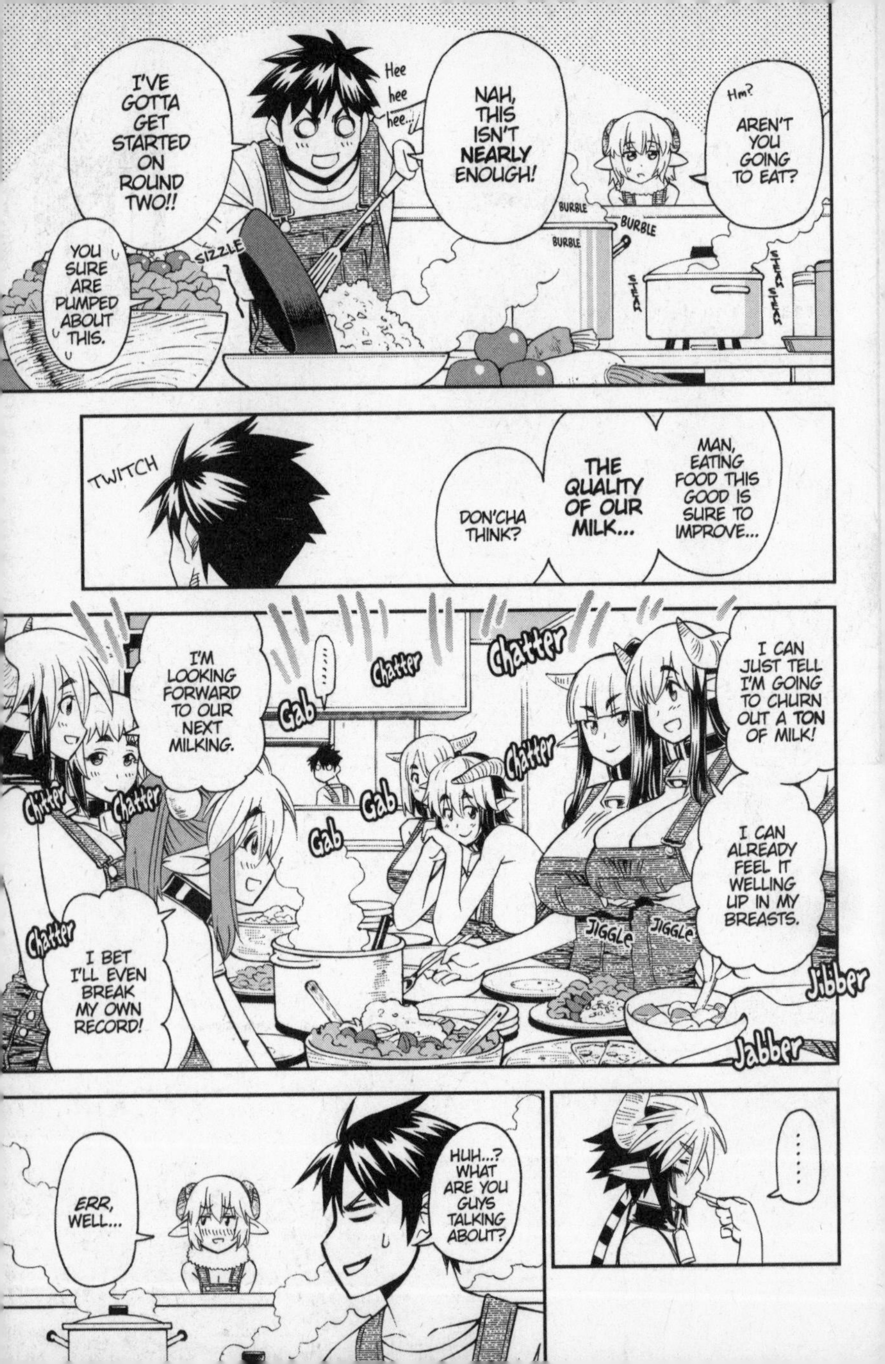
Hm?
AREN'T YOU GOING TO EAT?
STEAM
STEAM
STEAM
BURBLE
BURBLE
BURBLE
NAH, THIS ISN'T NEARLY ENOUGH!
Hee hee hee...
I'VE GOTTA GET STARTED ON ROUND TWO!!
SIZZLE
YOU SURE ARE PUMPED ABOUT THIS.
MAN, EATING FOOD THIS GOOD IS SURE TO IMPROVE...
THE QUALITY OF OUR MILK...
DON'CHA THINK?
TWITCH
I CAN JUST TELL I'M GOING TO CHURN OUT A TON OF MILK!
I CAN ALREADY FEEL IT WELLING UP IN MY BREASTS.
Jibber
Jabber
JIGGLE
JIGGLE
Chatter
Chatter
Chatter
Gab
Gab
......
Gab
I'M LOOKING FORWARD TO OUR NEXT MILKING.
Chatter
Chatter
Chatter
I BET I'LL EVEN BREAK MY OWN RECORD!
......
HUH...? WHAT ARE YOU GUYS TALKING ABOUT?
ERR, WELL...

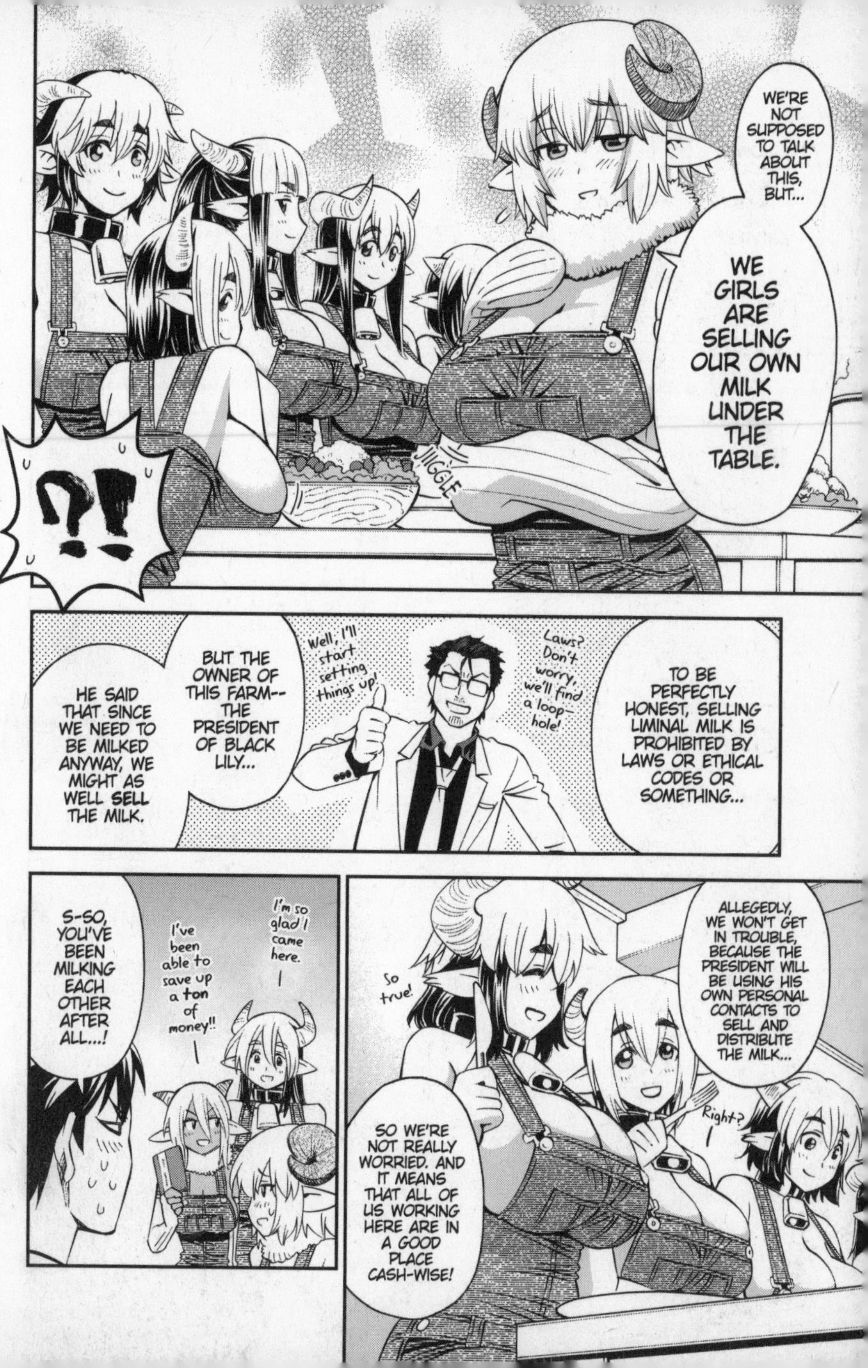
WE'RE NOT SUPPOSED TO TALK ABOUT THIS, BUT...
WE GIRLS ARE SELLING OUR OWN MILK UNDER THE TABLE.
JIGGLE
?!!
TO BE PERFECTLY HONEST, SELLING LIMINAL MILK IS PROHIBITED BY LAWS OR ETHICAL CODES OR SOMETHING...
Laws? Don't worry, we'll find a loop-hole!
Well, I'll start setting things up!
BUT THE OWNER OF THIS FARM-- THE PRESIDENT OF BLACK LILY...
HE SAID THAT SINCE WE NEED TO BE MILKED ANYWAY, WE MIGHT AS WELL SELL THE MILK.
ALLEGEDLY, WE WON'T GET IN TROUBLE, BECAUSE THE PRESIDENT WILL BE USING HIS OWN PERSONAL CONTACTS TO SELL AND DISTRIBUTE THE MILK...
Right?
So true!
SO WE'RE NOT REALLY WORRIED. AND IT MEANS THAT ALL OF US WORKING HERE ARE IN A GOOD PLACE CASH-WISE!
I'm so glad I came here.
I've been able to save up a ton of money!!
S-SO, YOU'VE BEEN MILKING EACH OTHER AFTER ALL...!

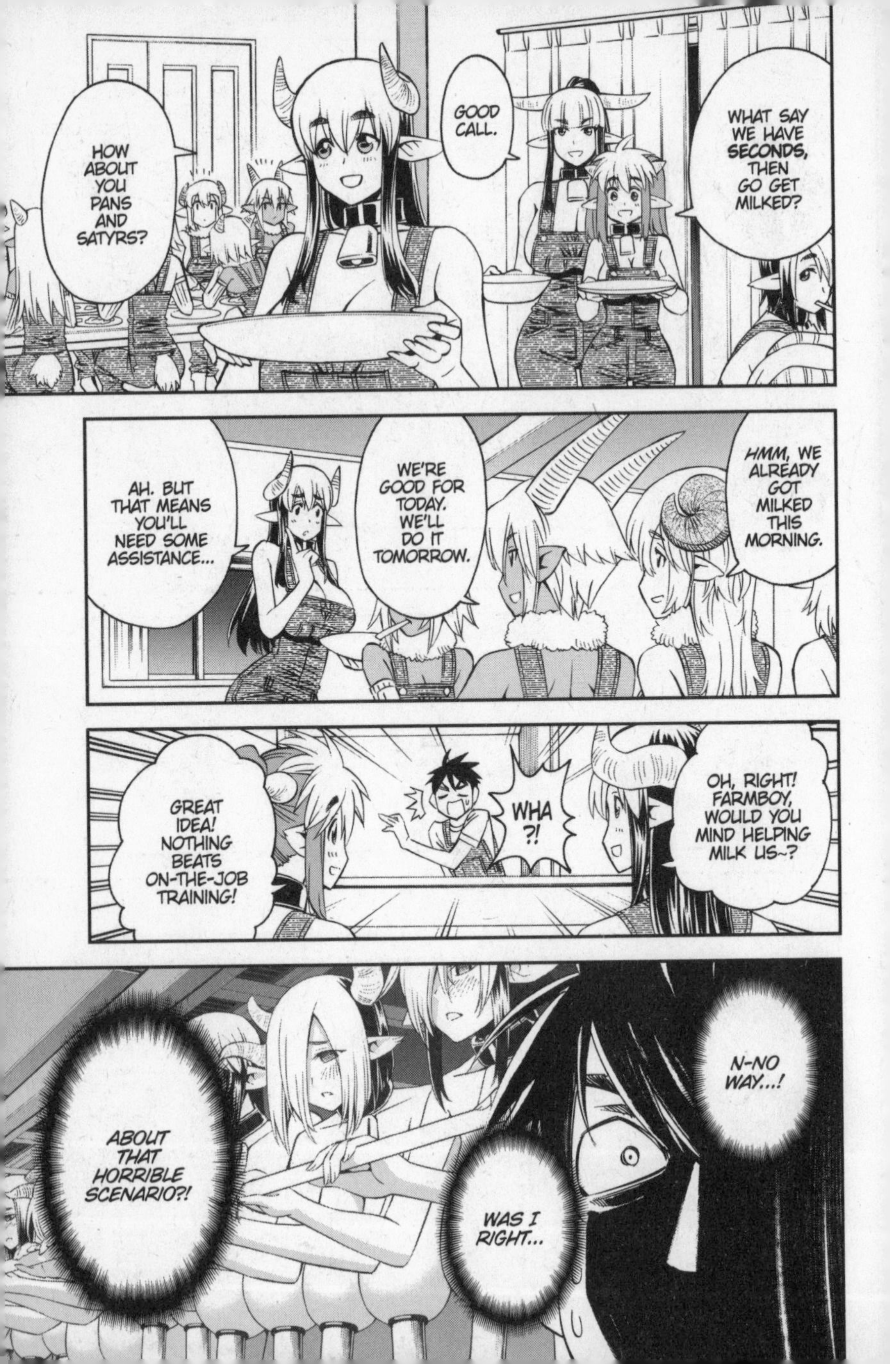
WHAT SAY WE HAVE SECONDS, THEN GO GET MILKED?
GOOD CALL.
HOW ABOUT YOU PANS AND SATYRS?
HMM, WE ALREADY GOT MILKED THIS MORNING.
WE'RE GOOD FOR TODAY. WE'LL DO IT TOMORROW.
AH. BUT THAT MEANS YOU'LL NEED SOME ASSISTANCE...
OH, RIGHT! FARMBOY, WOULD YOU MIND HELPING MILK US~?
WHA ?!
GREAT IDEA! NOTHING BEATS ON-THE-JOB TRAINING!
N-NO WAY...!
WAS I RIGHT...
ABOUT THAT HORRIBLE SCENARIO?!

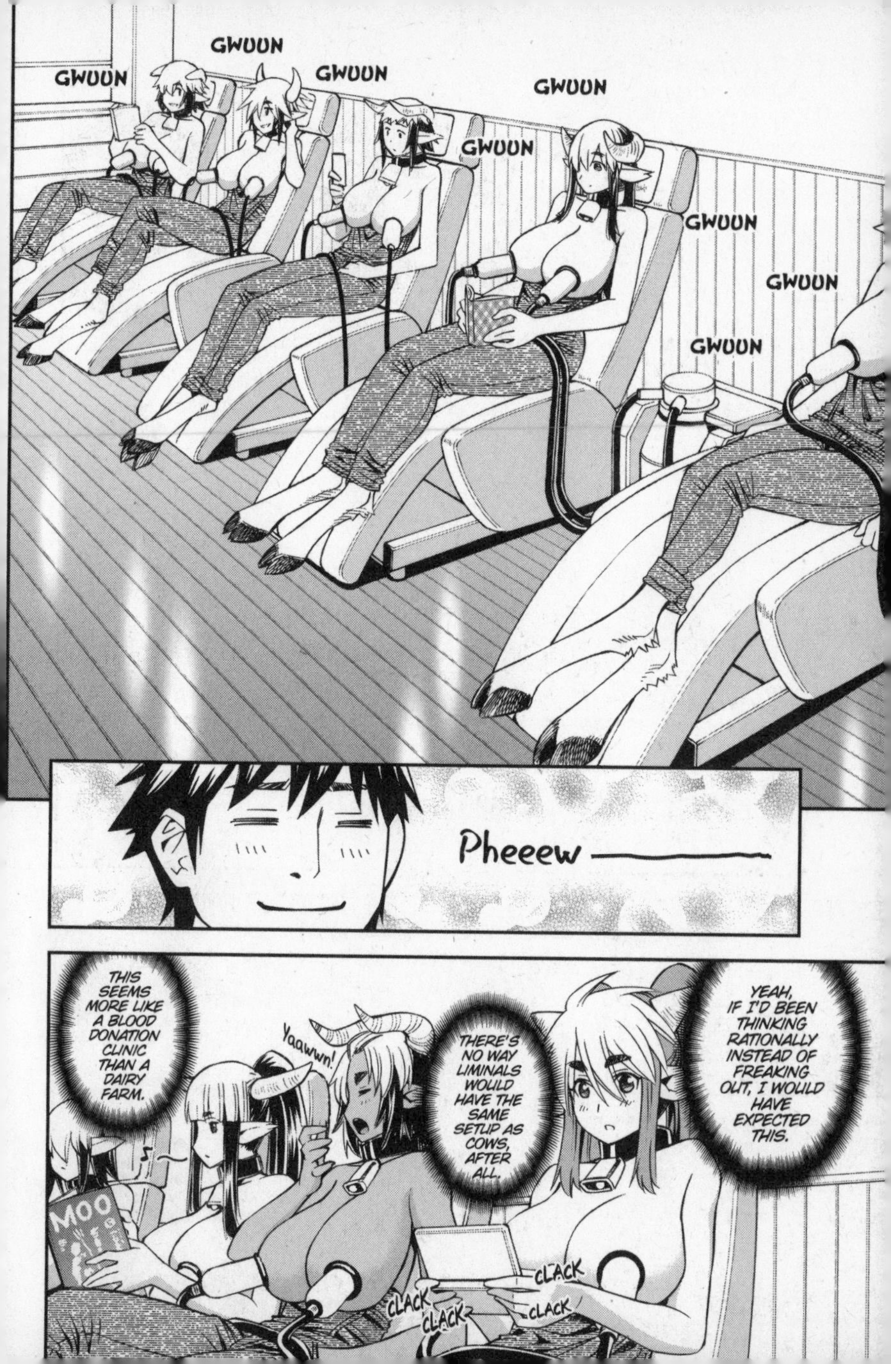
GWUUN
GWUUN
GWUUN
GWUUN
GWUUN
GWUUN
GWUUN
GWUUN
Pheeew
YEAH, IF I'D BEEN THINKING RATIONALLY INSTEAD OF FREAKING OUT, I WOULD HAVE EXPECTED THIS.
THERE'S NO WAY LIMINALS WOULD HAVE THE SAME SETUP AS COWS, AFTER ALL.
Yaaawwn!
THIS SEEMS MORE LIKE A BLOOD DONATION CLINIC THAN A DAIRY FARM.
MOO
CLACK
CLACK
CLACK
CLACK
CLACK

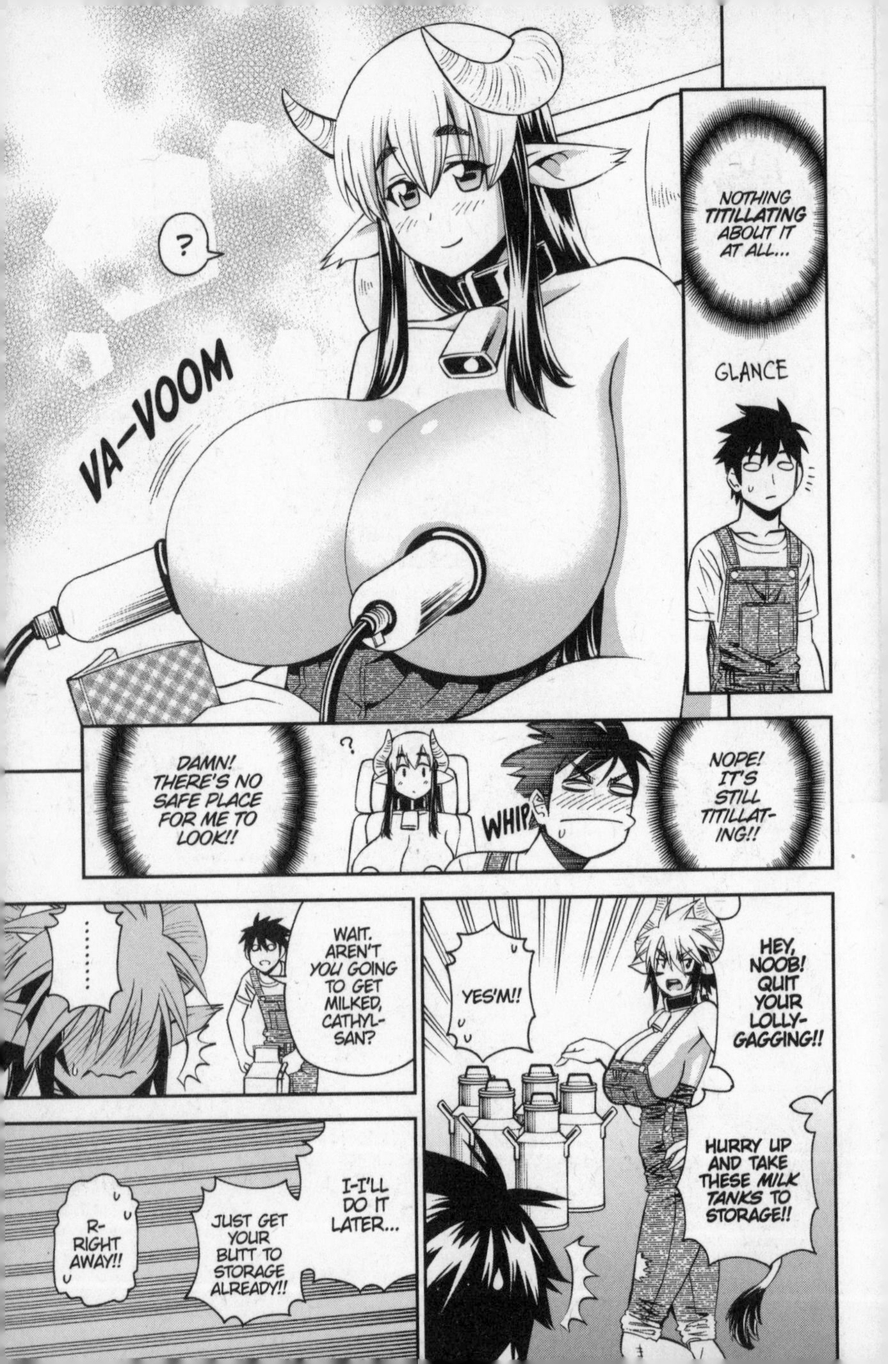
NOTHING TITILLATING ABOUT IT AT ALL...
GLANCE
?
VA-VOOM
NOPE! IT'S STILL TITILLAT-ING!!
WHIP
?
DAMN! THERE'S NO SAFE PLACE FOR ME TO LOOK!!
HEY, NOOB! QUIT YOUR LOLLY-GAGGING!!
YES'M!!
HURRY UP AND TAKE THESE MILK TANKS TO STORAGE!!
WAIT. AREN'T YOU GOING TO GET MILKED, CATHYL-SAN?
......
I-I'LL DO IT LATER...
JUST GET YOUR BUTT TO STORAGE ALREADY!!
R-RIGHT AWAY!!

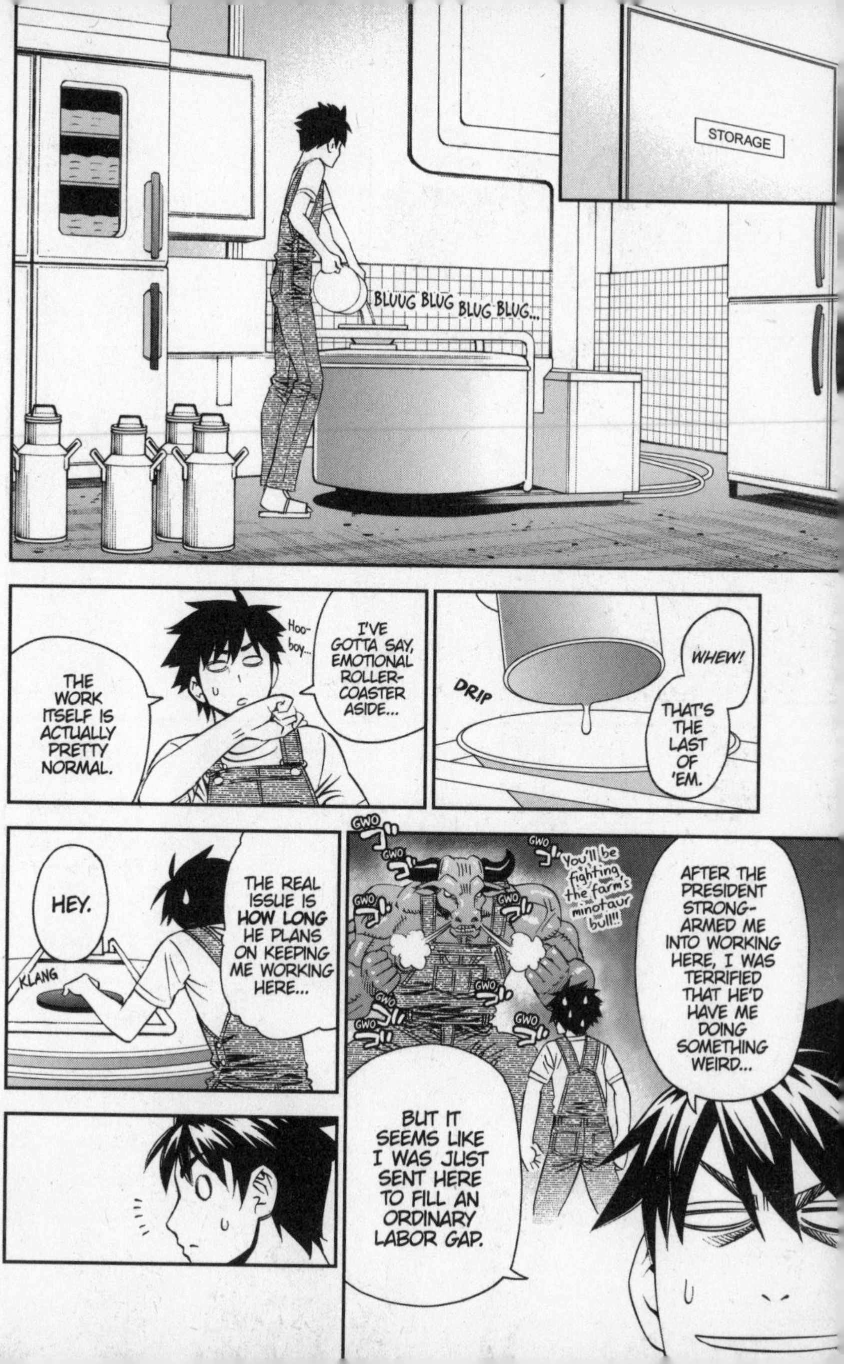
STORAGE
BLUUG BLUG BLUG BLUG...
DRIP
WHEW!
THAT'S THE LAST OF 'EM.
I'VE GOTTA SAY, EMOTIONAL ROLLER-COASTER ASIDE...
Hoo-boy...
THE WORK ITSELF IS ACTUALLY PRETTY NORMAL.
AFTER THE PRESIDENT STRONG-ARMED ME INTO WORKING HERE, I WAS TERRIFIED THAT HE'D HAVE ME DOING SOMETHING WEIRD...
GWO GWO GWO GWO GWO GWO GWO GWO GWO
You'll be fighting the farm's minotaur bull!!!
BUT IT SEEMS LIKE I WAS JUST SENT HERE TO FILL AN ORDINARY LABOR GAP.
THE REAL ISSUE IS HOW LONG HE PLANS ON KEEPING ME WORKING HERE...
HEY.
KLANG

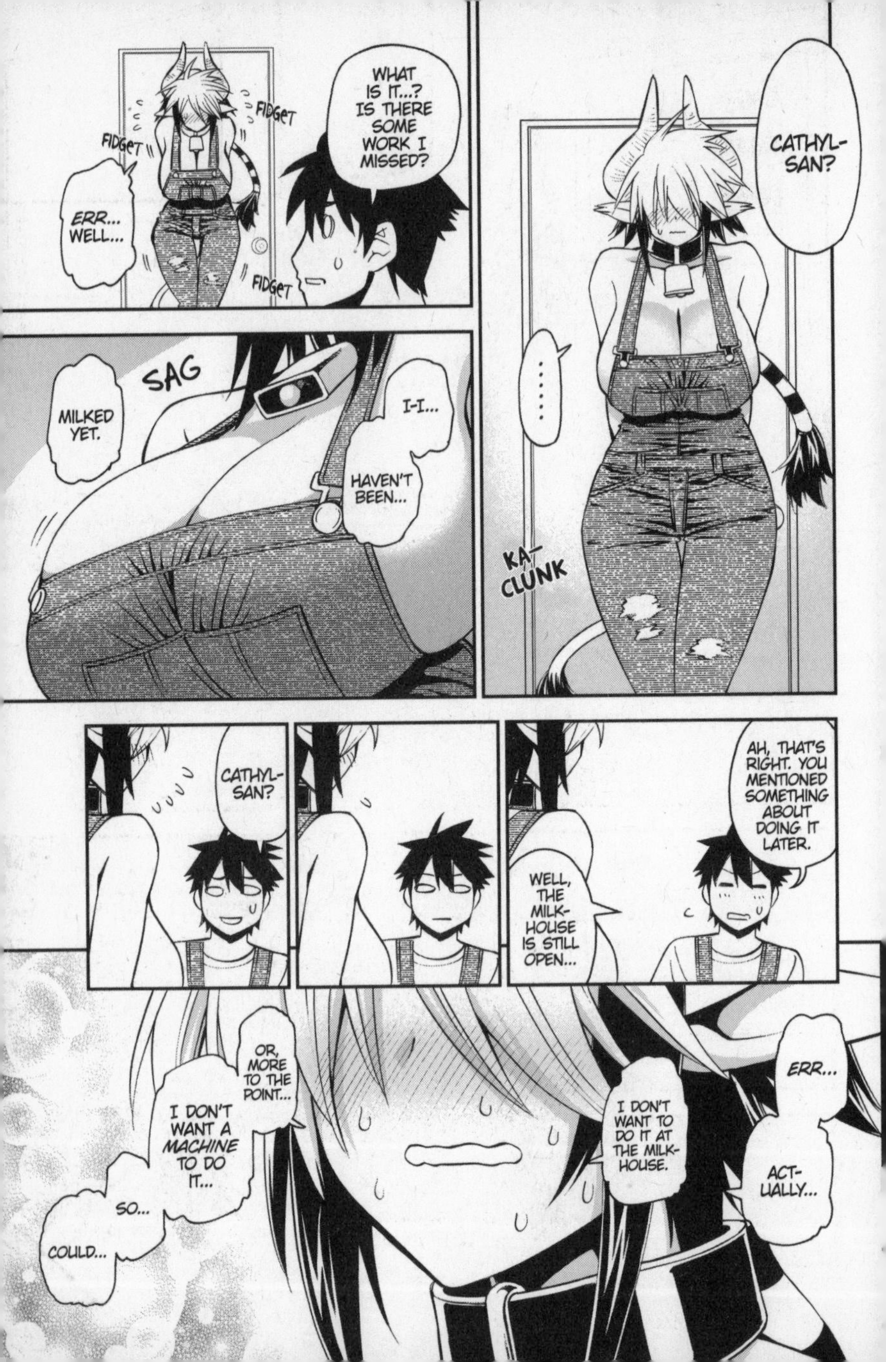
CATHYL-SAN?
......
KA-CLUNK
WHAT IS IT...? IS THERE SOME WORK I MISSED?
FIDGET
FIDGET
ERR... WELL...
FIDGET
I-I...
HAVEN'T BEEN...
MILKED YET.
SAG
AH, THAT'S RIGHT. YOU MENTIONED SOMETHING ABOUT DOING IT LATER.
WELL, THE MILK-HOUSE IS STILL OPEN...
CATHYL-SAN?
ERR...
ACT-UALLY...
I DON'T WANT TO DO IT AT THE MILK-HOUSE.
OR, MORE TO THE POINT...
I DON'T WANT A *MACHINE* TO DO IT...
SO...
COULD...

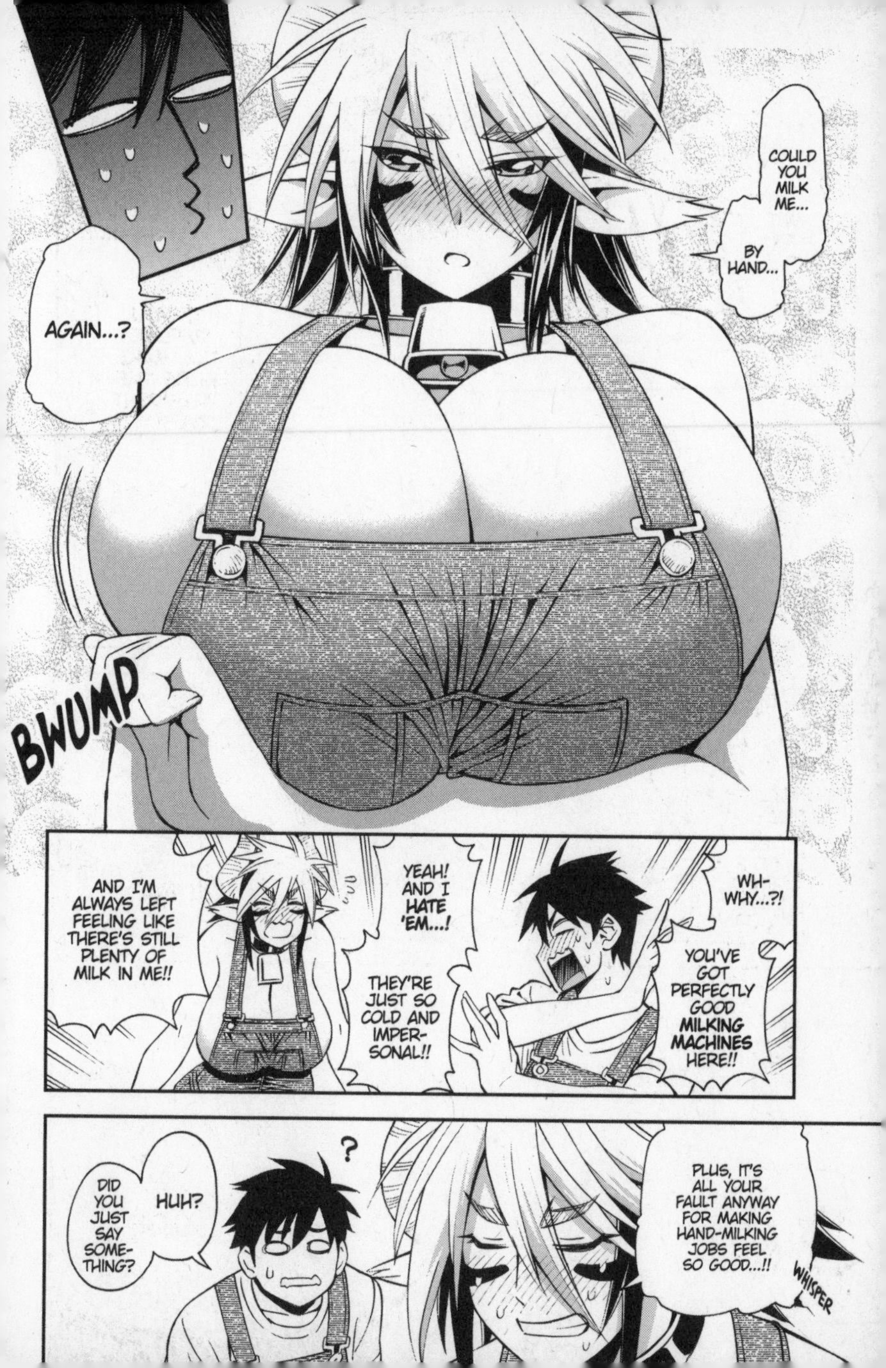
COULD YOU MILK ME...
BY HAND...
AGAIN...?
BWUMP
WH-WHY...?!
YOU'VE GOT PERFECTLY GOOD MILKING MACHINES HERE!!
YEAH! AND I HATE 'EM...!
THEY'RE JUST SO COLD AND IMPER-SONAL!!
AND I'M ALWAYS LEFT FEELING LIKE THERE'S STILL PLENTY OF MILK IN ME!!
PLUS, IT'S ALL YOUR FAULT ANYWAY FOR MAKING HAND-MILKING JOBS FEEL SO GOOD...!!
WHISPER
?
HUH?
DID YOU JUST SAY SOME-THING?

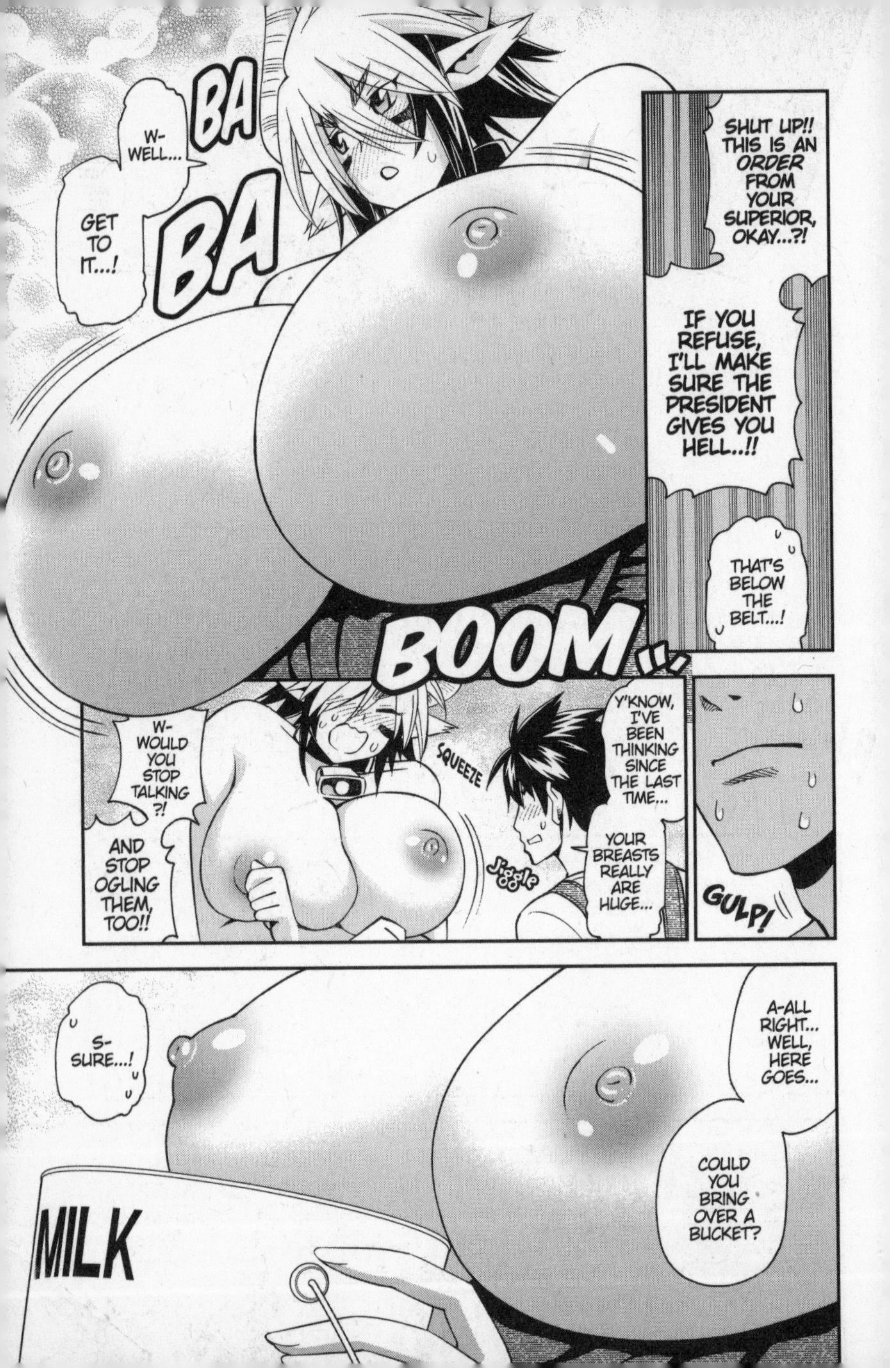
SHUT UP!! THIS IS AN ORDER FROM YOUR SUPERIOR, OKAY...?!
IF YOU REFUSE, I'LL MAKE SURE THE PRESIDENT GIVES YOU HELL...!!
THAT'S BELOW THE BELT...!
BA
BA
W-WELL...
GET TO IT...!
BOOM...
GULP!
Y'KNOW, I'VE BEEN THINKING SINCE THE LAST TIME...
YOUR BREASTS REALLY ARE HUGE...
SQUEEZE
JIGGLE
W-WOULD YOU STOP TALKING?!
AND STOP OGLING THEM, TOO!!
A-ALL RIGHT... WELL, HERE GOES...
COULD YOU BRING OVER A BUCKET?
S-SURE...!
MILK

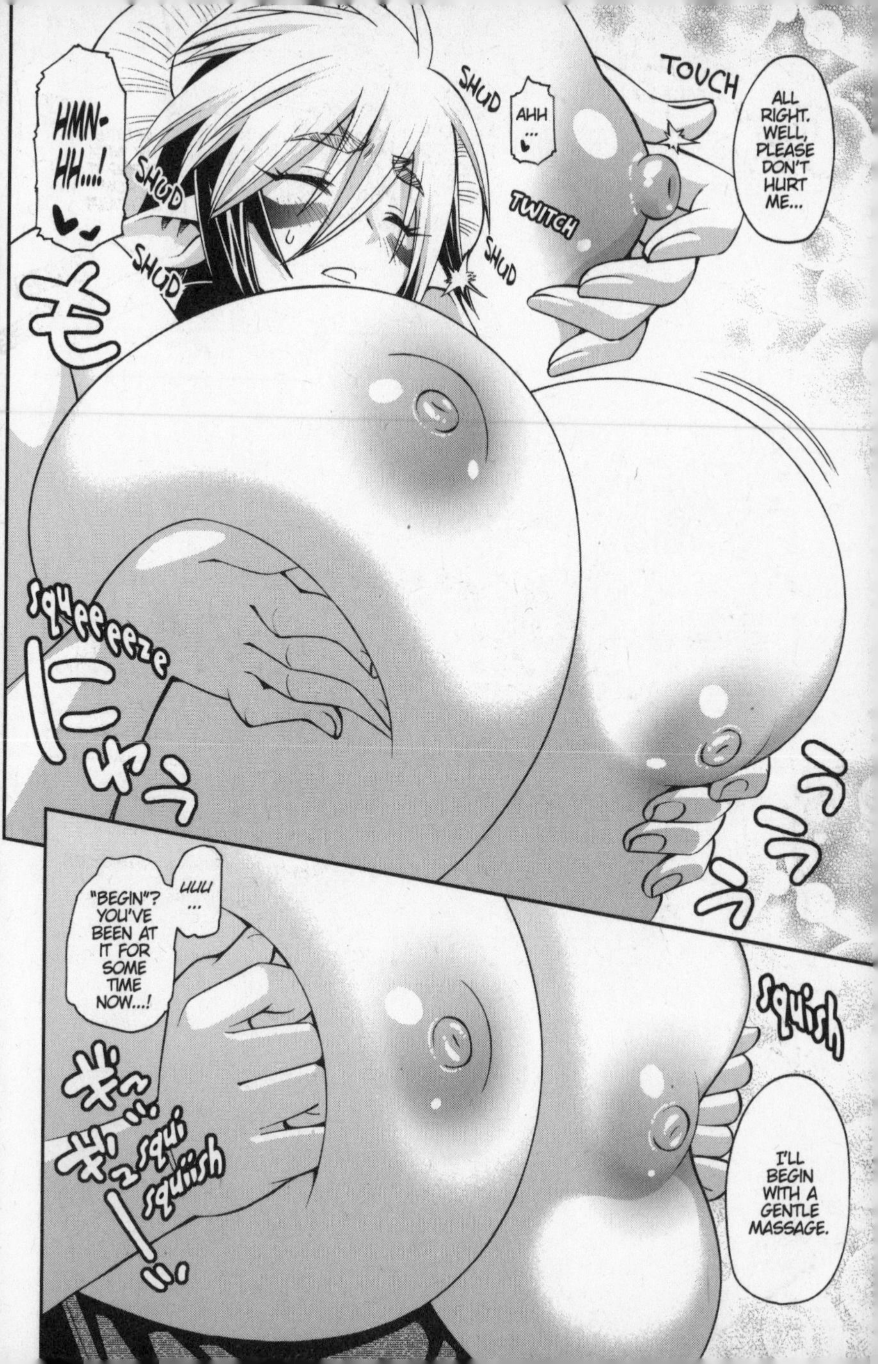
TOUCH
ALL RIGHT. WELL, PLEASE DON'T HURT ME...
SHUD
AHH ...♥
TWITCH
SHUD
HMN-HH...! ♥♥
SHUD
SHUD
squeeeeze
I'LL BEGIN WITH A GENTLE MASSAGE.
squish
UUU ...
"BEGIN"? YOU'VE BEEN AT IT FOR SOME TIME NOW...!
squi squiish

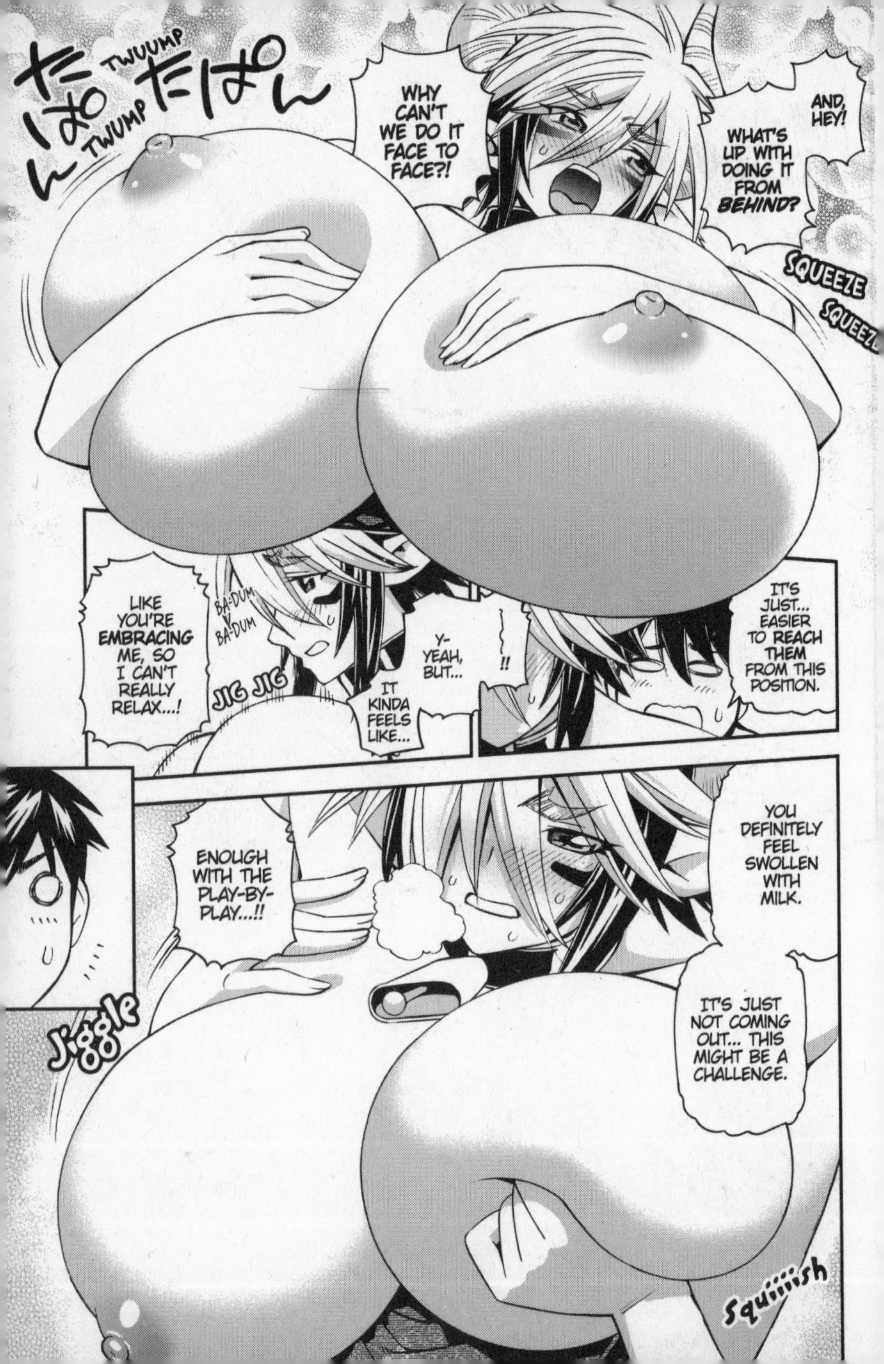
TWUUMP
TWUMP
AND, HEY!
WHAT'S UP WITH DOING IT FROM BEHIND?
WHY CAN'T WE DO IT FACE TO FACE?!
SQUEEZE
SQUEEZ
IT'S JUST... EASIER TO REACH THEM FROM THIS POSITION.
...!!
Y-YEAH, BUT...
IT KINDA FEELS LIKE...
LIKE YOU'RE EMBRACING ME, SO I CAN'T REALLY RELAX...!
BA-DUM BA-DUM
JIG JIG
YOU DEFINITELY FEEL SWOLLEN WITH MILK.
ENOUGH WITH THE PLAY-BY-PLAY...!!
IT'S JUST NOT COMING OUT... THIS MIGHT BE A CHALLENGE.
Jiggle
Squiiiiish

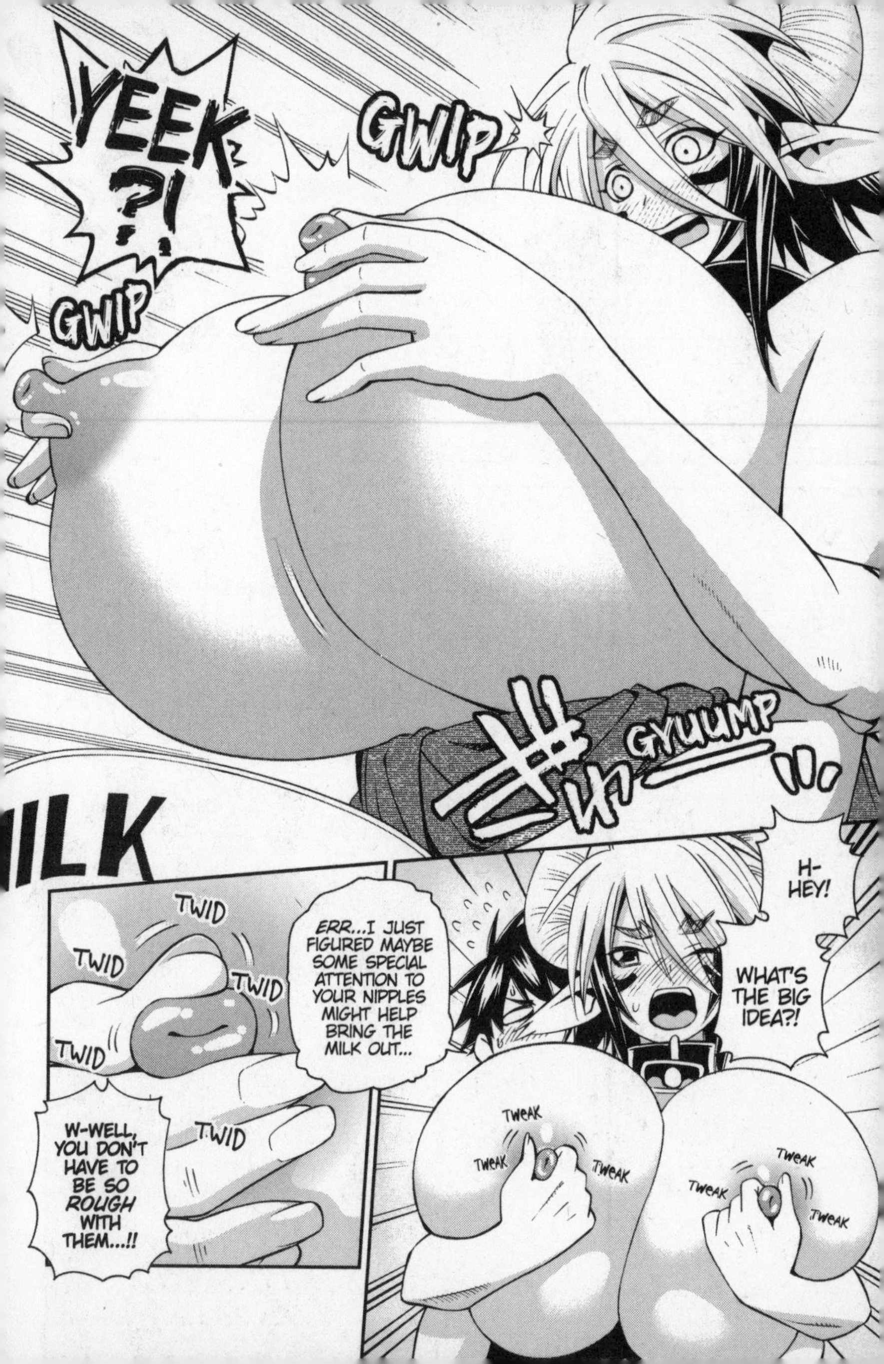
GWIP
YEEK?!
GWIP
GYUUMP
ILK
H-HEY!
WHAT'S THE BIG IDEA?!
ERR...I JUST FIGURED MAYBE SOME SPECIAL ATTENTION TO YOUR NIPPLES MIGHT HELP BRING THE MILK OUT...
TWEAK TWEAK TWEAK
TWEAK TWEAK TWEAK
TWID TWID TWID TWID
W-WELL, YOU DON'T HAVE TO BE SO *ROUGH* WITH THEM...!!
TWID

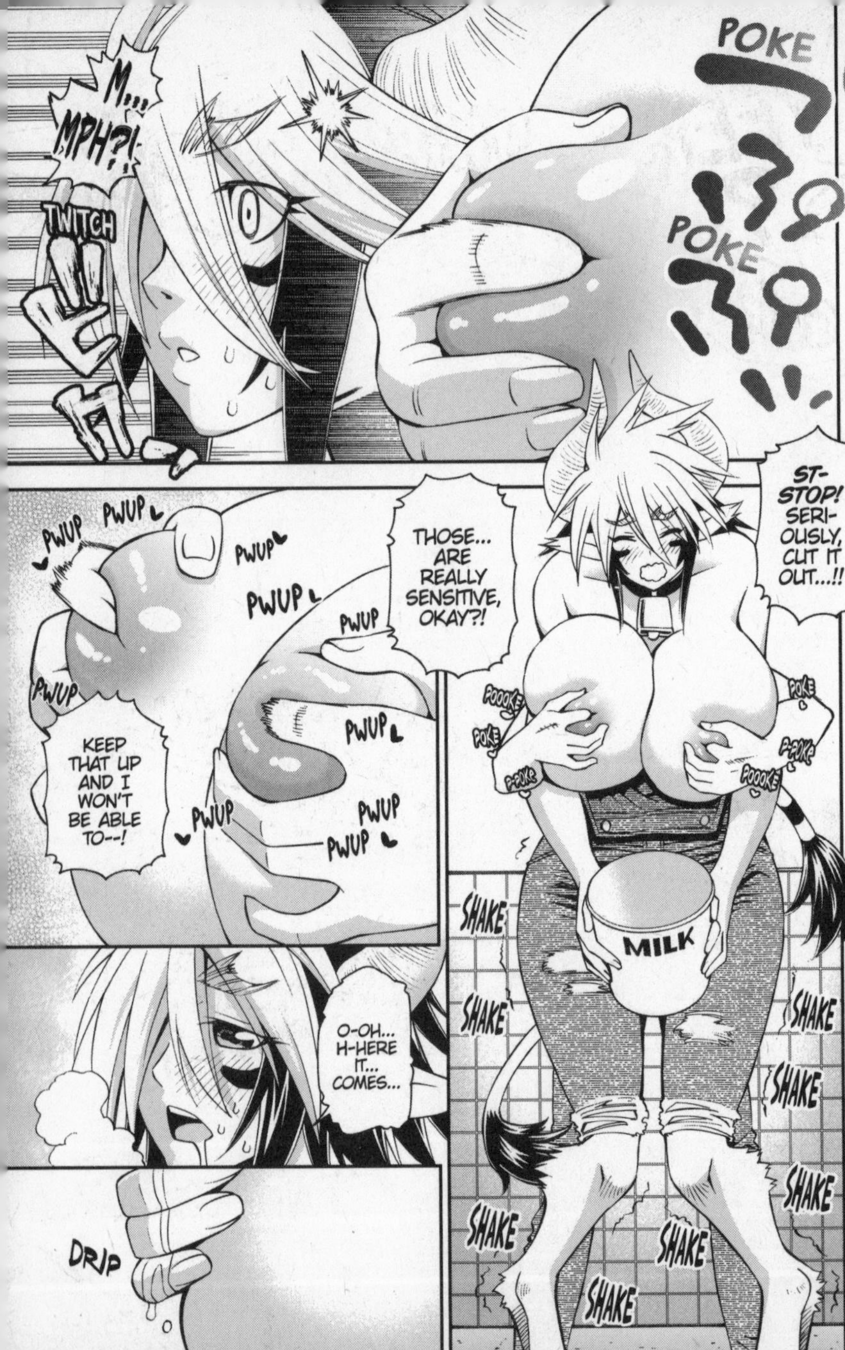
POKE
POKE
M... MPH?!
TWITCH
ST-STOP! SERIOUSLY, CUT IT OUT...!!
POKE
POOOKE
P-POKE
POOOKE
POKE
P-POKE
MILK
SHAKE
SHAKE
SHAKE
SHAKE
SHAKE
SHAKE
SHAKE
SHAKE
SHAKE
THOSE... ARE REALLY SENSITIVE, OKAY?!
PWUP
PWUP
PWUP
PWUP
PWUP
PWUP
PWUP
PWUP
PWUP
PWUP
KEEP THAT UP AND I WON'T BE ABLE TO--!
O-OH... H-HERE IT... COMES...
DRIP

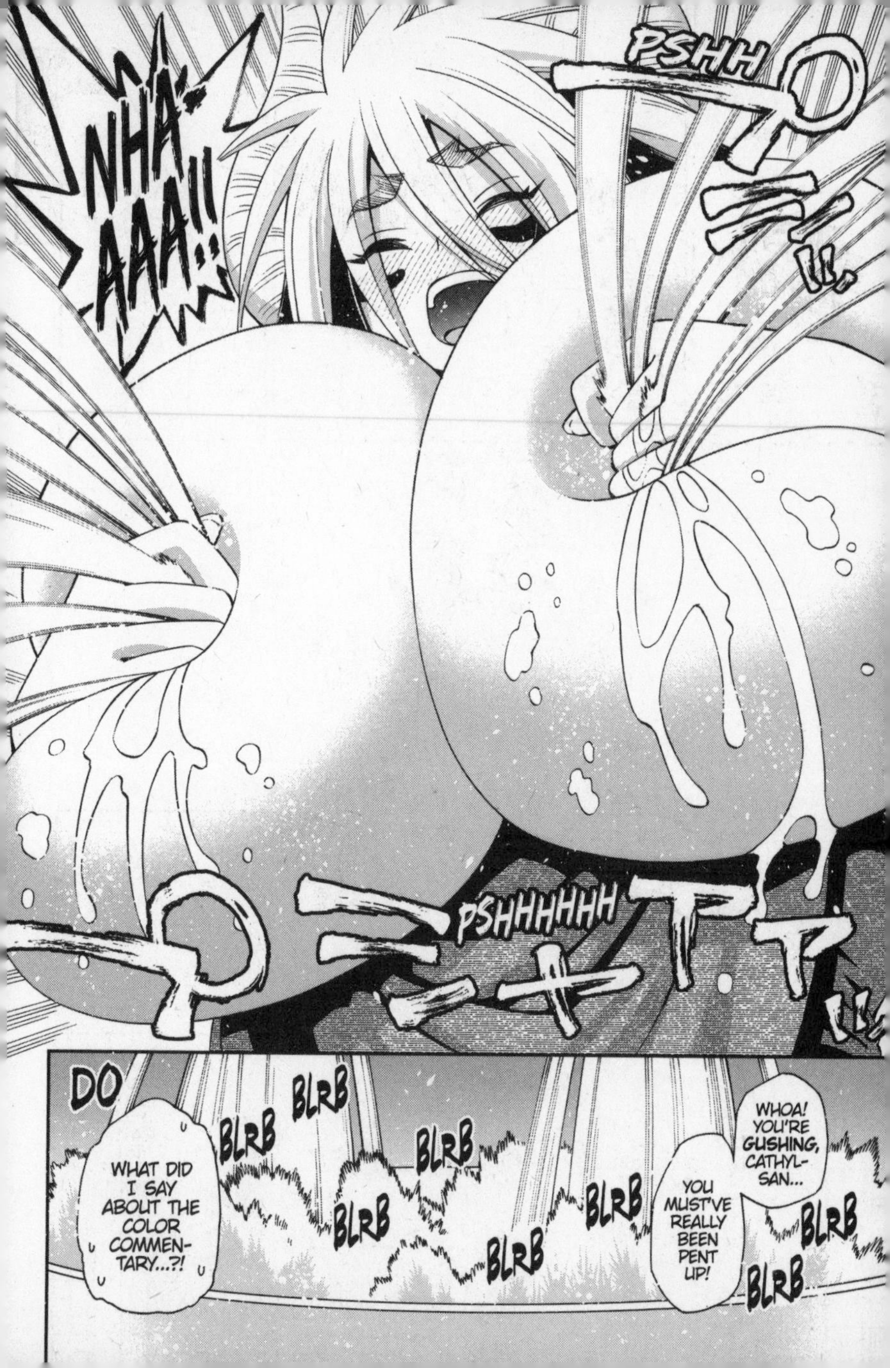
PSHH
NHAAA!!
PSHHHHHH
WHOA! YOU'RE GUSHING, CATHYL-SAN...
YOU MUST'VE REALLY BEEN PENT UP!
BLRB
BLRB
BLRB
BLRB
BLRB
BLRB
BLRB
BLRB
WHAT DID I SAY ABOUT THE COLOR COMMENTARY...?!
DO

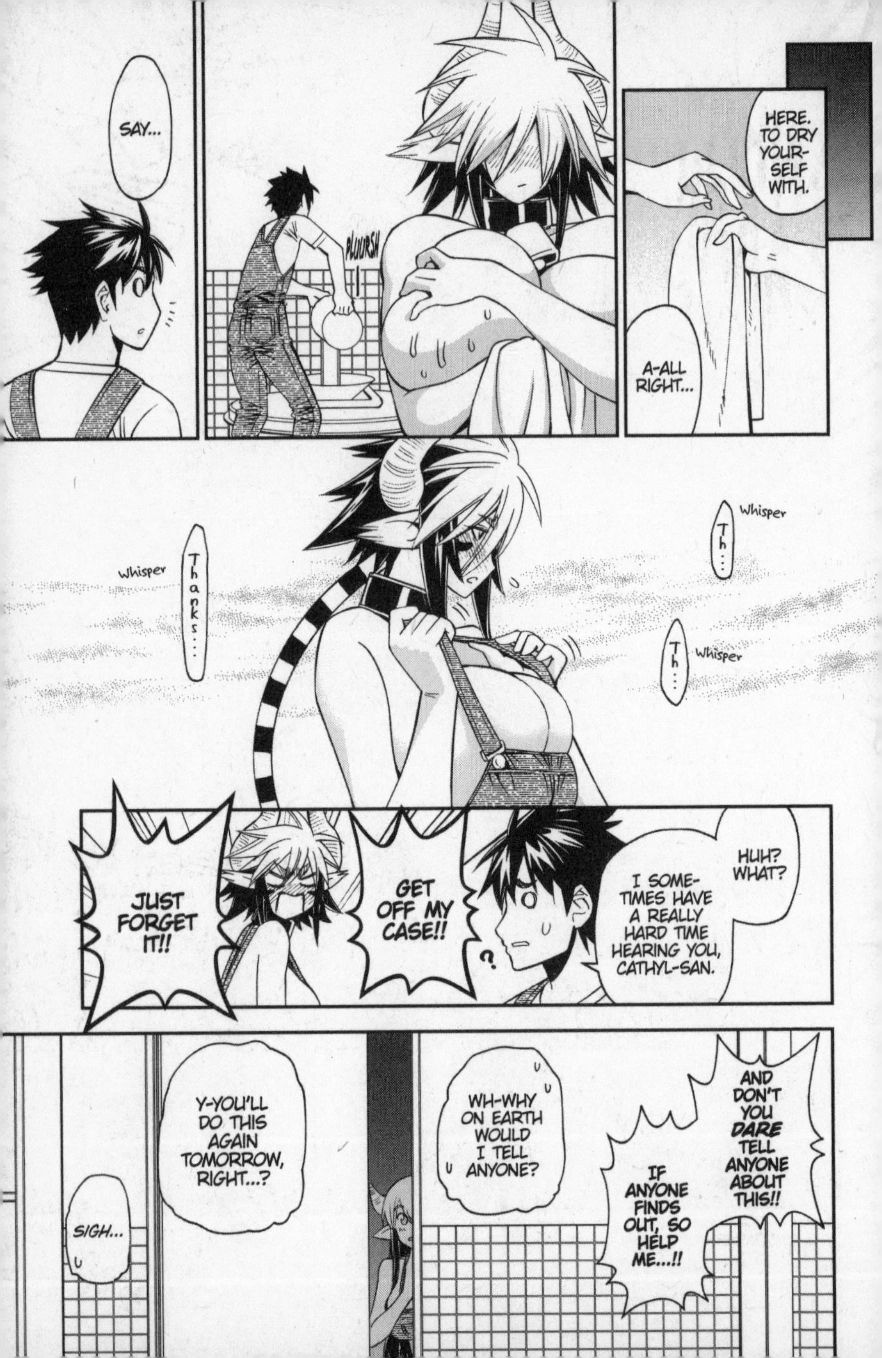
HERE. TO DRY YOUR-SELF WITH.
A-ALL RIGHT...
PLUURSH
SAY...
Whisper
Th...
Whisper
Th...
Whisper
Thanks...
HUH? WHAT?
I SOME-TIMES HAVE A REALLY HARD TIME HEARING YOU, CATHYL-SAN.
GET OFF MY CASE!!
JUST FORGET IT!!
AND DON'T YOU *DARE* TELL ANYONE ABOUT THIS!!
IF ANYONE FINDS OUT, SO HELP ME...!!
WH-WHY ON EARTH WOULD I TELL ANYONE?
Y-YOU'LL DO THIS AGAIN TOMORROW, RIGHT...?
SIGH...

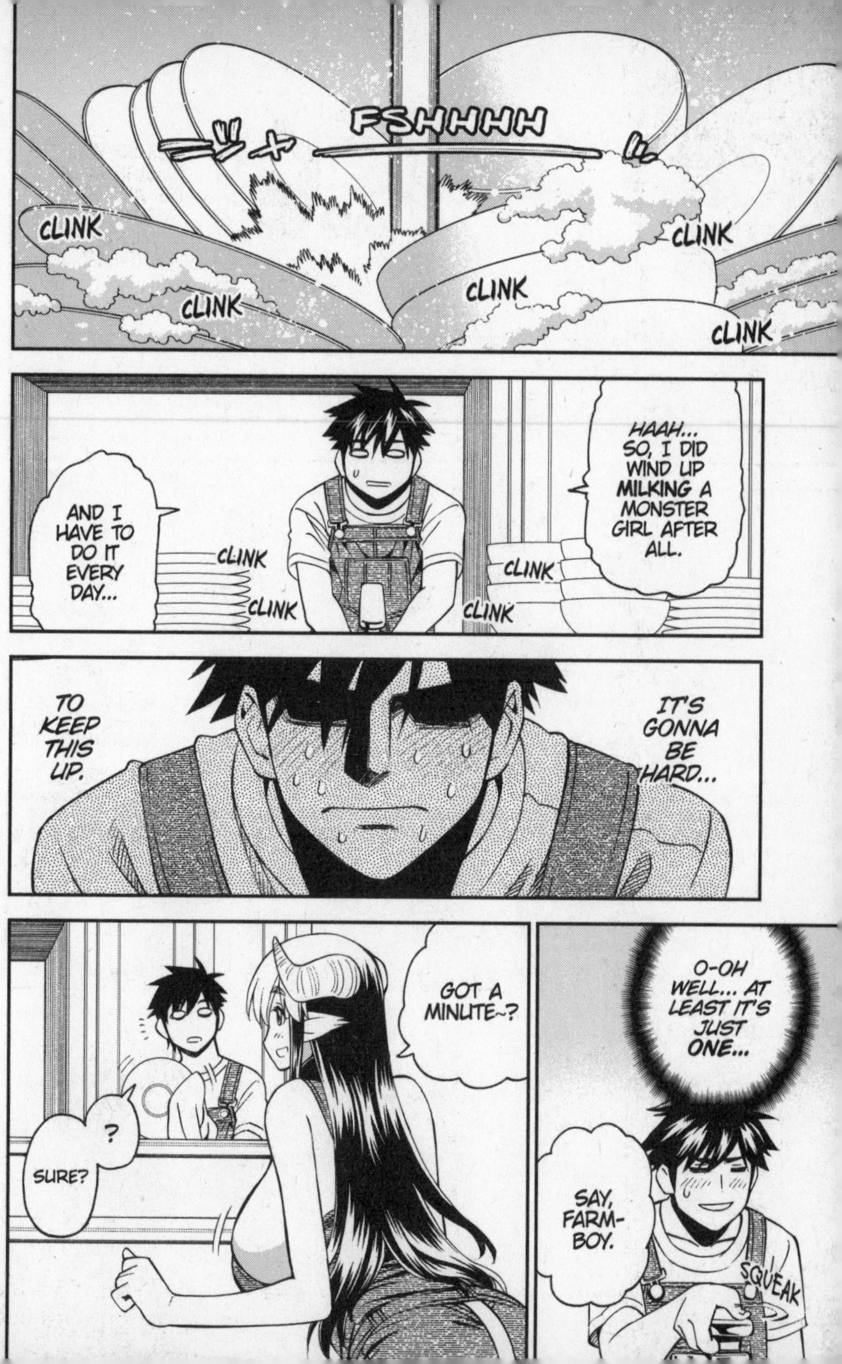
FSHHHH
CLINK
CLINK
CLINK
CLINK
CLINK
HAAH... SO, I DID WIND UP MILKING A MONSTER GIRL AFTER ALL.
AND I HAVE TO DO IT EVERY DAY...
CLINK
CLINK
CLINK
CLINK
IT'S GONNA BE HARD...
TO KEEP THIS UP.
O-OH WELL... AT LEAST IT'S JUST ONE...
SAY, FARM-BOY.
SQUEAK
GOT A MINUTE~?
?
SURE?

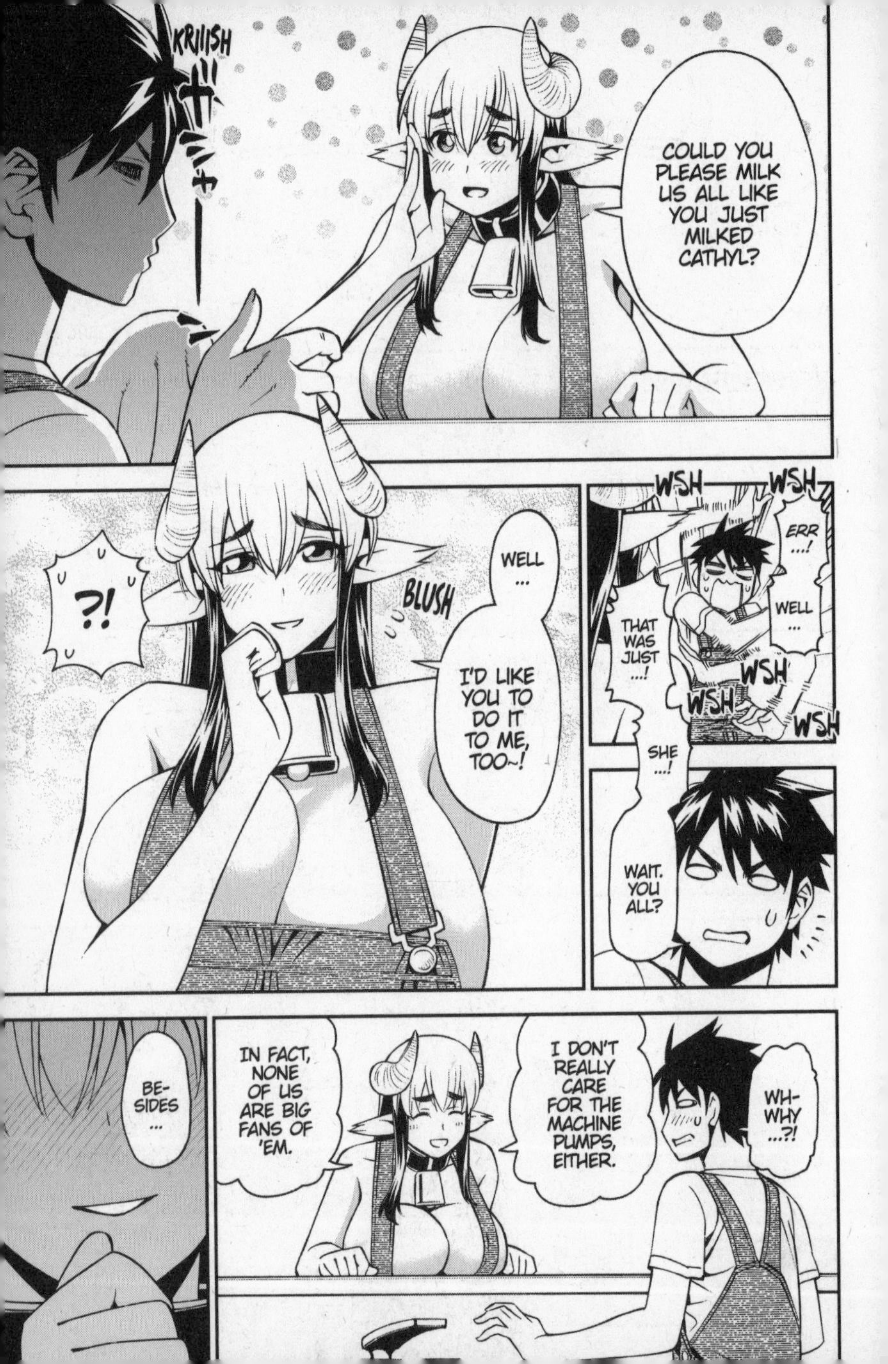
COULD YOU PLEASE MILK US ALL LIKE YOU JUST MILKED CATHYL?
KRIIISH
WSH
WSH
ERR ...!
WELL ...
THAT WAS JUST ...!
WSH
WSH
WSH
SHE ...!
WAIT. YOU ALL?
WELL ...
I'D LIKE YOU TO DO IT TO ME, TOO~!
BLUSH
?!
WH-WHY ...?!
I DON'T REALLY CARE FOR THE MACHINE PUMPS, EITHER.
IN FACT, NONE OF US ARE BIG FANS OF 'EM.
BE-SIDES ...

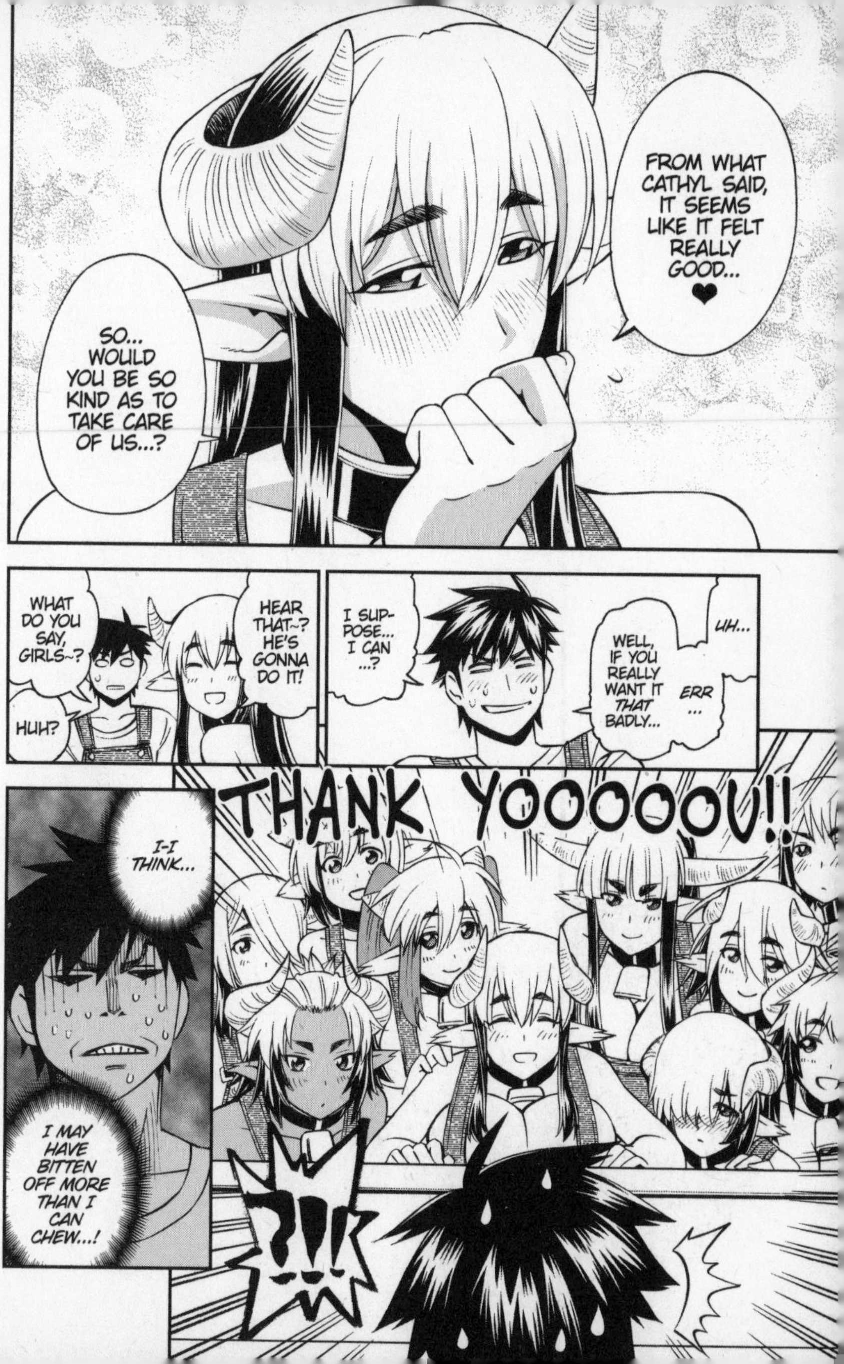
FROM WHAT CATHYL SAID, IT SEEMS LIKE IT FELT REALLY GOOD... ❤
SO... WOULD YOU BE SO KIND AS TO TAKE CARE OF US...?
UH...
WELL, IF YOU REALLY WANT IT *THAT* BADLY...
ERR ...
I SUP-POSE... I CAN ...?
HEAR THAT~? HE'S GONNA DO IT!
WHAT DO YOU SAY, GIRLS~?
HUH?
THANK YOOOOOU!!
?!!
I-I THINK...
I MAY HAVE BITTEN OFF MORE THAN I CAN CHEW...!

Monster Musume

Everyday Life with Monster Girls

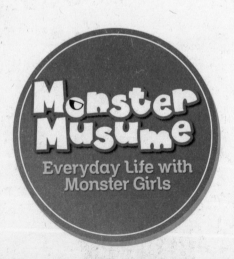

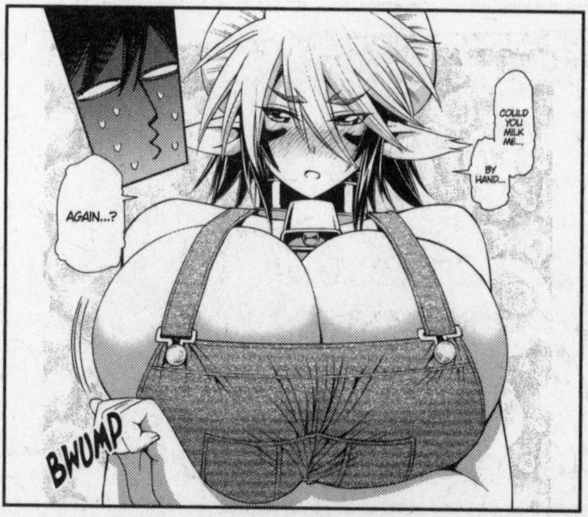
COULD YOU MILK ME...
BY HAND...
AGAIN...?
BWUMP

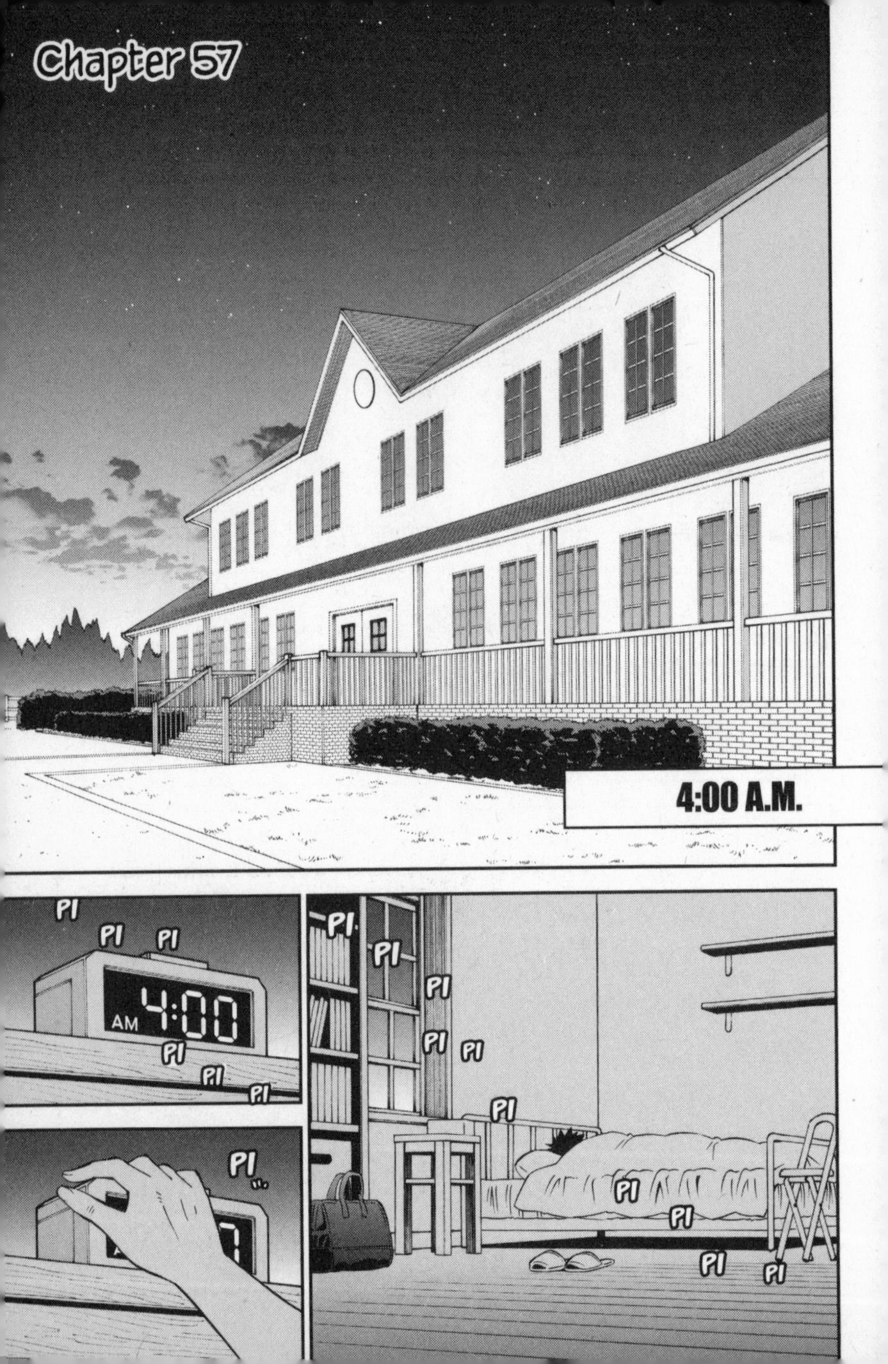
Chapter 57
4:00 A.M.
PI
PI
PI
PI
PI PI
PI
PI
PI
PI
PI
PI
PI
PI
AM 4:00
PI
PI
PI
PI..

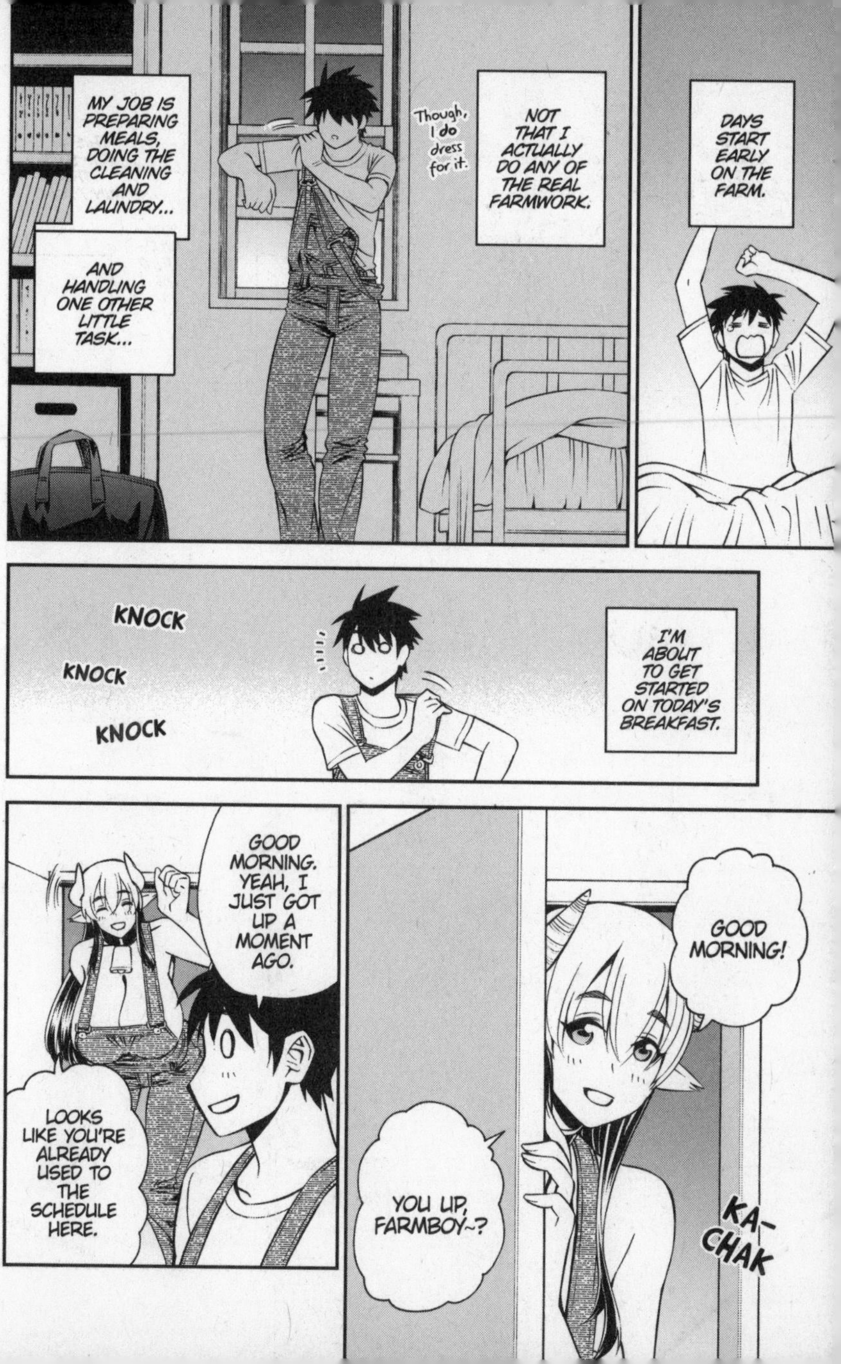
DAYS START EARLY ON THE FARM.
NOT THAT I ACTUALLY DO ANY OF THE REAL FARMWORK.
Though, I do dress for it.
MY JOB IS PREPARING MEALS, DOING THE CLEANING AND LAUNDRY...
AND HANDLING ONE OTHER LITTLE TASK...
I'M ABOUT TO GET STARTED ON TODAY'S BREAKFAST.
KNOCK
KNOCK
KNOCK
KA-CHAK
GOOD MORNING!
YOU UP, FARMBOY~?
GOOD MORNING. YEAH, I JUST GOT UP A MOMENT AGO.
LOOKS LIKE YOU'RE ALREADY USED TO THE SCHEDULE HERE.

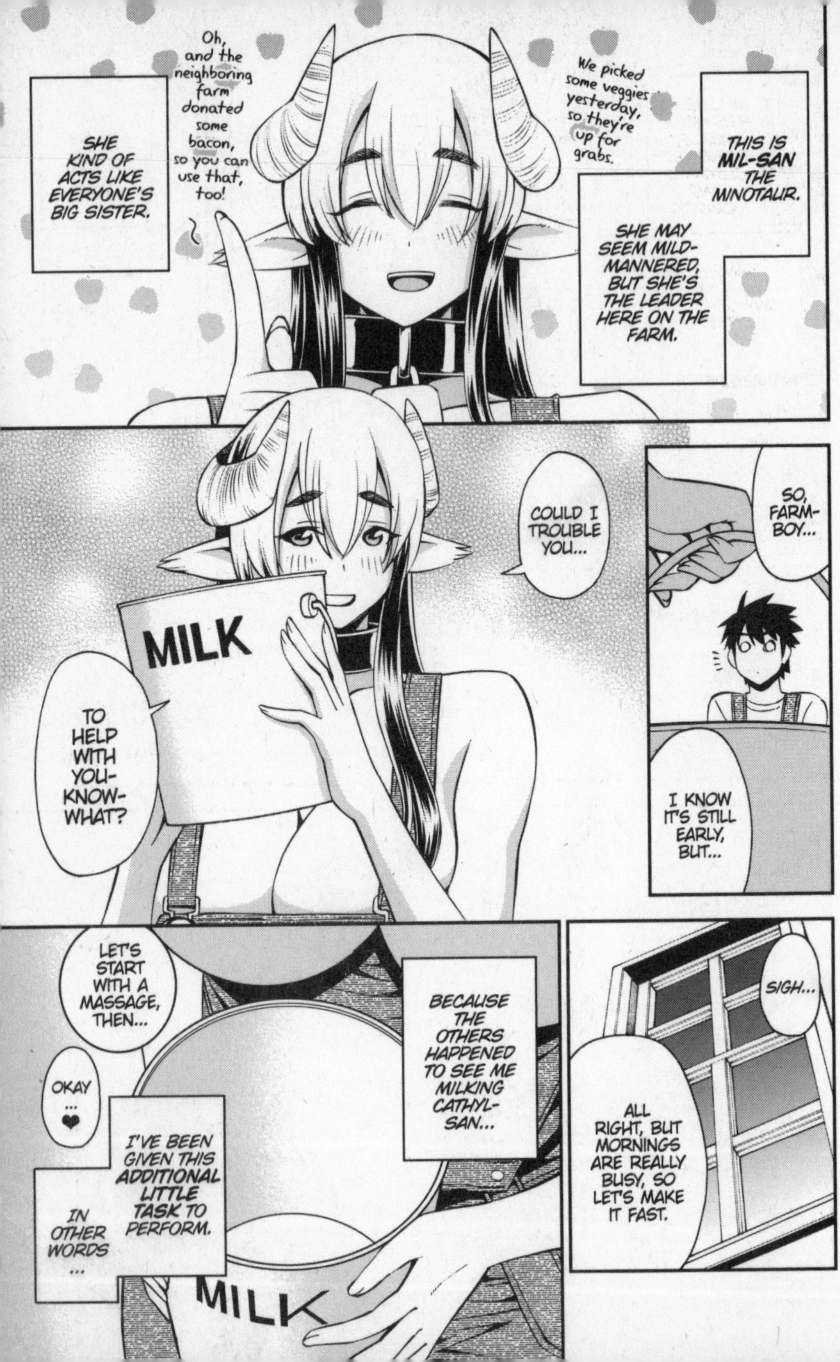
THIS IS MIL-SAN THE MINOTAUR.
SHE MAY SEEM MILD-MANNERED, BUT SHE'S THE LEADER HERE ON THE FARM.
We picked some veggies yesterday, so they're up for grabs.
Oh, and the neighboring farm donated some bacon, so you can use that, too!
SHE KIND OF ACTS LIKE EVERYONE'S BIG SISTER.
SO, FARM-BOY...
I KNOW IT'S STILL EARLY, BUT...
COULD I TROUBLE YOU...
MILK
TO HELP WITH YOU-KNOW-WHAT?
SIGH...
ALL RIGHT, BUT MORNINGS ARE REALLY BUSY, SO LET'S MAKE IT FAST.
BECAUSE THE OTHERS HAPPENED TO SEE ME MILKING CATHYL-SAN...
I'VE BEEN GIVEN THIS ADDITIONAL LITTLE TASK TO PERFORM.
LET'S START WITH A MASSAGE, THEN...
OKAY ... ❤
IN OTHER WORDS ...
MILK

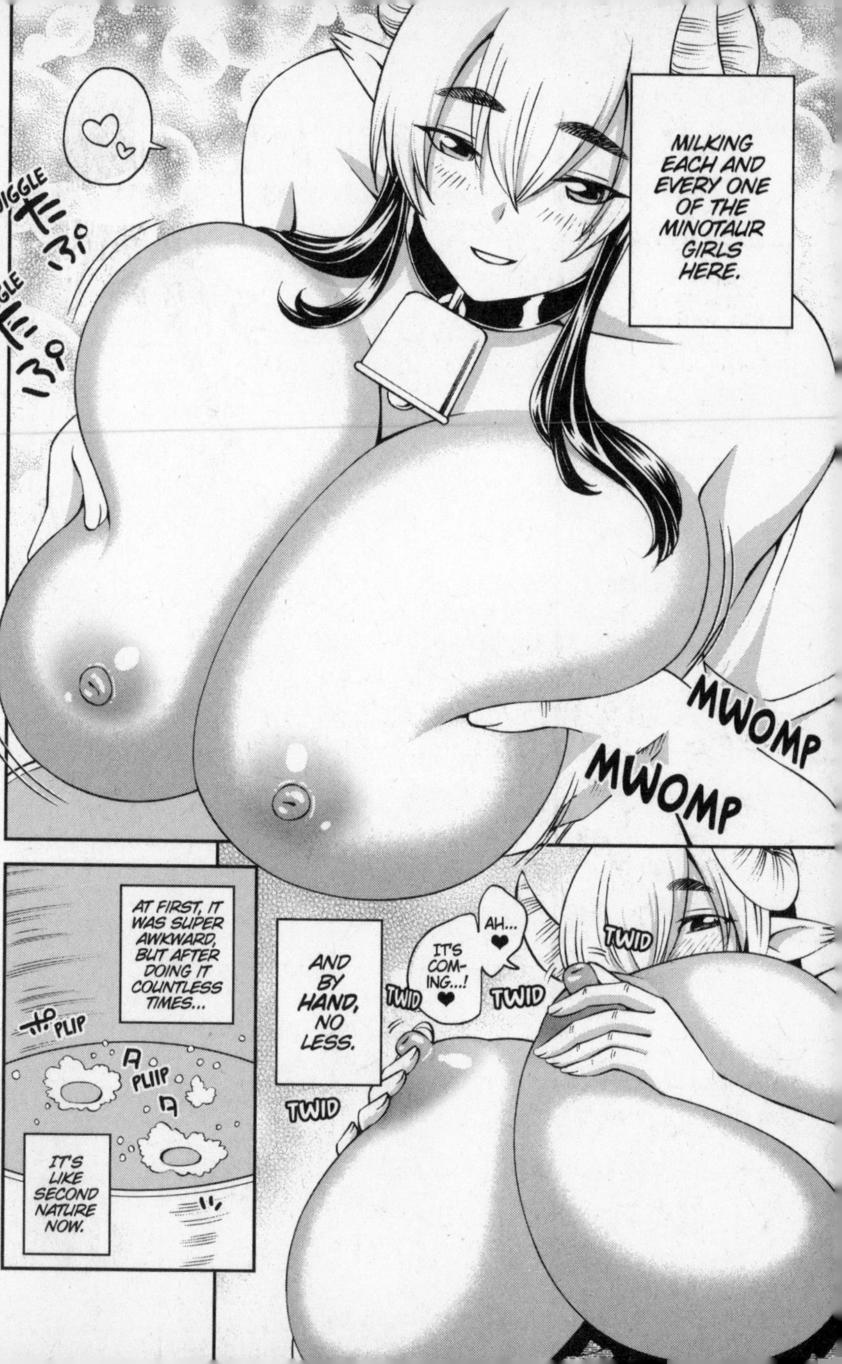
MILKING EACH AND EVERY ONE OF THE MINOTAUR GIRLS HERE.
MWOMP
MWOMP
JIGGLE
JIGGLE
AH... ❤
IT'S COMING...! ❤
TWID
AND BY HAND, NO LESS.
TWID
TWID
TWID
AT FIRST, IT WAS SUPER AWKWARD, BUT AFTER DOING IT COUNTLESS TIMES...
PLIP
PLIIP
IT'S LIKE SECOND NATURE NOW.

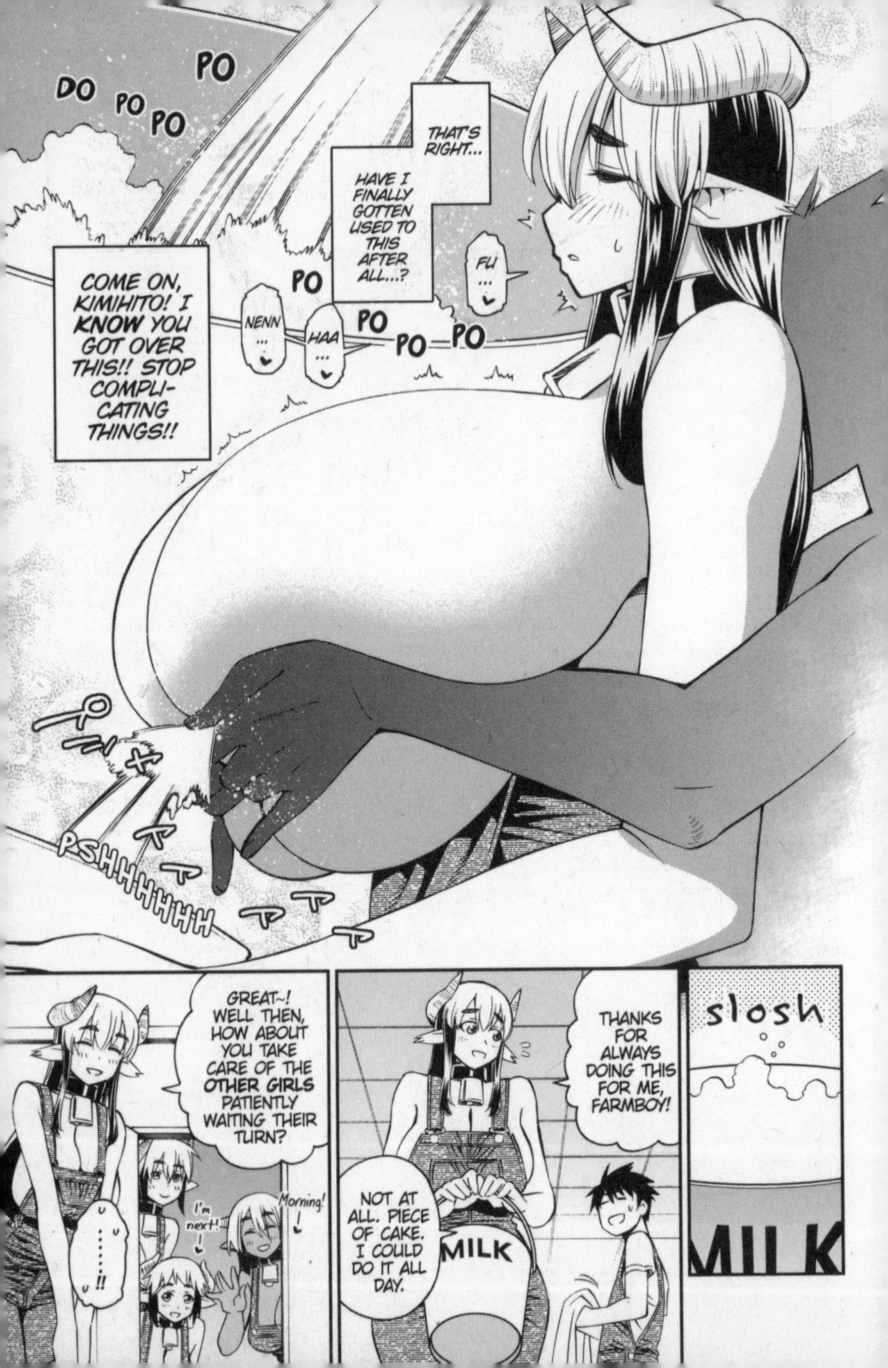

PO
DO PO PO
THAT'S RIGHT...
HAVE I FINALLY GOTTEN USED TO THIS AFTER ALL...?
FU ... ♥
PO PO PO PO
HAA ... ♥
NENN ... ♥
COME ON, KIMIHITO! I **KNOW** YOU GOT OVER THIS!! STOP COMPLI-CATING THINGS!!
PSHHHHHHH
slosh
MILK
THANKS FOR ALWAYS DOING THIS FOR ME, FARMBOY!
NOT AT ALL. PIECE OF CAKE. I COULD DO IT ALL DAY.
MILK
GREAT~! WELL THEN, HOW ABOUT YOU TAKE CARE OF THE **OTHER GIRLS** PATIENTLY WAITING THEIR TURN?
Morning! !
I'm next! ♥
......!!

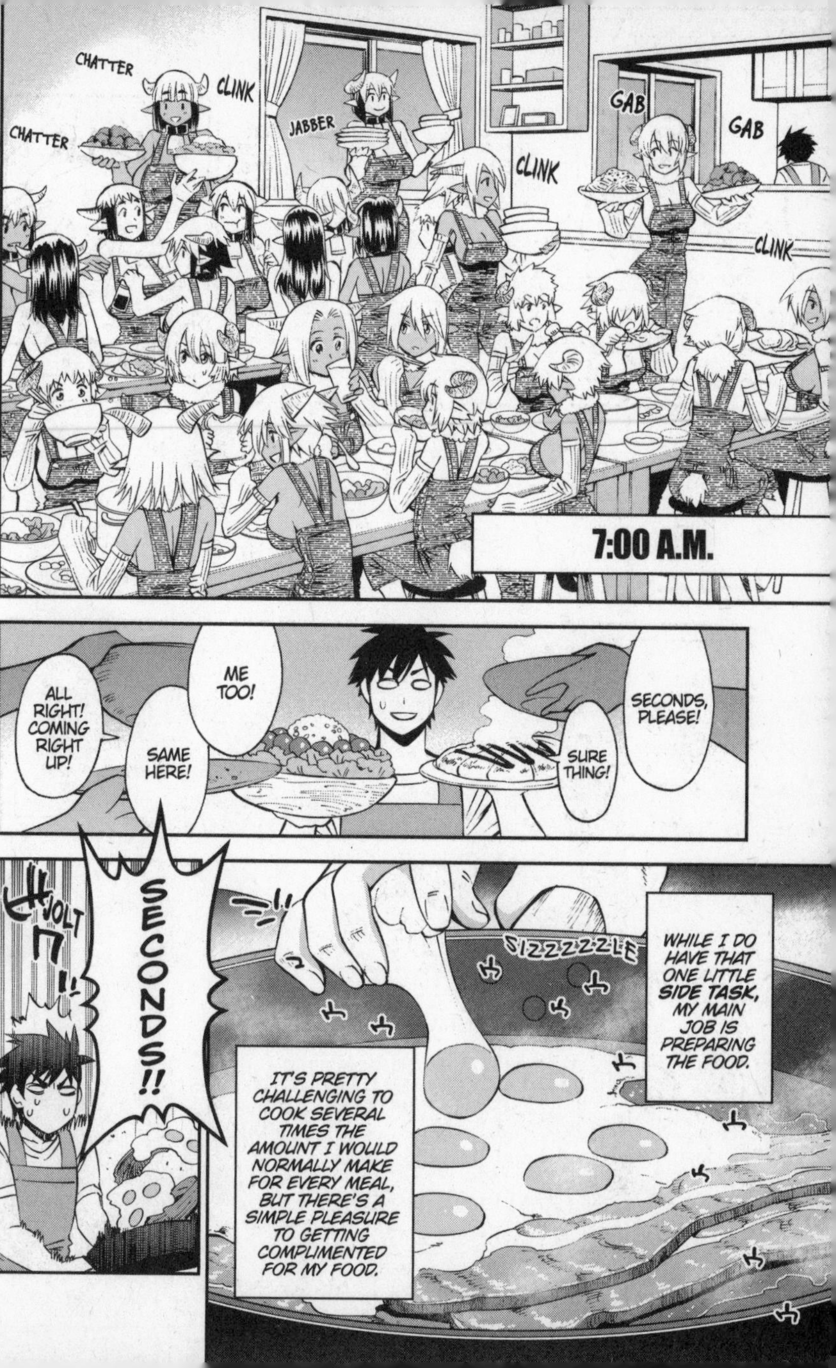
GAB
GAB
CLINK
CLINK
JABBER
CLINK
CHATTER
CHATTER
7:00 A.M.
SECONDS, PLEASE!
SURE THING!
ME TOO!
SAME HERE!
ALL RIGHT! COMING RIGHT UP!
WHILE I DO HAVE THAT ONE LITTLE SIDE TASK, MY MAIN JOB IS PREPARING THE FOOD.
SIZZZZZLE
IT'S PRETTY CHALLENGING TO COOK SEVERAL TIMES THE AMOUNT I WOULD NORMALLY MAKE FOR EVERY MEAL, BUT THERE'S A SIMPLE PLEASURE TO GETTING COMPLIMENTED FOR MY FOOD.
SECONDS!!
JOLT

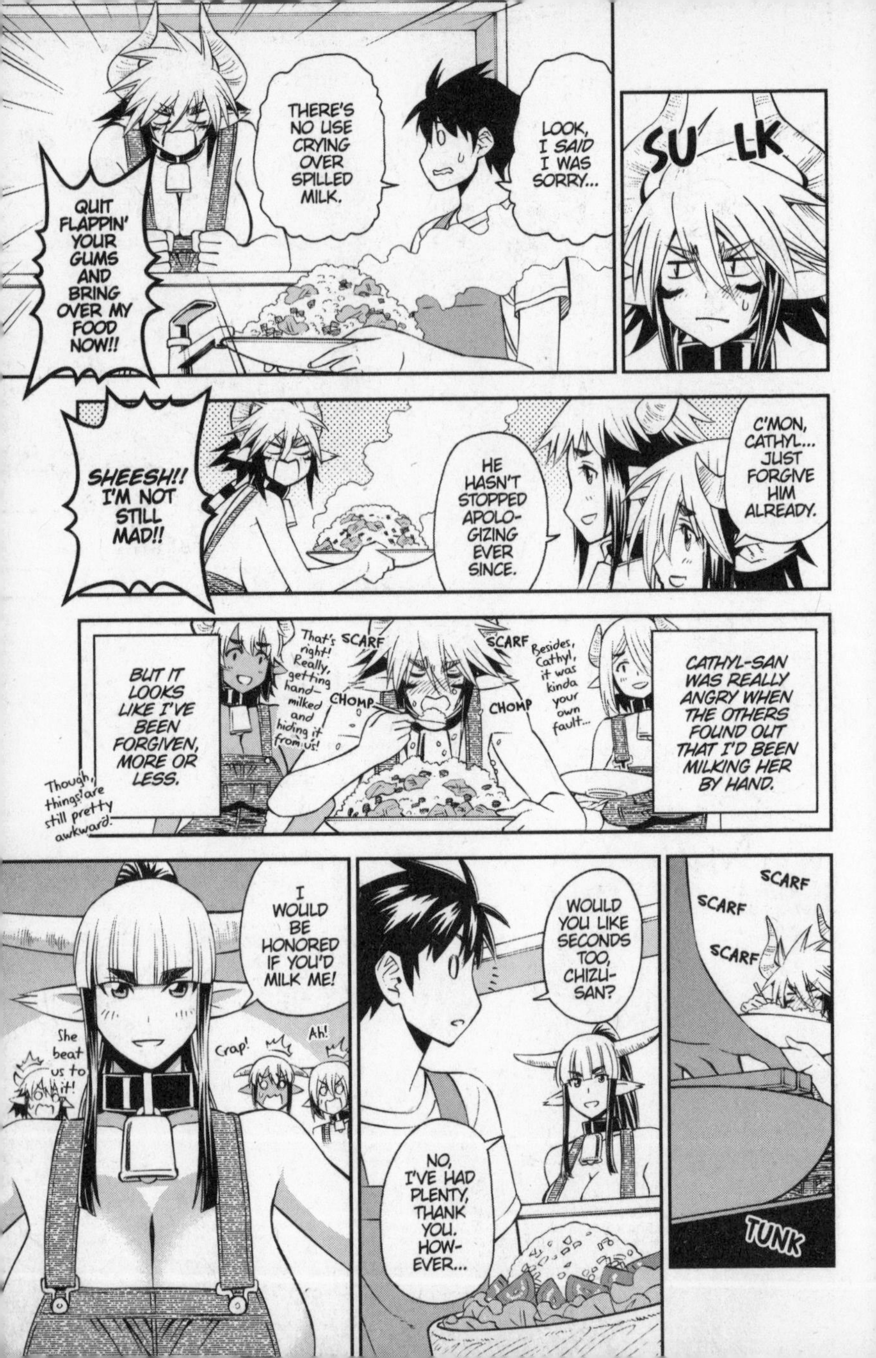
SULK
LOOK, I SAID I WAS SORRY...
THERE'S NO USE CRYING OVER SPILLED MILK.
QUIT FLAPPIN' YOUR GUMS AND BRING OVER MY FOOD NOW!!
C'MON, CATHYL... JUST FORGIVE HIM ALREADY.
HE HASN'T STOPPED APOLOGIZING EVER SINCE.
SHEESH!! I'M NOT STILL MAD!!
CATHYL-SAN WAS REALLY ANGRY WHEN THE OTHERS FOUND OUT THAT I'D BEEN MILKING HER BY HAND.
Besides, Cathyl, it was kinda your own fault...
SCARF
CHOMP
SCARF
That's right! Really, getting hand-milked and hiding it from us!
CHOMP
BUT IT LOOKS LIKE I'VE BEEN FORGIVEN, MORE OR LESS.
Though, things are still pretty awkward.
SCARF
SCARF
SCARF
TUNK
WOULD YOU LIKE SECONDS TOO, CHIZU-SAN?
NO, I'VE HAD PLENTY, THANK YOU. HOW-EVER...
I WOULD BE HONORED IF YOU'D MILK ME!
Ah!
Crap!
She beat us to it!

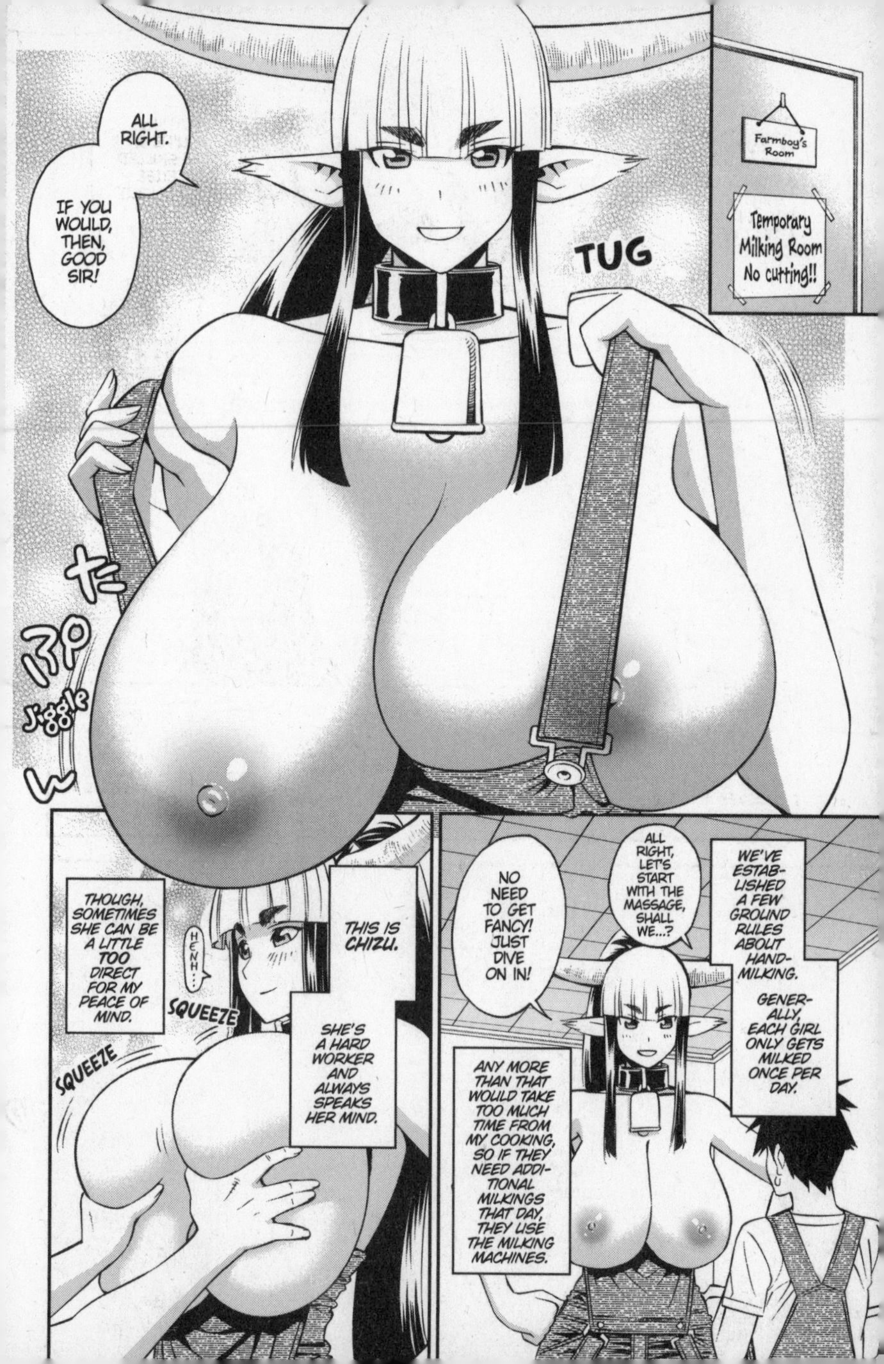
Farmboy's Room
Temporary Milking Room No cutting!!
TUG
ALL RIGHT.
IF YOU WOULD, THEN, GOOD SIR!
Jiggle
WE'VE ESTABLISHED A FEW GROUND RULES ABOUT HAND-MILKING.
GENERALLY, EACH GIRL ONLY GETS MILKED ONCE PER DAY.
ALL RIGHT, LET'S START WITH THE MASSAGE, SHALL WE...?
NO NEED TO GET FANCY! JUST DIVE ON IN!
ANY MORE THAN THAT WOULD TAKE TOO MUCH TIME FROM MY COOKING, SO IF THEY NEED ADDITIONAL MILKINGS THAT DAY, THEY USE THE MILKING MACHINES.
THIS IS CHIZU.
THOUGH, SOMETIMES SHE CAN BE A LITTLE TOO DIRECT FOR MY PEACE OF MIND.
HENH...
SQUEEZE
SHE'S A HARD WORKER AND ALWAYS SPEAKS HER MIND.
SQUEEZE

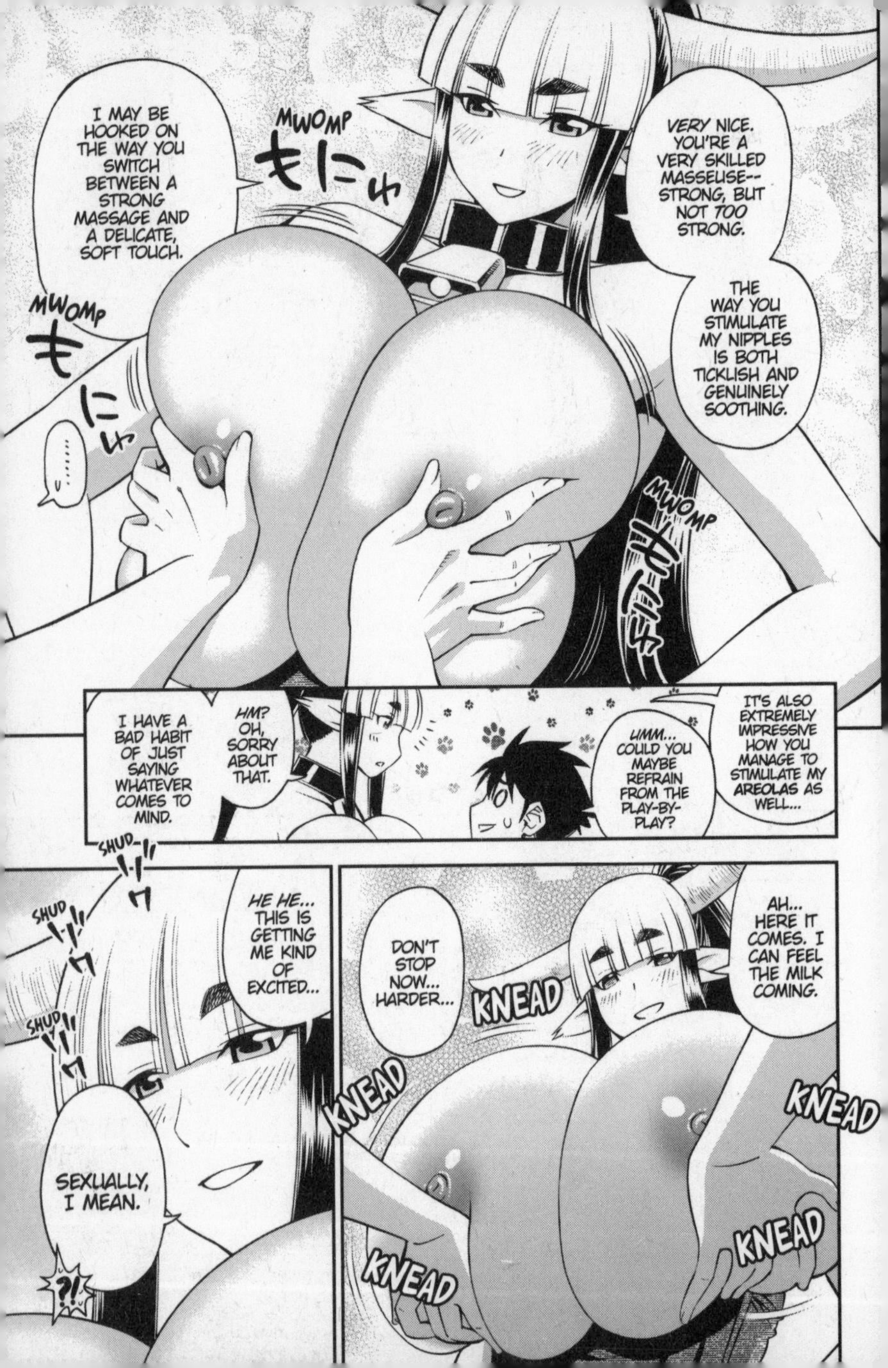
VERY NICE. YOU'RE A VERY SKILLED MASSEUSE-- STRONG, BUT NOT TOO STRONG.
THE WAY YOU STIMULATE MY NIPPLES IS BOTH TICKLISH AND GENUINELY SOOTHING.
MWOMP
もにゅ
MWOMP
もにゅ
I MAY BE HOOKED ON THE WAY YOU SWITCH BETWEEN A STRONG MASSAGE AND A DELICATE, SOFT TOUCH.
MWOMP
もにゅ
......
IT'S ALSO EXTREMELY IMPRESSIVE HOW YOU MANAGE TO STIMULATE MY AREOLAS AS WELL...
UMM... COULD YOU MAYBE REFRAIN FROM THE PLAY-BY-PLAY?
HM? OH, SORRY ABOUT THAT.
I HAVE A BAD HABIT OF JUST SAYING WHATEVER COMES TO MIND.
AH... HERE IT COMES. I CAN FEEL THE MILK COMING.
KNEAD
DON'T STOP NOW... HARDER...
KNEAD
KNEAD
KNEAD
KNEAD
SHUD
SHUD
SHUD
HE HE... THIS IS GETTING ME KIND OF EXCITED...
SEXUALLY, I MEAN.
?!

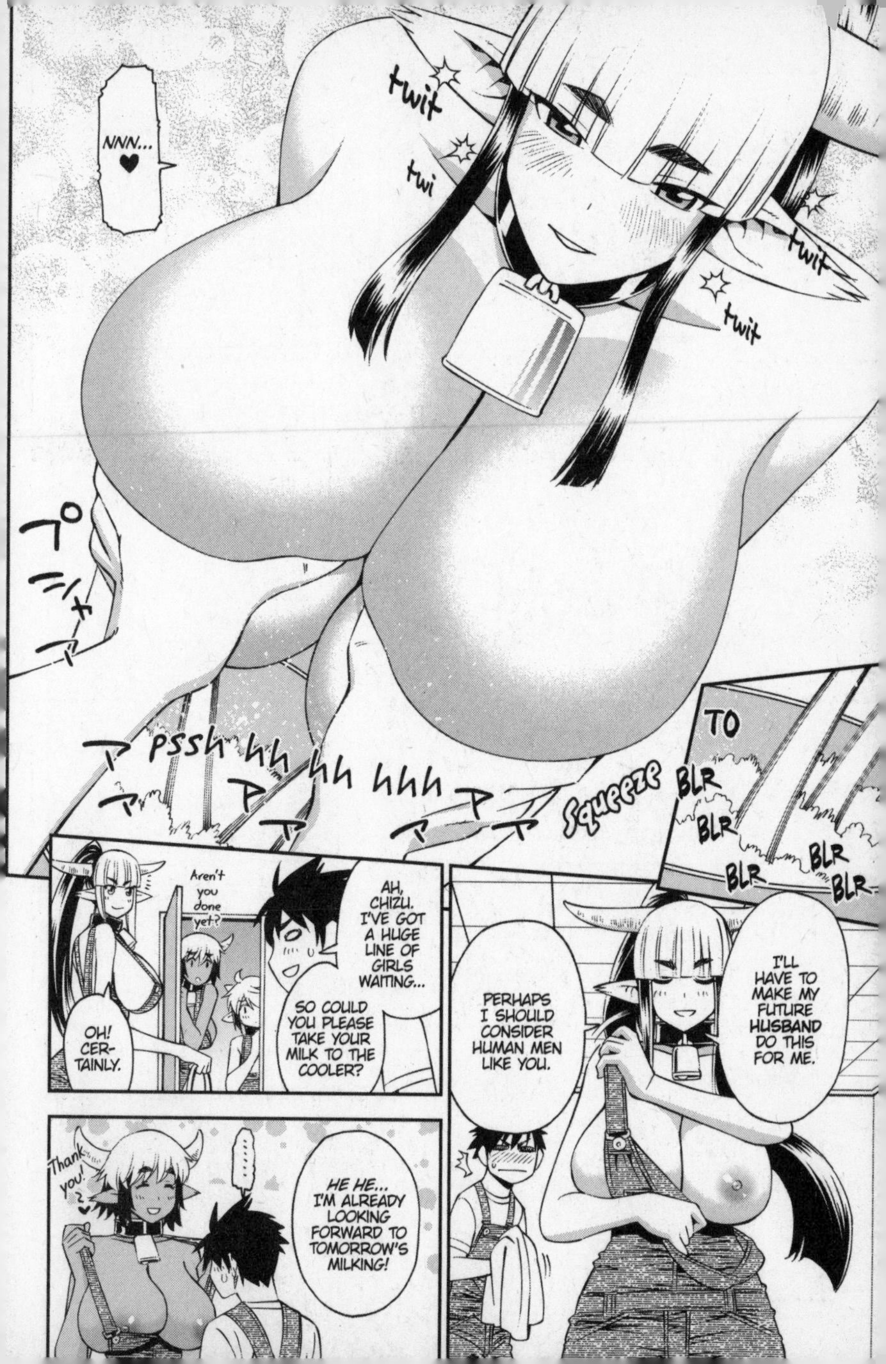
NNN... ♥
twit
twi
twit
twit
PSSH HH HH HHH
squeeze
TO
BLR
BLR
BLR
BLR
BLR
I'LL HAVE TO MAKE MY FUTURE HUSBAND DO THIS FOR ME.
PERHAPS I SHOULD CONSIDER HUMAN MEN LIKE YOU.
AH, CHIZU. I'VE GOT A HUGE LINE OF GIRLS WAITING...
SO COULD YOU PLEASE TAKE YOUR MILK TO THE COOLER?
Aren't you done yet?
OH! CER-TAINLY.
...
HE HE... I'M ALREADY LOOKING FORWARD TO TOMORROW'S MILKING!
Thank you!

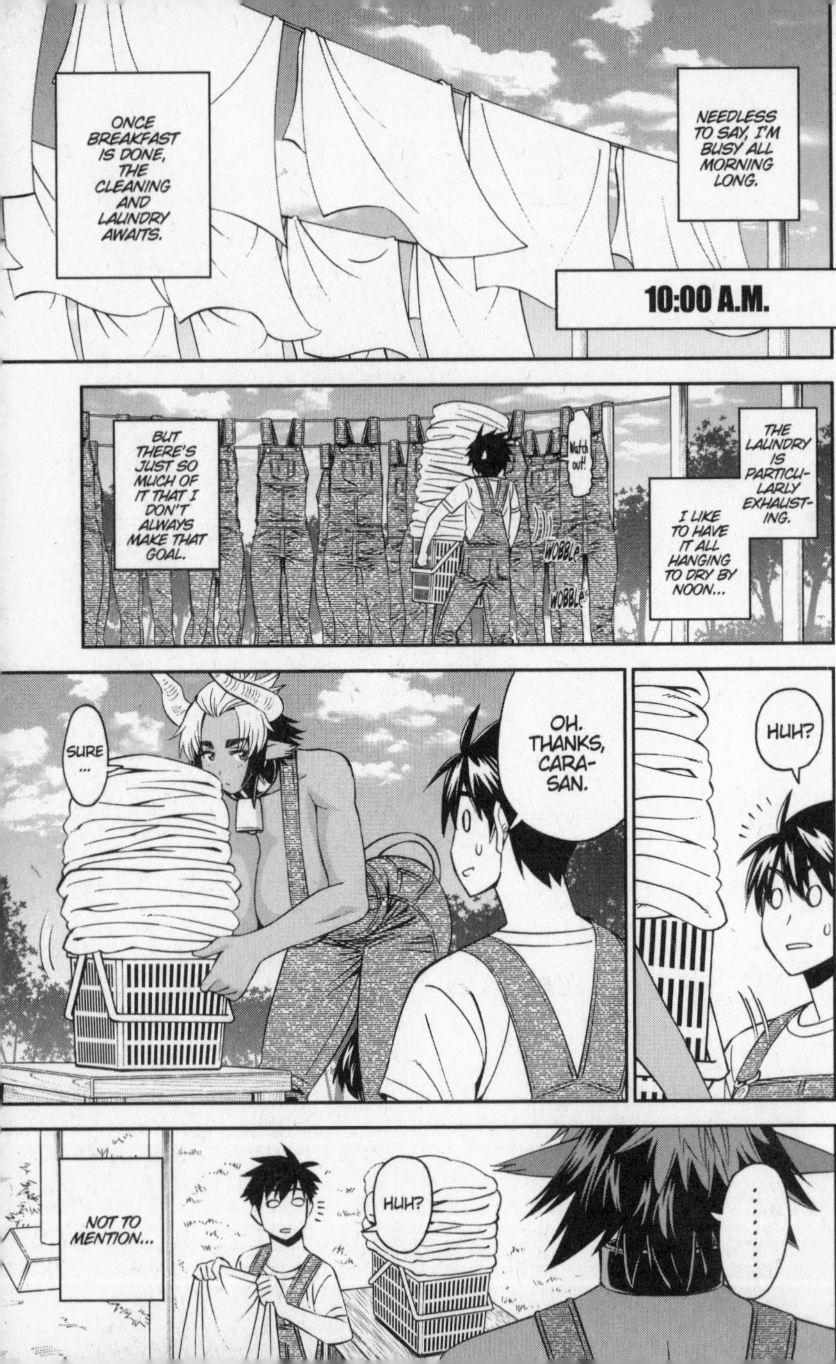
NEEDLESS TO SAY, I'M BUSY ALL MORNING LONG.
ONCE BREAKFAST IS DONE, THE CLEANING AND LAUNDRY AWAITS.
10:00 A.M.
THE LAUNDRY IS PARTICU-LARLY EXHAUST-ING.
I LIKE TO HAVE IT ALL HANGING TO DRY BY NOON...
Watch out!
WOBBLE
WOBBLE
BUT THERE'S JUST SO MUCH OF IT THAT I DON'T ALWAYS MAKE THAT GOAL.
HUH?
OH. THANKS, CARA-SAN.
SURE...
......
HUH?
NOT TO MENTION...

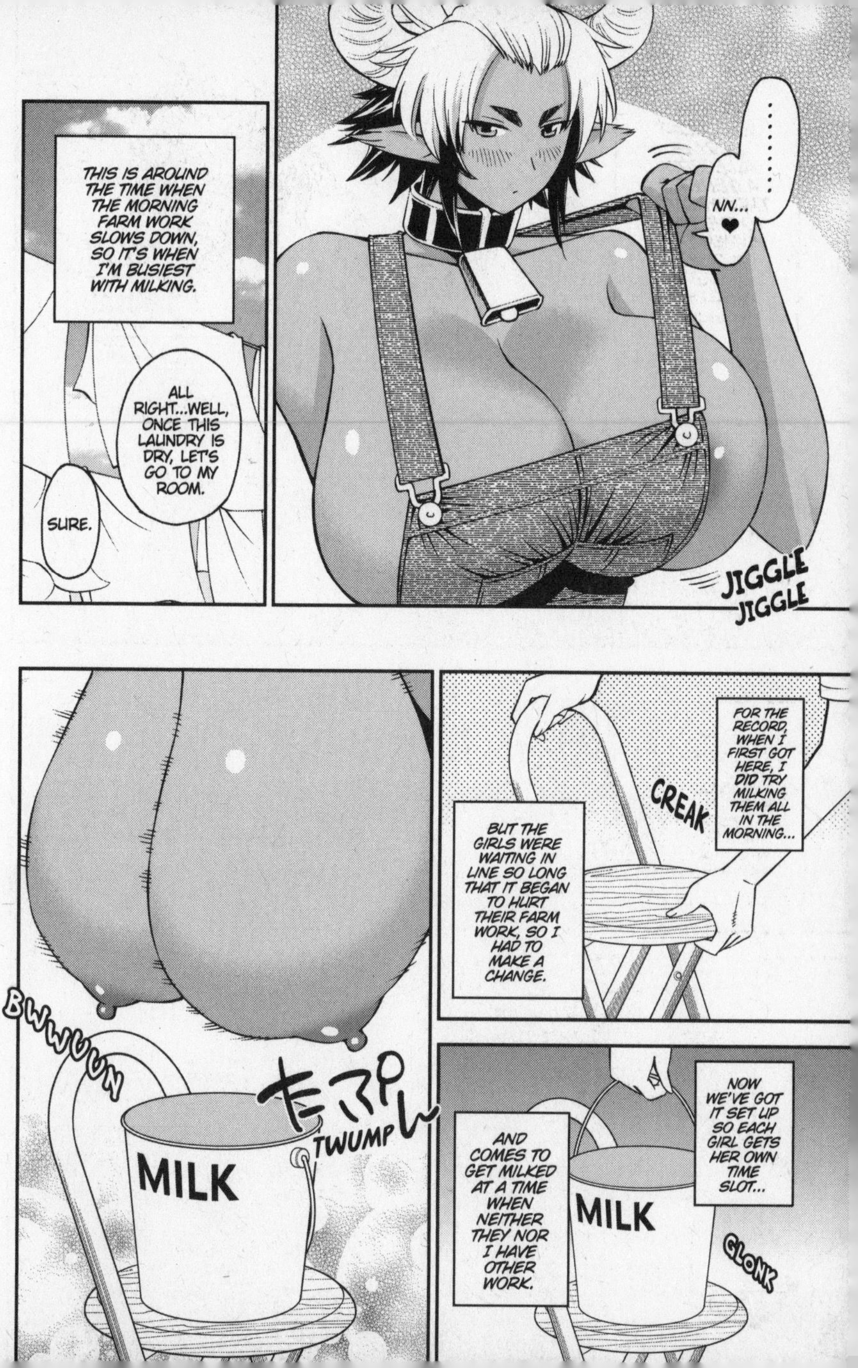
......
NN... ❤
JIGGLE JIGGLE
THIS IS AROUND THE TIME WHEN THE MORNING FARM WORK SLOWS DOWN, SO IT'S WHEN I'M BUSIEST WITH MILKING.
ALL RIGHT...WELL, ONCE THIS LAUNDRY IS DRY, LET'S GO TO MY ROOM.
SURE.
FOR THE RECORD, WHEN I FIRST GOT HERE, I DID TRY MILKING THEM ALL IN THE MORNING...
CREAK
BUT THE GIRLS WERE WAITING IN LINE SO LONG THAT IT BEGAN TO HURT THEIR FARM WORK, SO I HAD TO MAKE A CHANGE.
NOW WE'VE GOT IT SET UP SO EACH GIRL GETS HER OWN TIME SLOT...
AND COMES TO GET MILKED AT A TIME WHEN NEITHER THEY NOR I HAVE OTHER WORK.
MILK
CLONK
BWWUUN
TWUMP
MILK

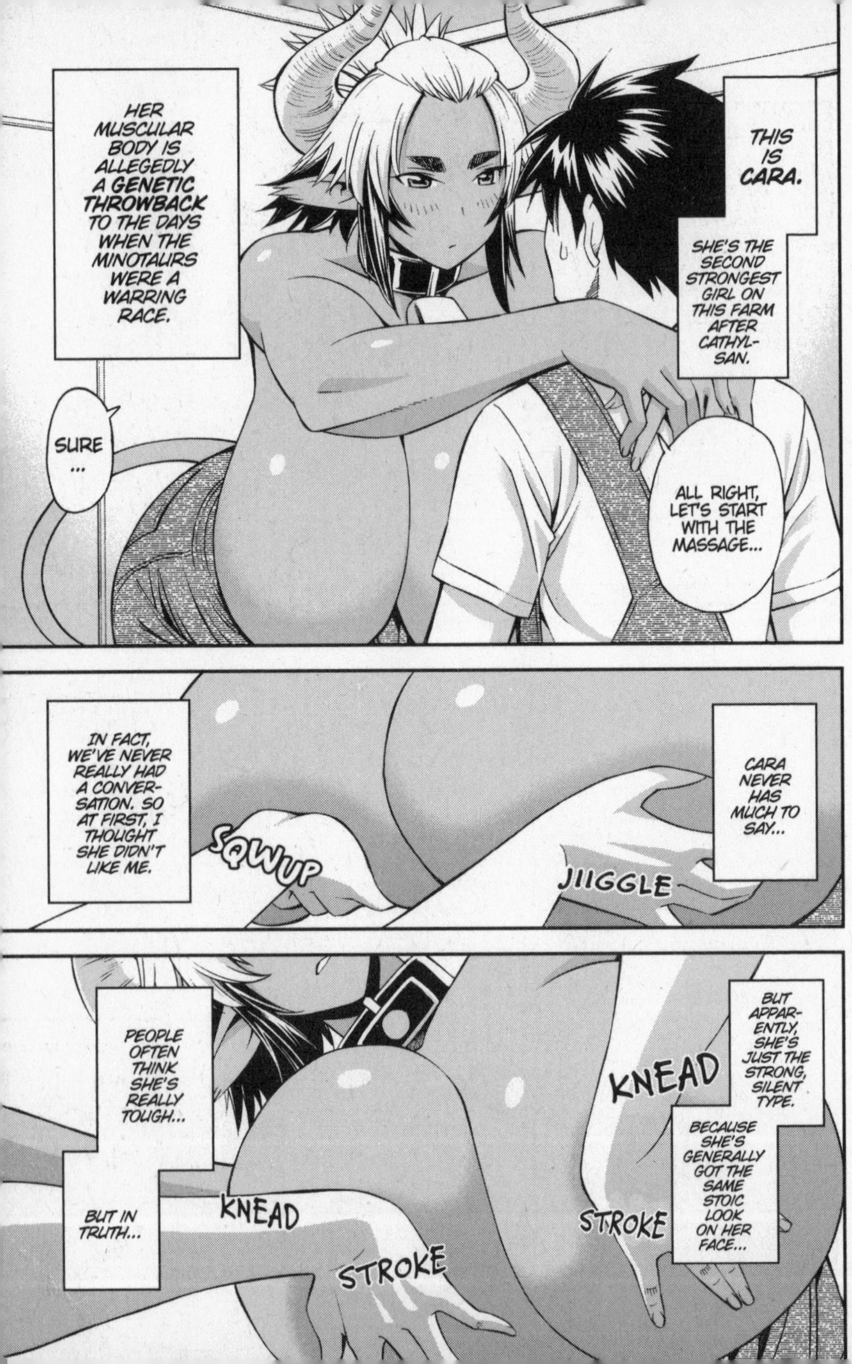

THIS IS CARA.
SHE'S THE SECOND STRONGEST GIRL ON THIS FARM AFTER CATHYL-SAN.
HER MUSCULAR BODY IS ALLEGEDLY A GENETIC THROWBACK TO THE DAYS WHEN THE MINOTAURS WERE A WARRING RACE.
ALL RIGHT, LET'S START WITH THE MASSAGE...
SURE ...
CARA NEVER HAS MUCH TO SAY...
JIIGGLE
IN FACT, WE'VE NEVER REALLY HAD A CONVER-SATION. SO AT FIRST, I THOUGHT SHE DIDN'T LIKE ME.
SQWUP
BUT APPAR-ENTLY, SHE'S JUST THE STRONG, SILENT TYPE.
KNEAD
BECAUSE SHE'S GENERALLY GOT THE SAME STOIC LOOK ON HER FACE...
STROKE
PEOPLE OFTEN THINK SHE'S REALLY TOUGH...
KNEAD
BUT IN TRUTH...
STROKE

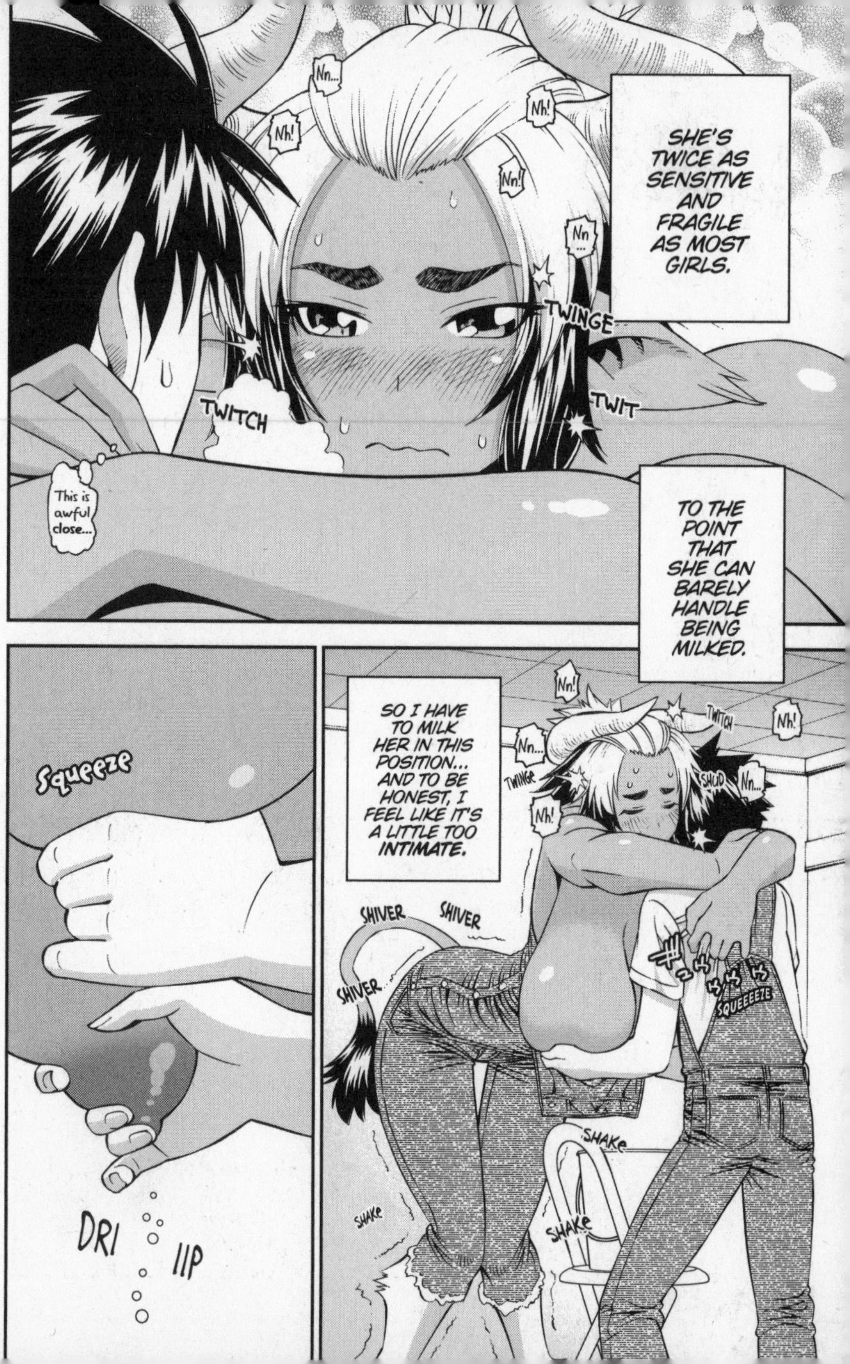
SHE'S TWICE AS SENSITIVE AND FRAGILE AS MOST GIRLS.
Nn...
Nh!
Nh!
Nn!
Nn...
TWINGE
TWIT
TWITCH
This is awful close...
TO THE POINT THAT SHE CAN BARELY HANDLE BEING MILKED.
SO I HAVE TO MILK HER IN THIS POSITION... AND TO BE HONEST, I FEEL LIKE IT'S A LITTLE TOO INTIMATE.
Nh!
TWITCH
Nn!
Nn...
Nn...
SHUD
TWINGE
Nh!
SHIVER
SHIVER
SHIVER
SQUEEEEZE
SHAKE
SHAKE
SHAKE
Squeeze
DRI
IIP

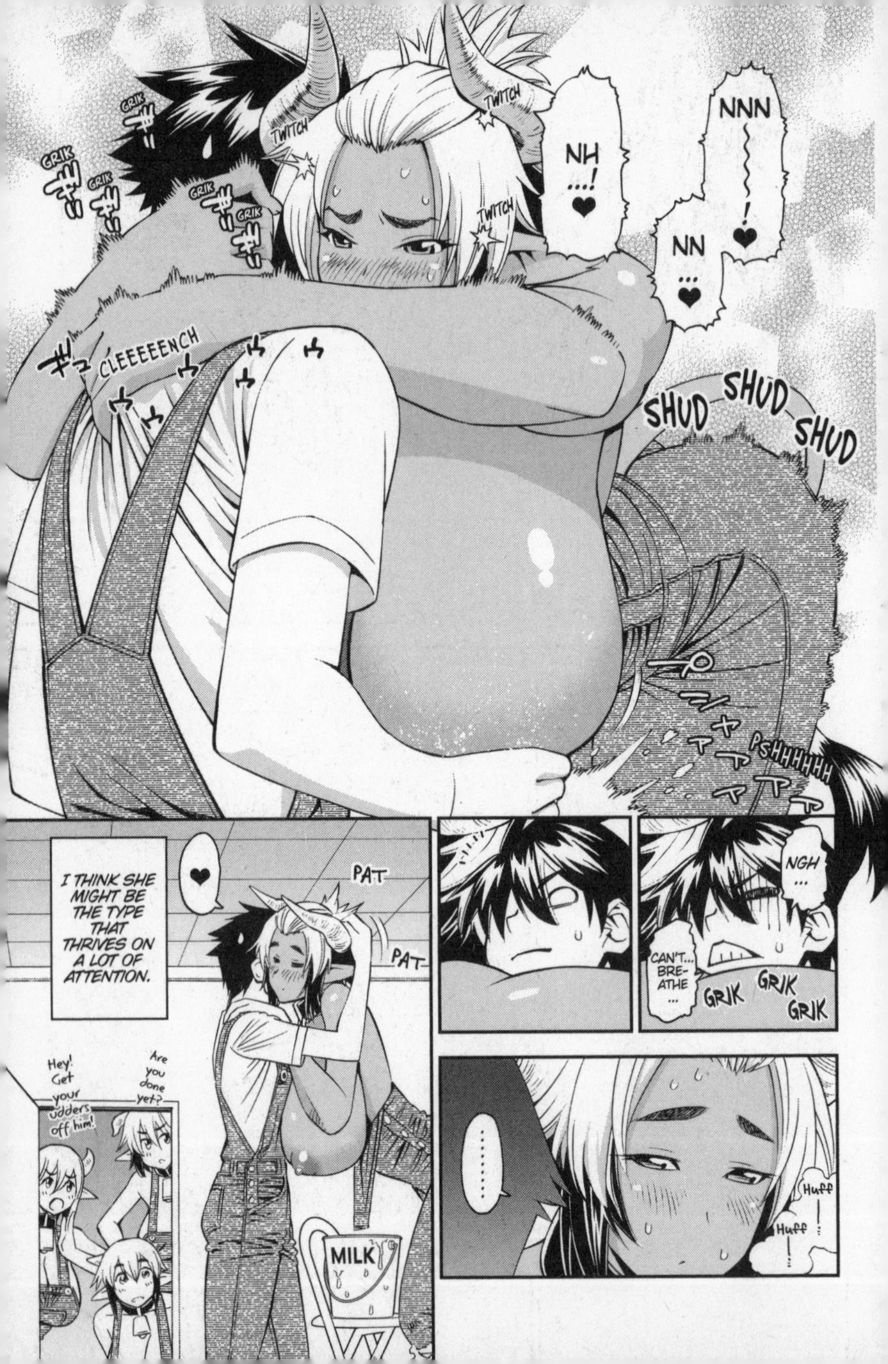
NNN~~~!♥
NH...!♥
NN...♥
TWITCH
TWITCH
TWITCH
GRIK
GRIK
GRIK
GRIK
GRIK
CLEEEEENCH
SHUD SHUD SHUD
PSHHHHHH
NGH...
CAN'T... BRE-ATHE...
GRIK GRIK GRIK
....
Huff...!
Huff...!
I THINK SHE MIGHT BE THE TYPE THAT THRIVES ON A LOT OF ATTENTION.
♥
PAT
PAT
Are you done yet?
Hey! Get your udders off him!
MILK

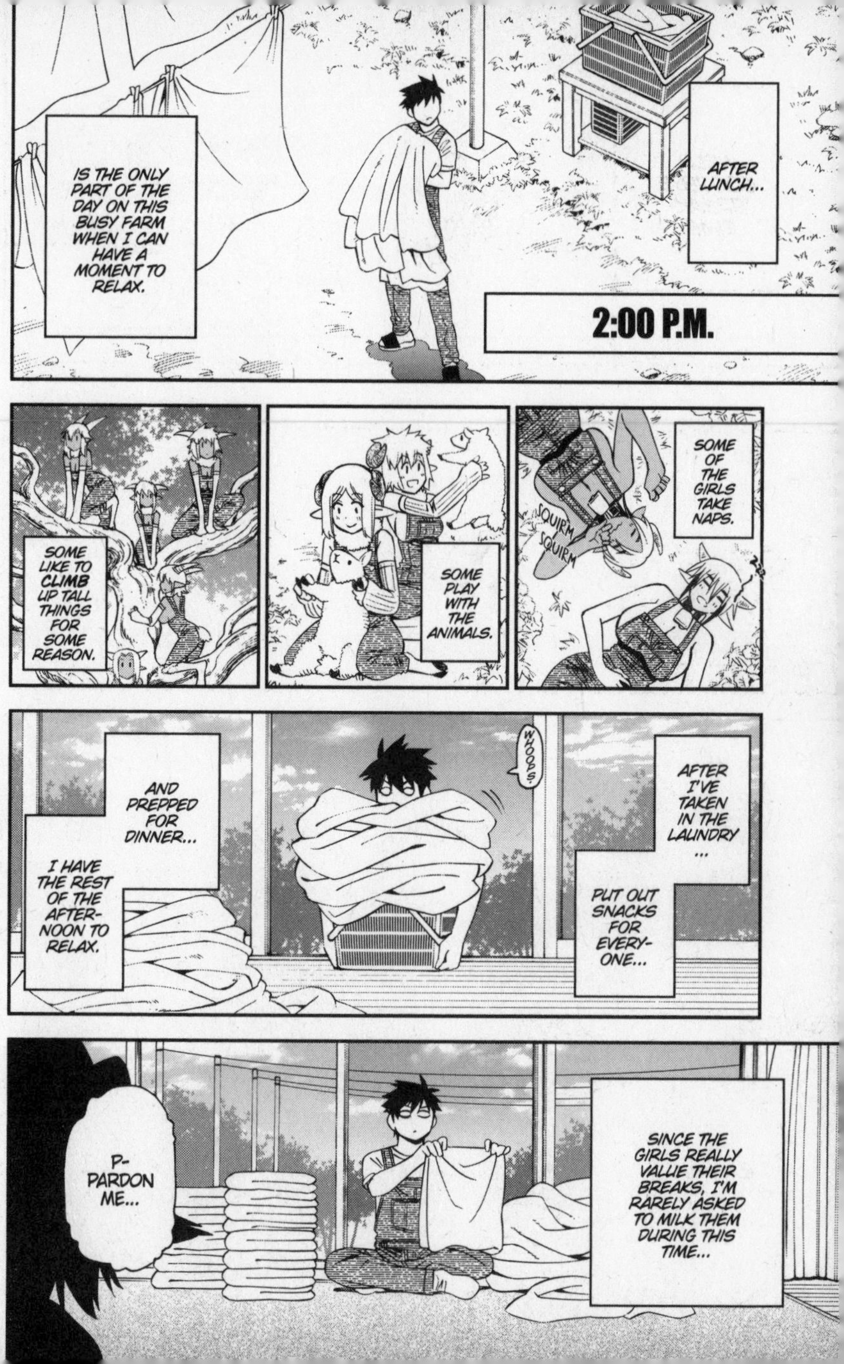
AFTER LUNCH...
2:00 P.M.
IS THE ONLY PART OF THE DAY ON THIS BUSY FARM WHEN I CAN HAVE A MOMENT TO RELAX.
SOME OF THE GIRLS TAKE NAPS.
SQUIRM SQUIRM
SOME PLAY WITH THE ANIMALS.
SOME LIKE TO CLIMB UP TALL THINGS FOR SOME REASON.
AFTER I'VE TAKEN IN THE LAUNDRY...
WHOOPS.
PUT OUT SNACKS FOR EVERYONE...
AND PREPPED FOR DINNER...
I HAVE THE REST OF THE AFTERNOON TO RELAX.
SINCE THE GIRLS REALLY VALUE THEIR BREAKS, I'M RARELY ASKED TO MILK THEM DURING THIS TIME...
P-PARDON ME...

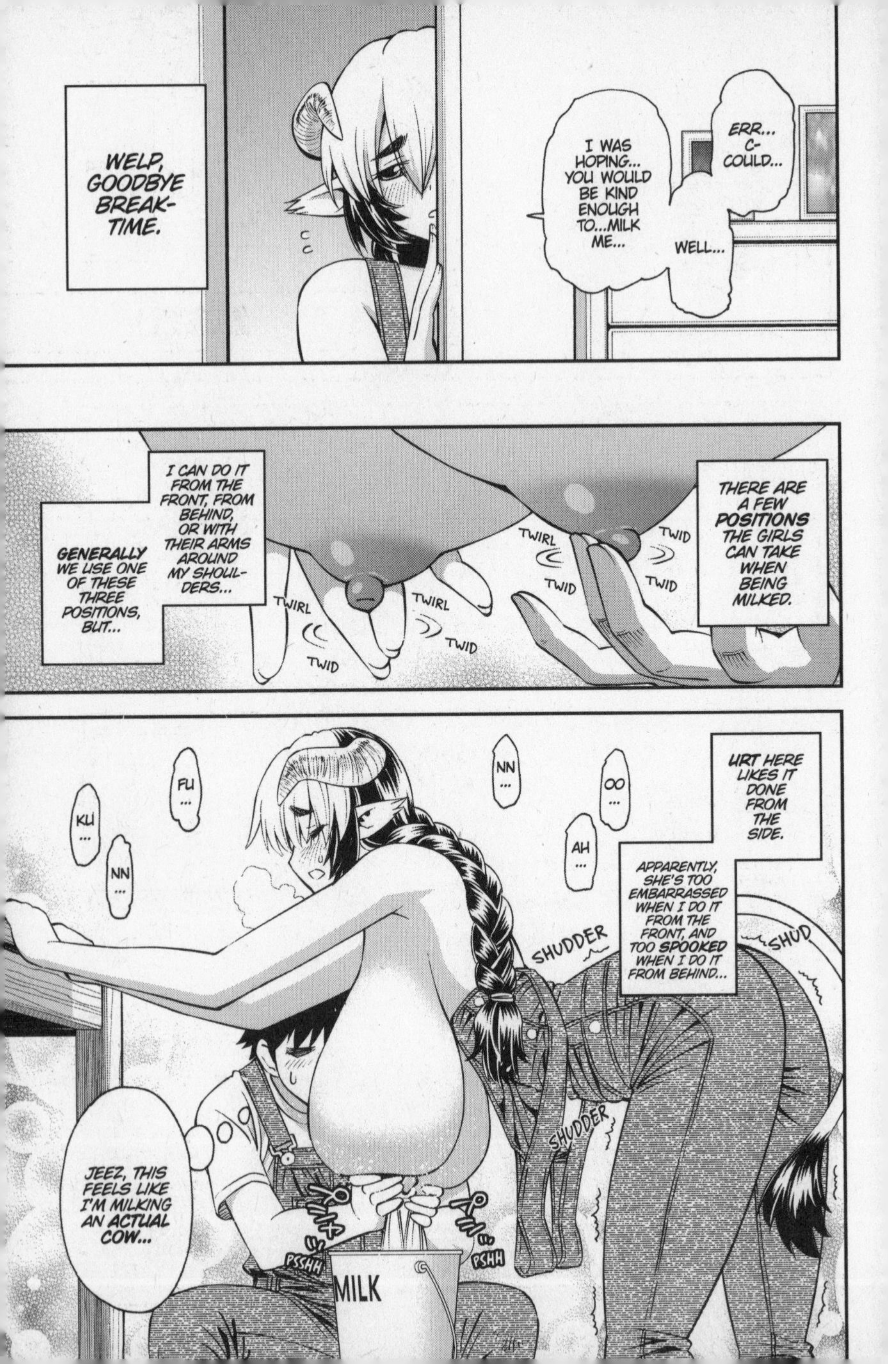
ERR... C-COULD...
WELL...
I WAS HOPING... YOU WOULD BE KIND ENOUGH TO...MILK ME...
WELP, GOODBYE BREAK-TIME.
THERE ARE A FEW POSITIONS THE GIRLS CAN TAKE WHEN BEING MILKED.
TWID
TWID
TWIRL
TWID
TWIRL
TWID
TWIRL
TWID
I CAN DO IT FROM THE FRONT, FROM BEHIND, OR WITH THEIR ARMS AROUND MY SHOULDERS...
GENERALLY WE USE ONE OF THESE THREE POSITIONS, BUT...
URT HERE LIKES IT DONE FROM THE SIDE.
APPARENTLY, SHE'S TOO EMBARRASSED WHEN I DO IT FROM THE FRONT, AND TOO SPOOKED WHEN I DO IT FROM BEHIND...
SHUD
OO...
AH...
NN...
FU...
KU...
NN...
SHUDDER
SHUDDER
JEEZ, THIS FEELS LIKE I'M MILKING AN ACTUAL COW...
PSHH
PSHH
MILK

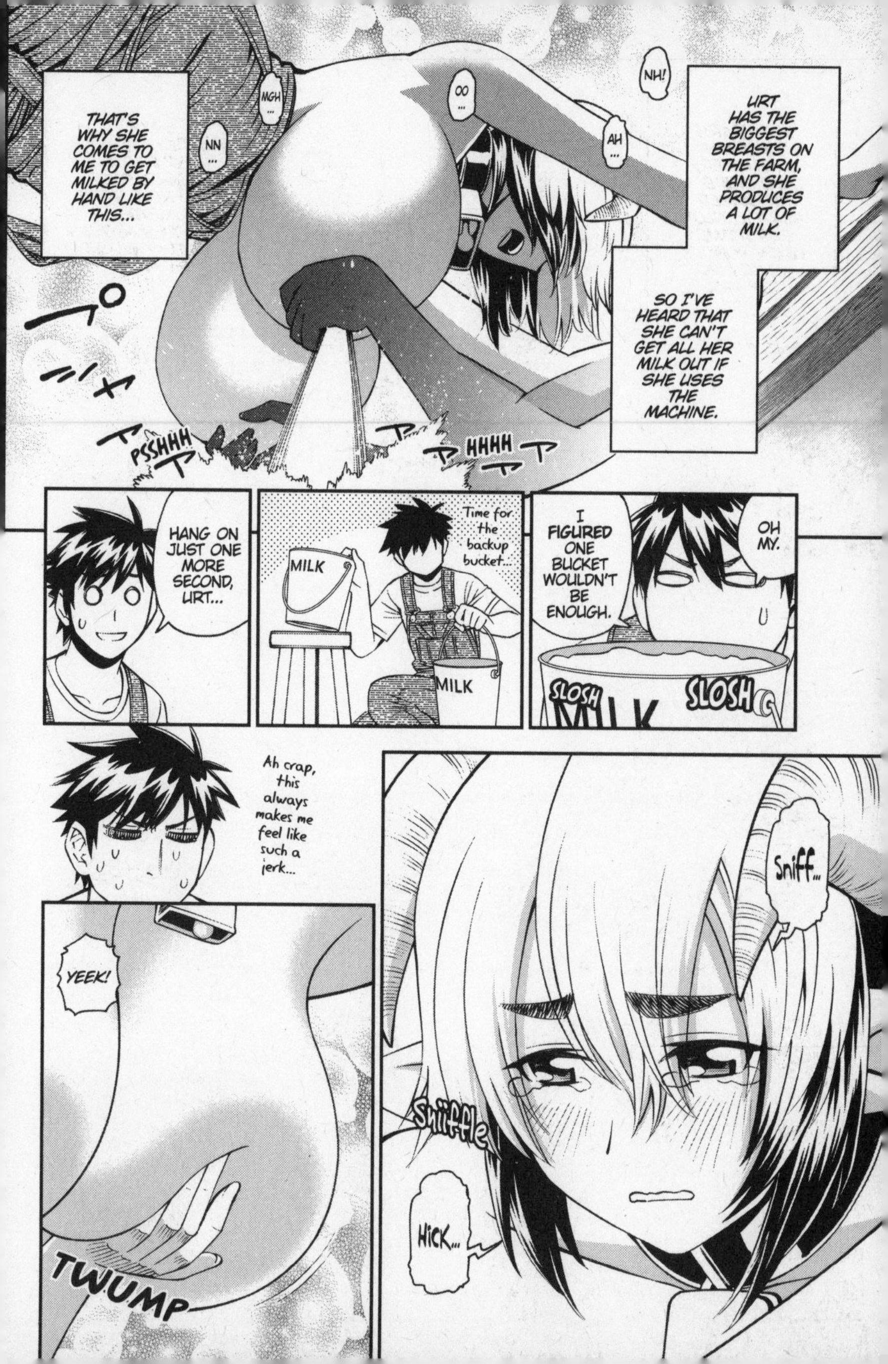
NH!
URT HAS THE BIGGEST BREASTS ON THE FARM, AND SHE PRODUCES A LOT OF MILK.
AH...
OO...
SO I'VE HEARD THAT SHE CAN'T GET ALL HER MILK OUT IF SHE USES THE MACHINE.
MGH...
NN...
THAT'S WHY SHE COMES TO ME TO GET MILKED BY HAND LIKE THIS...
HHHH
PSSHHH
OH MY.
I FIGURED ONE BUCKET WOULDN'T BE ENOUGH.
SLOSH
SLOSH
Time for the backup bucket...
MILK
MILK
HANG ON JUST ONE MORE SECOND, URT...
Sniff...
Sniiffle
Hick...
Ah crap, this always makes me feel like such a jerk...
YEEK!
TWUMP

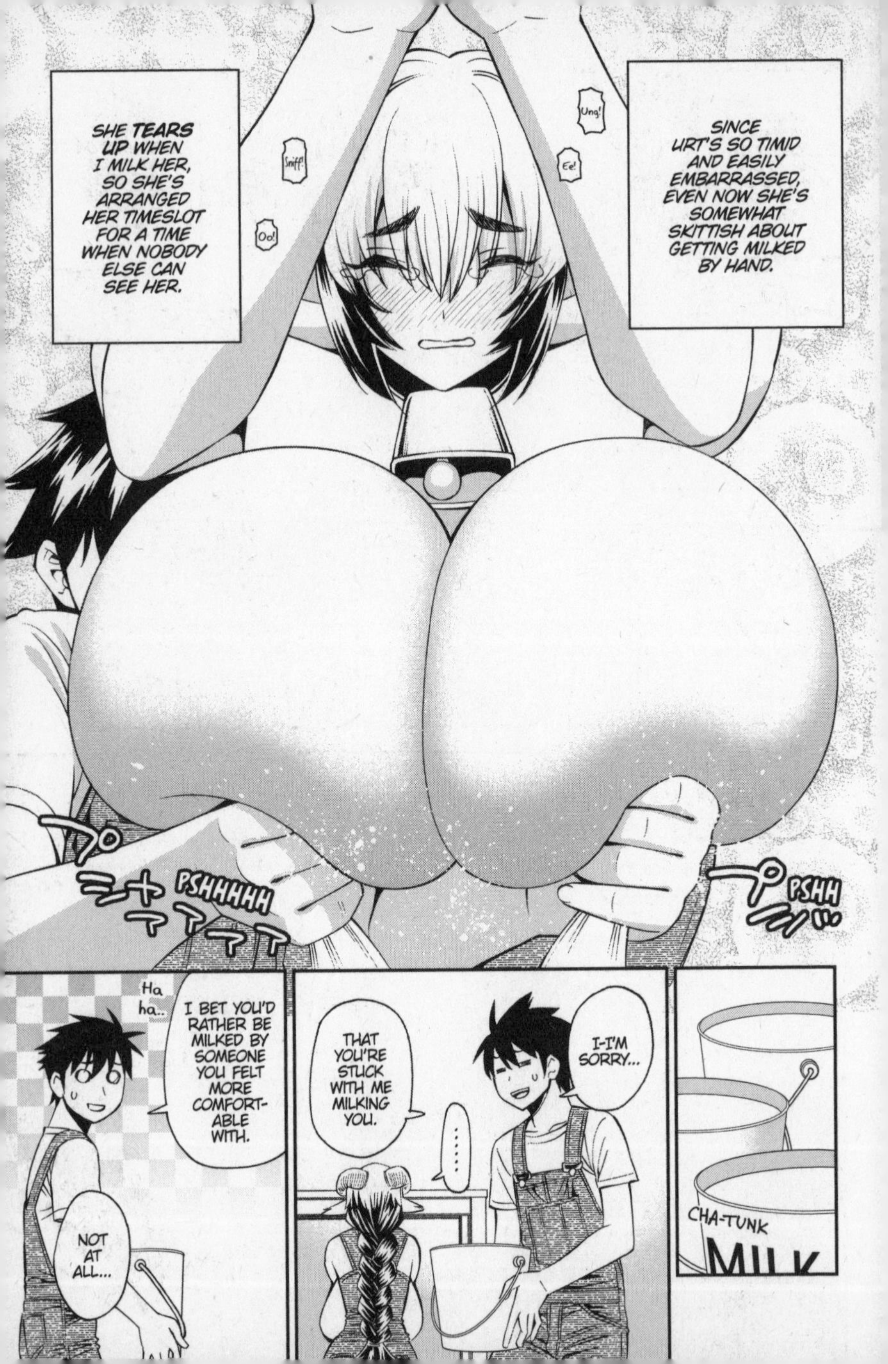
SINCE URT'S SO TIMID AND EASILY EMBARRASSED, EVEN NOW SHE'S SOMEWHAT SKITTISH ABOUT GETTING MILKED BY HAND.
Ung!
Ee!
SHE TEARS UP WHEN I MILK HER, SO SHE'S ARRANGED HER TIMESLOT FOR A TIME WHEN NOBODY ELSE CAN SEE HER.
Sniff!
Oo!
PSHH
PSHHHHH
CHA-TUNK
MILK
I-I'M SORRY...
THAT YOU'RE STUCK WITH ME MILKING YOU.
......
Ha ha..
I BET YOU'D RATHER BE MILKED BY SOMEONE YOU FELT MORE COMFORT-ABLE WITH.
NOT AT ALL...

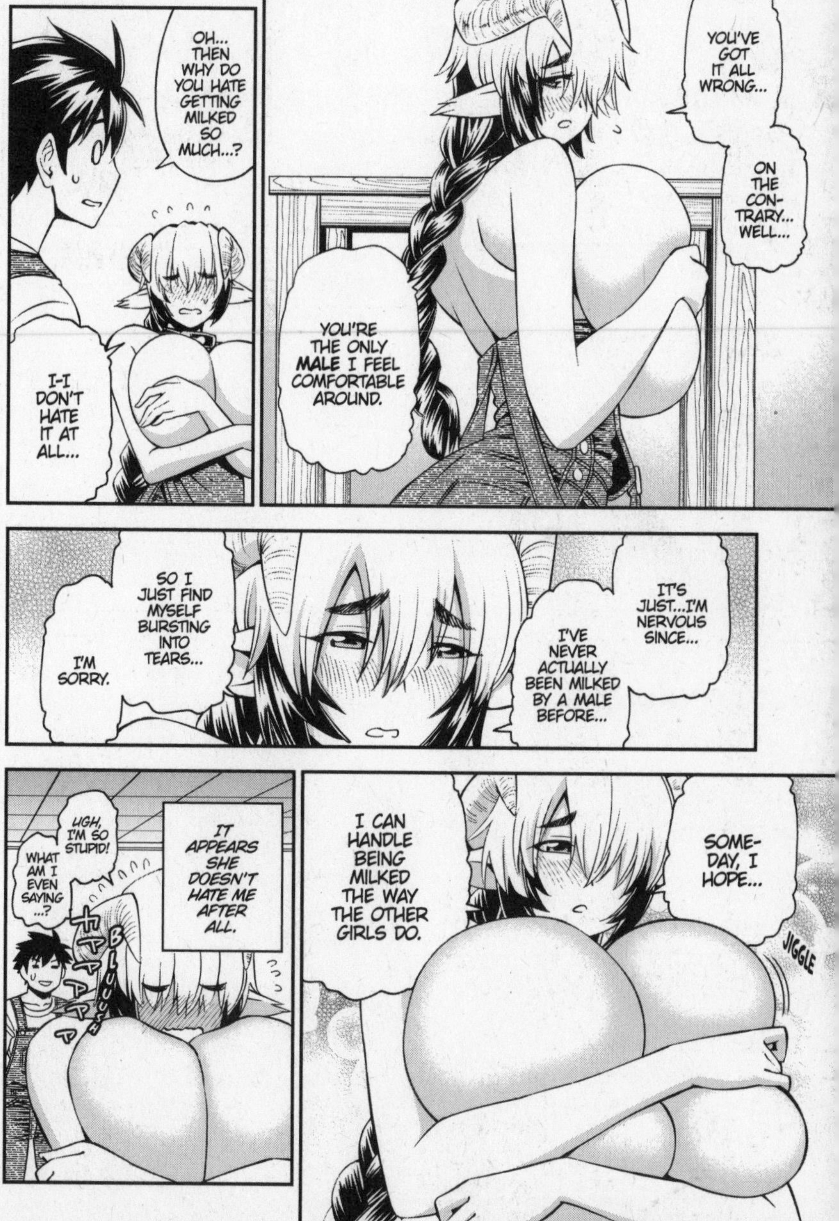
YOU'VE GOT IT ALL WRONG...
ON THE CON-TRARY... WELL...
YOU'RE THE ONLY MALE I FEEL COMFORTABLE AROUND.
OH... THEN WHY DO YOU HATE GETTING MILKED SO MUCH...?
I-I DON'T HATE IT AT ALL...
IT'S JUST...I'M NERVOUS SINCE...
I'VE NEVER ACTUALLY BEEN MILKED BY A MALE BEFORE...
SO I JUST FIND MYSELF BURSTING INTO TEARS...
I'M SORRY.
SOME-DAY, I HOPE...
I CAN HANDLE BEING MILKED THE WAY THE OTHER GIRLS DO.
JIGGLE
IT APPEARS SHE DOESN'T HATE ME AFTER ALL.
UGH, I'M SO STUPID!
WHAT AM I EVEN SAYING ...?

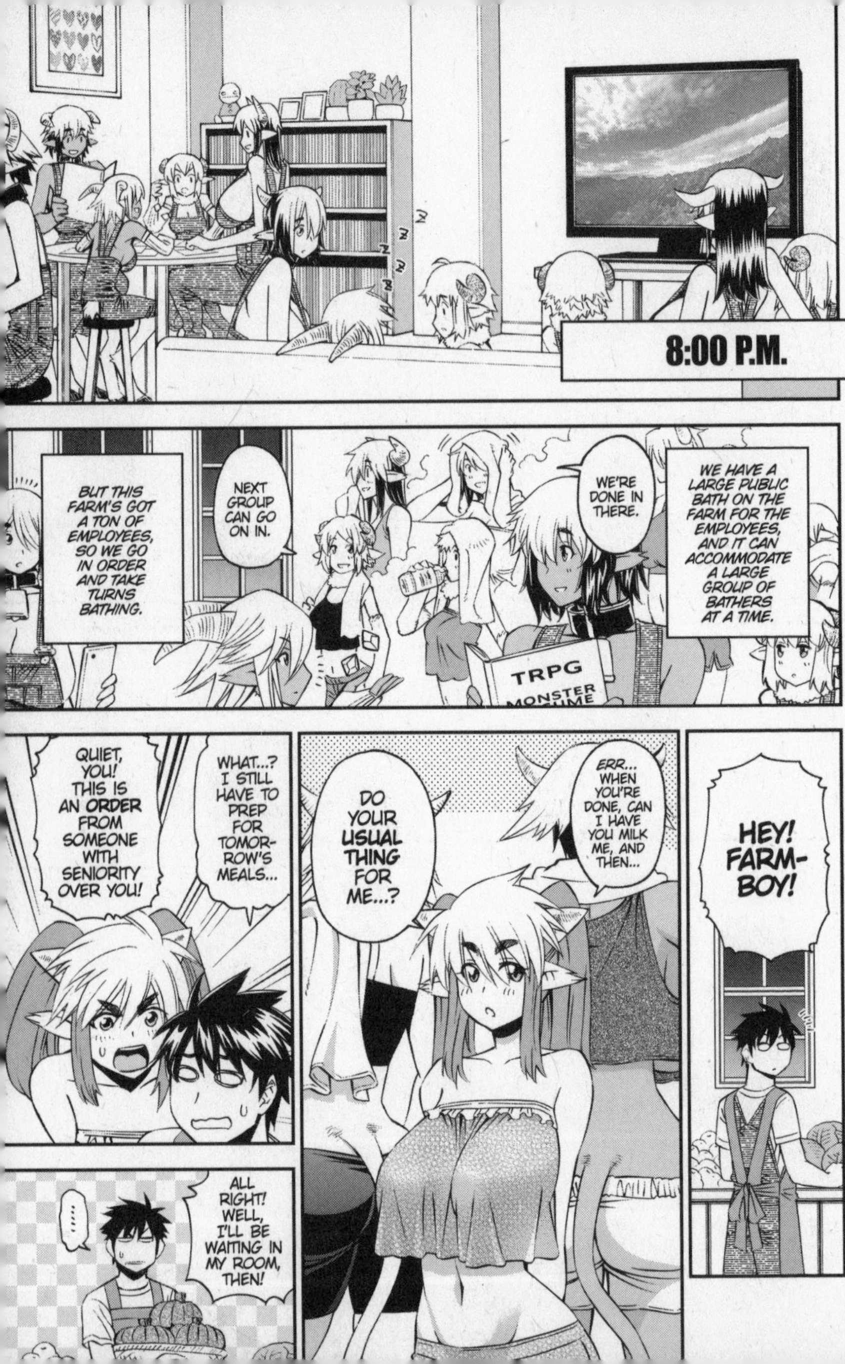

8:00 P.M.
WE HAVE A LARGE PUBLIC BATH ON THE FARM FOR THE EMPLOYEES, AND IT CAN ACCOMMODATE A LARGE GROUP OF BATHERS AT A TIME.
WE'RE DONE IN THERE.
TRPG
MONSTER
NEXT GROUP CAN GO ON IN.
BUT THIS FARM'S GOT A TON OF EMPLOYEES, SO WE GO IN ORDER AND TAKE TURNS BATHING.
HEY! FARM-BOY!
ERR... WHEN YOU'RE DONE, CAN I HAVE YOU MILK ME, AND THEN...
DO YOUR USUAL THING FOR ME...?
WHAT...? I STILL HAVE TO PREP FOR TOMORROW'S MEALS...
QUIET, YOU! THIS IS AN ORDER FROM SOMEONE WITH SENIORITY OVER YOU!
ALL RIGHT! WELL, I'LL BE WAITING IN MY ROOM, THEN!
......

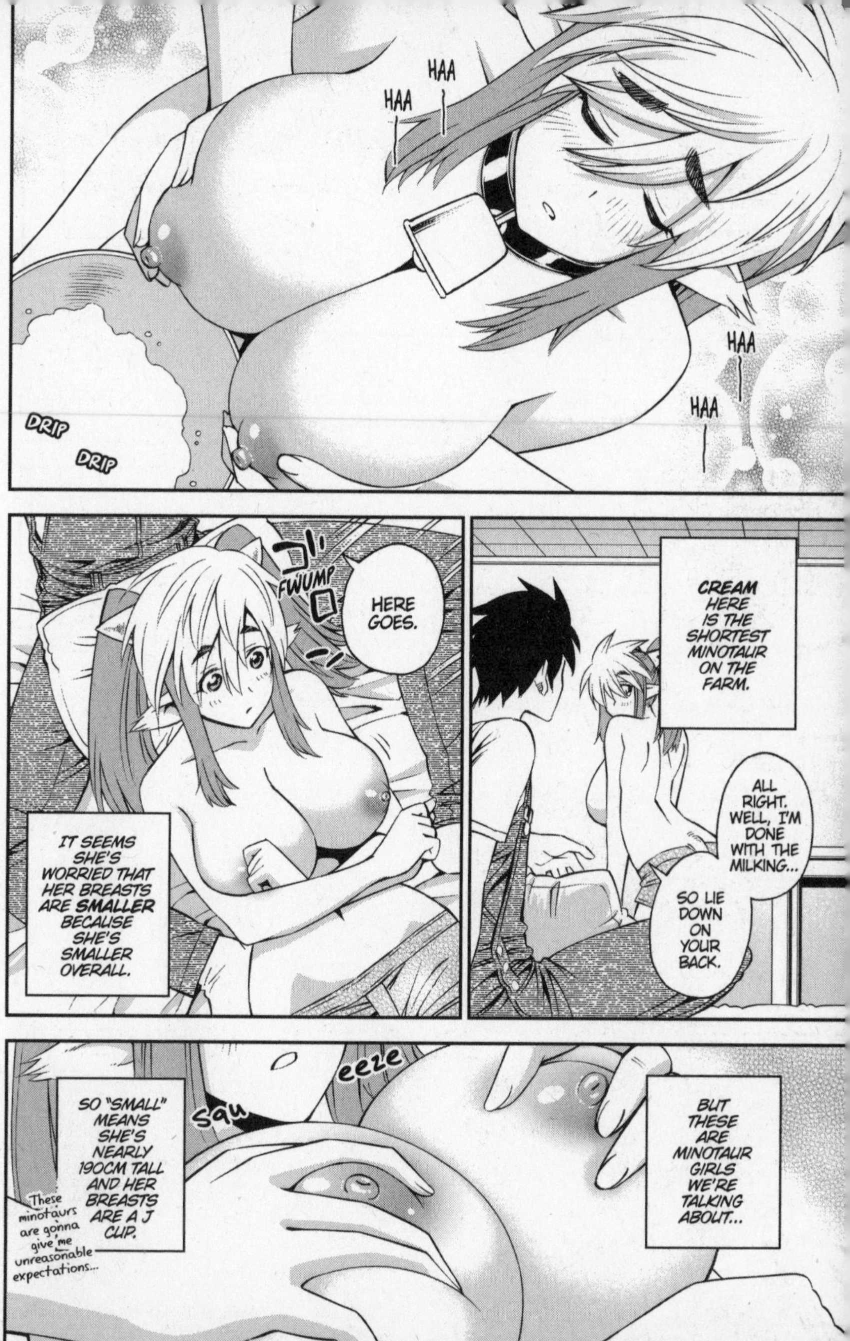

HAA
HAA
HAA
HAA
DRIP
DRIP
CREAM HERE IS THE SHORTEST MINOTAUR ON THE FARM.
ALL RIGHT. WELL, I'M DONE WITH THE MILKING...
SO LIE DOWN ON YOUR BACK.
HERE GOES.
FWUMP
IT SEEMS SHE'S WORRIED THAT HER BREASTS ARE SMALLER BECAUSE SHE'S SMALLER OVERALL.
BUT THESE ARE MINOTAUR GIRLS WE'RE TALKING ABOUT...
squeeze
SO "SMALL" MEANS SHE'S NEARLY 190CM TALL AND HER BREASTS ARE A J CUP.
These minotaurs are gonna give me unreasonable expectations...

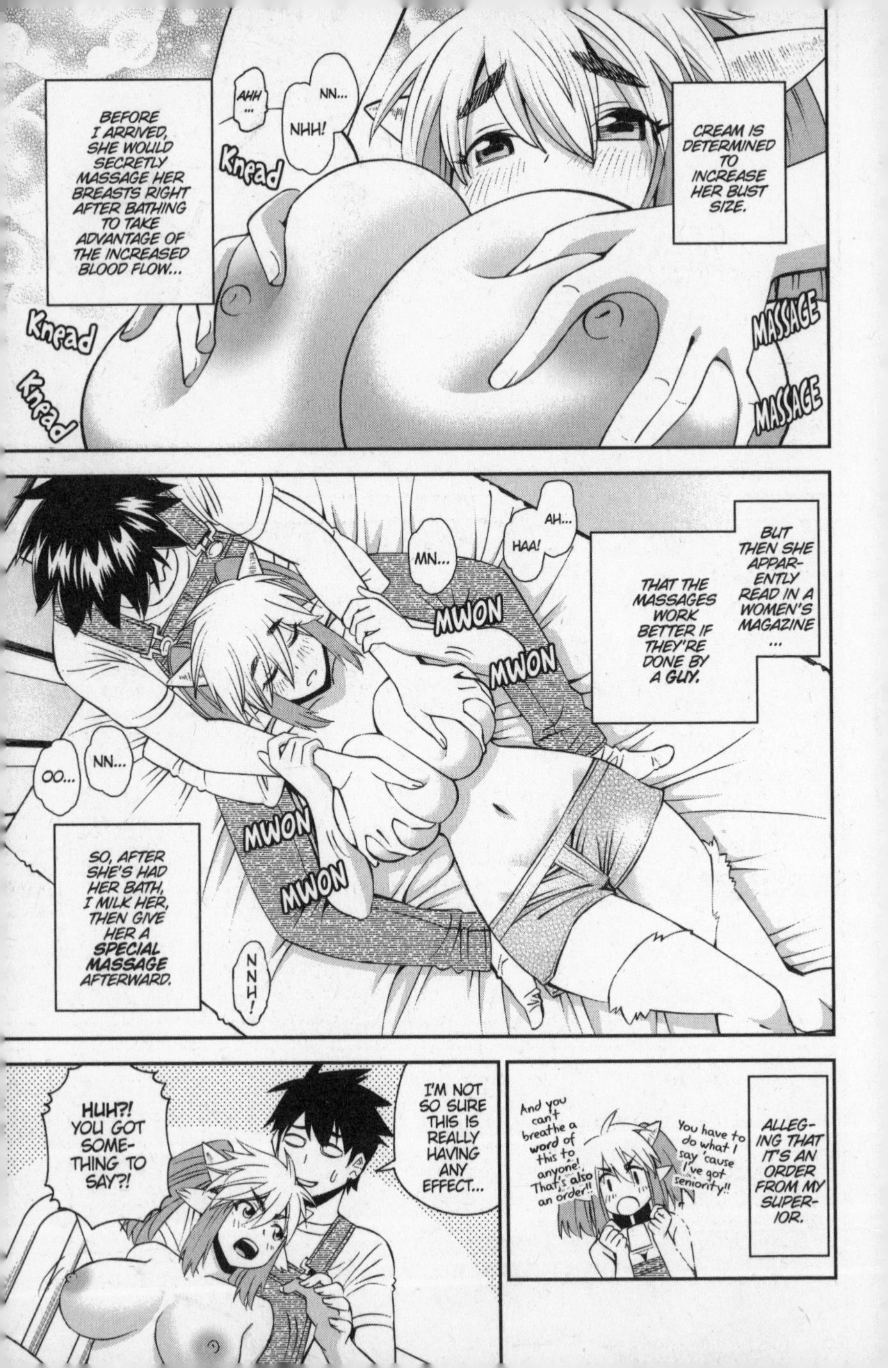
CREAM IS DETERMINED TO INCREASE HER BUST SIZE.
NN...
NHH!
AHH ...
BEFORE I ARRIVED, SHE WOULD SECRETLY MASSAGE HER BREASTS RIGHT AFTER BATHING TO TAKE ADVANTAGE OF THE INCREASED BLOOD FLOW...
Knead
MASSAGE
MASSAGE
Knead
Knead
BUT THEN SHE APPARENTLY READ IN A WOMEN'S MAGAZINE ...
THAT THE MASSAGES WORK BETTER IF THEY'RE DONE BY A GUY.
AH...
HAA!
MN...
MWON
MWON
NN...
OO...
MWON
MWON
SO, AFTER SHE'S HAD HER BATH, I MILK HER, THEN GIVE HER A SPECIAL MASSAGE AFTERWARD.
NNH!
ALLEGING THAT IT'S AN ORDER FROM MY SUPERIOR.
You have to do what I say 'cause I've got seniority!!
And you can't breathe a word of this to anyone! That's also an order!!
I'M NOT SO SURE THIS IS REALLY HAVING ANY EFFECT...
HUH?! YOU GOT SOME-THING TO SAY?!

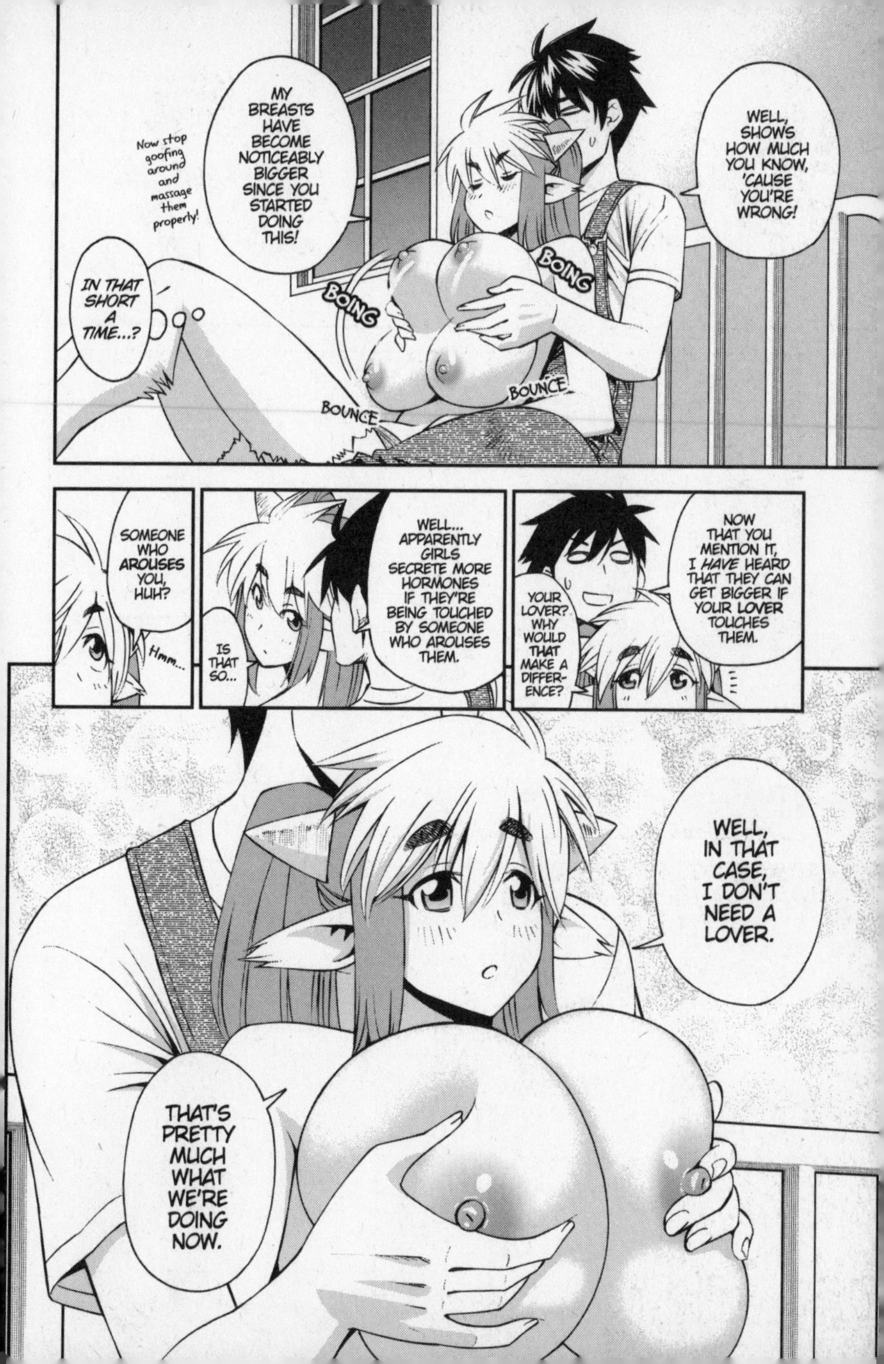
WELL, SHOWS HOW MUCH YOU KNOW, 'CAUSE YOU'RE WRONG!
MY BREASTS HAVE BECOME NOTICEABLY BIGGER SINCE YOU STARTED DOING THIS!
Now stop goofing around and massage them properly!
BOING
BOING
IN THAT SHORT A TIME...?
BOUNCE
BOUNCE
NOW THAT YOU MENTION IT, I *HAVE* HEARD THAT THEY CAN GET BIGGER IF YOUR LOVER TOUCHES THEM.
YOUR LOVER? WHY WOULD THAT MAKE A DIFFERENCE?
WELL... APPARENTLY GIRLS SECRETE MORE HORMONES IF THEY'RE BEING TOUCHED BY SOMEONE WHO AROUSES THEM.
IS THAT SO...
SOMEONE WHO AROUSES YOU, HUH?
Hmm...
WELL, IN THAT CASE, I DON'T NEED A LOVER.
THAT'S PRETTY MUCH WHAT WE'RE DOING NOW.

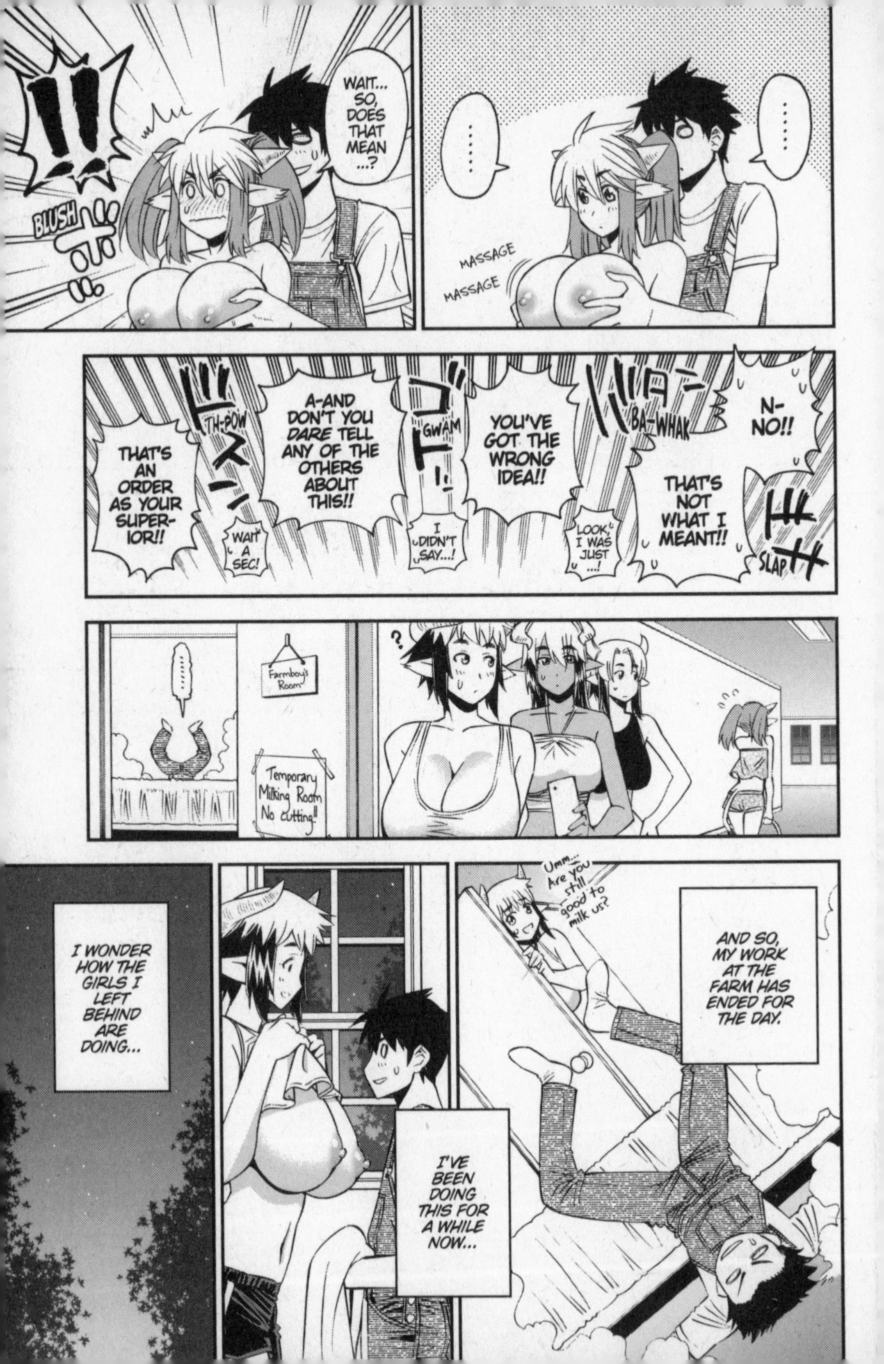

......
......
MASSAGE
MASSAGE
WAIT... SO, DOES THAT MEAN ...?
!!
BLUSH
N-NO!!
THAT'S NOT WHAT I MEANT!!
SLAP
BA-WHAK
LOOK, I WAS JUST ...!
YOU'VE GOT THE WRONG IDEA!!
GWAM
I DIDN'T SAY...!
A-AND DON'T YOU *DARE* TELL ANY OF THE OTHERS ABOUT THIS!!
TH-POW
WAIT A SEC!
THAT'S AN ORDER AS YOUR SUPER-IOR!!
?
Farmboy's Room
Temporary Milking Room No cutting!!
......
AND SO, MY WORK AT THE FARM HAS ENDED FOR THE DAY.
Umm... Are you still good to milk us?
I'VE BEEN DOING THIS FOR A WHILE NOW...
I WONDER HOW THE GIRLS I LEFT BEHIND ARE DOING...

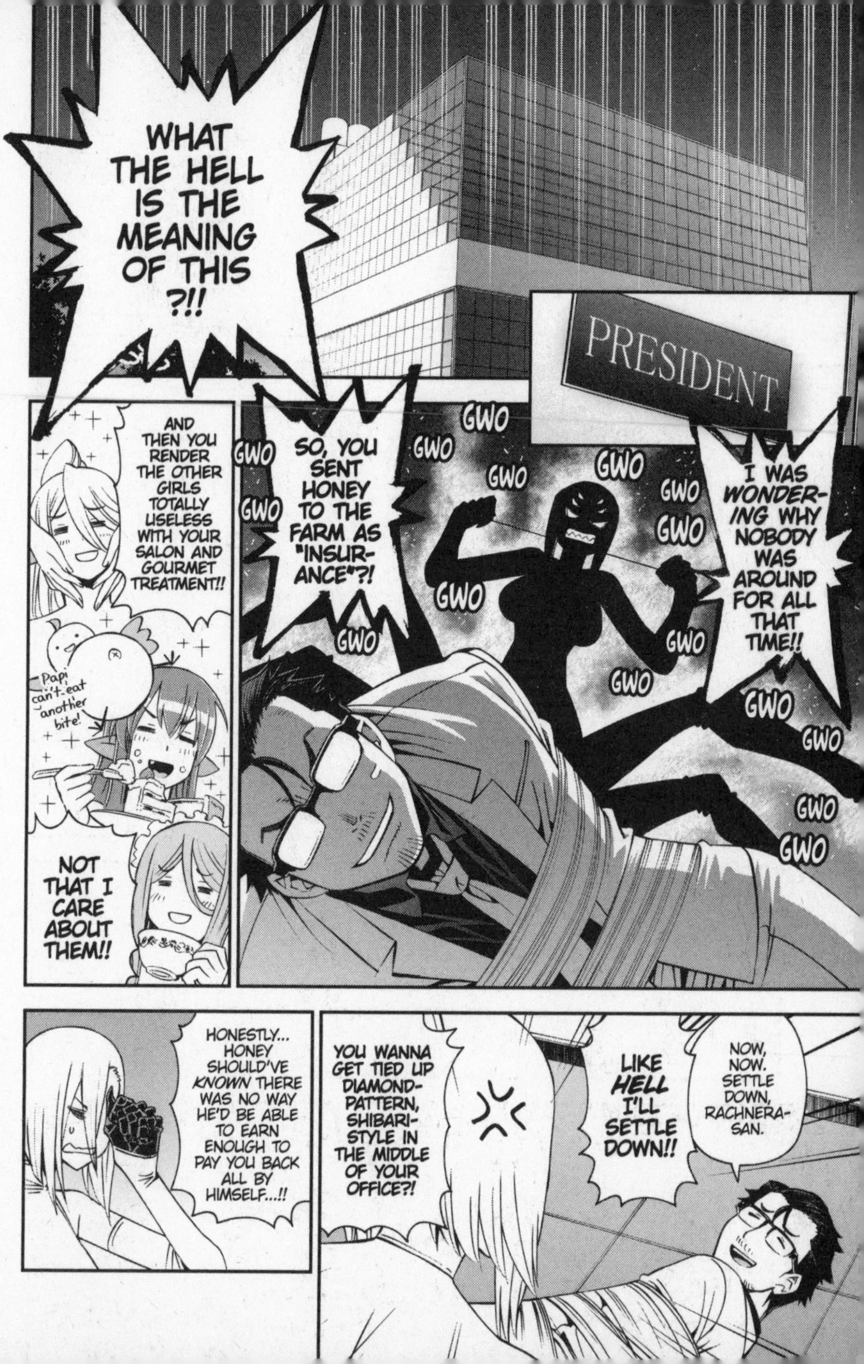
WHAT THE HELL IS THE MEANING OF THIS ?!!
PRESIDENT
I WAS *WONDERING* WHY NOBODY WAS AROUND FOR ALL THAT TIME!!
GWO
GWO
GWO
GWO
GWO
GWO
GWO
GWO
GWO
GWO
GWO
GWO
GWO
GWO
GWO
SO, YOU SENT HONEY TO THE FARM AS "INSURANCE"?!
AND THEN YOU RENDER THE OTHER GIRLS TOTALLY USELESS WITH YOUR SALON AND GOURMET TREATMENT!!
Papi can't eat another bite!
NOT THAT I CARE ABOUT THEM!!
NOW, NOW. SETTLE DOWN, RACHNERA-SAN.
LIKE ***HELL*** I'LL SETTLE DOWN!!
YOU WANNA GET TIED UP DIAMOND-PATTERN, SHIBARI-STYLE IN THE MIDDLE OF YOUR OFFICE?!
HONESTLY... HONEY SHOULD'VE *KNOWN* THERE WAS NO WAY HE'D BE ABLE TO EARN ENOUGH TO PAY YOU BACK ALL BY HIMSELF...!!

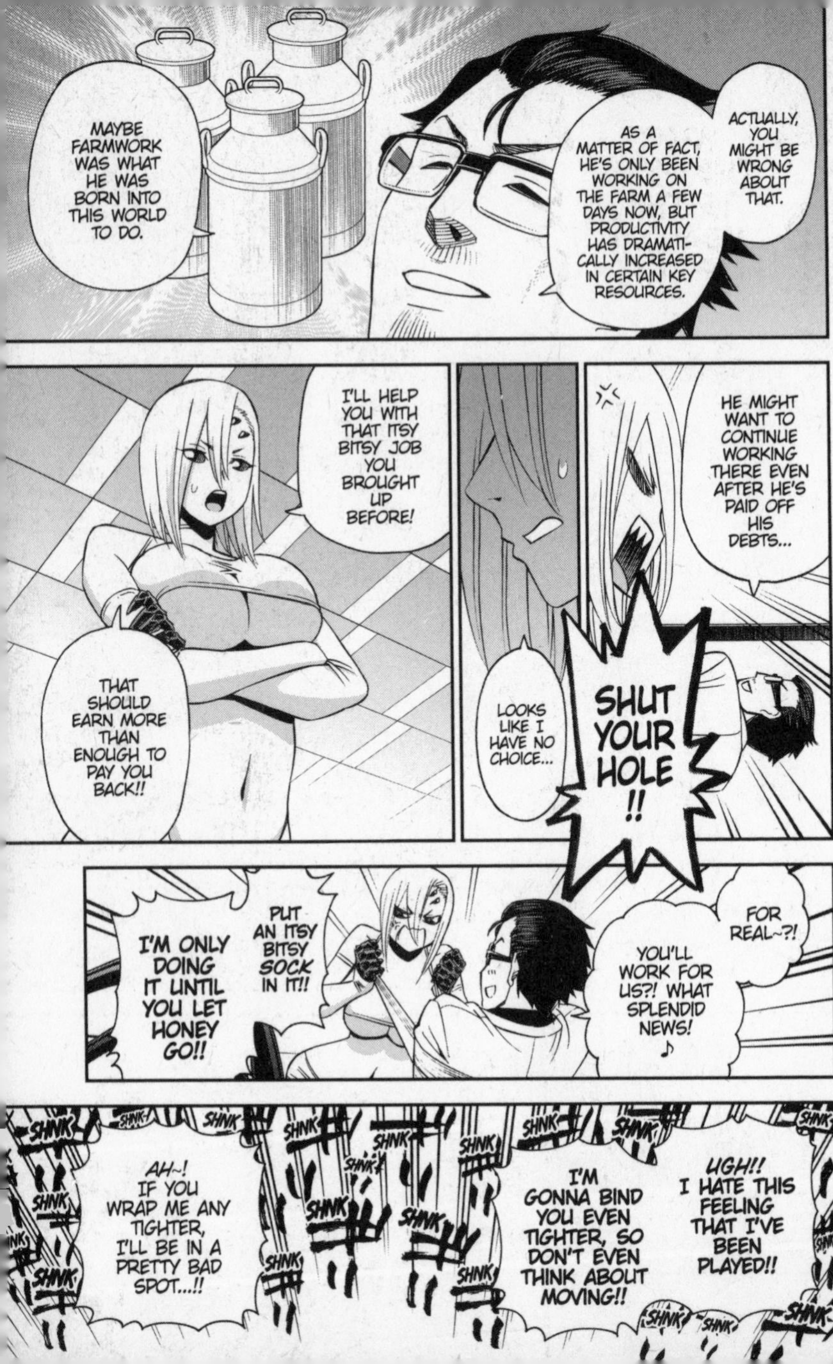
ACTUALLY, YOU MIGHT BE WRONG ABOUT THAT.
AS A MATTER OF FACT, HE'S ONLY BEEN WORKING ON THE FARM A FEW DAYS NOW, BUT PRODUCTIVITY HAS DRAMATICALLY INCREASED IN CERTAIN KEY RESOURCES.
MAYBE FARMWORK WAS WHAT HE WAS BORN INTO THIS WORLD TO DO.
HE MIGHT WANT TO CONTINUE WORKING THERE EVEN AFTER HE'S PAID OFF HIS DEBTS...
LOOKS LIKE I HAVE NO CHOICE...
SHUT YOUR HOLE!!
I'LL HELP YOU WITH THAT ITSY BITSY JOB YOU BROUGHT UP BEFORE!
THAT SHOULD EARN MORE THAN ENOUGH TO PAY YOU BACK!!
FOR REAL~?!
YOU'LL WORK FOR US?! WHAT SPLENDID NEWS! ♪
PUT AN ITSY BITSY SOCK IN IT!!
I'M ONLY DOING IT UNTIL YOU LET HONEY GO!!
SHNK
UGH!! I HATE THIS FEELING THAT I'VE BEEN PLAYED!!
I'M GONNA BIND YOU EVEN TIGHTER, SO DON'T EVEN THINK ABOUT MOVING!!
AH~! IF YOU WRAP ME ANY TIGHTER, I'LL BE IN A PRETTY BAD SPOT...!!

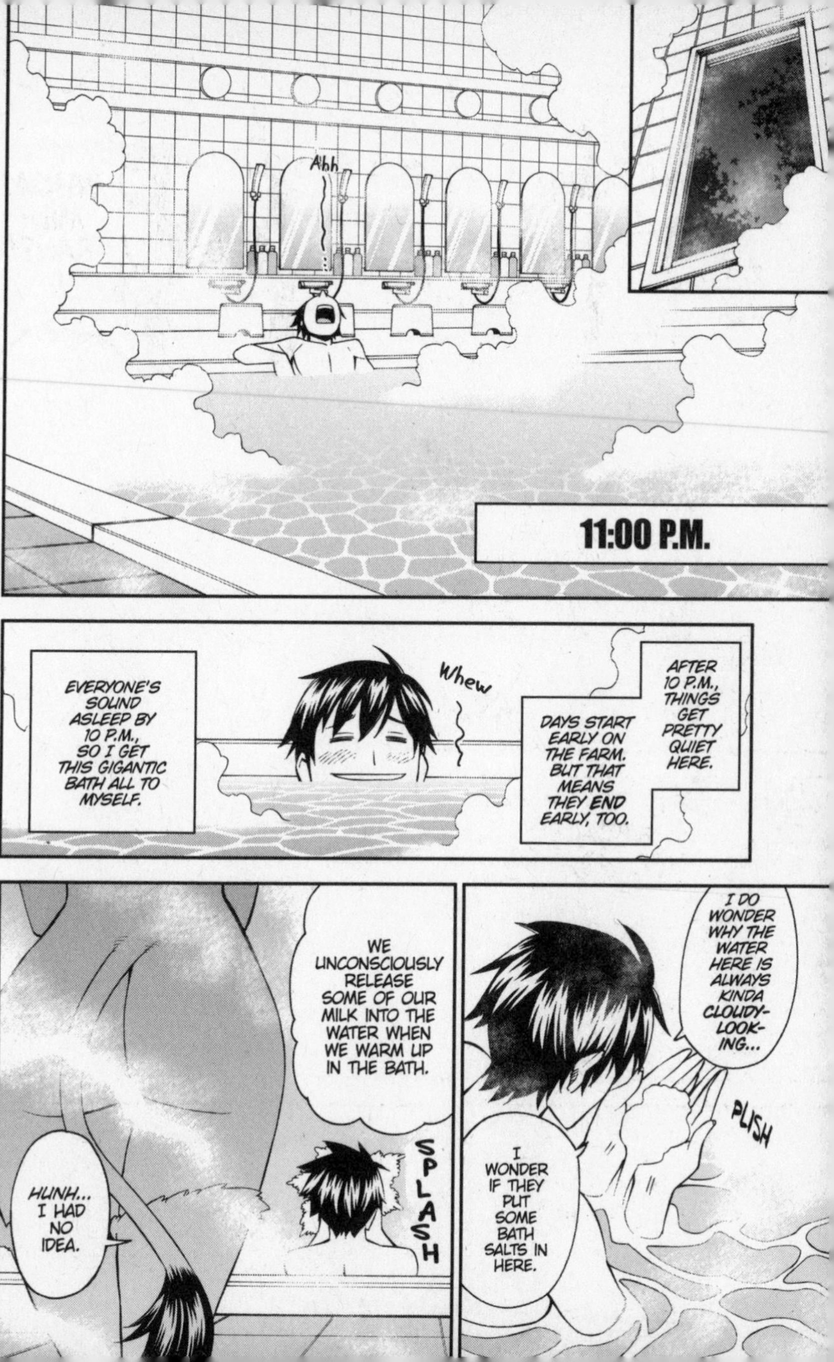
Ahh
11:00 P.M.
AFTER 10 P.M., THINGS GET PRETTY QUIET HERE.
DAYS START EARLY ON THE FARM. BUT THAT MEANS THEY END EARLY, TOO.
Whew
EVERYONE'S SOUND ASLEEP BY 10 P.M., SO I GET THIS GIGANTIC BATH ALL TO MYSELF.
I DO WONDER WHY THE WATER HERE IS ALWAYS KINDA CLOUDY-LOOKING...
PLISH
I WONDER IF THEY PUT SOME BATH SALTS IN HERE.
WE UNCONSCIOUSLY RELEASE SOME OF OUR MILK INTO THE WATER WHEN WE WARM UP IN THE BATH.
SPLASH
HUNH... I HAD NO IDEA.

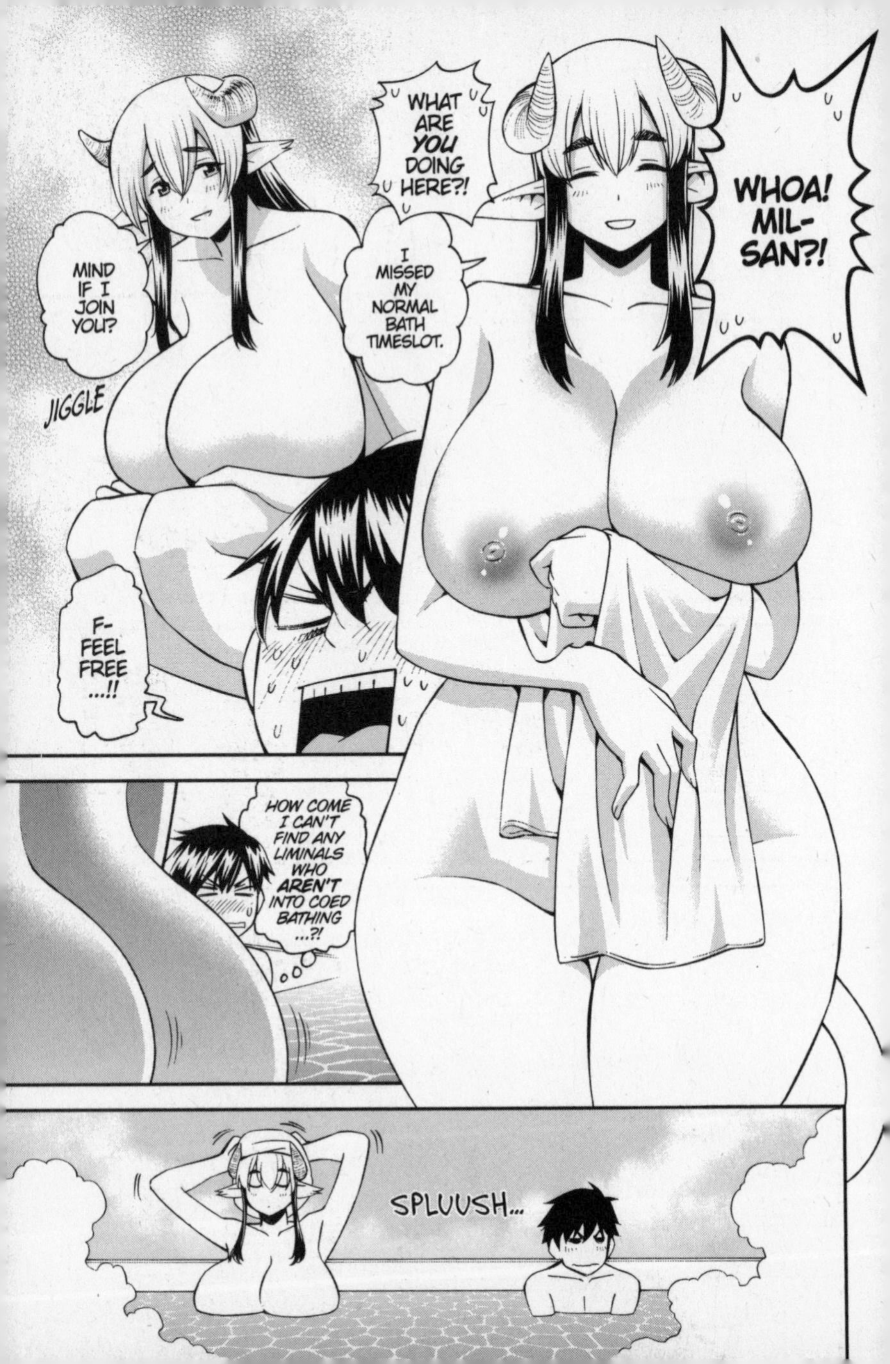
WHOA! MIL-SAN?!
WHAT ARE YOU DOING HERE?!
I MISSED MY NORMAL BATH TIMESLOT.
MIND IF I JOIN YOU?
JIGGLE
F-FEEL FREE ...!!
HOW COME I CAN'T FIND ANY LIMINALS WHO AREN'T INTO COED BATHING ...?!
SPLUUSH...

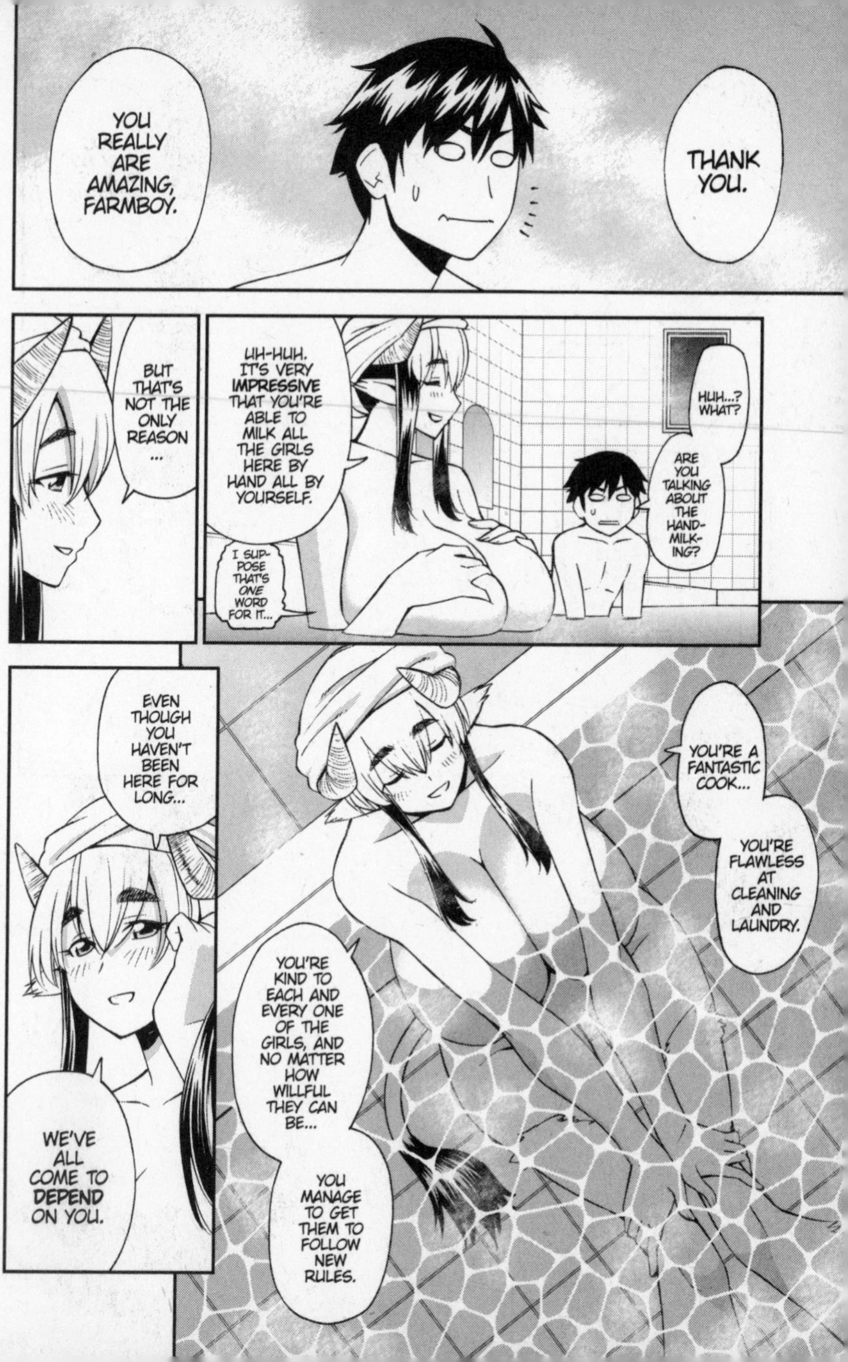
THANK YOU.
YOU REALLY ARE AMAZING, FARMBOY.
HUH...? WHAT?
ARE YOU TALKING ABOUT THE HAND-MILKING?
UH-HUH. IT'S VERY IMPRESSIVE THAT YOU'RE ABLE TO MILK ALL THE GIRLS HERE BY HAND ALL BY YOURSELF.
I SUPPOSE THAT'S ONE WORD FOR IT...
BUT THAT'S NOT THE ONLY REASON...
YOU'RE A FANTASTIC COOK...
YOU'RE FLAWLESS AT CLEANING AND LAUNDRY.
YOU'RE KIND TO EACH AND EVERY ONE OF THE GIRLS, AND NO MATTER HOW WILLFUL THEY CAN BE...
YOU MANAGE TO GET THEM TO FOLLOW NEW RULES.
EVEN THOUGH YOU HAVEN'T BEEN HERE FOR LONG...
WE'VE ALL COME TO DEPEND ON YOU.

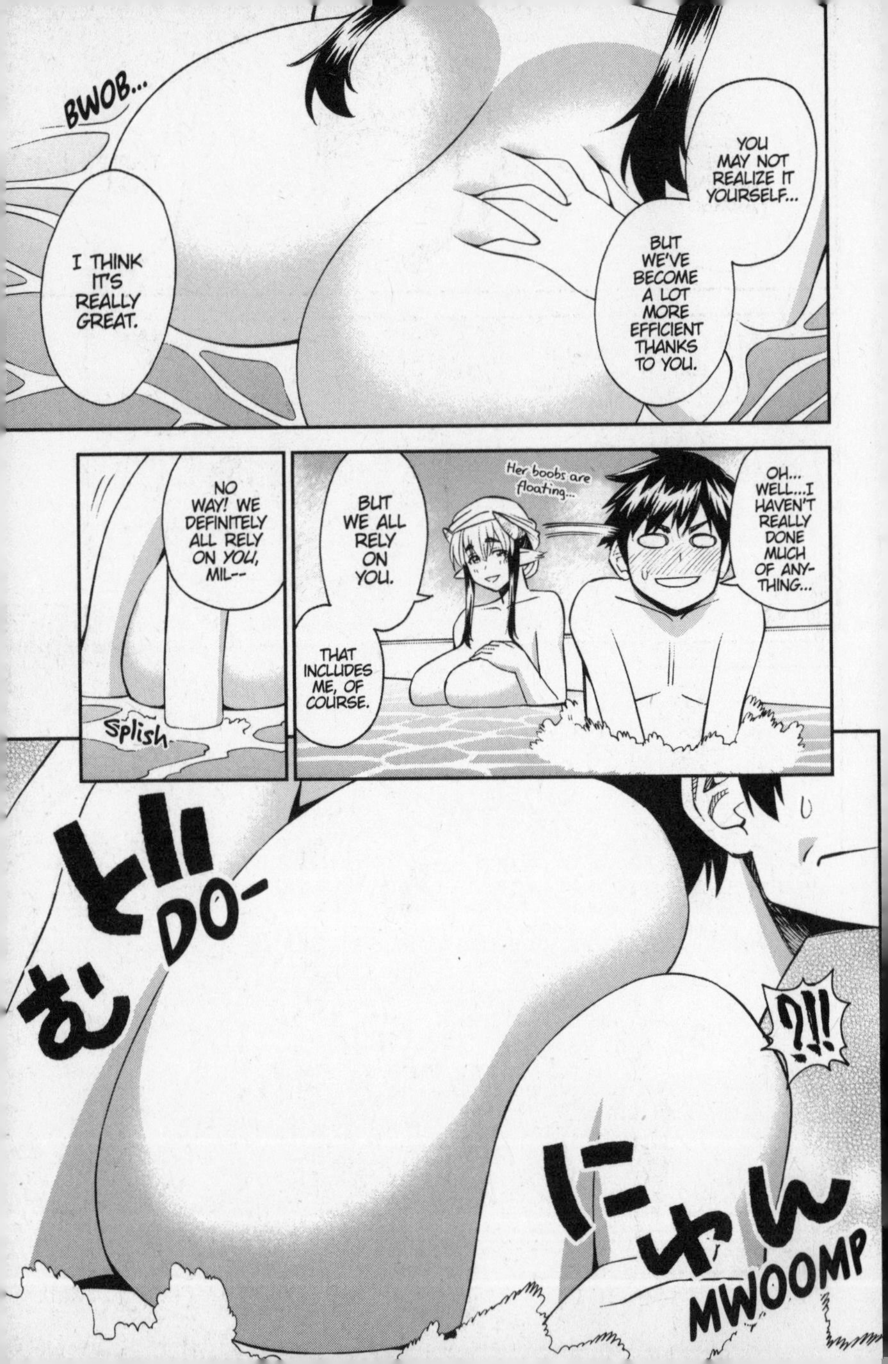

YOU MAY NOT REALIZE IT YOURSELF...
BUT WE'VE BECOME A LOT MORE EFFICIENT THANKS TO YOU.
I THINK IT'S REALLY GREAT.
BWOB...
OH... WELL...I HAVEN'T REALLY DONE MUCH OF ANY-THING...
Her boobs are floating...
BUT WE ALL RELY ON YOU.
THAT INCLUDES ME, OF COURSE.
NO WAY! WE DEFINITELY ALL RELY ON YOU, MIL--
Splish
?!!
にゅん
MWOOMP
どむ
DO-

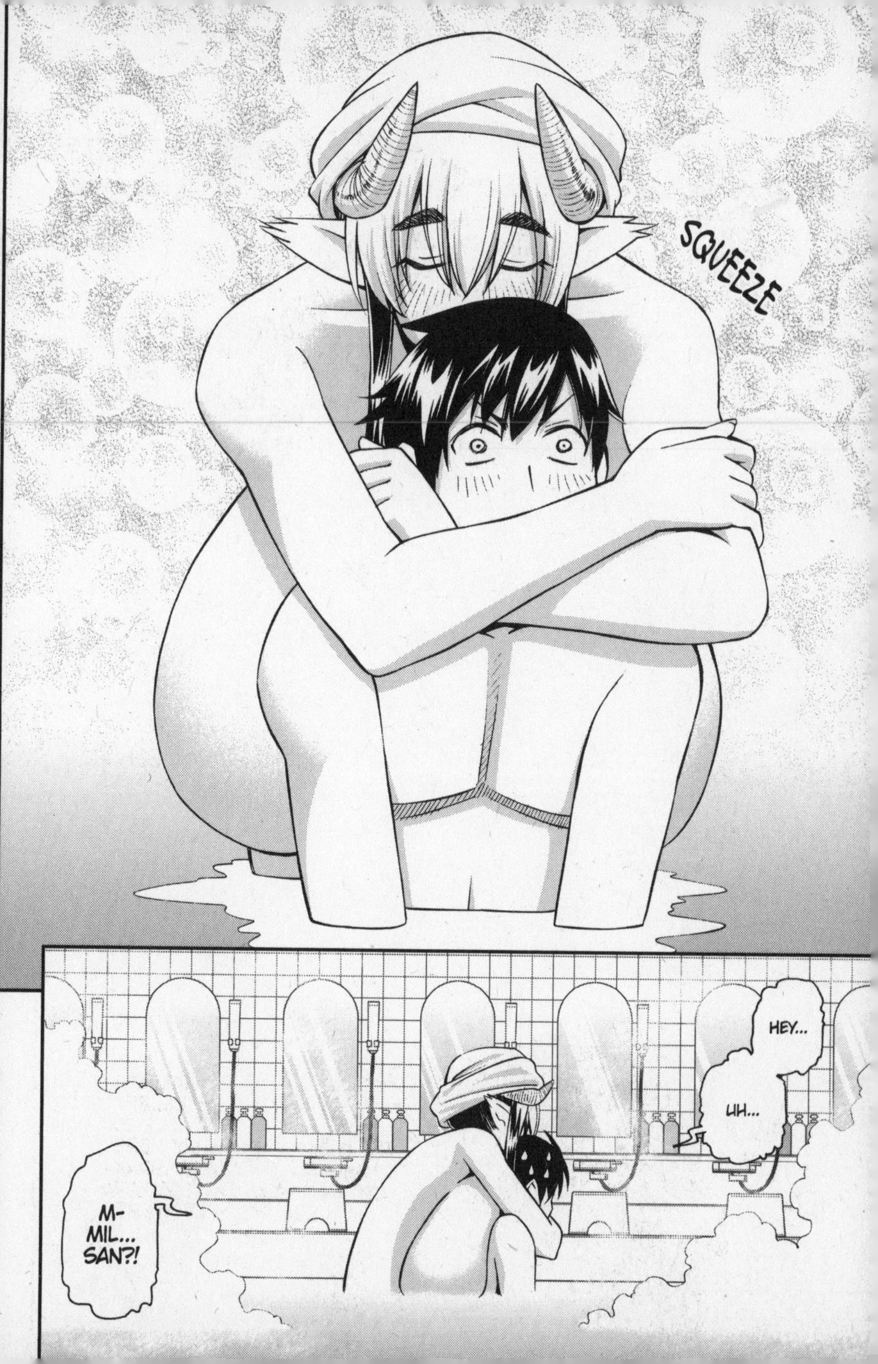
SQUEEZE
HEY...
UH...
M-MIL... SAN?!

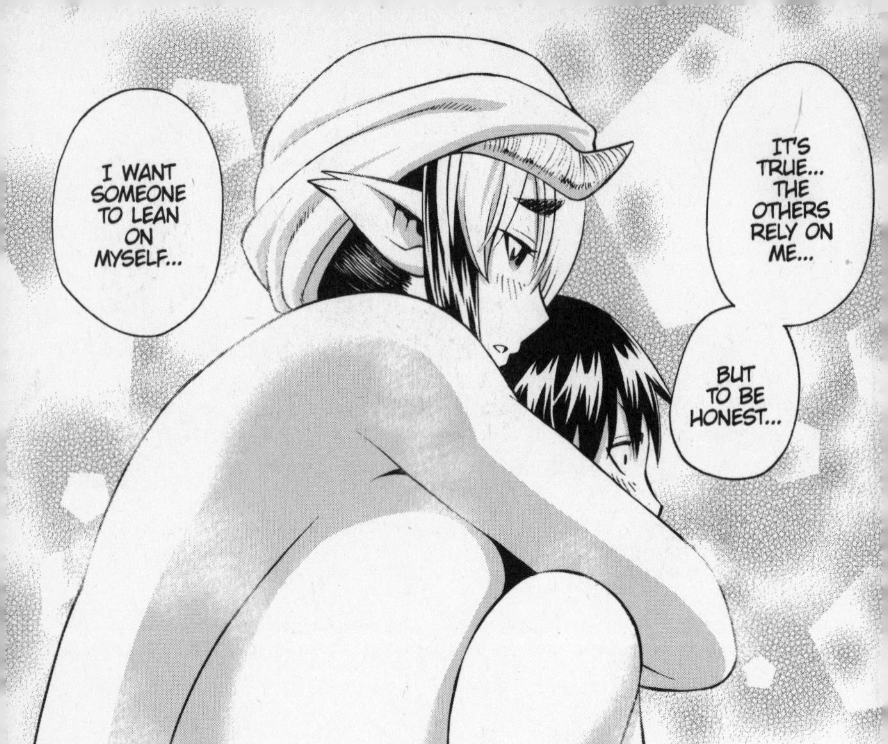
IT'S TRUE... THE OTHERS RELY ON ME...
BUT TO BE HONEST...
I WANT SOMEONE TO LEAN ON MYSELF...
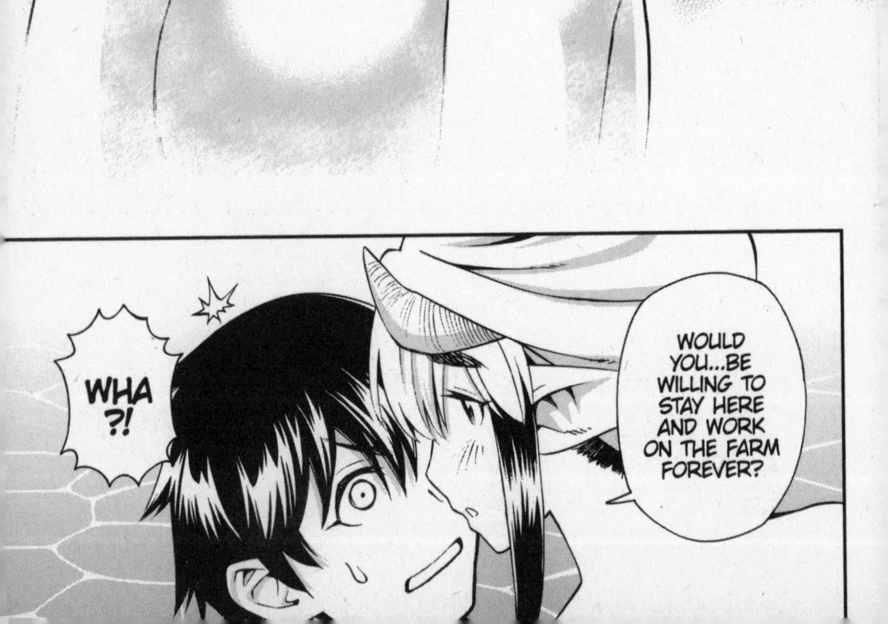
WOULD YOU...BE WILLING TO STAY HERE AND WORK ON THE FARM FOREVER?
WHA ?!

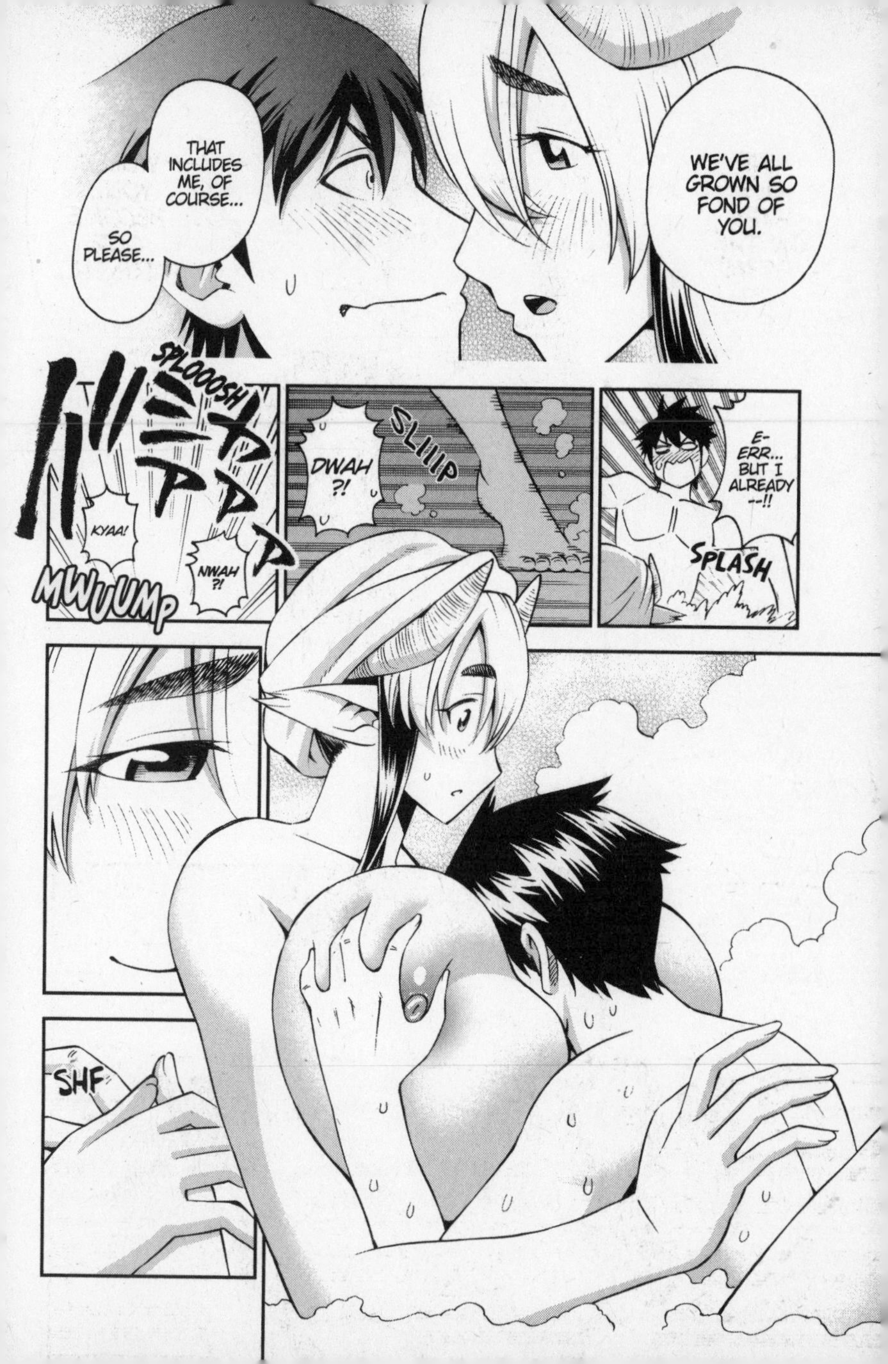
WE'VE ALL GROWN SO FOND OF YOU.
THAT INCLUDES ME, OF COURSE...
SO PLEASE...
E-ERR... BUT I ALREADY --!!
SPLASH
SLIIIP
DWAH ?!
SPLOOOSH
KYAA!
NWAH ?!
MWUUMP
SHF

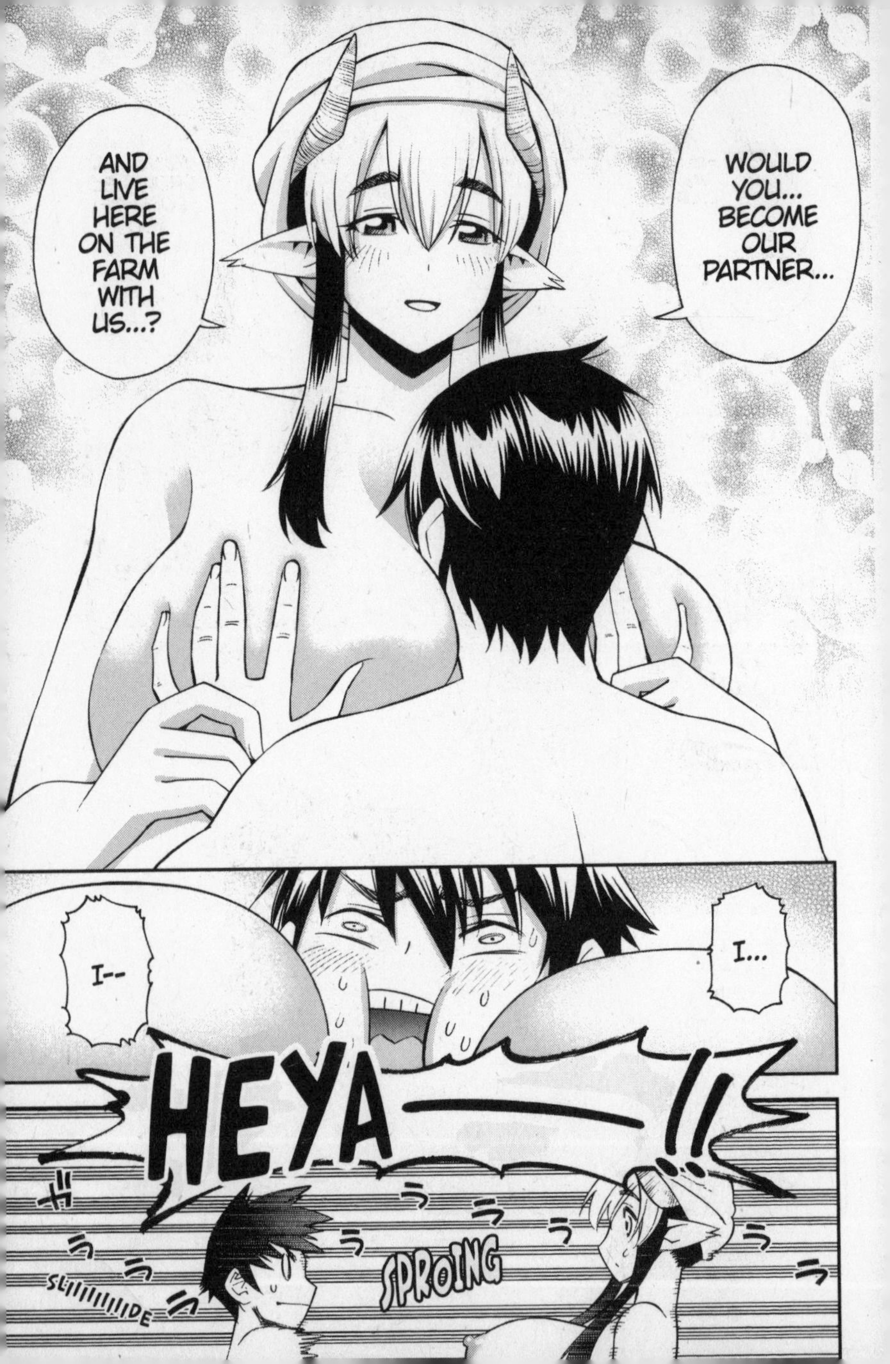
WOULD YOU... BECOME OUR PARTNER...
AND LIVE HERE ON THE FARM WITH US...?
I...
I--
HEYA——!!
SPROING
SLIIIIIIIIIIDE

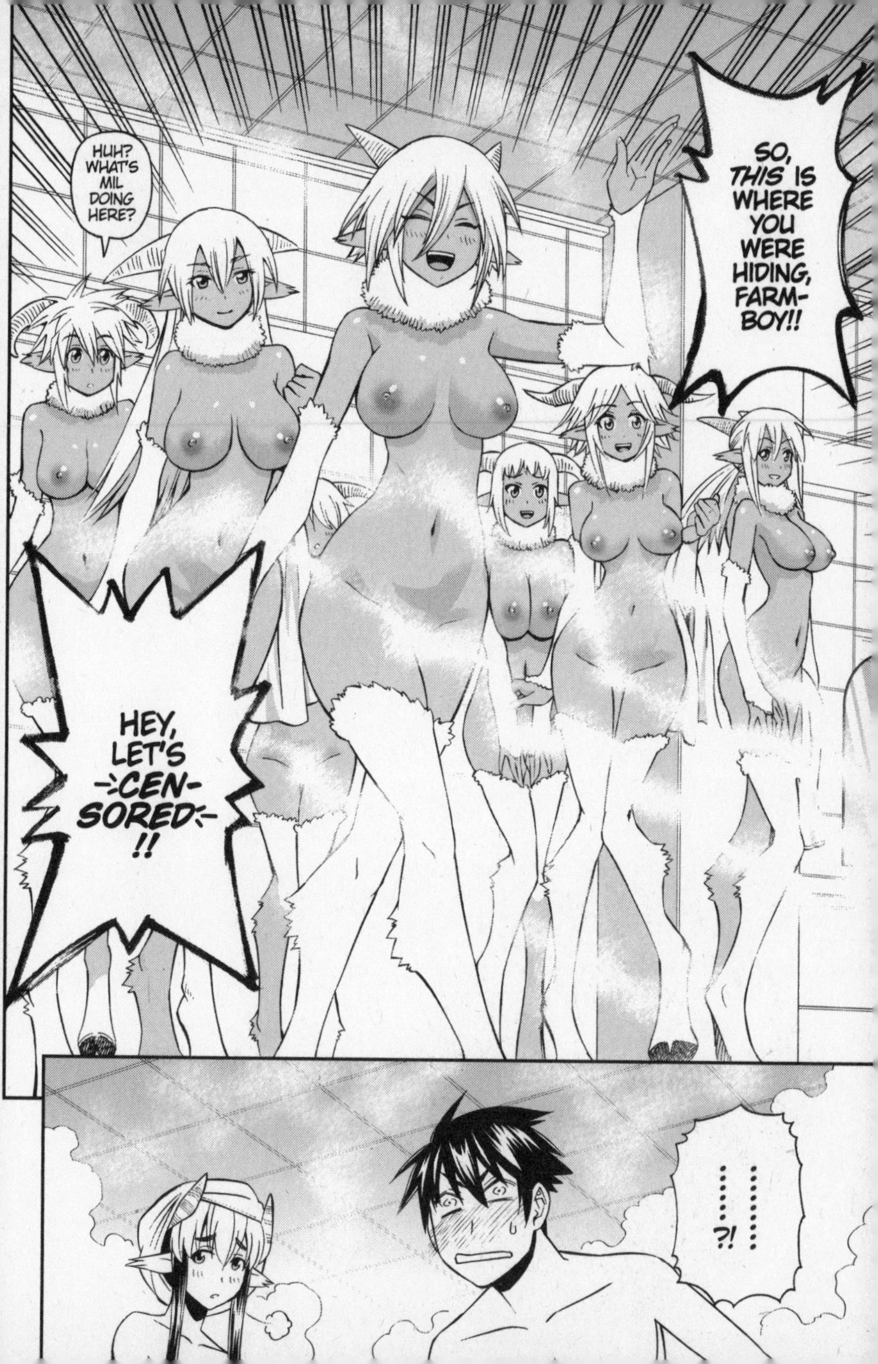
SO, THIS IS WHERE YOU WERE HIDING, FARM-BOY!!
HUH? WHAT'S MIL DOING HERE?
HEY, LET'S -CEN-SORED- !!
......?!

Monster Musume

Everyday Life with Monster Girls

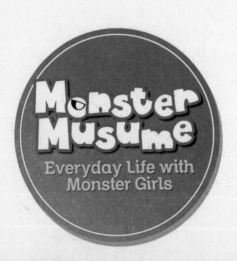

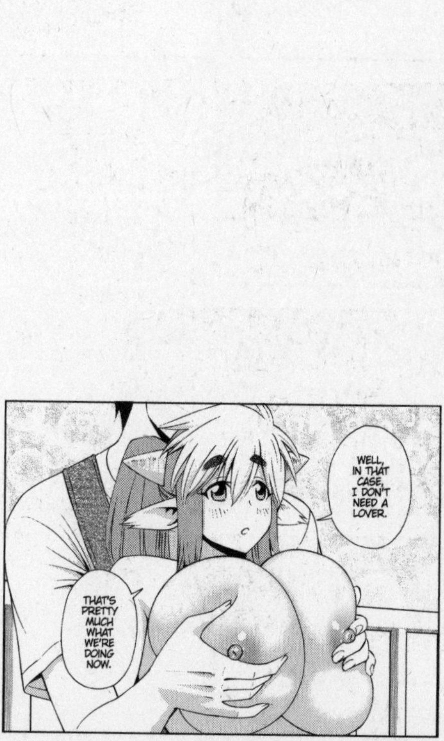
WELL, IN THAT CASE, I DON'T NEED A LOVER.
THAT'S PRETTY MUCH WHAT WE'RE DOING NOW.

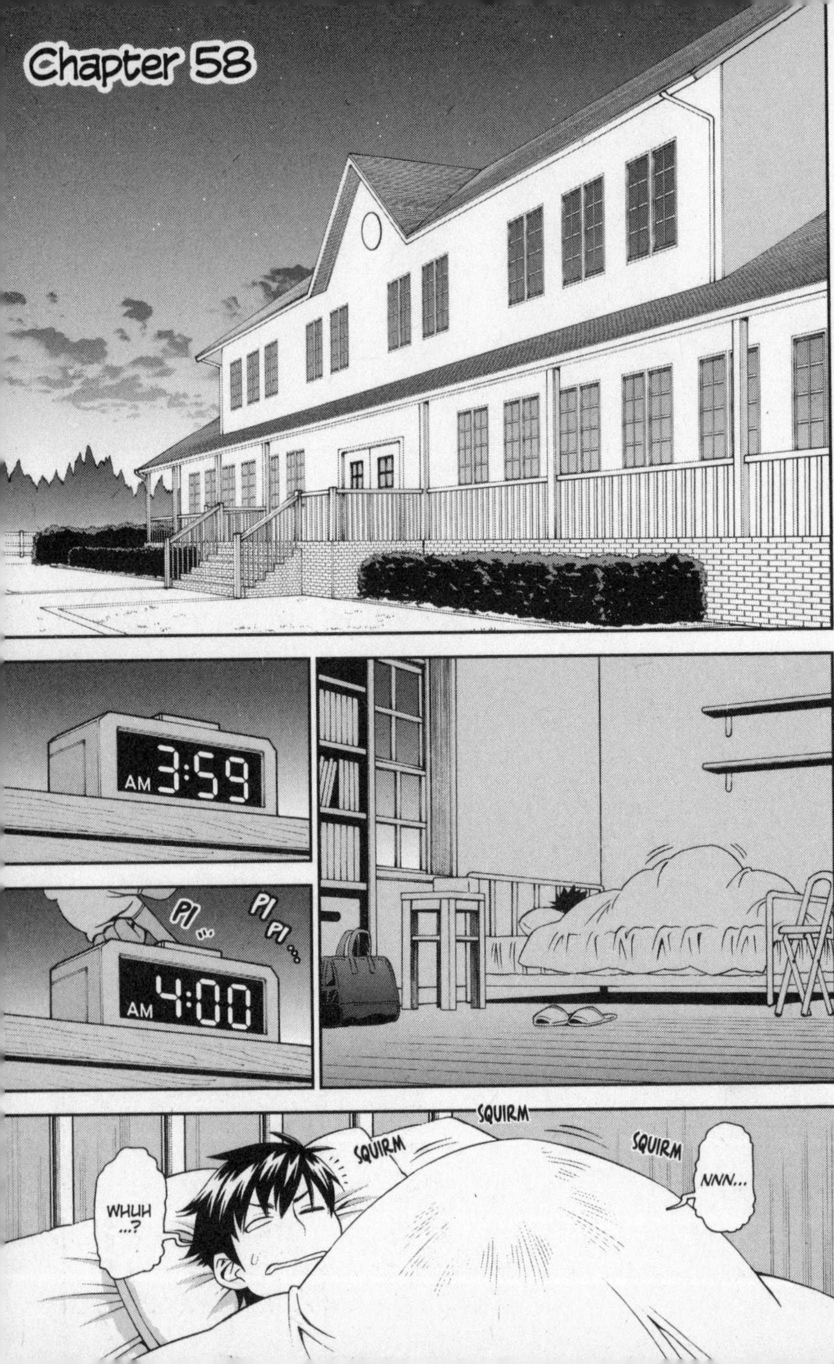
Chapter 58
AM 3:59
PI PI...
PI...
AM 4:00
NNN...
SQUIRM
SQUIRM
SQUIRM
WHUH ...?

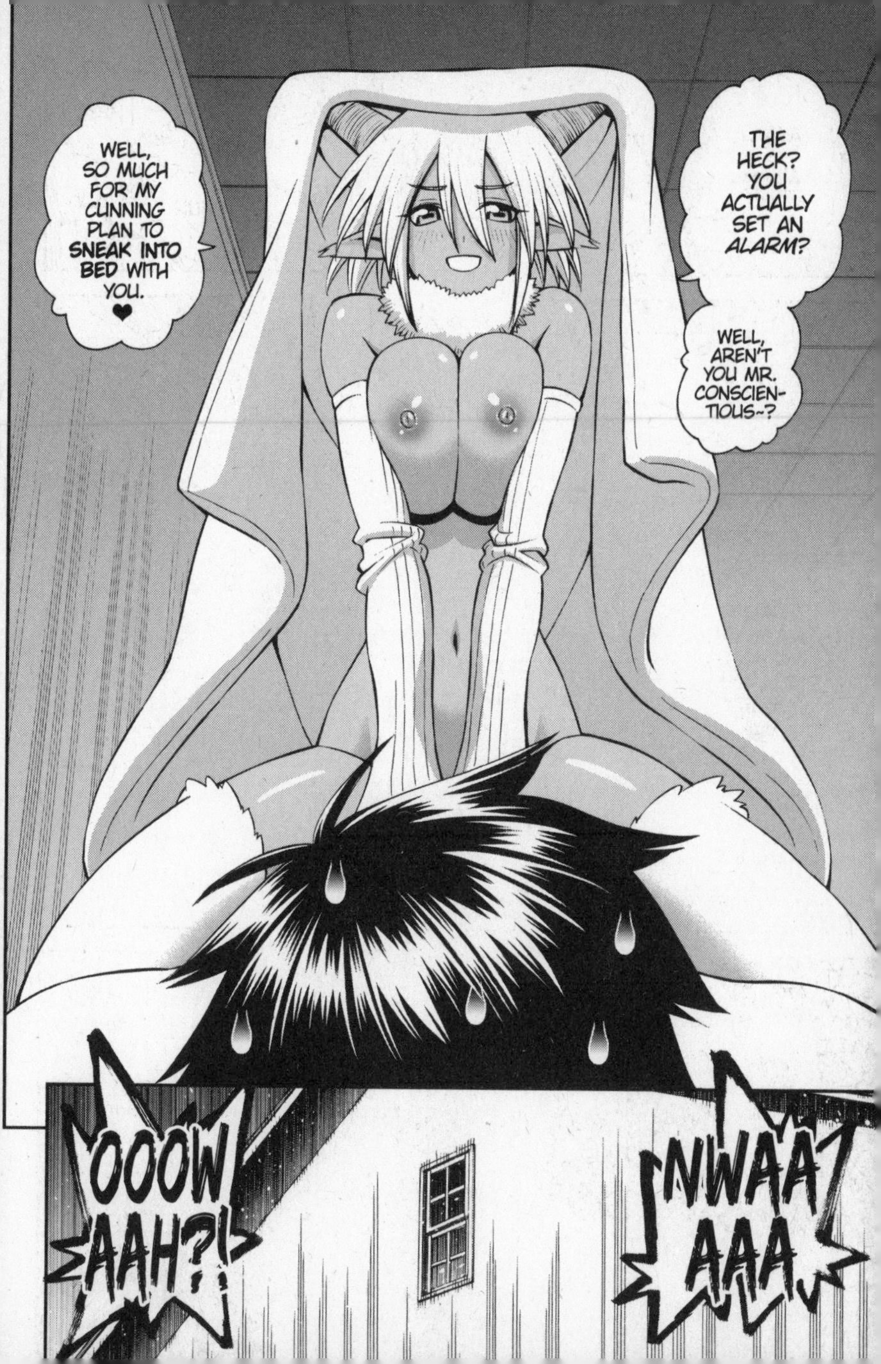
THE HECK? YOU ACTUALLY SET AN ALARM?
WELL, AREN'T YOU MR. CONSCIEN-TIOUS~?
WELL, SO MUCH FOR MY CUNNING PLAN TO SNEAK INTO BED WITH YOU. ❤
NWAAAAA
OOOW AAH?!

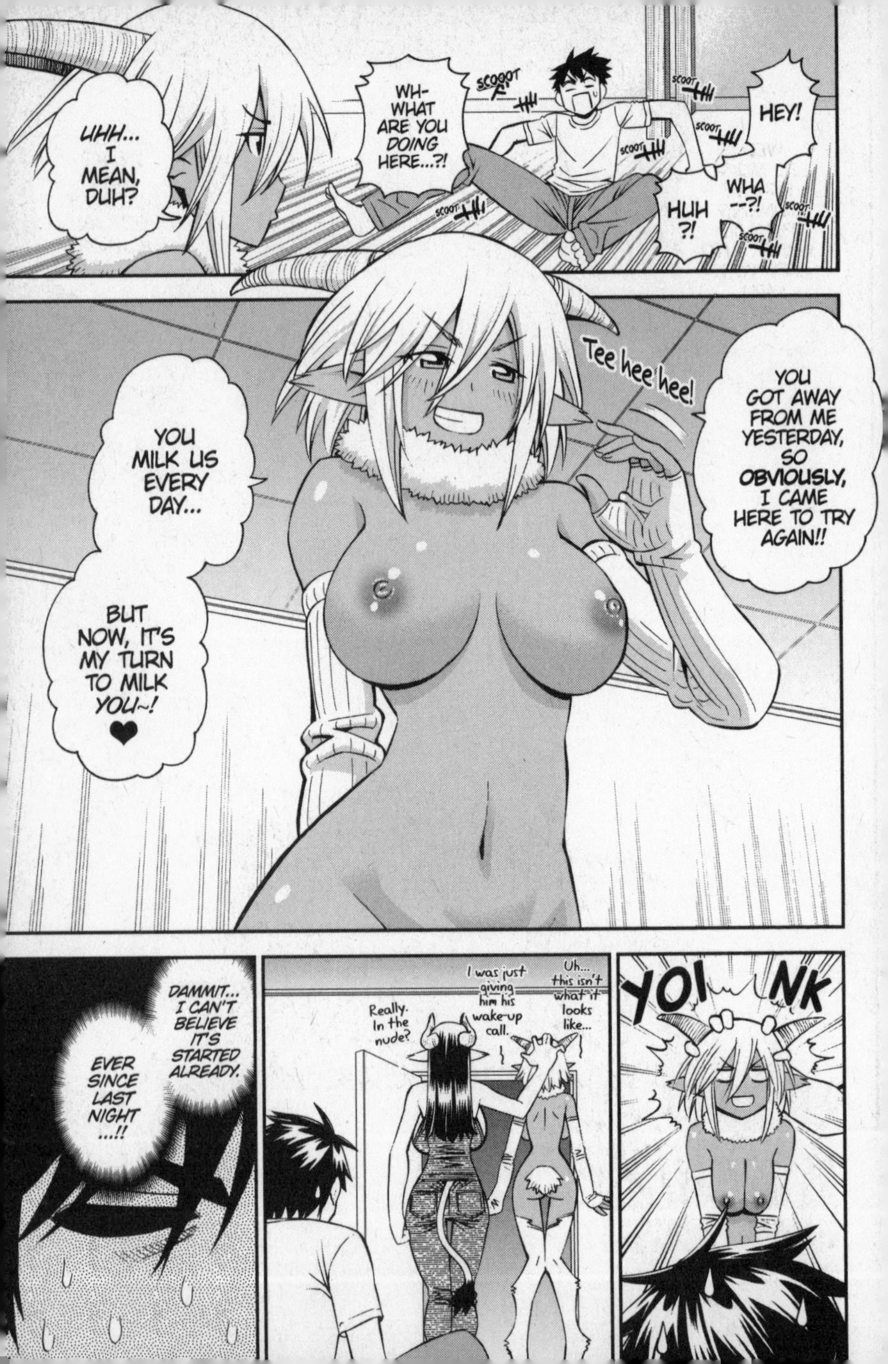
HEY!
SCOOT
SCOOT
SCOOT
WHA --?!
HUH ?!
SCOOOT
WH- WHAT ARE YOU DOING HERE...?!
SCOOT
UHH... I MEAN, DUH?
YOU GOT AWAY FROM ME YESTERDAY, SO OBVIOUSLY, I CAME HERE TO TRY AGAIN!!
Tee hee hee!
YOU MILK US EVERY DAY...
BUT NOW, IT'S MY TURN TO MILK YOU~! ❤
YOINK
Uh... this isn't what it looks like...
I was just giving him his wake-up call.
Really. In the nude?
DAMMIT... I CAN'T BELIEVE IT'S STARTED ALREADY.
EVER SINCE LAST NIGHT ...!!

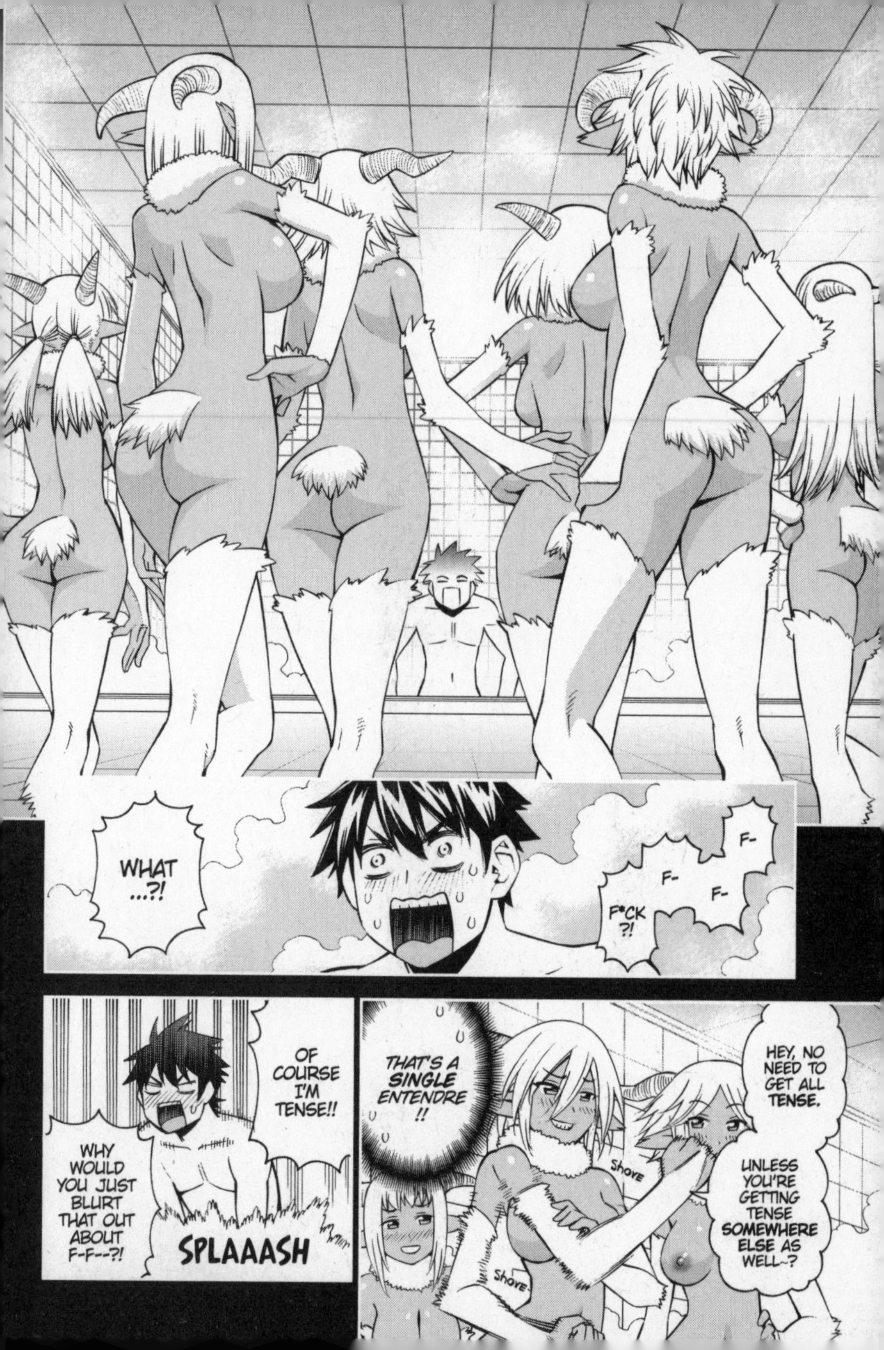
F- F- F- F*CK ?!
WHAT ...?!
HEY, NO NEED TO GET ALL TENSE.
THAT'S A SINGLE ENTENDRE !!
Shove
UNLESS YOU'RE GETTING TENSE SOMEWHERE ELSE AS WELL~?
Shove
OF COURSE I'M TENSE!!
WHY WOULD YOU JUST BLURT THAT OUT ABOUT F-F--?!
SPLAAASH

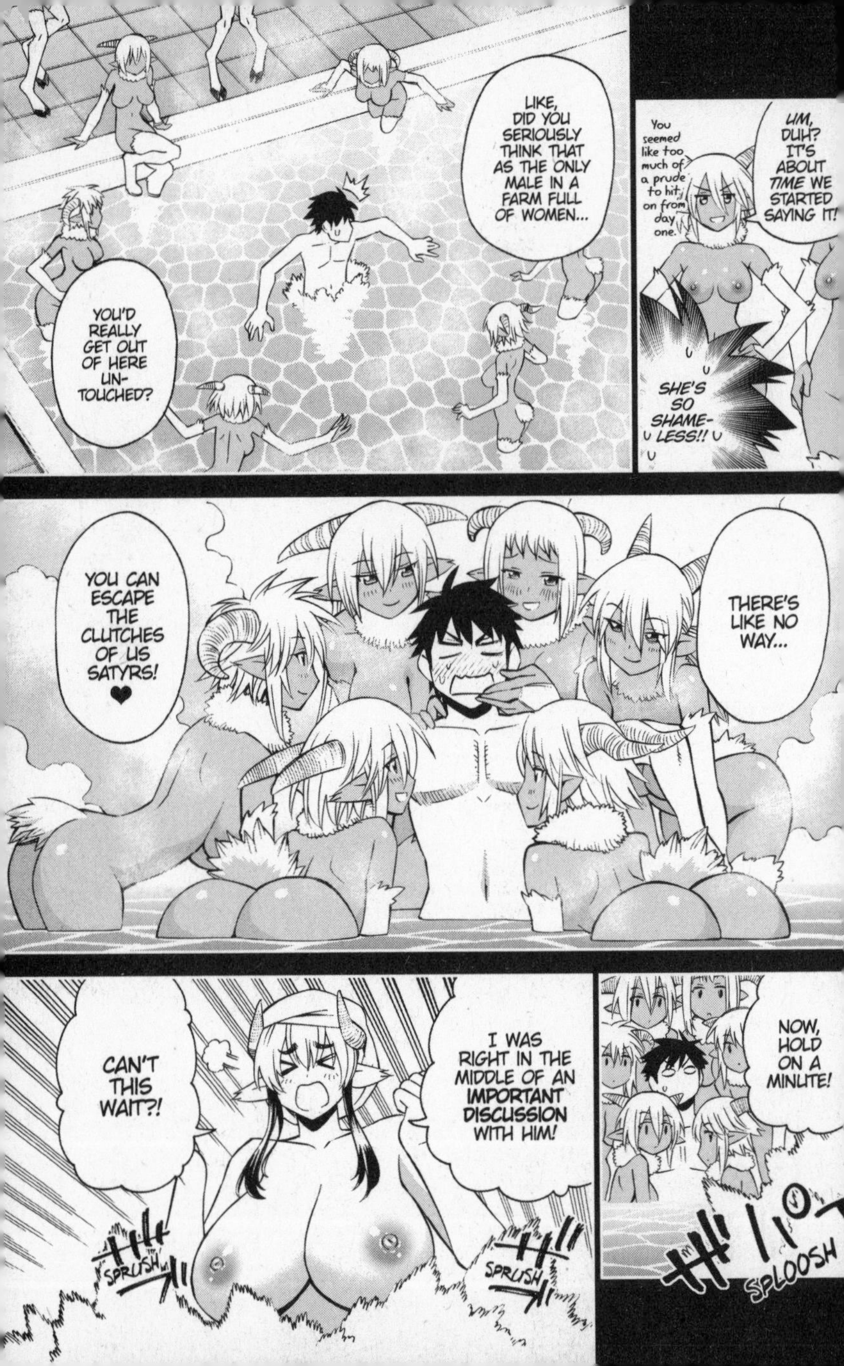
UM, DUH? IT'S ABOUT TIME WE STARTED SAYING IT!
You seemed like too much of a prude to hit on from day one.
SHE'S SO SHAMELESS!!
LIKE, DID YOU SERIOUSLY THINK THAT AS THE ONLY MALE IN A FARM FULL OF WOMEN...
YOU'D REALLY GET OUT OF HERE UN-TOUCHED?
THERE'S LIKE NO WAY...
YOU CAN ESCAPE THE CLUTCHES OF US SATYRS! ❤
NOW, HOLD ON A MINUTE!
SPLOOSH
I WAS RIGHT IN THE MIDDLE OF AN IMPORTANT DISCUSSION WITH HIM!
CAN'T THIS WAIT?!
SPRUSH
SPRUSH

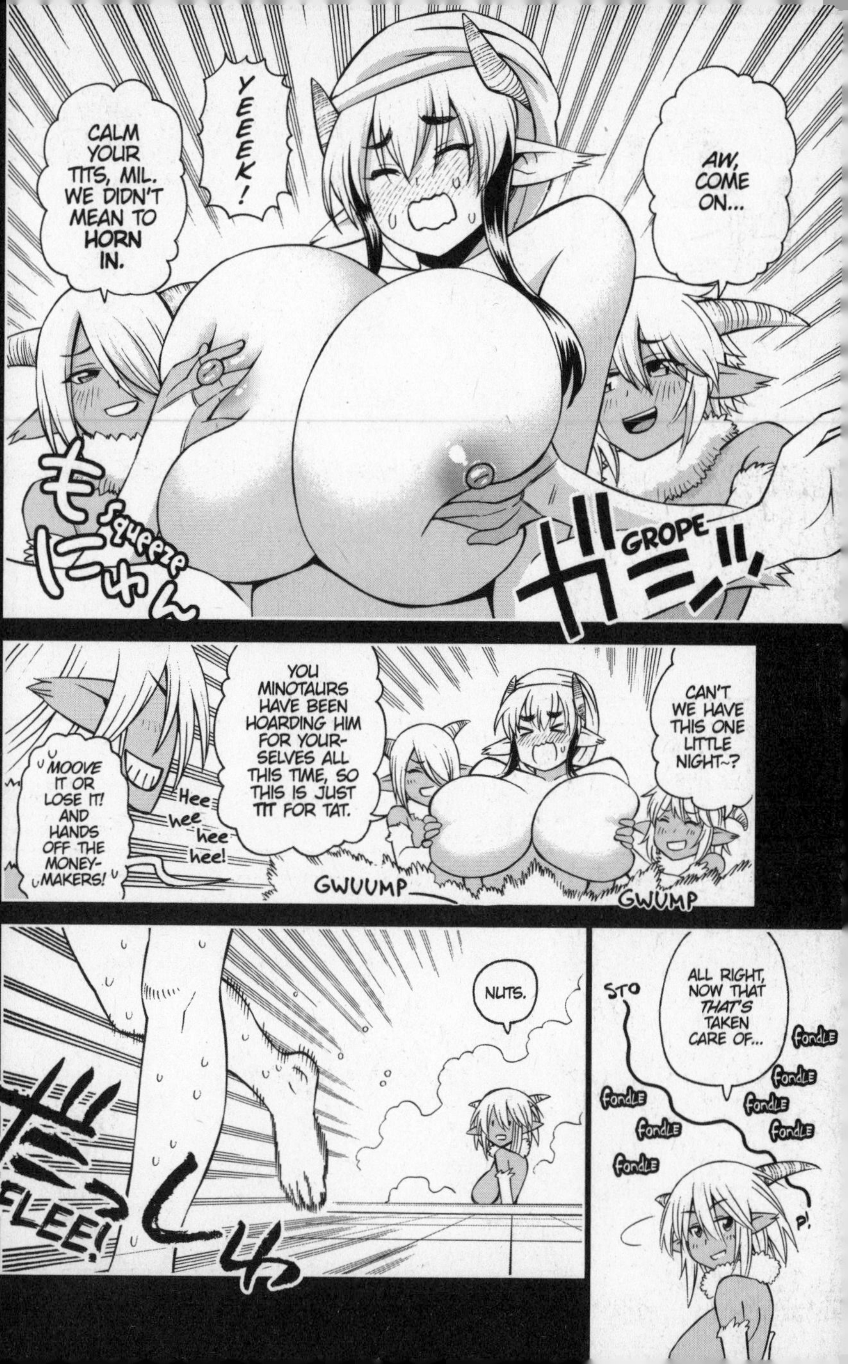
AW, COME ON...
YEEEK!
CALM YOUR TITS, MIL. WE DIDN'T MEAN TO HORN IN.
GROPE
squeeze
CAN'T WE HAVE THIS ONE LITTLE NIGHT~?
YOU MINOTAURS HAVE BEEN HOARDING HIM FOR YOURSELVES ALL THIS TIME, SO THIS IS JUST TIT FOR TAT.
Hee hee hee hee!
MOOVE IT OR LOSE IT! AND HANDS OFF THE MONEY-MAKERS!
GWUMP
GWUUMP
ALL RIGHT, NOW THAT THAT'S TAKEN CARE OF...
STOP!
fondle
fondle
fondle
fondle
fondle
fondle
fondle
NUTS.
FLEE!

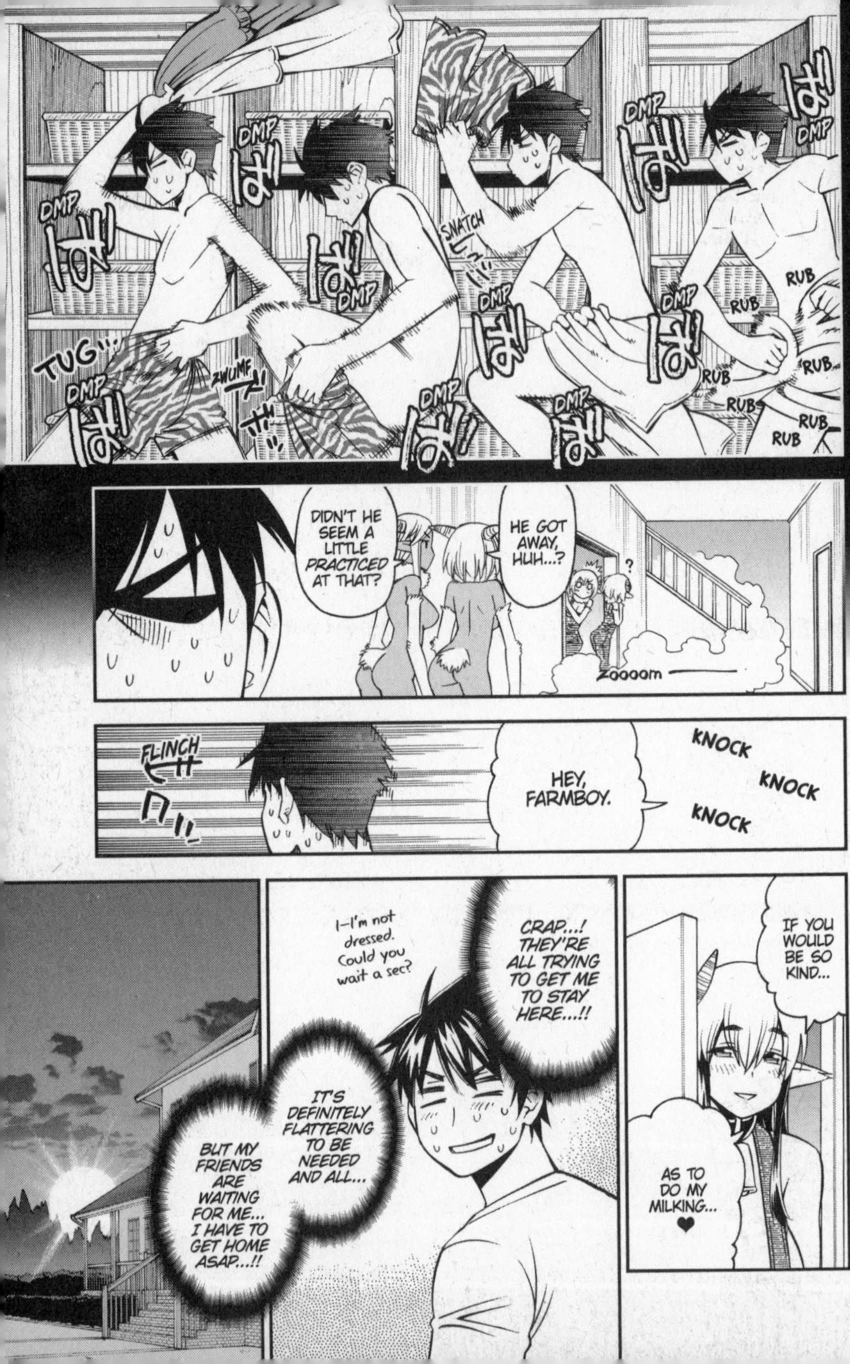
ば
DMP
DMP
ば
RUB
RUB
RUB
RUB
RUB
RUB
DMP
ば
DMP
ば
DMP
ば
SNATCH
DMP
ば
DMP
ば
ZWUMF
TUG...
DMP
ば
DMP
ば
?
HE GOT AWAY, HUH...?
DIDN'T HE SEEM A LITTLE PRACTICED AT THAT?
zoooom
KNOCK
KNOCK
KNOCK
HEY, FARMBOY.
FLINCH
IF YOU WOULD BE SO KIND...
AS TO DO MY MILKING... ♥
CRAP...! THEY'RE ALL TRYING TO GET ME TO STAY HERE...!!
I-I'm not dressed. Could you wait a sec?
IT'S DEFINITELY FLATTERING TO BE NEEDED AND ALL...
BUT MY FRIENDS ARE WAITING FOR ME... I HAVE TO GET HOME ASAP...!!

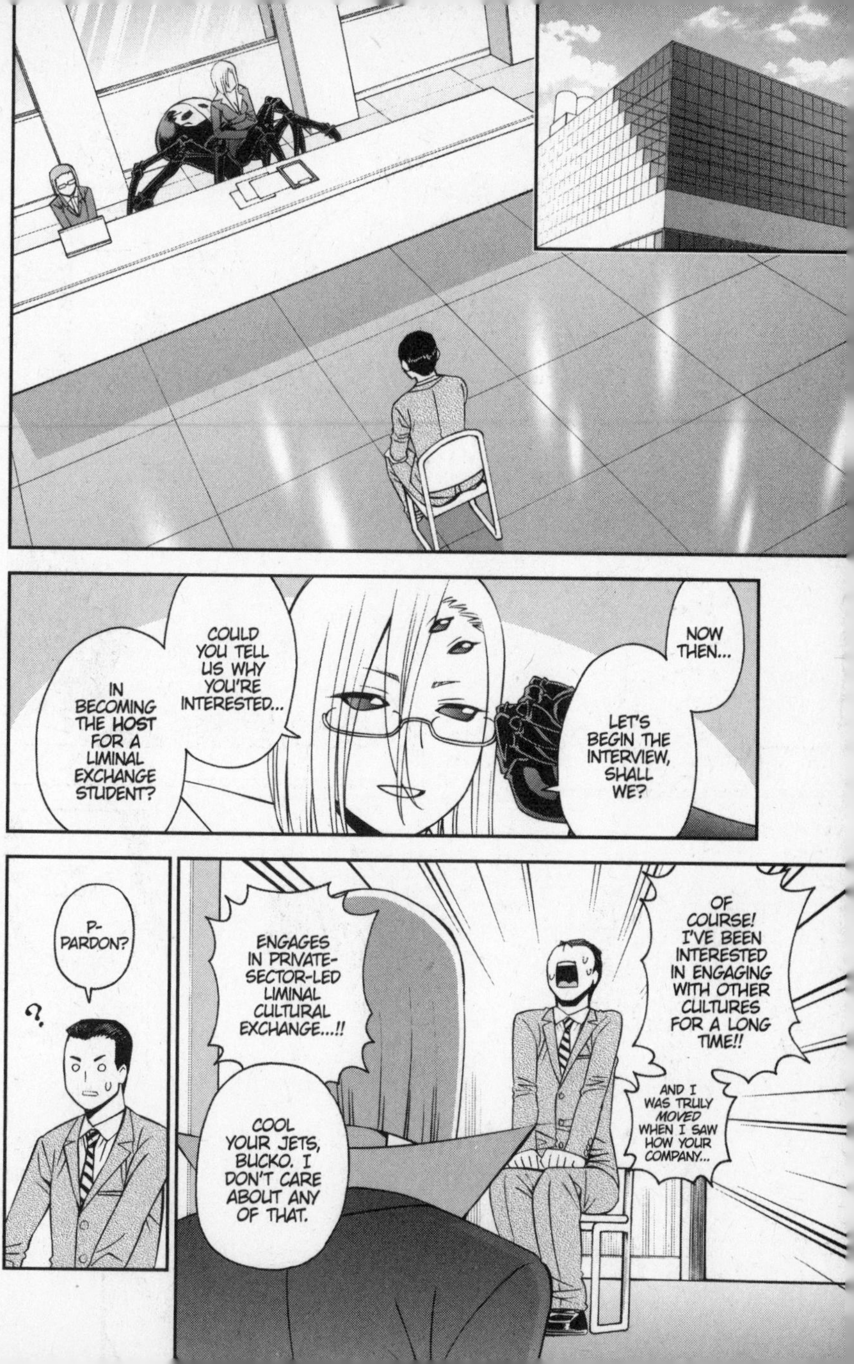
NOW THEN...
LET'S BEGIN THE INTERVIEW, SHALL WE?
COULD YOU TELL US WHY YOU'RE INTERESTED...
IN BECOMING THE HOST FOR A LIMINAL EXCHANGE STUDENT?
OF COURSE! I'VE BEEN INTERESTED IN ENGAGING WITH OTHER CULTURES FOR A LONG TIME!!
AND I WAS TRULY *MOVED* WHEN I SAW HOW YOUR COMPANY...
ENGAGES IN PRIVATE-SECTOR-LED LIMINAL CULTURAL EXCHANGE...!!
COOL YOUR JETS, BUCKO. I DON'T CARE ABOUT ANY OF THAT.
P-PARDON?
?

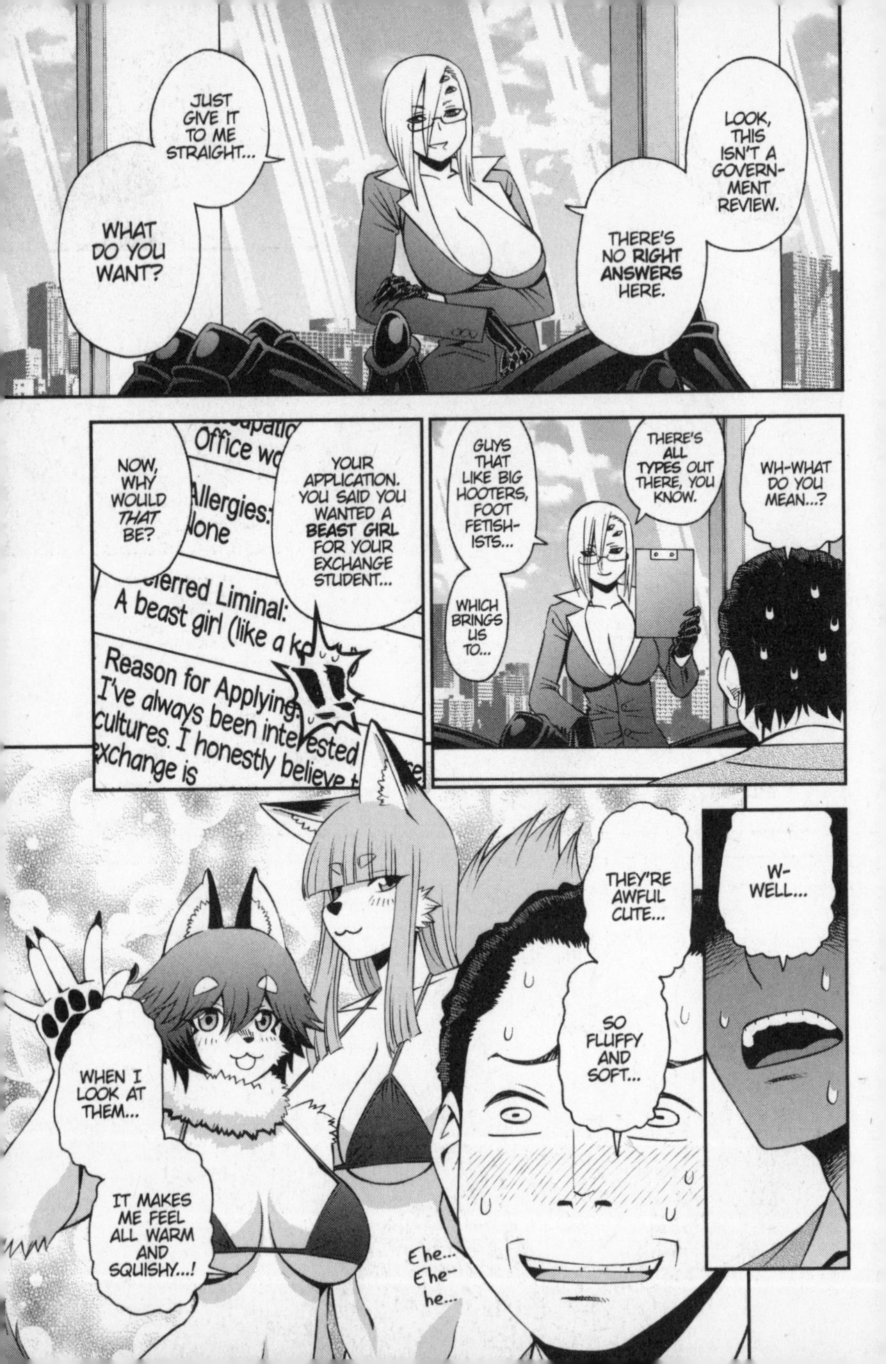
LOOK, THIS ISN'T A GOVERNMENT REVIEW.
THERE'S NO RIGHT ANSWERS HERE.
JUST GIVE IT TO ME STRAIGHT...
WHAT DO YOU WANT?
WH-WHAT DO YOU MEAN...?
THERE'S ALL TYPES OUT THERE, YOU KNOW.
GUYS THAT LIKE BIG HOOTERS, FOOT FETISHISTS...
WHICH BRINGS US TO...
YOUR APPLICATION. YOU SAID YOU WANTED A BEAST GIRL FOR YOUR EXCHANGE STUDENT...
NOW, WHY WOULD THAT BE?
Office wo
Allergies:
Liminal:
A beast girl (like a k
Reason for Applying
I've always been interested
cultures. I honestly believe
exchange is
W-WELL...
THEY'RE AWFUL CUTE...
SO FLUFFY AND SOFT...
WHEN I LOOK AT THEM...
IT MAKES ME FEEL ALL WARM AND SQUISHY...!
Ehe... Ehe-he...

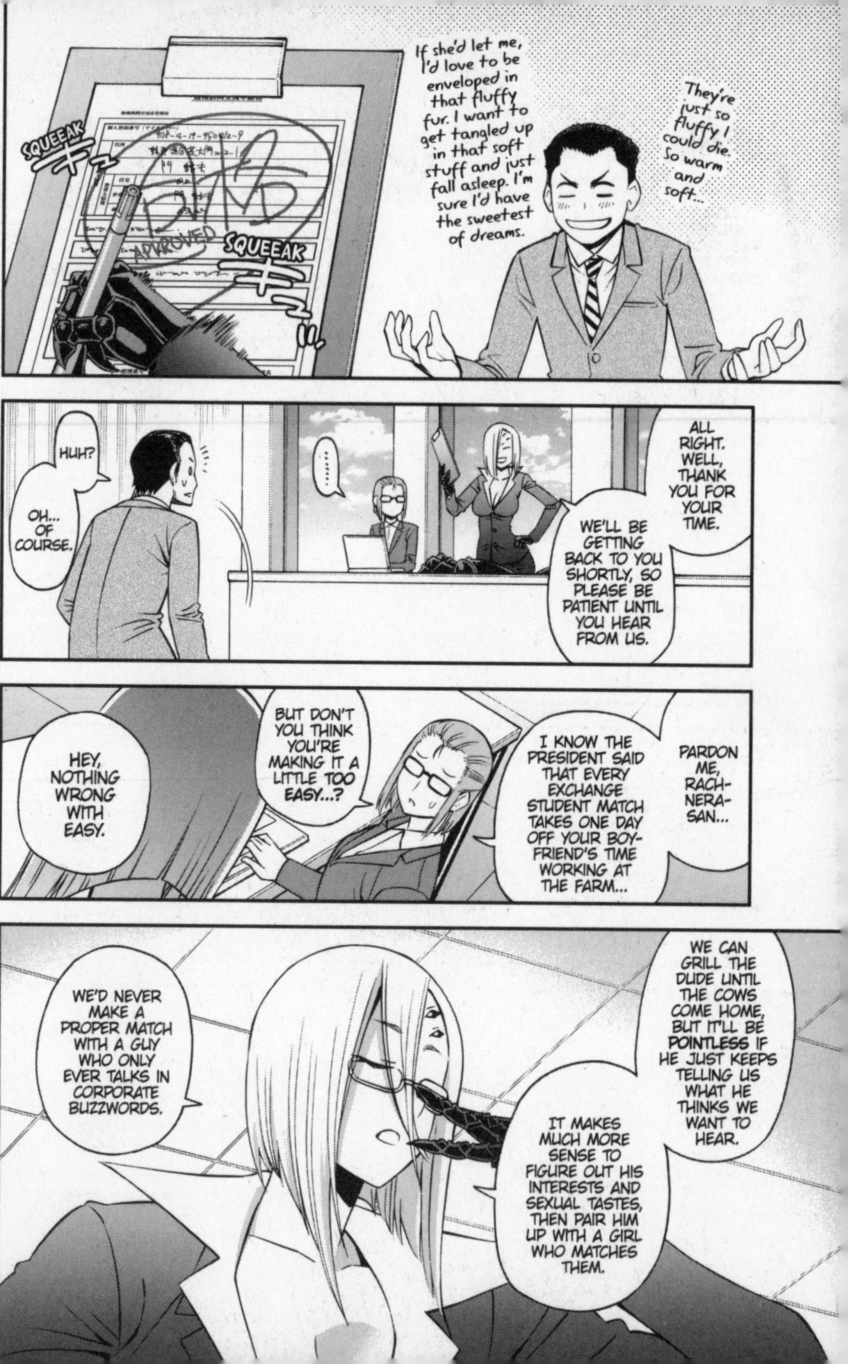
They're just so fluffy I could die. So warm and soft...
If she'd let me, I'd love to be enveloped in that fluffy fur. I want to get tangled up in that soft stuff and just fall asleep. I'm sure I'd have the sweetest of dreams.
SQUEEAK
APPROVED
SQUEEAK
ALL RIGHT. WELL, THANK YOU FOR YOUR TIME.
WE'LL BE GETTING BACK TO YOU SHORTLY, SO PLEASE BE PATIENT UNTIL YOU HEAR FROM US.
......
HUH?
OH... OF COURSE.
PARDON ME, RACHNERA-SAN...
I KNOW THE PRESIDENT SAID THAT EVERY EXCHANGE STUDENT MATCH TAKES ONE DAY OFF YOUR BOY-FRIEND'S TIME WORKING AT THE FARM...
BUT DON'T YOU THINK YOU'RE MAKING IT A LITTLE TOO EASY...?
HEY, NOTHING WRONG WITH EASY.
WE CAN GRILL THE DUDE UNTIL THE COWS COME HOME, BUT IT'LL BE POINTLESS IF HE JUST KEEPS TELLING US WHAT HE THINKS WE WANT TO HEAR.
IT MAKES MUCH MORE SENSE TO FIGURE OUT HIS INTERESTS AND SEXUAL TASTES, THEN PAIR HIM UP WITH A GIRL WHO MATCHES THEM.
WE'D NEVER MAKE A PROPER MATCH WITH A GUY WHO ONLY EVER TALKS IN CORPORATE BUZZWORDS.

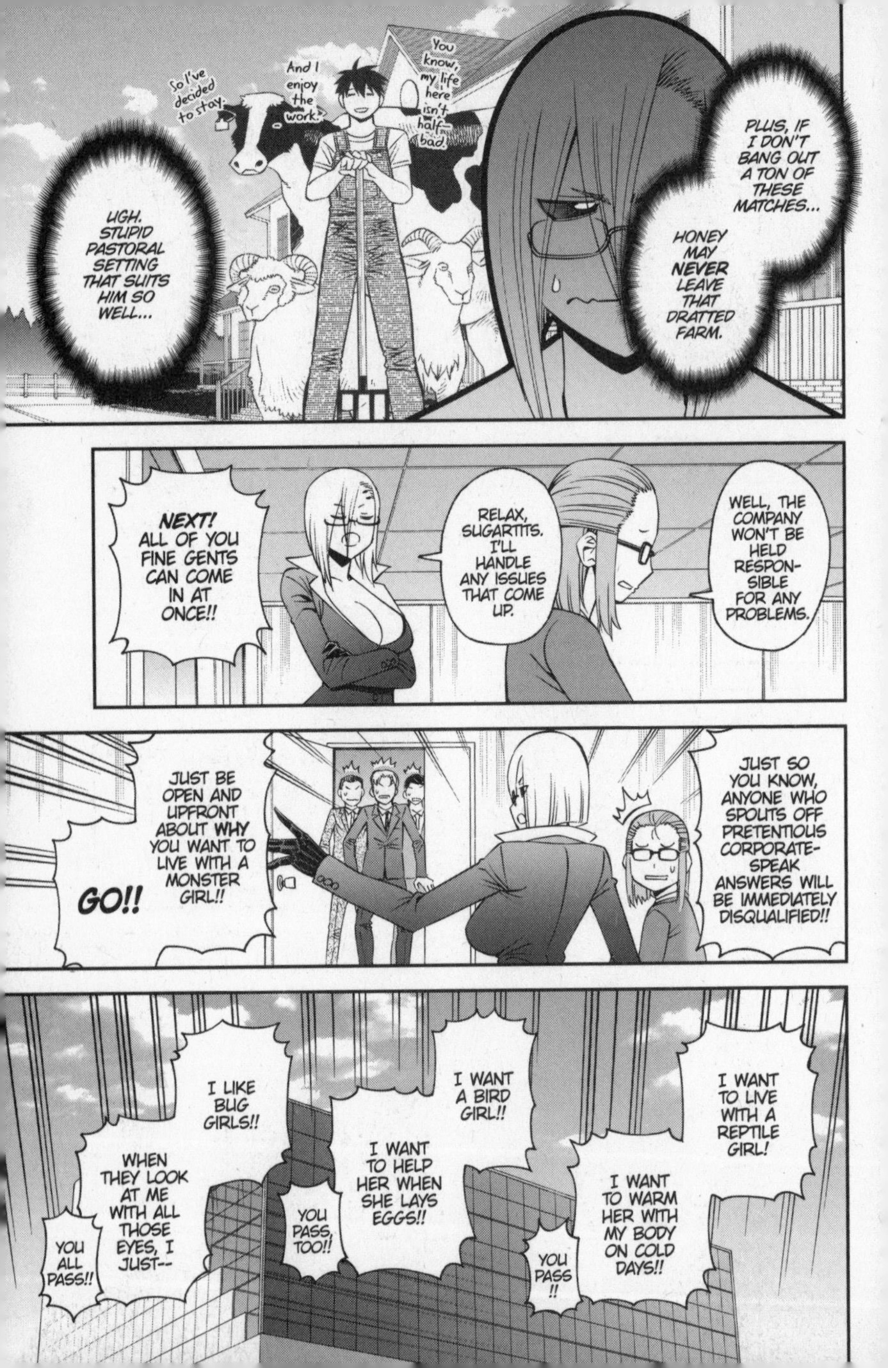
PLUS, IF I DON'T BANG OUT A TON OF THESE MATCHES...
HONEY MAY NEVER LEAVE THAT DRATTED FARM.
You know, my life here isn't half-bad.
And I enjoy the work.
So I've decided to stay.
UGH. STUPID PASTORAL SETTING THAT SUITS HIM SO WELL...
WELL, THE COMPANY WON'T BE HELD RESPONSIBLE FOR ANY PROBLEMS.
RELAX, SUGARTITS. I'LL HANDLE ANY ISSUES THAT COME UP.
NEXT! ALL OF YOU FINE GENTS CAN COME IN AT ONCE!!
JUST SO YOU KNOW, ANYONE WHO SPOUTS OFF PRETENTIOUS CORPORATE-SPEAK ANSWERS WILL BE IMMEDIATELY DISQUALIFIED!!
JUST BE OPEN AND UPFRONT ABOUT WHY YOU WANT TO LIVE WITH A MONSTER GIRL!!
GO!!
I WANT TO LIVE WITH A REPTILE GIRL!
I WANT TO WARM HER WITH MY BODY ON COLD DAYS!!
YOU PASS!!
I WANT A BIRD GIRL!!
I WANT TO HELP HER WHEN SHE LAYS EGGS!!
YOU PASS, TOO!!
I LIKE BUG GIRLS!!
WHEN THEY LOOK AT ME WITH ALL THOSE EYES, I JUST--
YOU ALL PASS!!

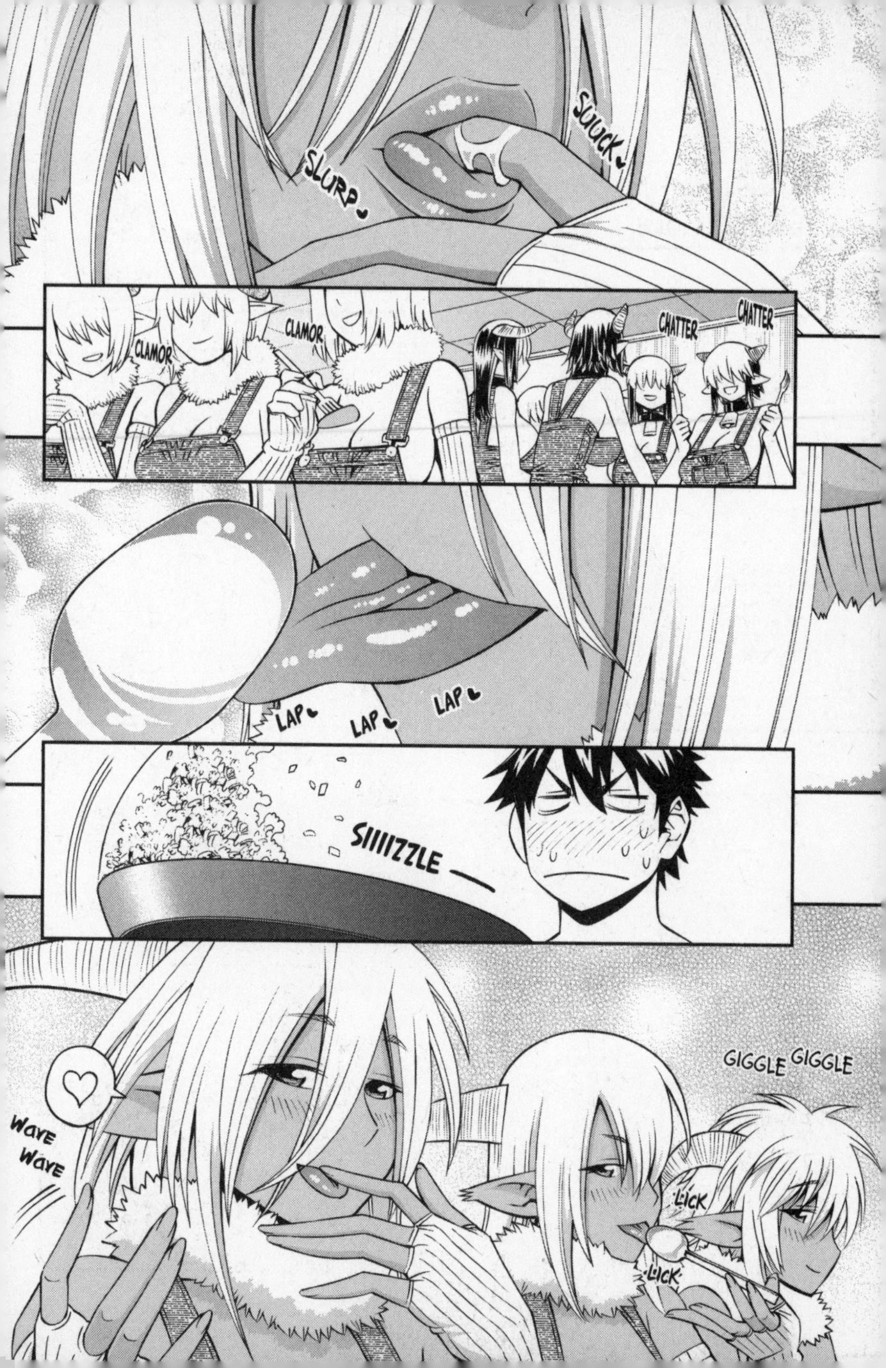
SUUCK♥
SLURP♥
CHATTER CHATTER
CLAMOR
CLAMOR
LAP♥
LAP♥
LAP♥
SIIIIZZLE
GIGGLE GIGGLE
LICK
LICK
♡
WAVE WAVE

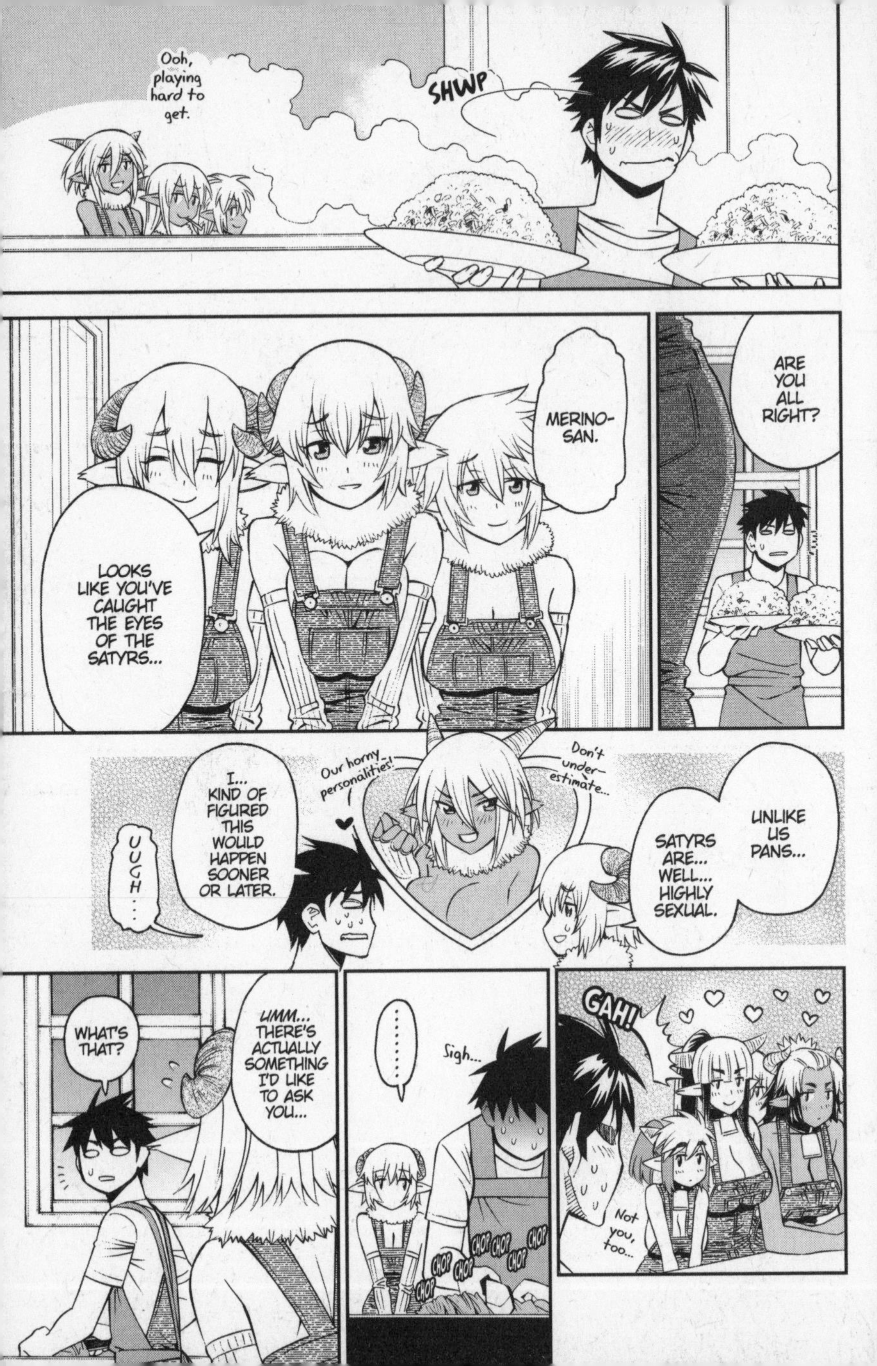
SHWP
Ooh, playing hard to get.
ARE YOU ALL RIGHT?
MERINO-SAN.
LOOKS LIKE YOU'VE CAUGHT THE EYES OF THE SATYRS...
UNLIKE US PANS...
SATYRS ARE... WELL... HIGHLY SEXUAL.
Don't under-estimate...
Our horny personalities!
I... KIND OF FIGURED THIS WOULD HAPPEN SOONER OR LATER.
UUGH...
GAH!
Not you, too...
Sigh...
......
CHOP CHOP CHOP CHOP CHOP CHOP
UMM... THERE'S ACTUALLY SOMETHING I'D LIKE TO ASK YOU...
WHAT'S THAT?

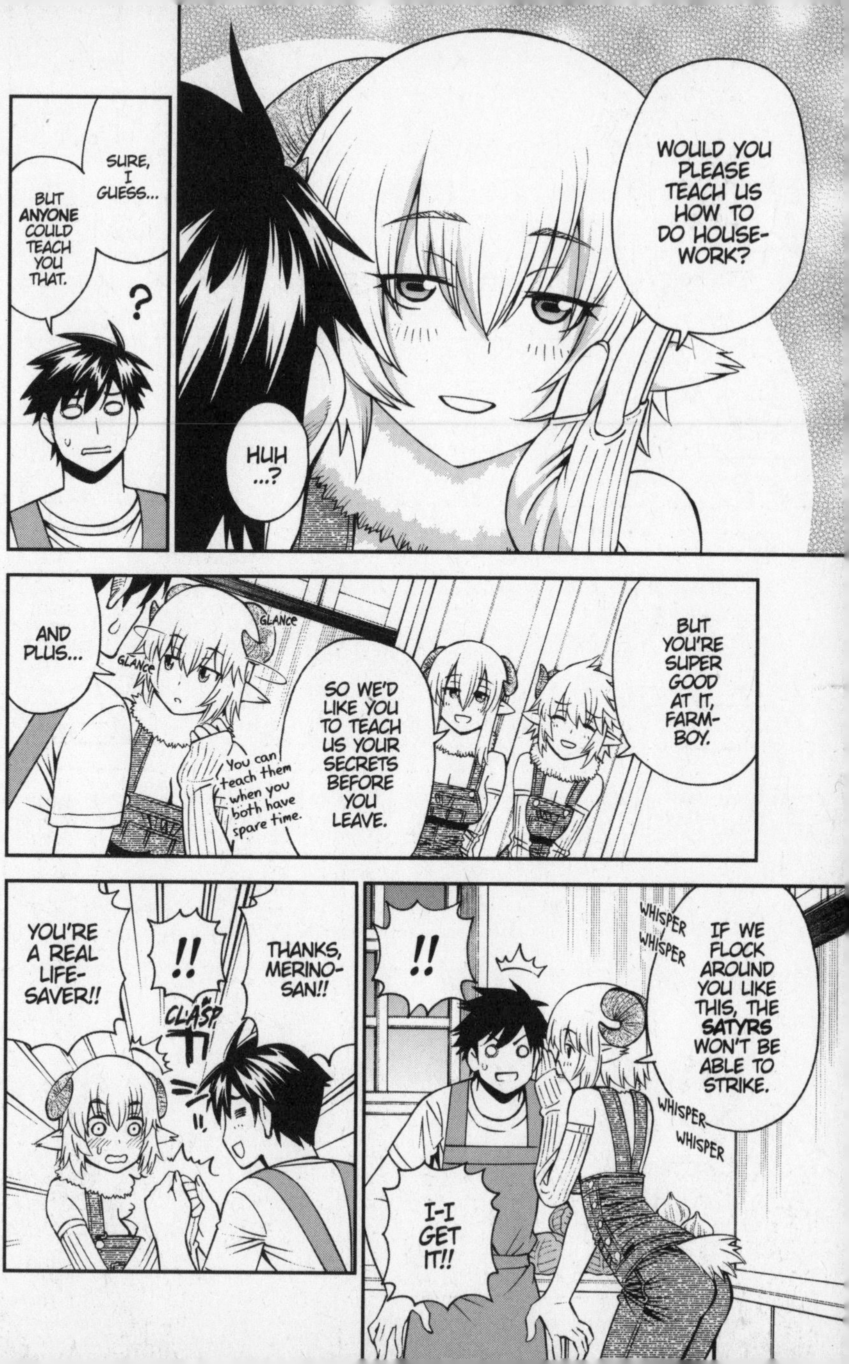
WOULD YOU PLEASE TEACH US HOW TO DO HOUSE-WORK?
HUH ...?
SURE, I GUESS...
BUT ANYONE COULD TEACH YOU THAT.
?
BUT YOU'RE SUPER GOOD AT IT, FARM-BOY.
SO WE'D LIKE YOU TO TEACH US YOUR SECRETS BEFORE YOU LEAVE.
GLANCE
GLANCE
AND PLUS...
You can teach them when you both have spare time.
WHISPER
WHISPER
IF WE FLOCK AROUND YOU LIKE THIS, THE SATYRS WON'T BE ABLE TO STRIKE.
WHISPER
WHISPER
!!
I-I GET IT!!
THANKS, MERINO-SAN!!
!!
YOU'RE A REAL LIFE-SAVER!!
CLASP

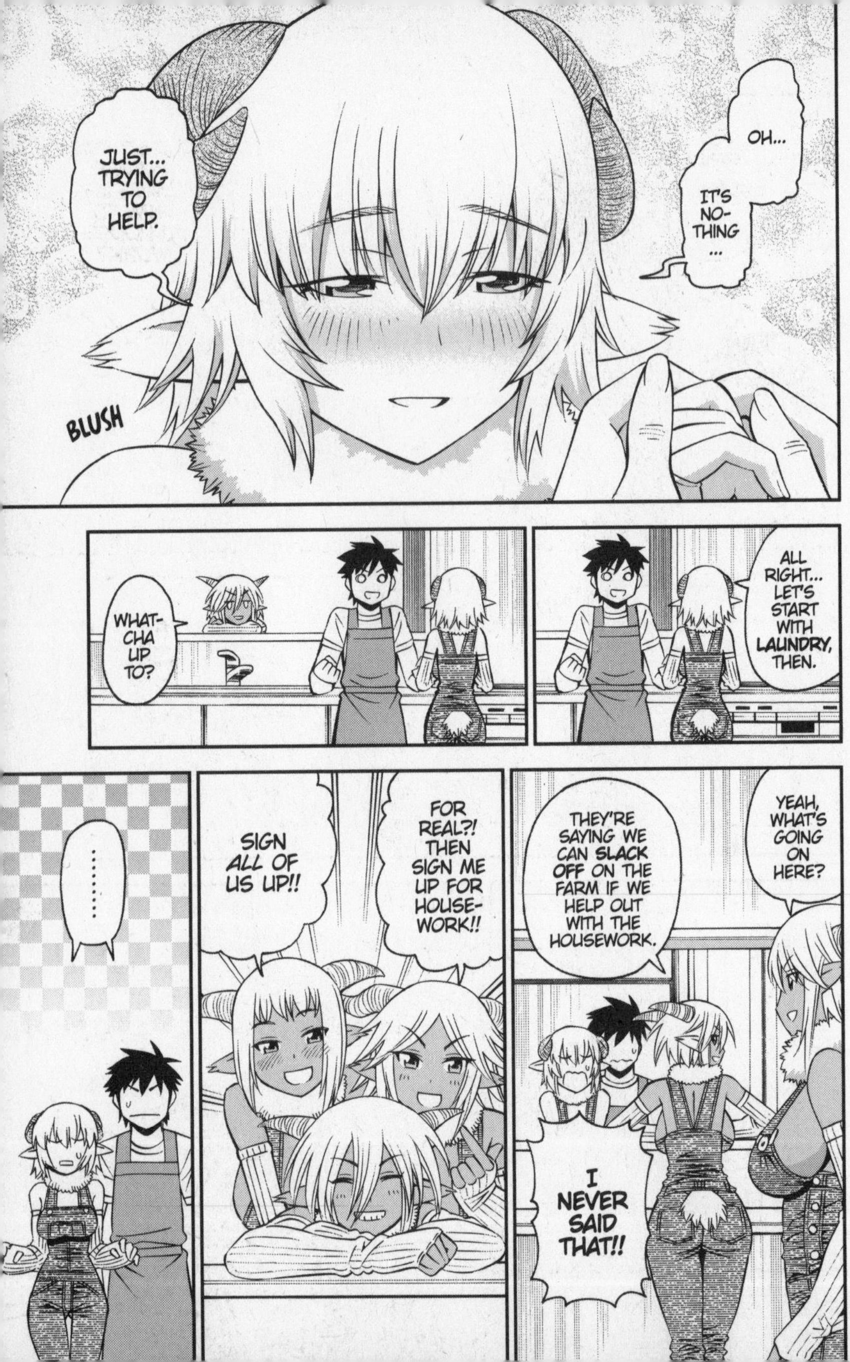
OH...
IT'S NOTHING...
JUST... TRYING TO HELP.
BLUSH
ALL RIGHT... LET'S START WITH LAUNDRY, THEN.
WHATCHA UP TO?
YEAH, WHAT'S GOING ON HERE?
THEY'RE SAYING WE CAN SLACK OFF ON THE FARM IF WE HELP OUT WITH THE HOUSEWORK.
I NEVER SAID THAT!!
FOR REAL?! THEN SIGN ME UP FOR HOUSEWORK!!
SIGN ALL OF US UP!!
....

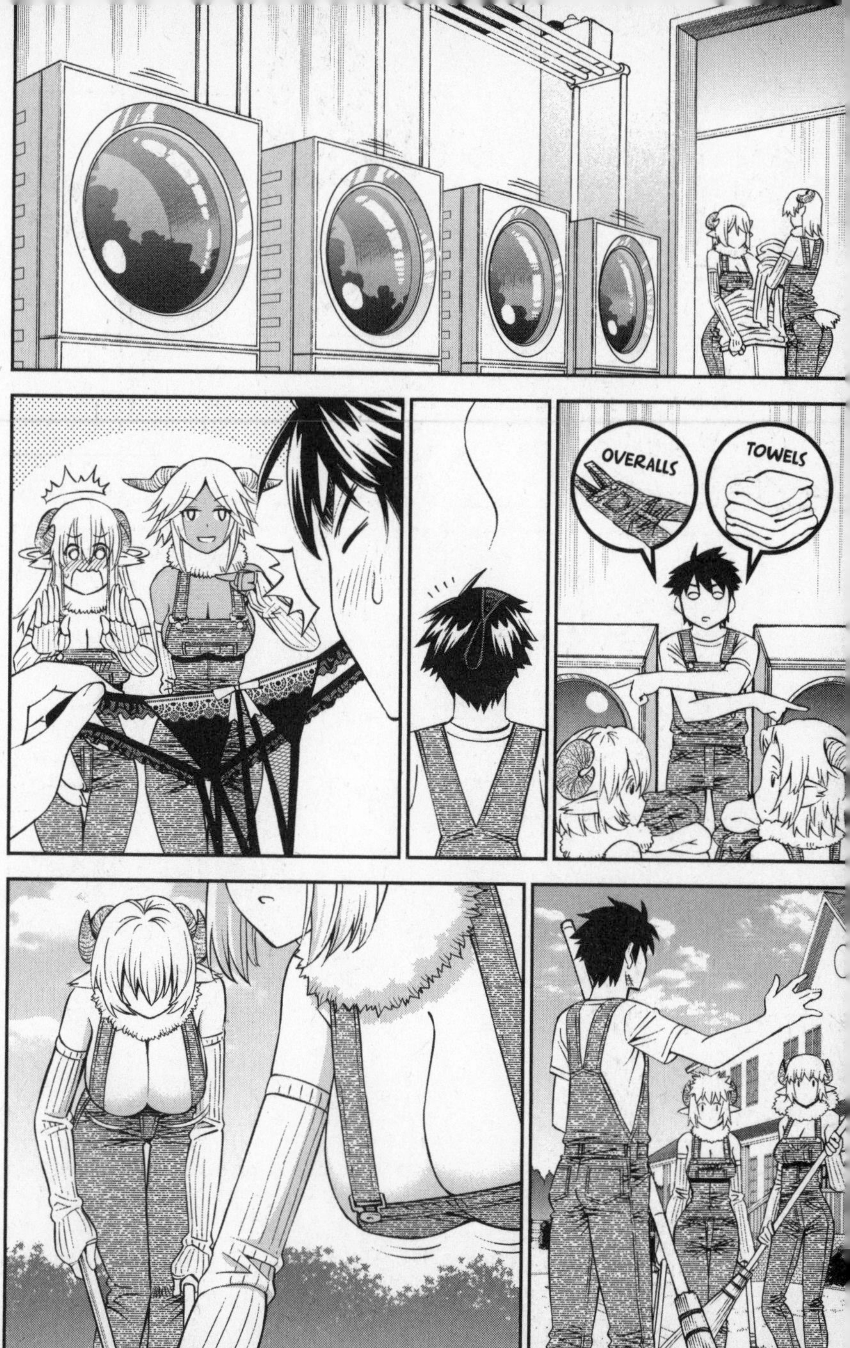
TOWELS
OVERALLS

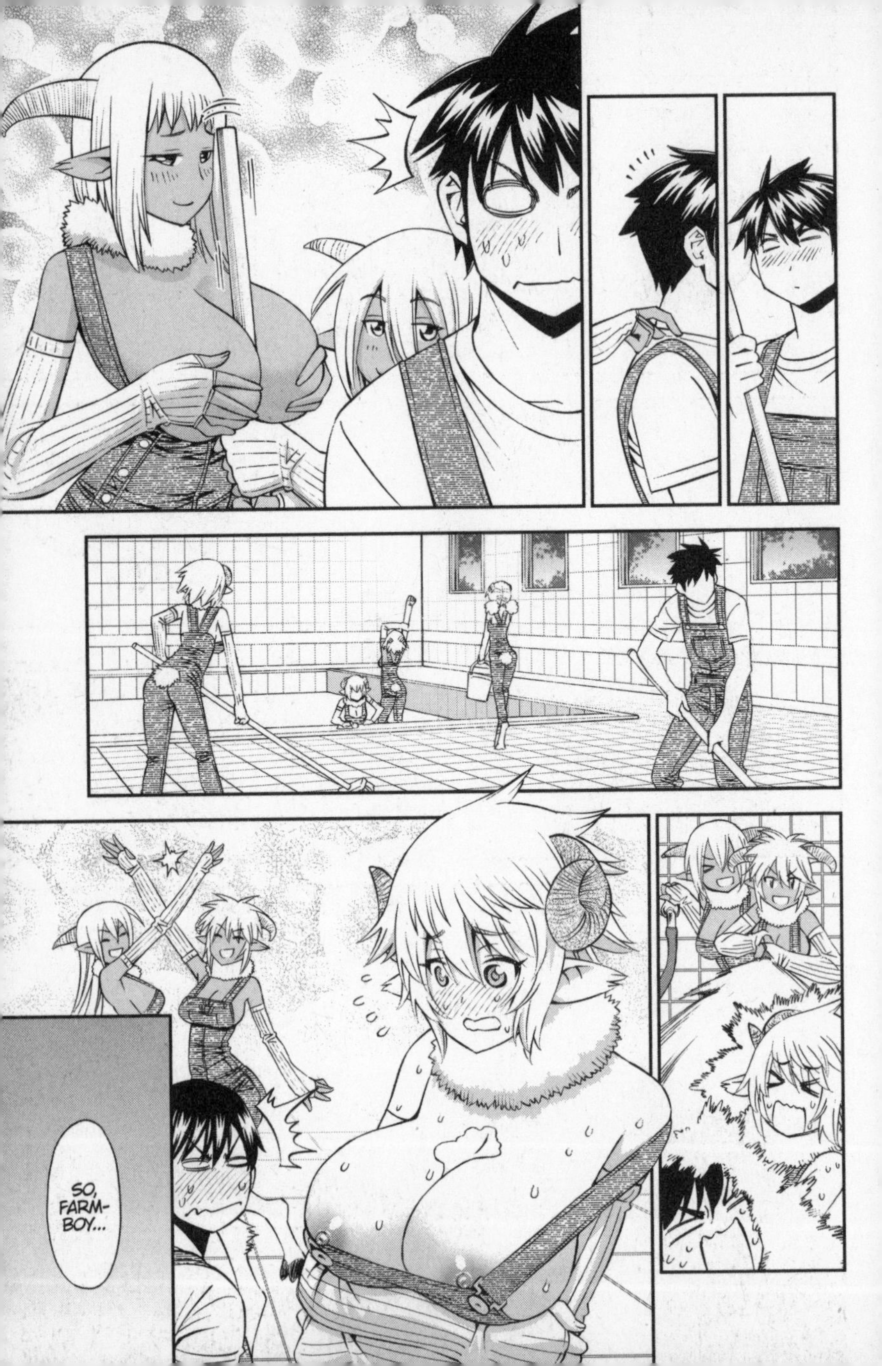
SO, FARM-BOY...

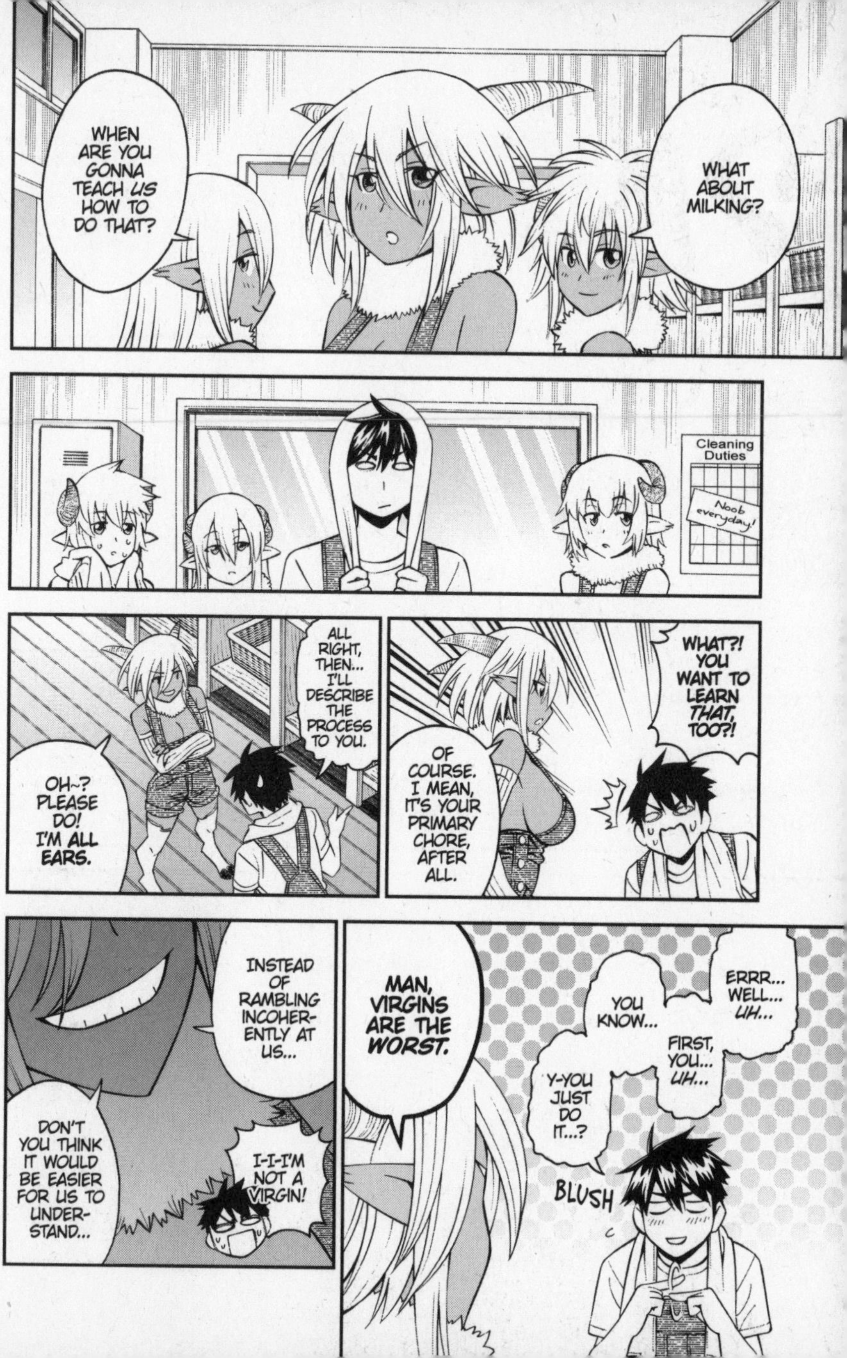
WHAT ABOUT MILKING?
WHEN ARE YOU GONNA TEACH US HOW TO DO THAT?
Cleaning Duties
Noob everyday!
WHAT?! YOU WANT TO LEARN THAT, TOO?!
OF COURSE. I MEAN, IT'S YOUR PRIMARY CHORE, AFTER ALL.
ALL RIGHT, THEN... I'LL DESCRIBE THE PROCESS TO YOU.
OH~? PLEASE DO! I'M ALL EARS.
ERRR... WELL... UH...
YOU KNOW...
FIRST, YOU... UH...
Y-YOU JUST DO IT...?
BLUSH
MAN, VIRGINS ARE THE WORST.
INSTEAD OF RAMBLING INCOHERENTLY AT US...
DON'T YOU THINK IT WOULD BE EASIER FOR US TO UNDERSTAND...
I-I-I'M NOT A VIRGIN!

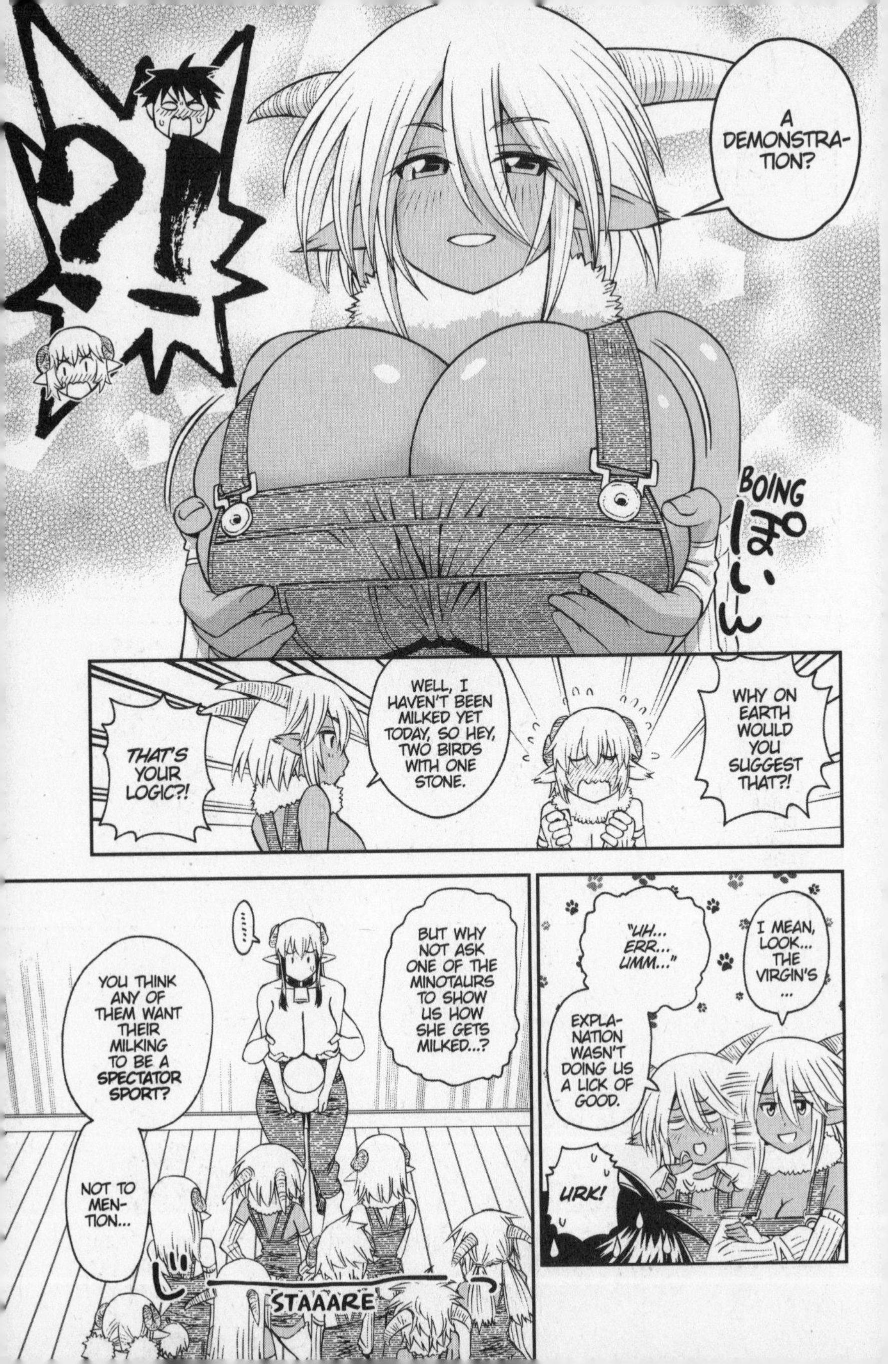
A DEMONSTRATION?
BOING
ぽいん
?!
WHY ON EARTH WOULD YOU SUGGEST THAT?!
WELL, I HAVEN'T BEEN MILKED YET TODAY, SO HEY, TWO BIRDS WITH ONE STONE.
THAT'S YOUR LOGIC?!
I MEAN, LOOK... THE VIRGIN'S ...
"UH... ERR... UMM..."
EXPLANATION WASN'T DOING US A LICK OF GOOD.
URK!
BUT WHY NOT ASK ONE OF THE MINOTAURS TO SHOW US HOW SHE GETS MILKED...?
......
YOU THINK ANY OF THEM WANT THEIR MILKING TO BE A SPECTATOR SPORT?
NOT TO MENTION...
STAAARE

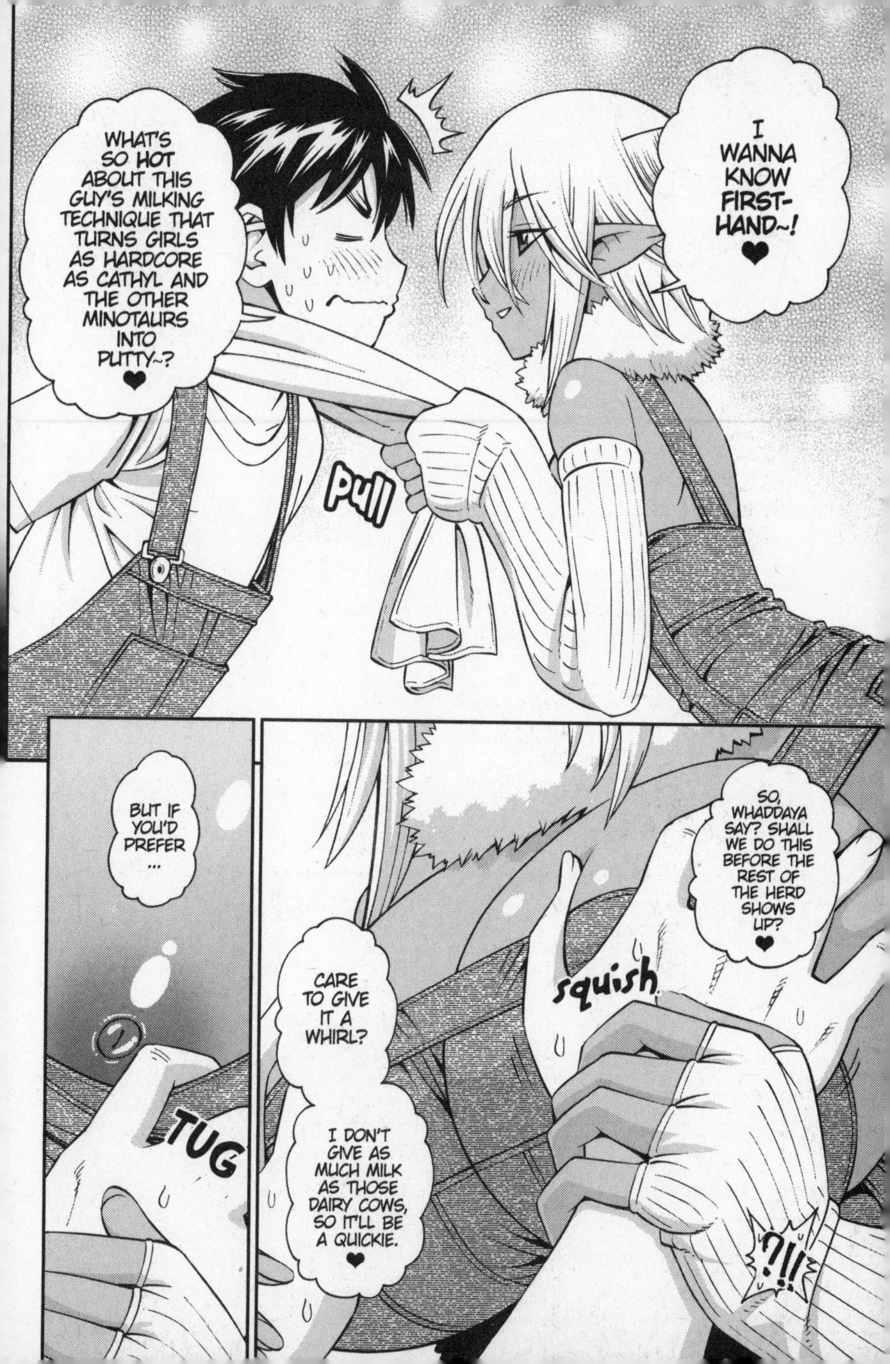
I WANNA KNOW FIRST-HAND~! ❤
WHAT'S SO HOT ABOUT THIS GUY'S MILKING TECHNIQUE THAT TURNS GIRLS AS HARDCORE AS CATHYL AND THE OTHER MINOTAURS INTO PUTTY~? ❤
pull
SO, WHADDAYA SAY? SHALL WE DO THIS BEFORE THE REST OF THE HERD SHOWS UP? ❤
CARE TO GIVE IT A WHIRL?
squish
I DON'T GIVE AS MUCH MILK AS THOSE DAIRY COWS, SO IT'LL BE A QUICKIE. ❤
?!!
BUT IF YOU'D PREFER ...
TUG

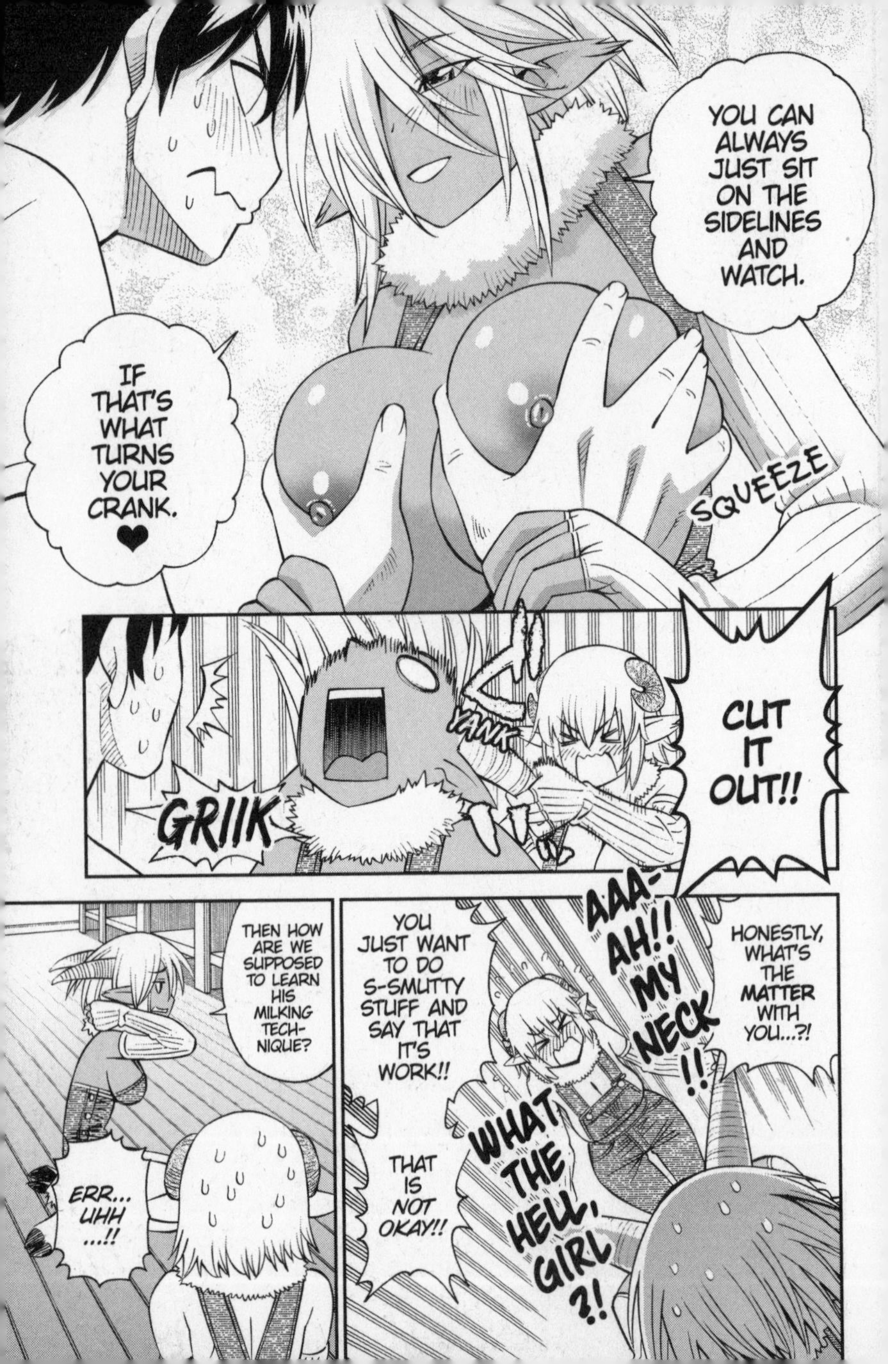
YOU CAN ALWAYS JUST SIT ON THE SIDELINES AND WATCH.
IF THAT'S WHAT TURNS YOUR CRANK. ❤
SQUEEZE
CUT IT OUT!!
YANK
GRIIK
HONESTLY, WHAT'S THE MATTER WITH YOU...?!
AAA-AH!! MY NECK!!
YOU JUST WANT TO DO S-SMUTTY STUFF AND SAY THAT IT'S WORK!!
WHAT THE HELL, GIRL?!
THAT IS NOT OKAY!!
THEN HOW ARE WE SUPPOSED TO LEARN HIS MILKING TECH-NIQUE?
ERR... UHH ...!!

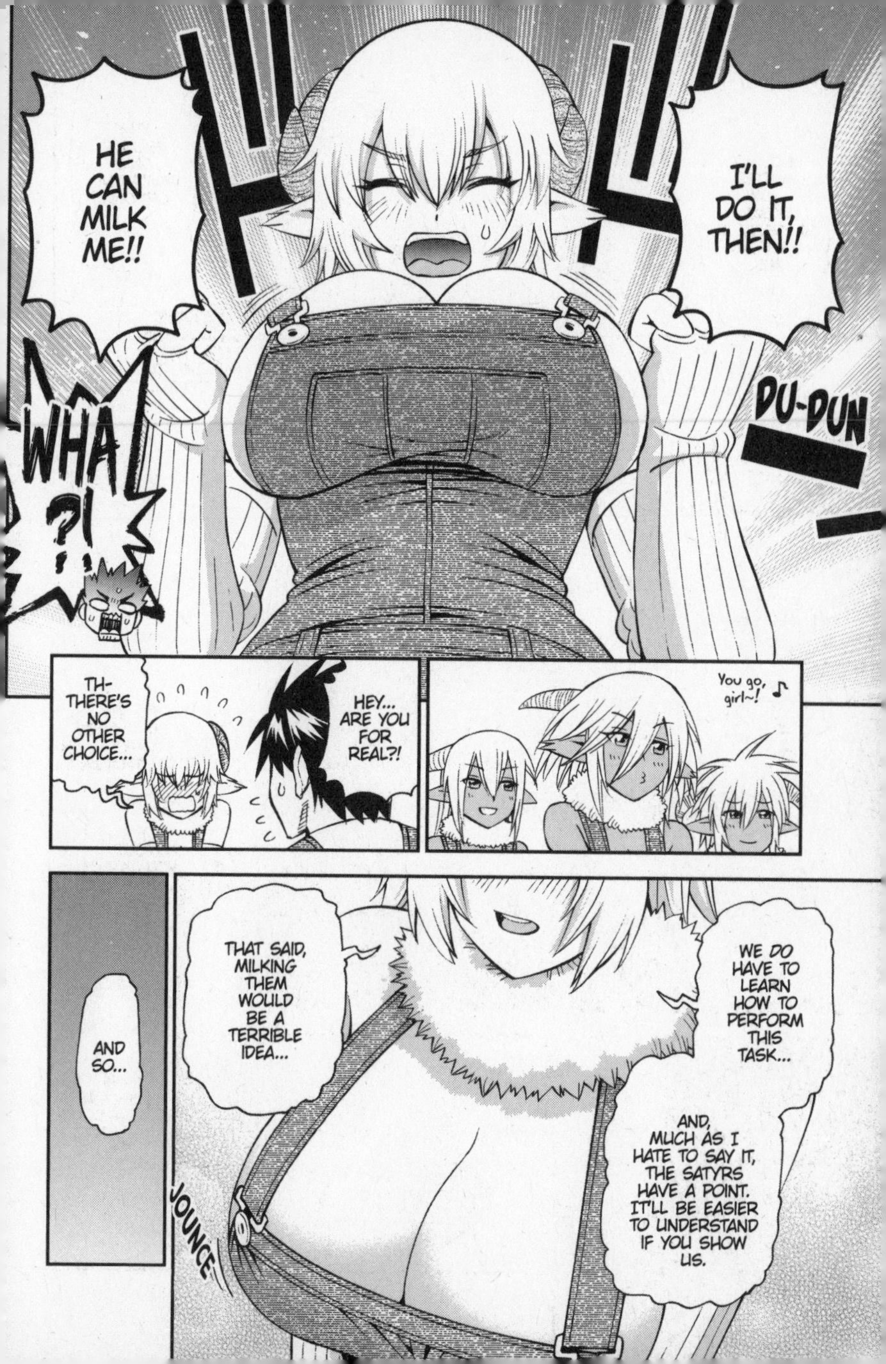
I'LL DO IT, THEN!!
HE CAN MILK ME!!
DU-DUN
WHA?!
You go, girl~! ♪
HEY... ARE YOU FOR REAL?!
TH-THERE'S NO OTHER CHOICE...
WE DO HAVE TO LEARN HOW TO PERFORM THIS TASK...
THAT SAID, MILKING THEM WOULD BE A TERRIBLE IDEA...
AND, MUCH AS I HATE TO SAY IT, THE SATYRS HAVE A POINT. IT'LL BE EASIER TO UNDERSTAND IF YOU SHOW US.
JOUNCE
AND SO...

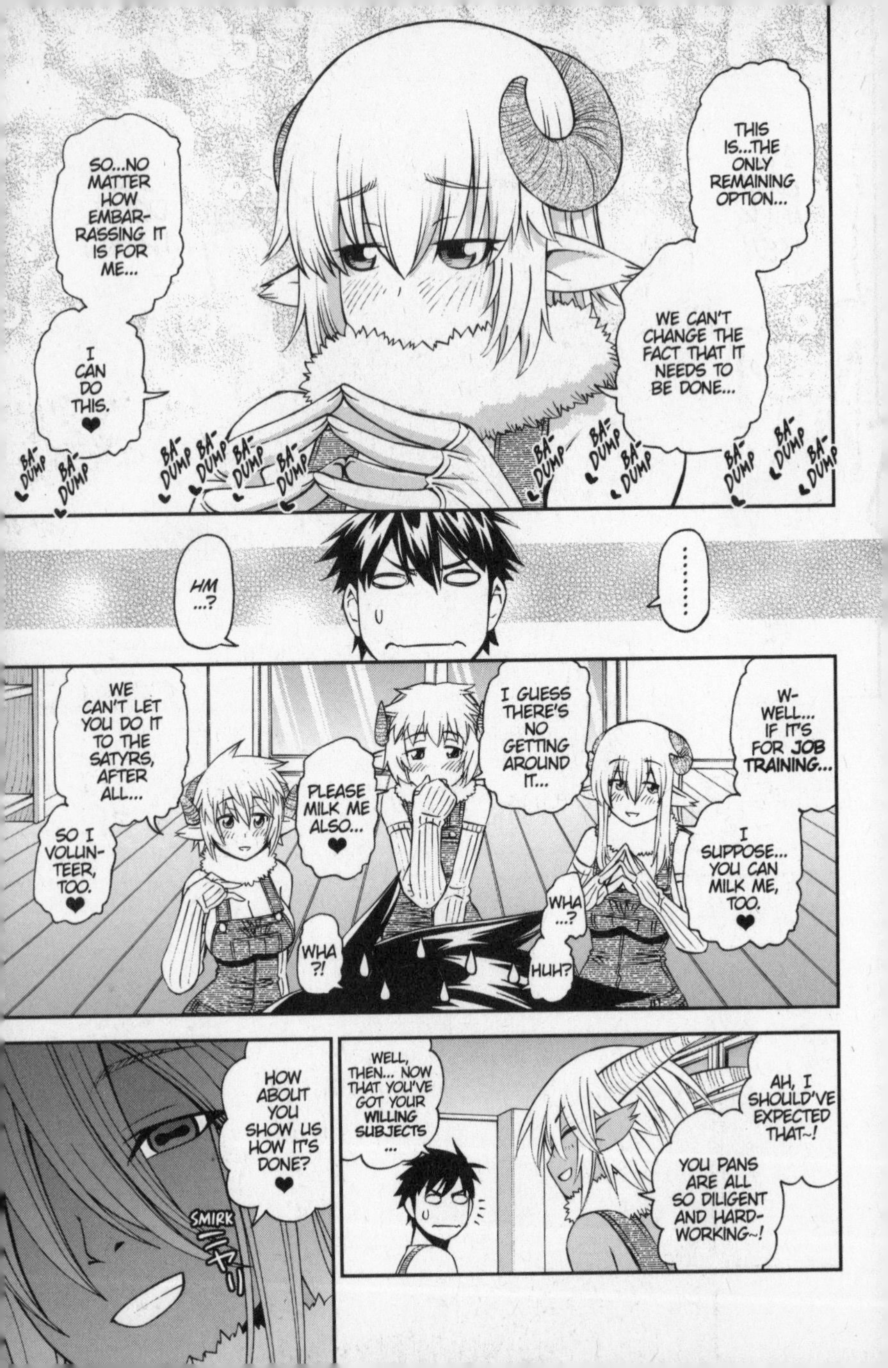
THIS IS...THE ONLY REMAINING OPTION...
WE CAN'T CHANGE THE FACT THAT IT NEEDS TO BE DONE...
SO...NO MATTER HOW EMBARRASSING IT IS FOR ME...
I CAN DO THIS. ❤
BA-DUMP ❤ BA-DUMP ❤ BA-DUMP ❤ BA-DUMP ❤ BA-DUMP ❤ BA-DUMP ❤ BA-DUMP ❤ BA-DUMP ❤ BA-DUMP ❤ BA-DUMP ❤ BA-DUMP ❤ BA-DUMP ❤
......
HM...?
W-WELL... IF IT'S FOR JOB TRAINING...
I SUPPOSE... YOU CAN MILK ME, TOO. ❤
I GUESS THERE'S NO GETTING AROUND IT...
PLEASE MILK ME ALSO... ❤
WE CAN'T LET YOU DO IT TO THE SATYRS, AFTER ALL...
SO I VOLUNTEER, TOO. ❤
WHA...?
HUH?
WHA?!
AH, I SHOULD'VE EXPECTED THAT~!
YOU PANS ARE ALL SO DILIGENT AND HARD-WORKING~!
WELL, THEN... NOW THAT YOU'VE GOT YOUR WILLING SUBJECTS...
HOW ABOUT YOU SHOW US HOW IT'S DONE? ❤
SMIRK

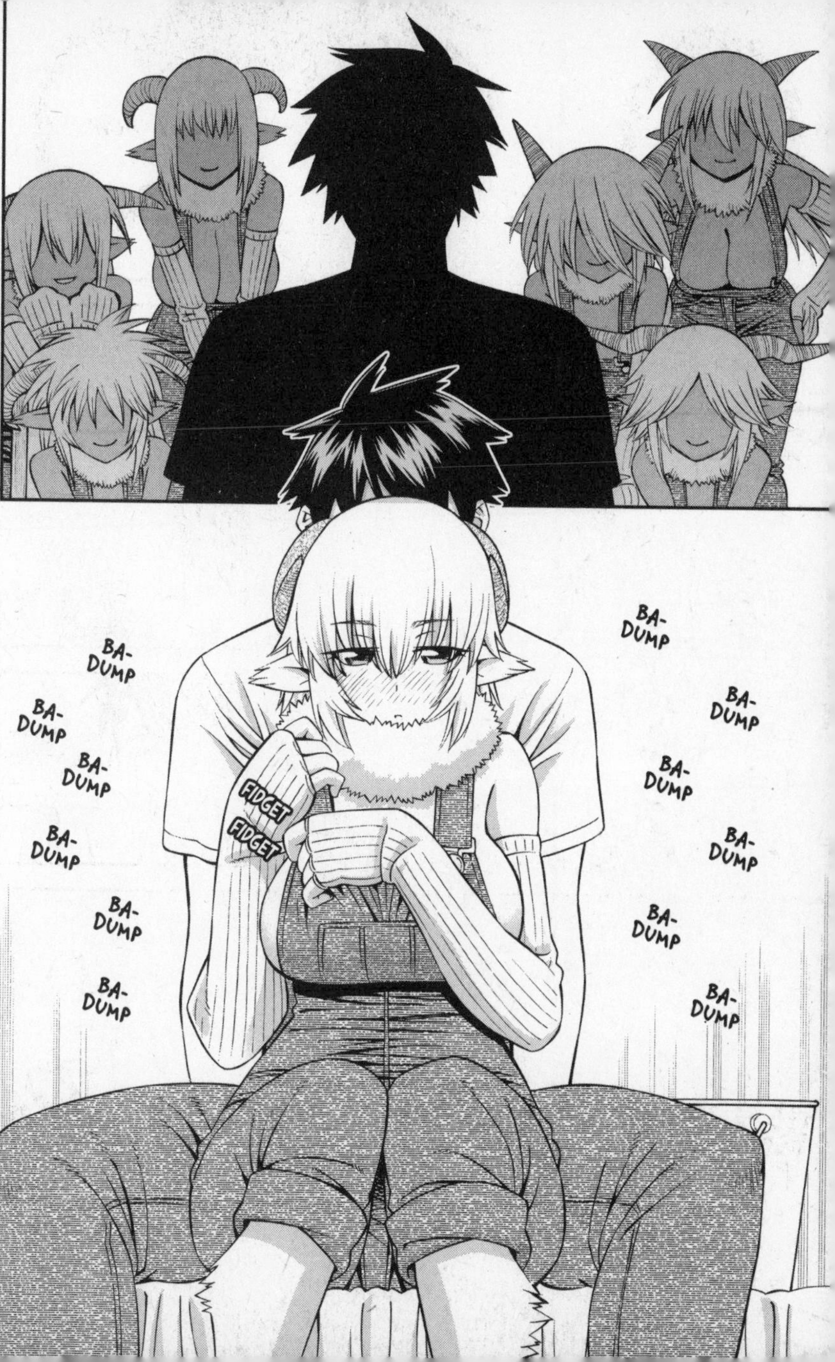
BA-
DUMP
BA-
DUMP
BA-
DUMP
BA-
DUMP
BA-
DUMP
BA-
DUMP
BA-
DUMP
FIDGET
FIDGET
BA-
DUMP
BA-
DUMP
BA-
DUMP
BA-
DUMP
BA-
DUMP
BA-
DUMP

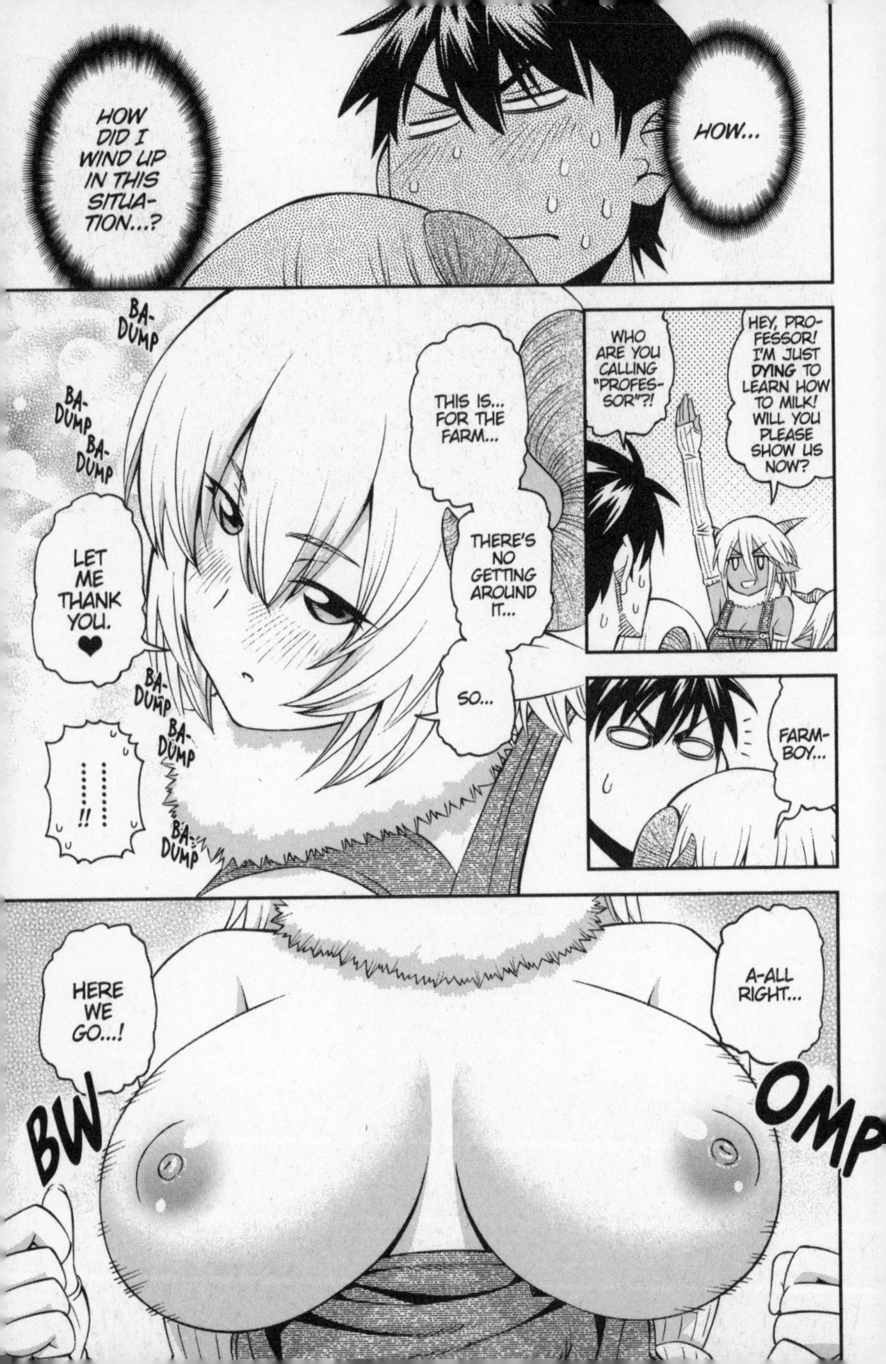
HOW...
HOW DID I WIND UP IN THIS SITUATION...?
HEY, PROFESSOR! I'M JUST DYING TO LEARN HOW TO MILK! WILL YOU PLEASE SHOW US NOW?
WHO ARE YOU CALLING "PROFESSOR"?!
FARM-BOY...
THIS IS... FOR THE FARM...
THERE'S NO GETTING AROUND IT...
SO...
BA-DUMP
BA-DUMP BA-DUMP
LET ME THANK YOU. ❤
BA-DUMP
BA-DUMP
BA-DUMP
......!!
A-ALL RIGHT...
HERE WE GO...!
BWOMP

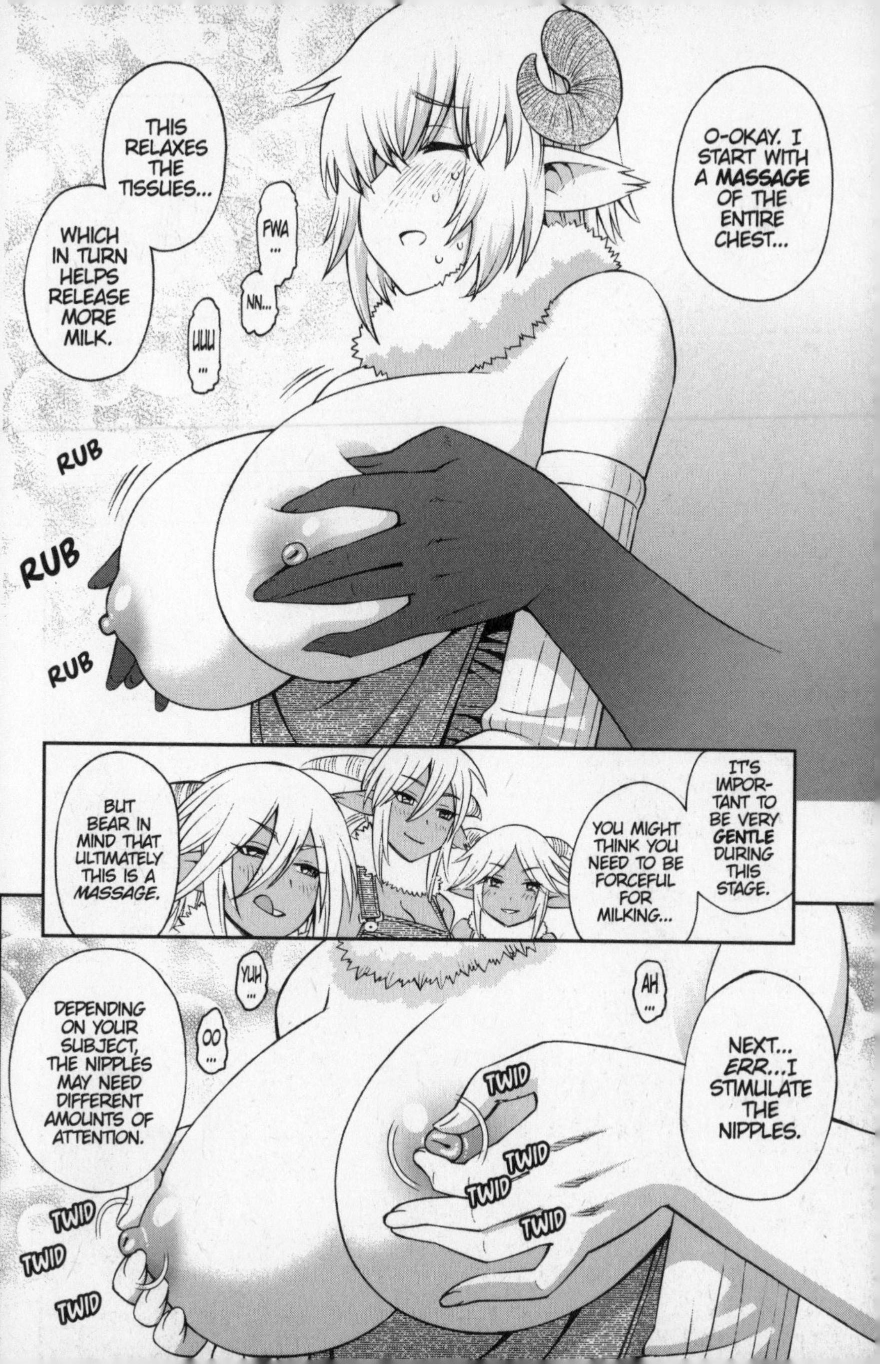
O-OKAY. I START WITH A **MASSAGE** OF THE ENTIRE CHEST...
FWA...
NN...
UUU...
THIS RELAXES THE TISSUES...
WHICH IN TURN HELPS RELEASE MORE MILK.
RUB
RUB
RUB
IT'S IMPORTANT TO BE VERY **GENTLE** DURING THIS STAGE.
YOU MIGHT THINK YOU NEED TO BE FORCEFUL FOR MILKING...
BUT BEAR IN MIND THAT ULTIMATELY THIS IS A *MASSAGE*.
AH...
NEXT... *ERR*...I STIMULATE THE NIPPLES.
YUH...
OO...
DEPENDING ON YOUR SUBJECT, THE NIPPLES MAY NEED DIFFERENT AMOUNTS OF ATTENTION.
TWID
TWID
TWID
TWID
TWID
TWID
TWID

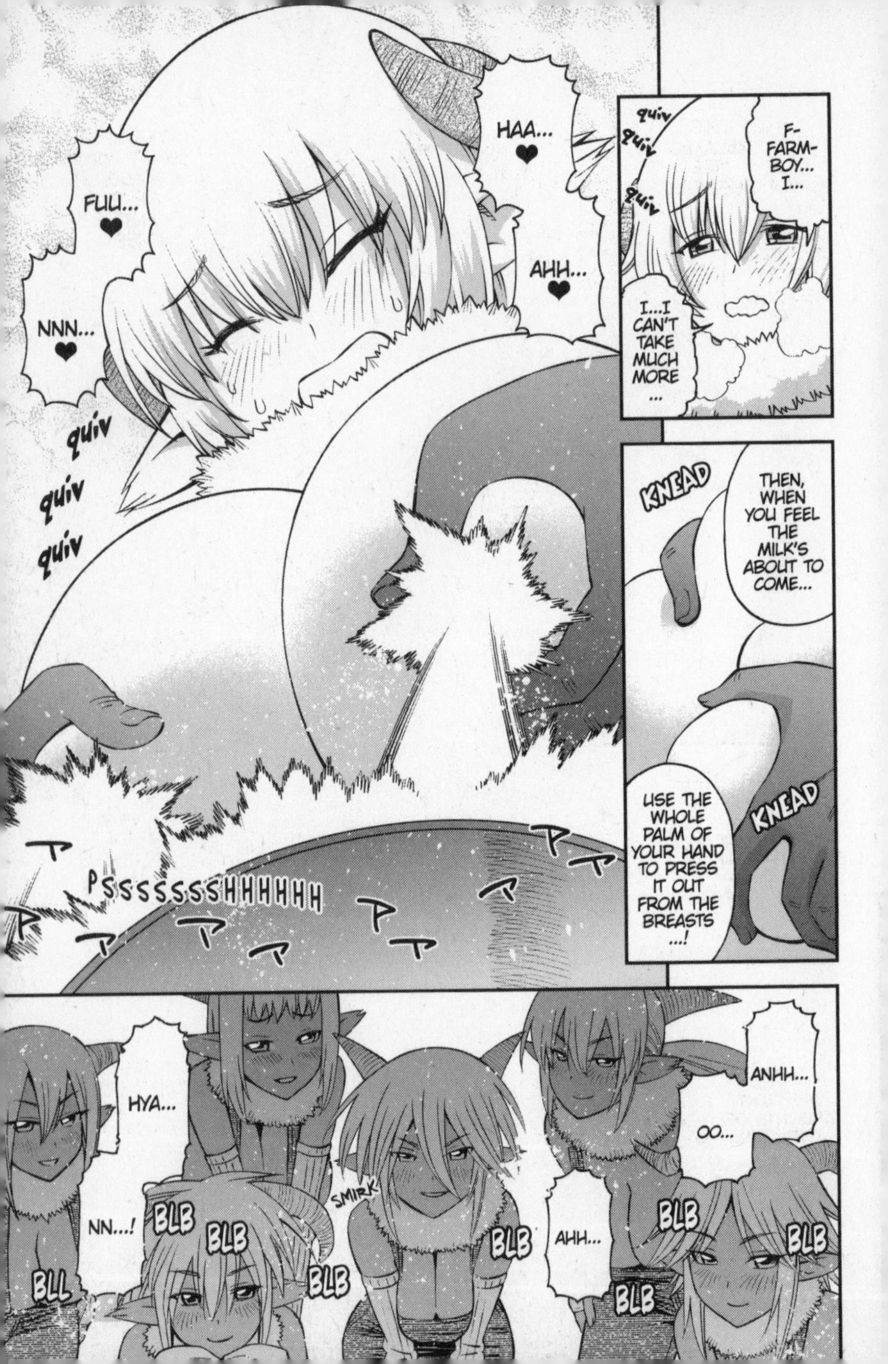
F-FARM-BOY... I...
quiv quiv quiv
I...I CAN'T TAKE MUCH MORE ...
KNEAD
THEN, WHEN YOU FEEL THE MILK'S ABOUT TO COME...
KNEAD
USE THE WHOLE PALM OF YOUR HAND TO PRESS IT OUT FROM THE BREASTS ...!
HAA... ❤
AHH... ❤
FUU... ❤
NNN... ❤
quiv quiv quiv
PSSSSSSSHHHHHH
ANHH...
OO...
BLB
BLB
AHH...
BLB
SMIRK
HYA...
NN...!
BLB
BLB
BLB
BLL

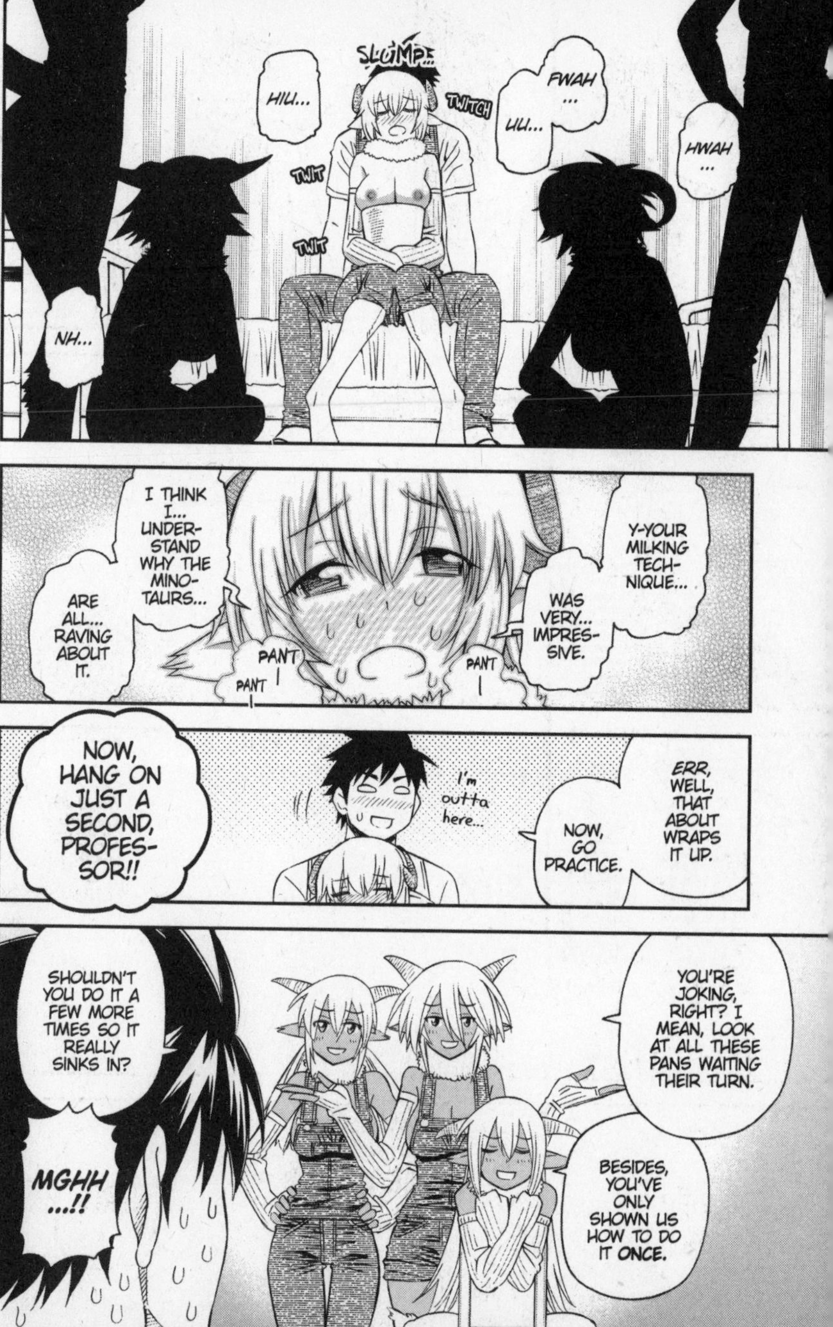
HWAH...
FWAH... UU...
SLUMP...
TWITCH
HIU...
TWIT
TWIT
NH...
Y-YOUR MILKING TECHNIQUE...
WAS VERY... IMPRESSIVE.
PANT
PANT
PANT
I THINK I... UNDERSTAND WHY THE MINOTAURS...
ARE ALL... RAVING ABOUT IT.
ERR, WELL, THAT ABOUT WRAPS IT UP.
NOW, GO PRACTICE.
I'm outta here...
NOW, HANG ON JUST A SECOND, PROFESSOR!!
YOU'RE JOKING, RIGHT? I MEAN, LOOK AT ALL THESE PANS WAITING THEIR TURN.
BESIDES, YOU'VE ONLY SHOWN US HOW TO DO IT ONCE.
SHOULDN'T YOU DO IT A FEW MORE TIMES SO IT REALLY SINKS IN?
MGHH...!!

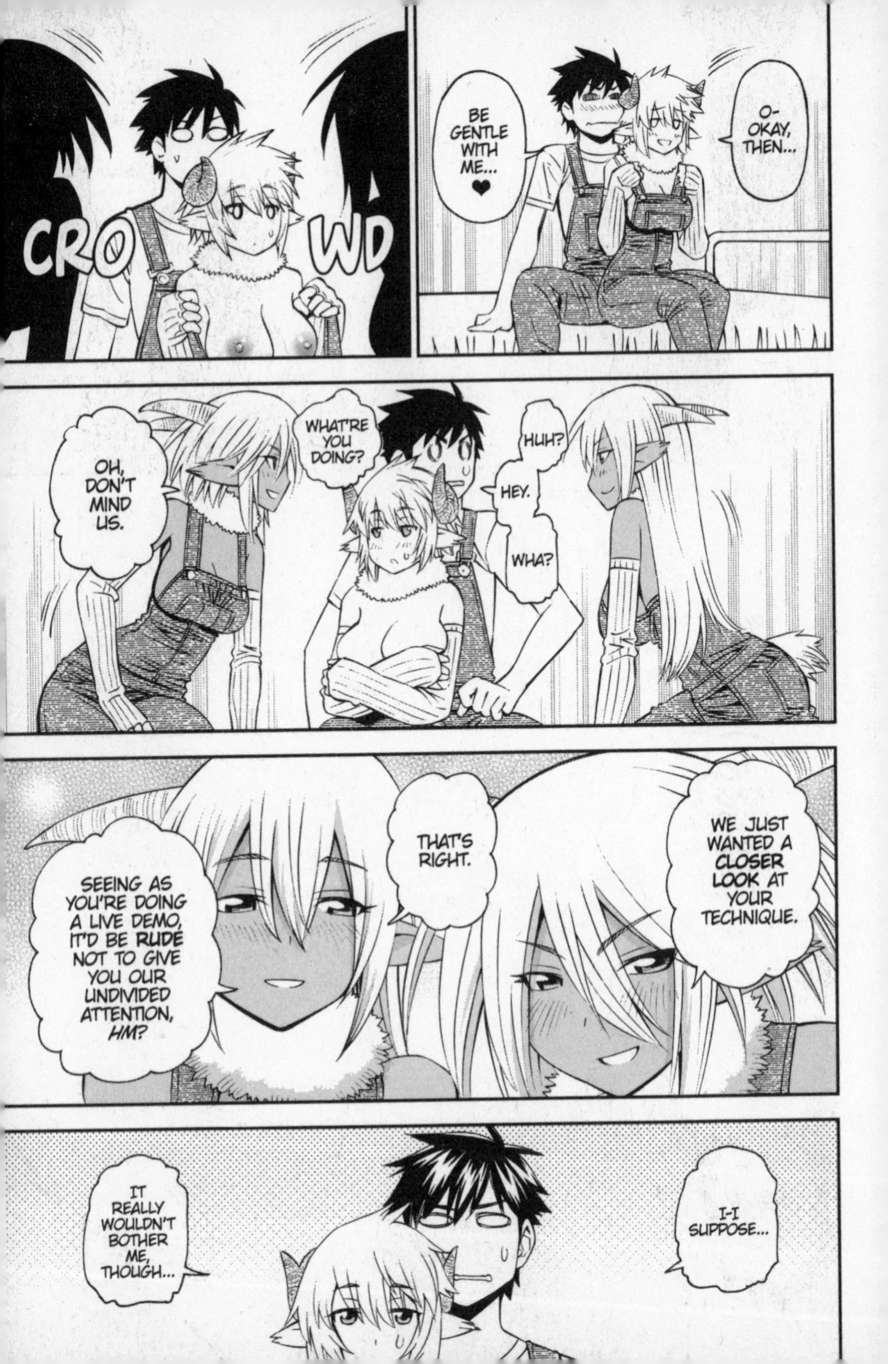
O-OKAY, THEN...
BE GENTLE WITH ME... ❤
CROWD
HUH?
HEY.
WHA?
WHAT'RE YOU DOING?
OH, DON'T MIND US.
WE JUST WANTED A CLOSER LOOK AT YOUR TECHNIQUE.
THAT'S RIGHT.
SEEING AS YOU'RE DOING A LIVE DEMO, IT'D BE RUDE NOT TO GIVE YOU OUR UNDIVIDED ATTENTION, HM?
I-I SUPPOSE...
IT REALLY WOULDN'T BOTHER ME, THOUGH...

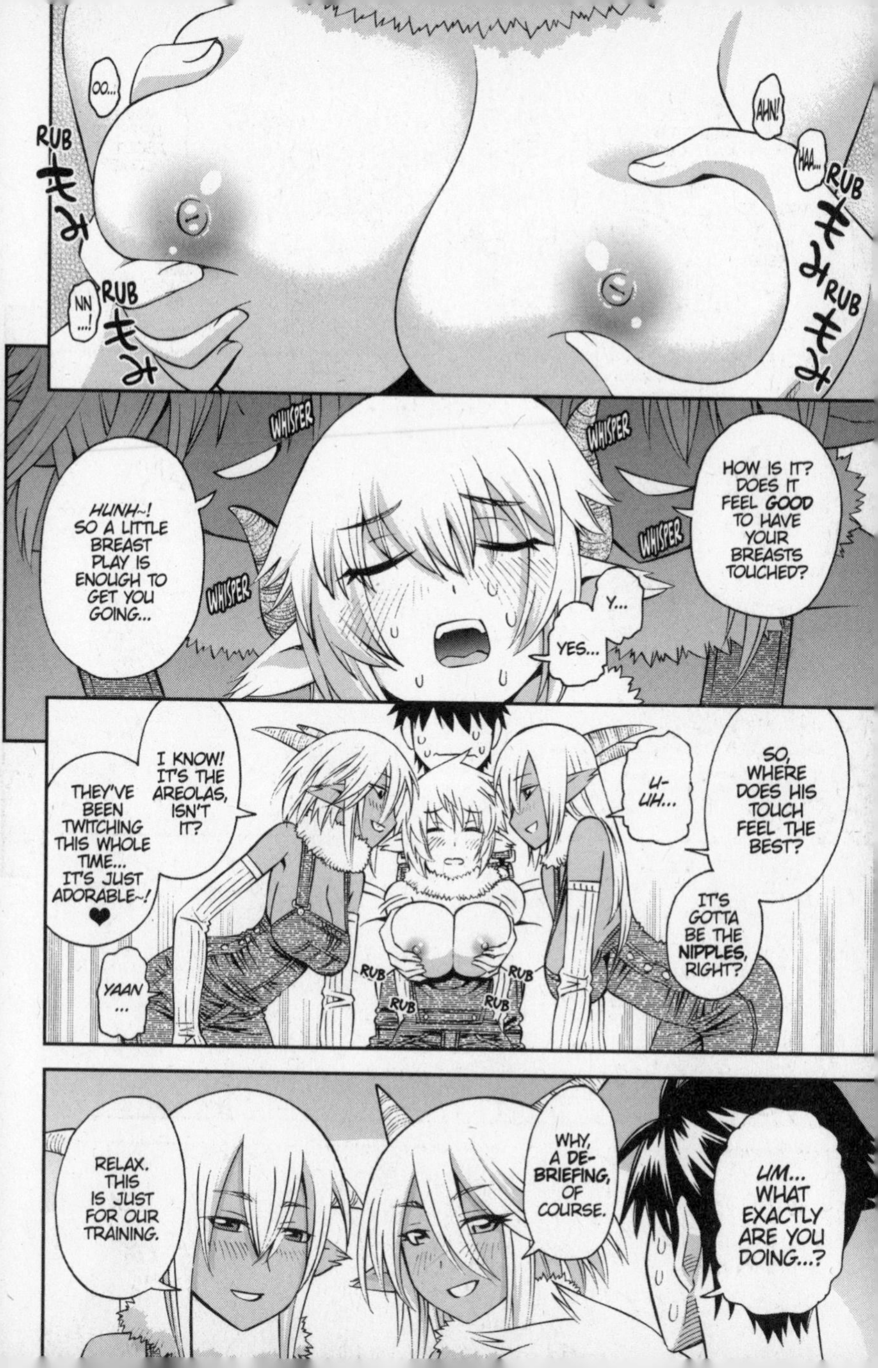
AHN!
HAA...
RUB
もみ
RUB
もみ
OO...
RUB
もみ
NN ...!
RUB
もみ
WHISPER
HOW IS IT? DOES IT FEEL GOOD TO HAVE YOUR BREASTS TOUCHED?
WHISPER
Y...
YES...
WHISPER
HUNH~! SO A LITTLE BREAST PLAY IS ENOUGH TO GET YOU GOING...
WHISPER
SO, WHERE DOES HIS TOUCH FEEL THE BEST?
IT'S GOTTA BE THE NIPPLES, RIGHT?
U-UH...
I KNOW! IT'S THE AREOLAS, ISN'T IT?
THEY'VE BEEN TWITCHING THIS WHOLE TIME... IT'S JUST ADORABLE~! ❤
RUB
RUB
RUB
RUB
YAAN ...
UM... WHAT EXACTLY ARE YOU DOING...?
WHY, A DE-BRIEFING, OF COURSE.
RELAX. THIS IS JUST FOR OUR TRAINING.

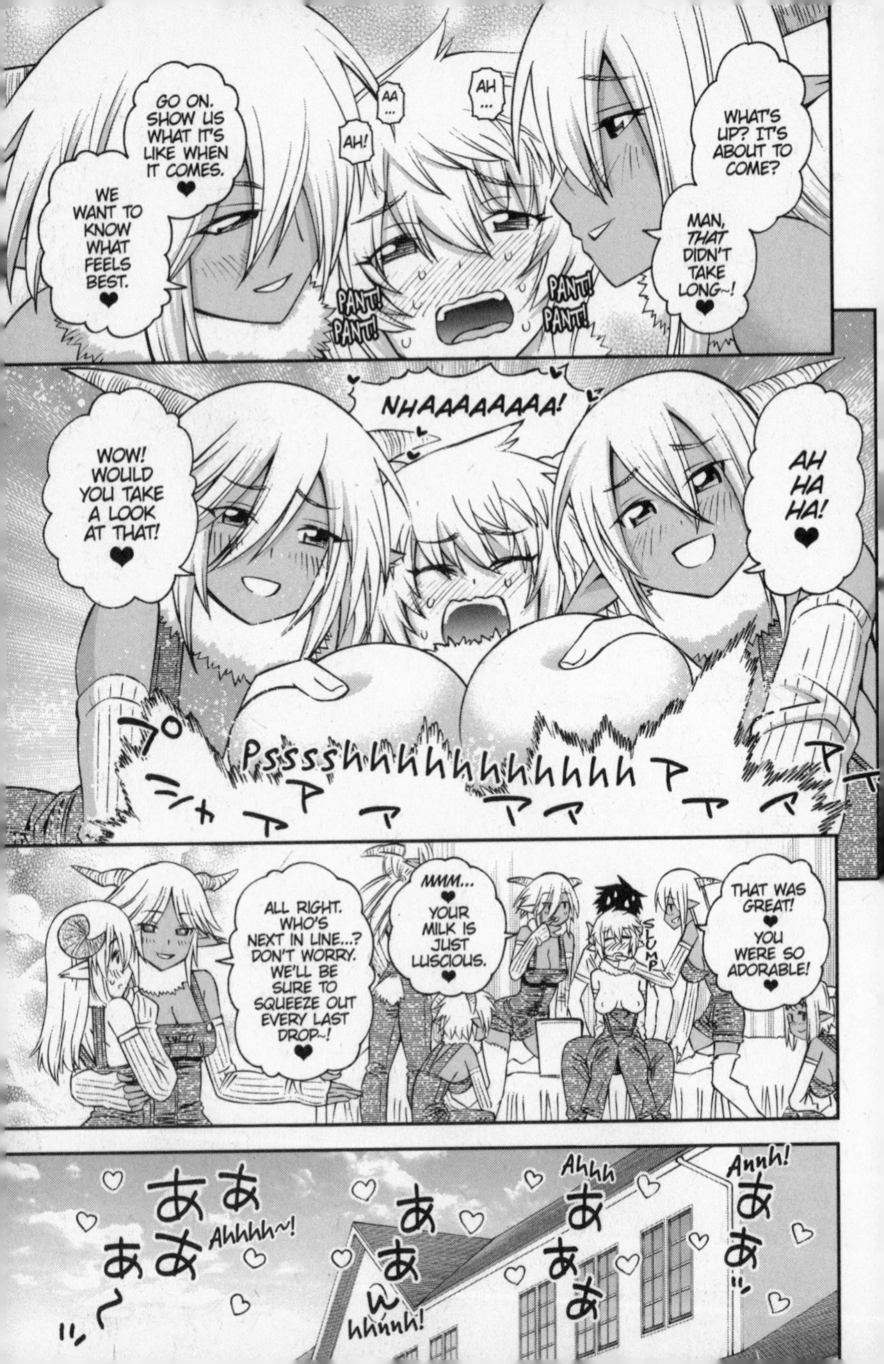
WHAT'S UP? IT'S ABOUT TO COME?
MAN, *THAT* DIDN'T TAKE LONG~! ❤
AH ...
AA ...
AH!
PANT! PANT!
PANT! PANT!
GO ON. SHOW US WHAT IT'S LIKE WHEN IT COMES. ❤
WE WANT TO KNOW WHAT FEELS BEST. ❤
AH HA HA! ❤
NHAAAAAAAA!
WOW! WOULD YOU TAKE A LOOK AT THAT! ❤
Psssshhhhhhhhhhhh
プシャアアアアアアアア
THAT WAS GREAT! ❤ YOU WERE SO ADORABLE! ❤
SLUMP
MMM... ❤ YOUR MILK IS JUST LUSCIOUS. ❤
ALL RIGHT. WHO'S NEXT IN LINE...? DON'T WORRY. WE'LL BE SURE TO SQUEEZE OUT EVERY LAST DROP~! ❤
Annh! あぁっ
Ahhh あぁぁ
あぁん Ahhhh!
ああああ～っ Ahhhh~!

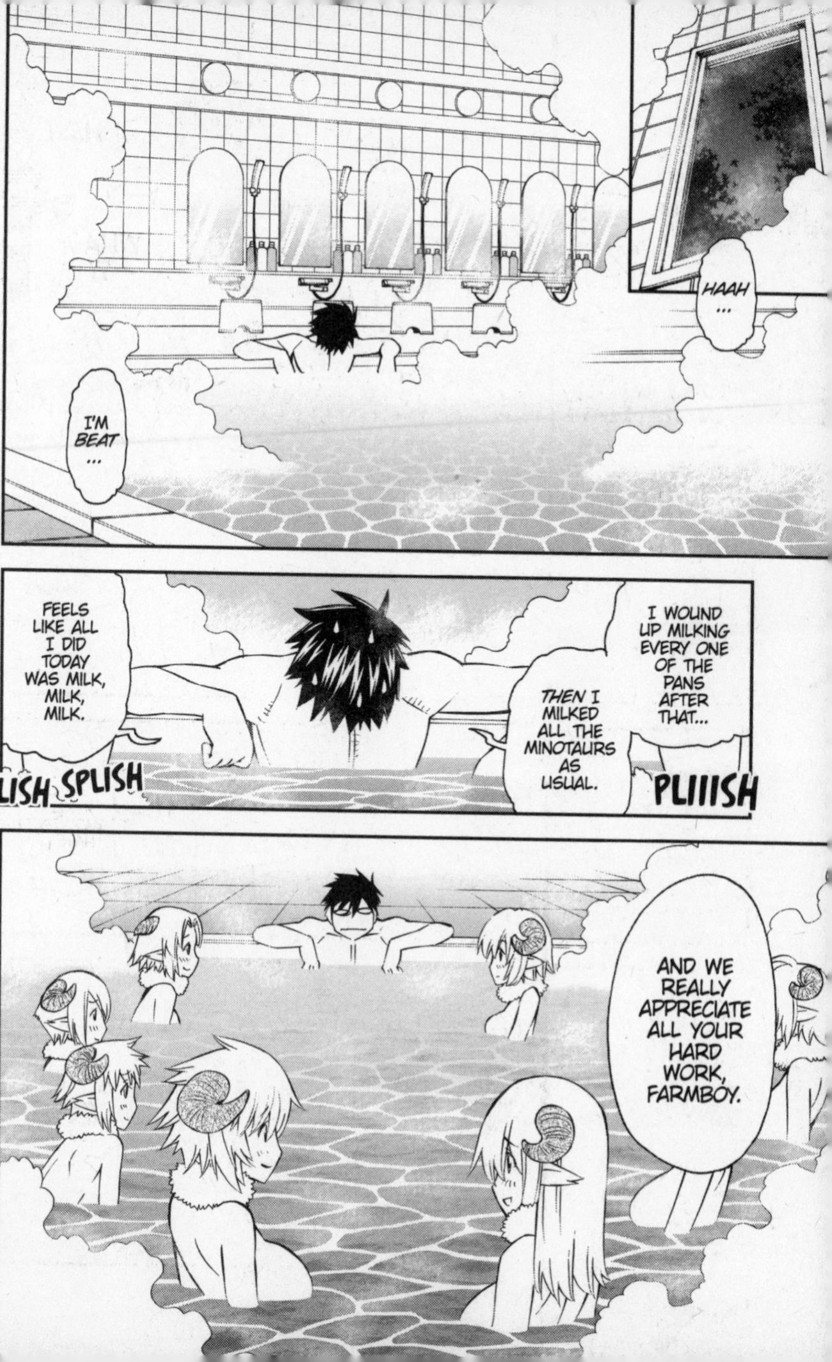
HAAH ...
I'M BEAT ...
PLIIISH
I WOUND UP MILKING EVERY ONE OF THE PANS AFTER THAT...
THEN I MILKED ALL THE MINOTAURS AS USUAL.
FEELS LIKE ALL I DID TODAY WAS MILK, MILK, MILK.
SPLISH SPLISH
AND WE REALLY APPRECIATE ALL YOUR HARD WORK, FARMBOY.

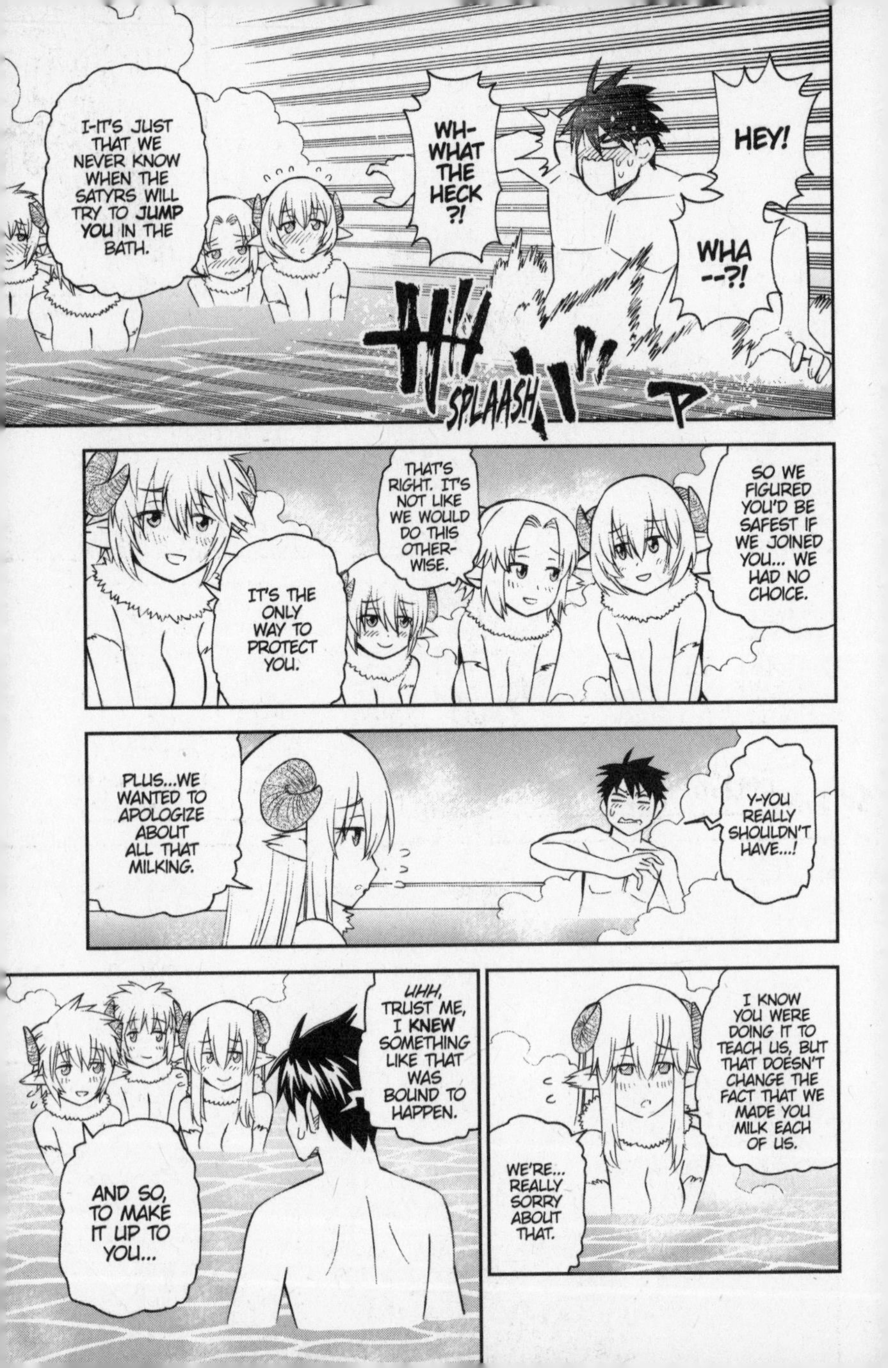
HEY!
WHA --?!
WH- WHAT THE HECK ?!
SPLAASH
I-IT'S JUST THAT WE NEVER KNOW WHEN THE SATYRS WILL TRY TO JUMP YOU IN THE BATH.
SO WE FIGURED YOU'D BE SAFEST IF WE JOINED YOU... WE HAD NO CHOICE.
THAT'S RIGHT. IT'S NOT LIKE WE WOULD DO THIS OTHER- WISE.
IT'S THE ONLY WAY TO PROTECT YOU.
Y-YOU REALLY SHOULDN'T HAVE...!
PLUS...WE WANTED TO APOLOGIZE ABOUT ALL THAT MILKING.
I KNOW YOU WERE DOING IT TO TEACH US, BUT THAT DOESN'T CHANGE THE FACT THAT WE MADE YOU MILK EACH OF US.
WE'RE... REALLY SORRY ABOUT THAT.
UHH, TRUST ME, I KNEW SOMETHING LIKE THAT WAS BOUND TO HAPPEN.
AND SO, TO MAKE IT UP TO YOU...

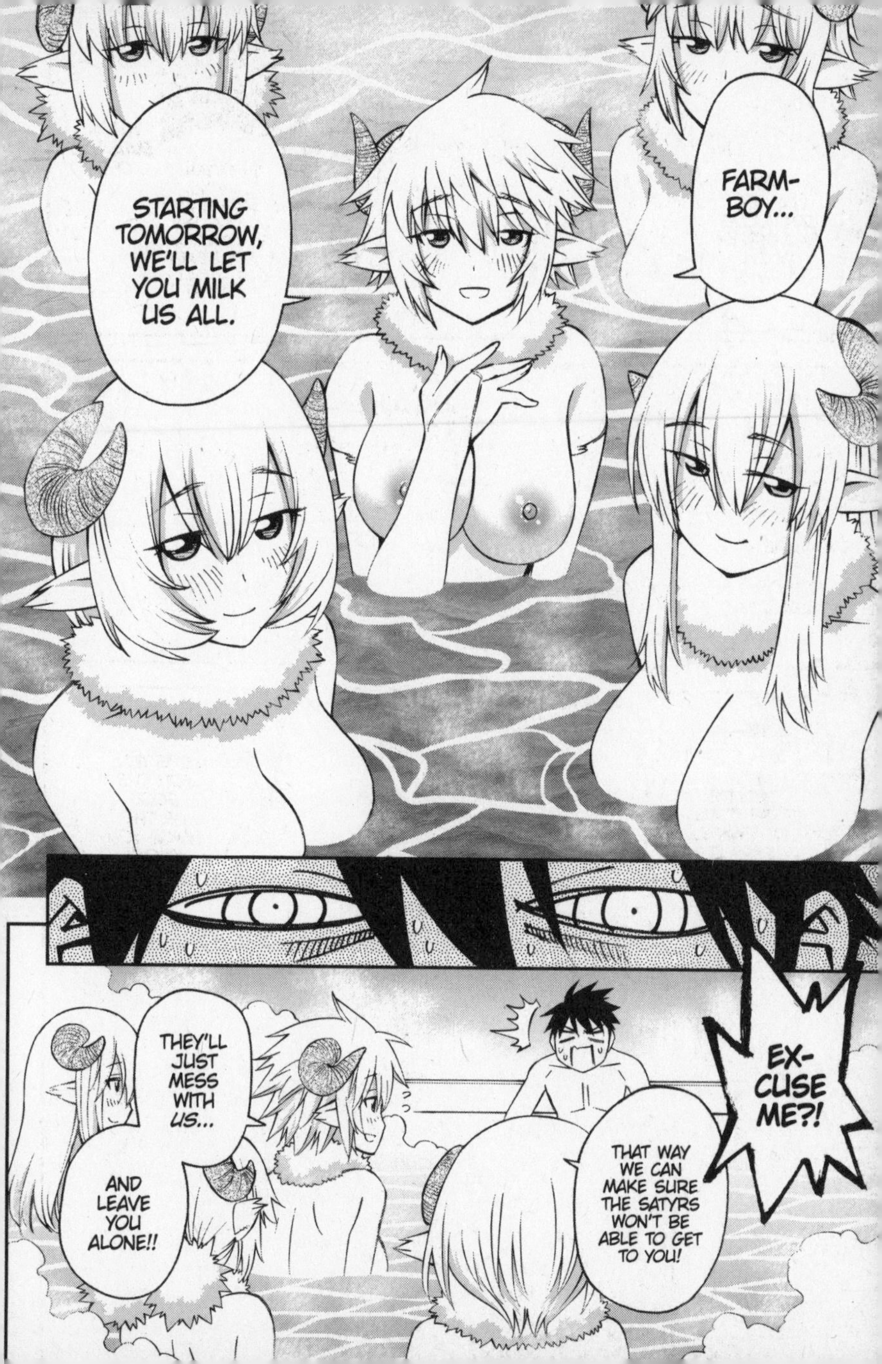
FARM-BOY...
STARTING TOMORROW, WE'LL LET YOU MILK US ALL.
EX-CUSE ME?!
THAT WAY WE CAN MAKE SURE THE SATYRS WON'T BE ABLE TO GET TO YOU!
THEY'LL JUST MESS WITH US...
AND LEAVE YOU ALONE!!

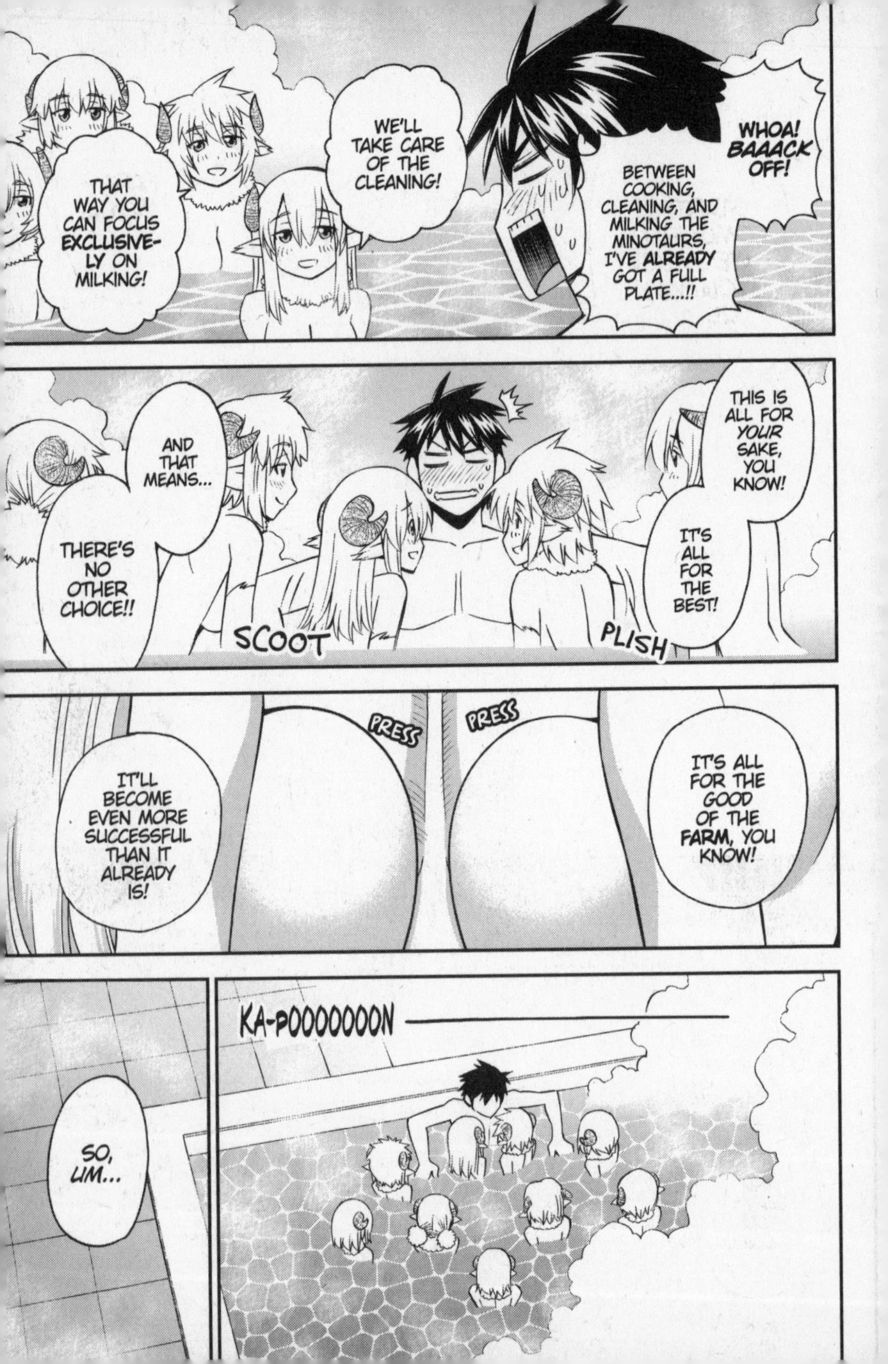

WHOA! BAAACK OFF!
BETWEEN COOKING, CLEANING, AND MILKING THE MINOTAURS, I'VE ALREADY GOT A FULL PLATE...!!
WE'LL TAKE CARE OF THE CLEANING!
THAT WAY YOU CAN FOCUS EXCLUSIVELY ON MILKING!
THIS IS ALL FOR YOUR SAKE, YOU KNOW!
IT'S ALL FOR THE BEST!
PLISH
SCOOT
AND THAT MEANS...
THERE'S NO OTHER CHOICE!!
PRESS
PRESS
IT'S ALL FOR THE GOOD OF THE FARM, YOU KNOW!
IT'LL BECOME EVEN MORE SUCCESSFUL THAN IT ALREADY IS!
KA-POOOOOOON
SO, UM...

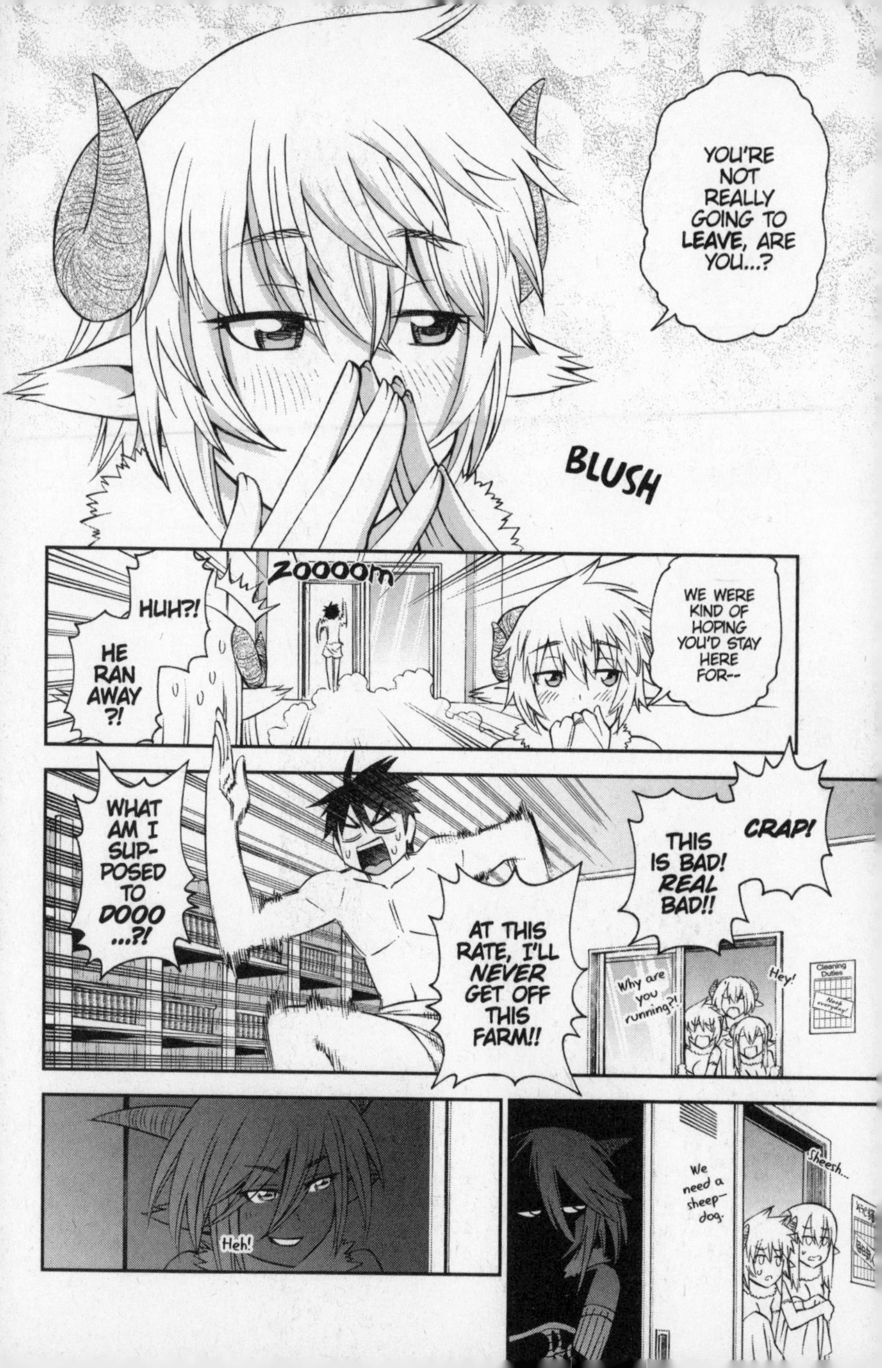
YOU'RE NOT REALLY GOING TO LEAVE, ARE YOU...?
BLUSH
WE WERE KIND OF HOPING YOU'D STAY HERE FOR--
ZOOOOm
HUH?!
HE RAN AWAY ?!
CRAP!
THIS IS BAD! REAL BAD!!
Hey!
Cleaning Duties
Why are you running?!
AT THIS RATE, I'LL NEVER GET OFF THIS FARM!!
WHAT AM I SUP-POSED TO DOOO ...?!
Sheesh...
We need a sheep-dog.
Heh!

Monster Musume

Everyday Life with Monster Girls

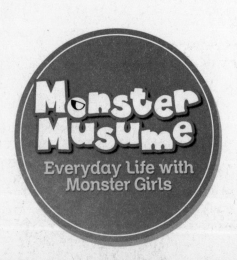

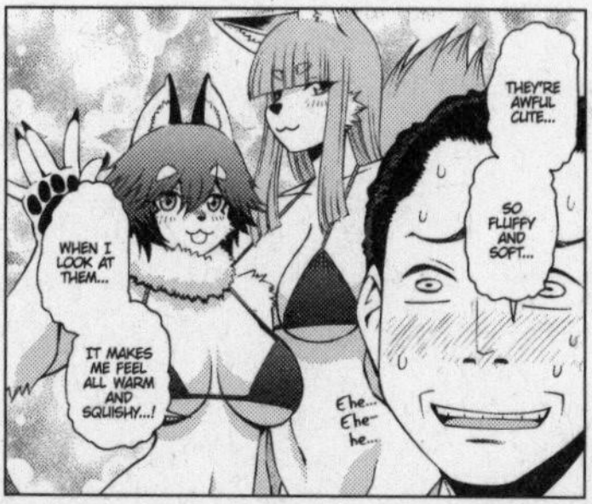
THEY'RE AWFUL CUTE...
SO FLUFFY AND SOFT...
Ehe... Ehe-he...
WHEN I LOOK AT THEM...
IT MAKES ME FEEL ALL WARM AND SQUISHY...!

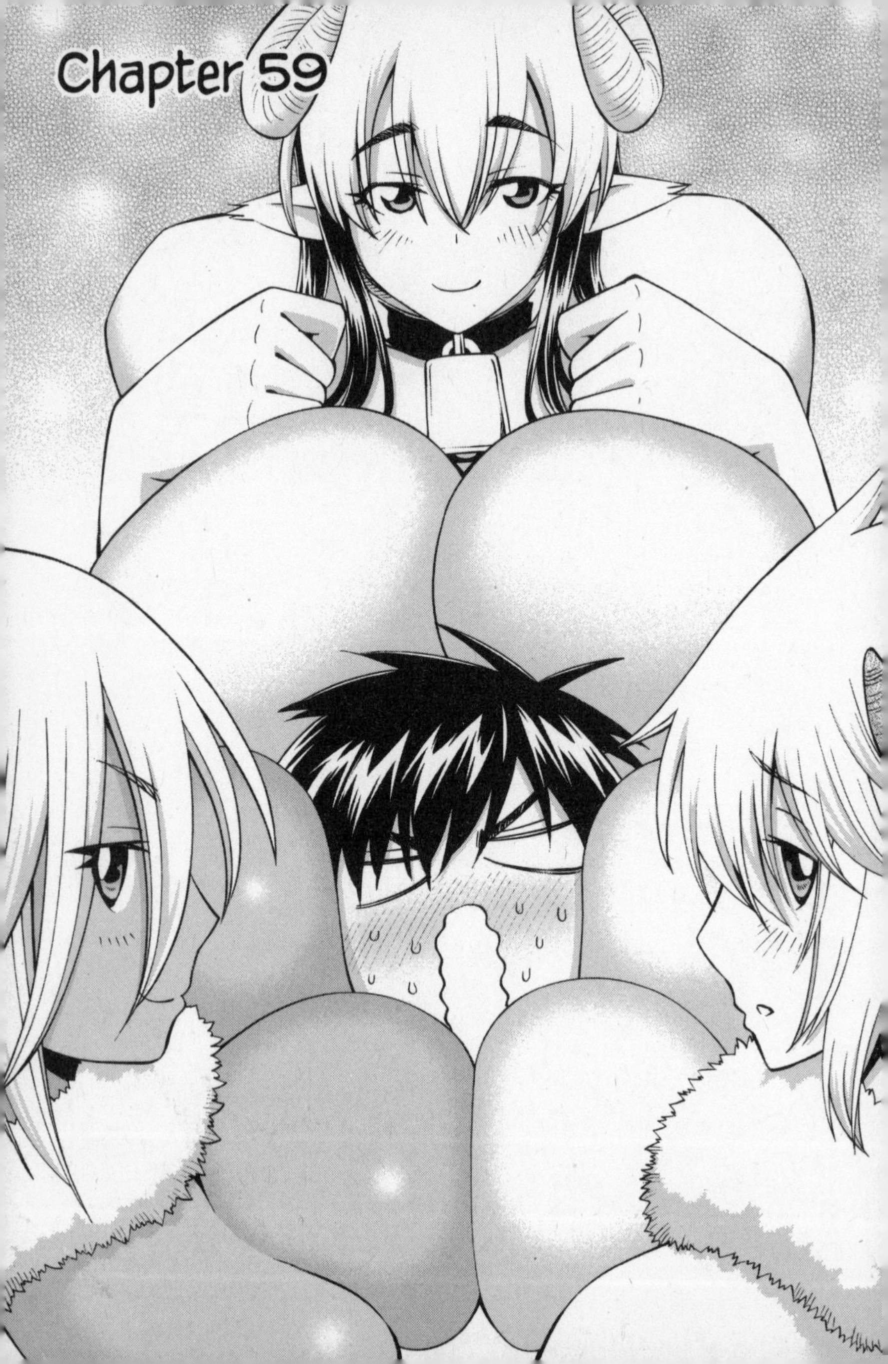
Chapter 59

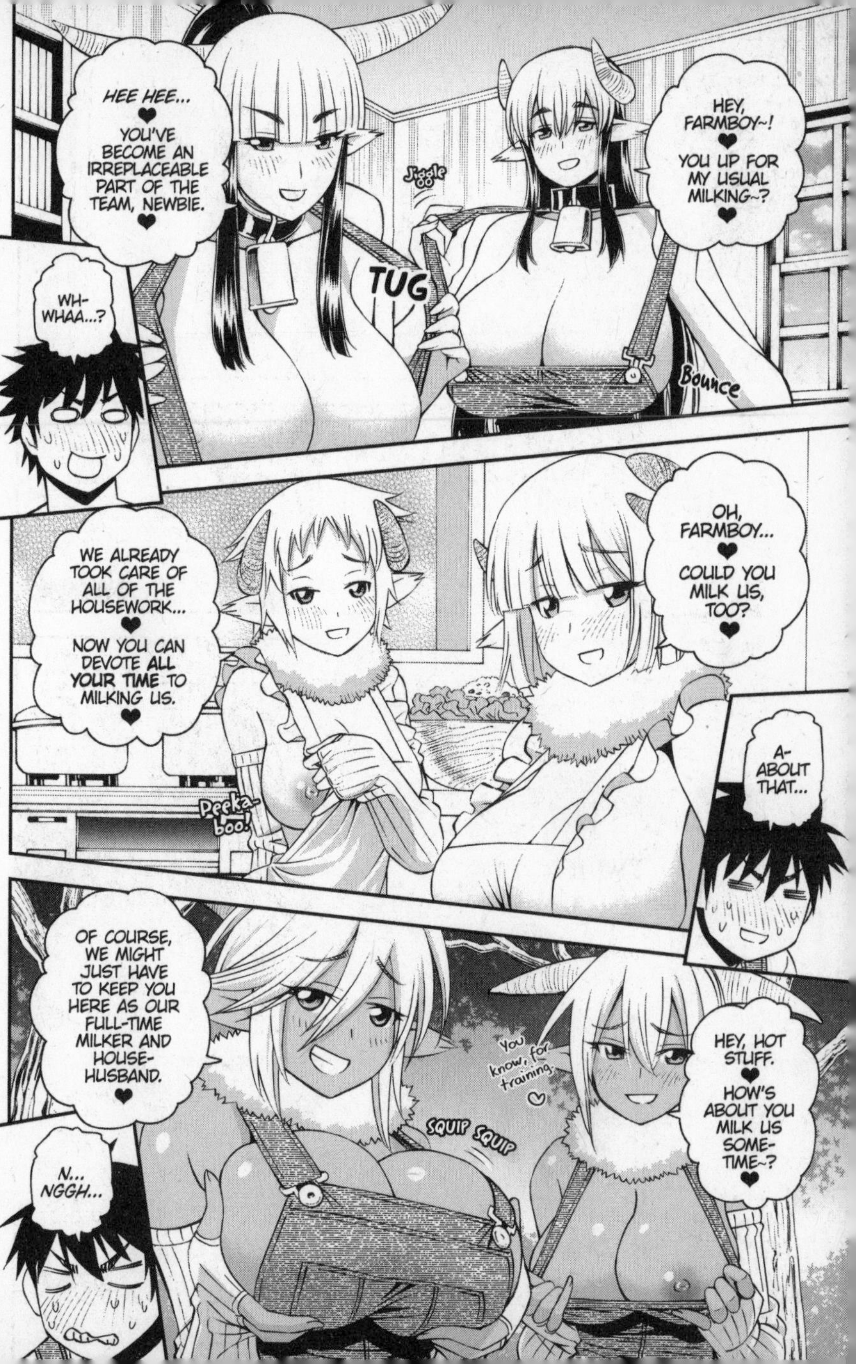
HEY, FARMBOY~! ♥ YOU UP FOR MY USUAL MILKING~? ♥
Jiggle
HEE HEE... ♥ YOU'VE BECOME AN IRREPLACEABLE PART OF THE TEAM, NEWBIE. ♥
TUG
Bounce
WH- WHAA...?
OH, FARMBOY... ♥ COULD YOU MILK US, TOO? ♥
WE ALREADY TOOK CARE OF ALL OF THE HOUSEWORK... ♥ NOW YOU CAN DEVOTE ALL YOUR TIME TO MILKING US. ♥
Peeka-boo!
A- ABOUT THAT...
HEY, HOT STUFF. ♥ HOW'S ABOUT YOU MILK US SOME-TIME~? ♥
You know, for training. ♥
OF COURSE, WE MIGHT JUST HAVE TO KEEP YOU HERE AS OUR FULL-TIME MILKER AND HOUSE-HUSBAND. ♥
SQUIP SQUIP
N... NGGH...

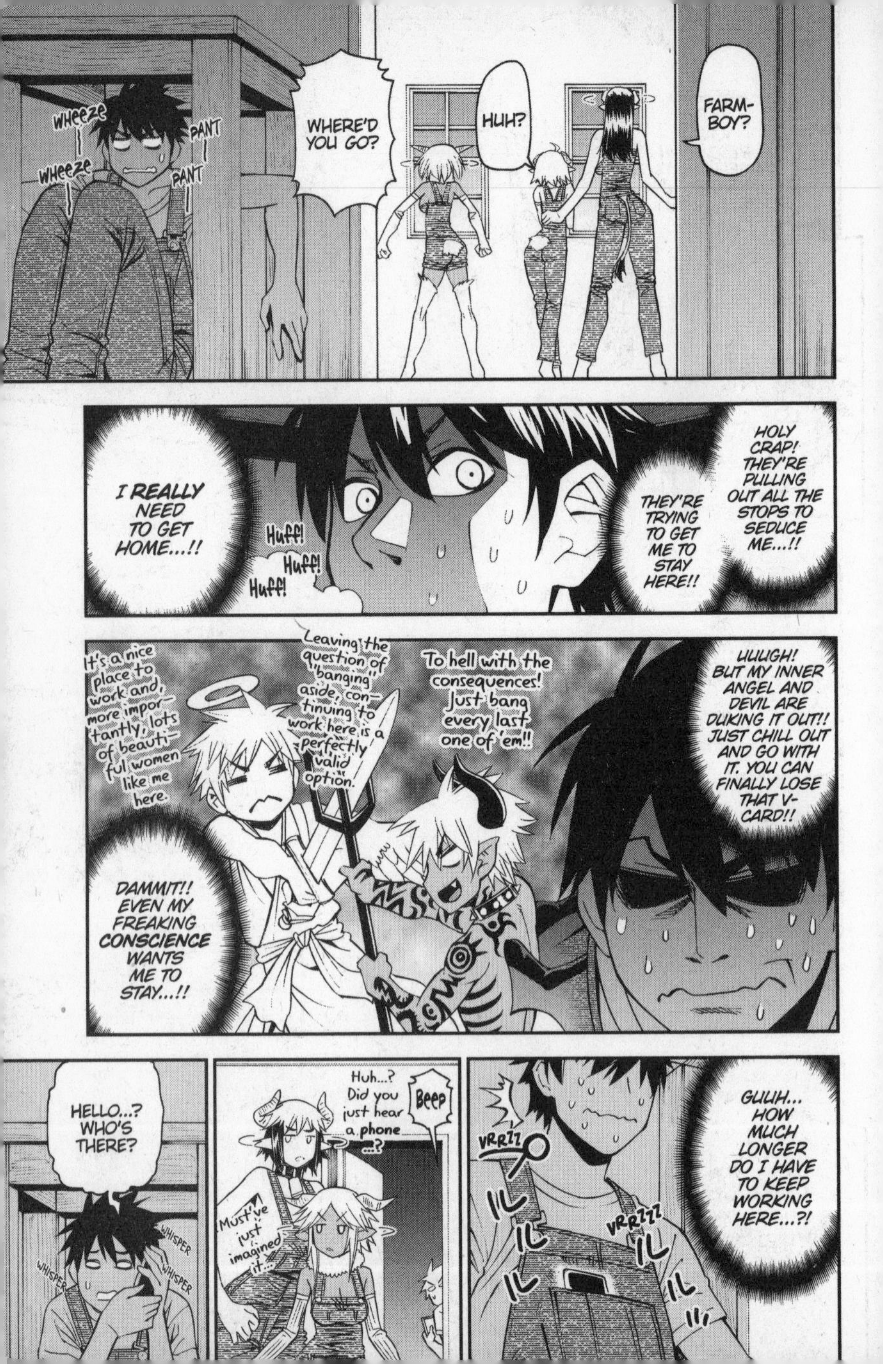
FARM-BOY?
HUH?
WHERE'D YOU GO?
PANT PANT
WHEEZE WHEEZE
HOLY CRAP! THEY'RE PULLING OUT ALL THE STOPS TO SEDUCE ME...!!
THEY'RE TRYING TO GET ME TO STAY HERE!!
Huff! Huff! Huff!
I **REALLY** NEED TO GET HOME...!!
UUUGH! BUT MY INNER ANGEL AND DEVIL ARE DUKING IT OUT!! JUST CHILL OUT AND GO WITH IT. YOU CAN FINALLY LOSE THAT V-CARD!!
To hell with the consequences! Just bang every last one of 'em!!
Leaving the question of "banging" aside, continuing to work here is a perfectly valid option.
It's a nice place to work and, more importantly, lots of beautiful women like me here.
DAMMIT!! EVEN MY FREAKING **CONSCIENCE** WANTS ME TO STAY...!!
GUUH... HOW MUCH LONGER DO I HAVE TO KEEP WORKING HERE...?!
VRRZZ
VRRZZZ
Beep
Huh...? Did you just hear a phone...?
Must've just imagined it...
HELLO...? WHO'S THERE?
WHISPER WHISPER
WHISPER

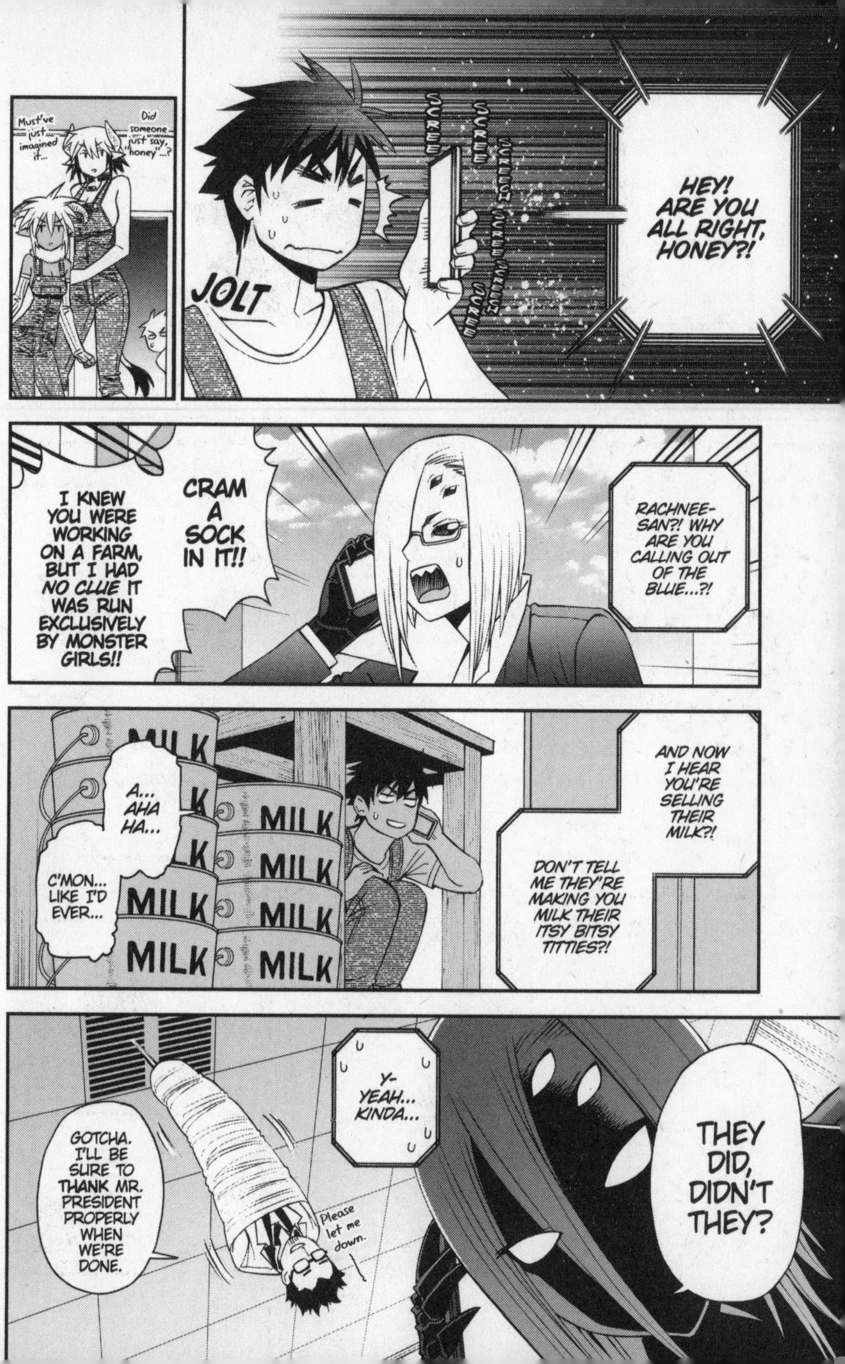
HEY! ARE YOU ALL RIGHT, HONEY?!
SCREE
SCREE
SCREECH SCREE SCREECH
SCREE
JOLT
Did someone just say, "honey"...?
Must've just imagined it...
RACHNEE-SAN?! WHY ARE YOU CALLING OUT OF THE BLUE...?!
CRAM A SOCK IN IT!!
I KNEW YOU WERE WORKING ON A FARM, BUT I HAD NO CLUE IT WAS RUN EXCLUSIVELY BY MONSTER GIRLS!!
AND NOW I HEAR YOU'RE SELLING THEIR MILK?!
DON'T TELL ME THEY'RE MAKING YOU MILK THEIR ITSY BITSY TITTIES?!
A... AHAHA...
C'MON... LIKE I'D EVER...
MILK
THEY DID, DIDN'T THEY?
Y-YEAH... KINDA...
Please let me down.
GOTCHA. I'LL BE SURE TO THANK MR. PRESIDENT PROPERLY WHEN WE'RE DONE.

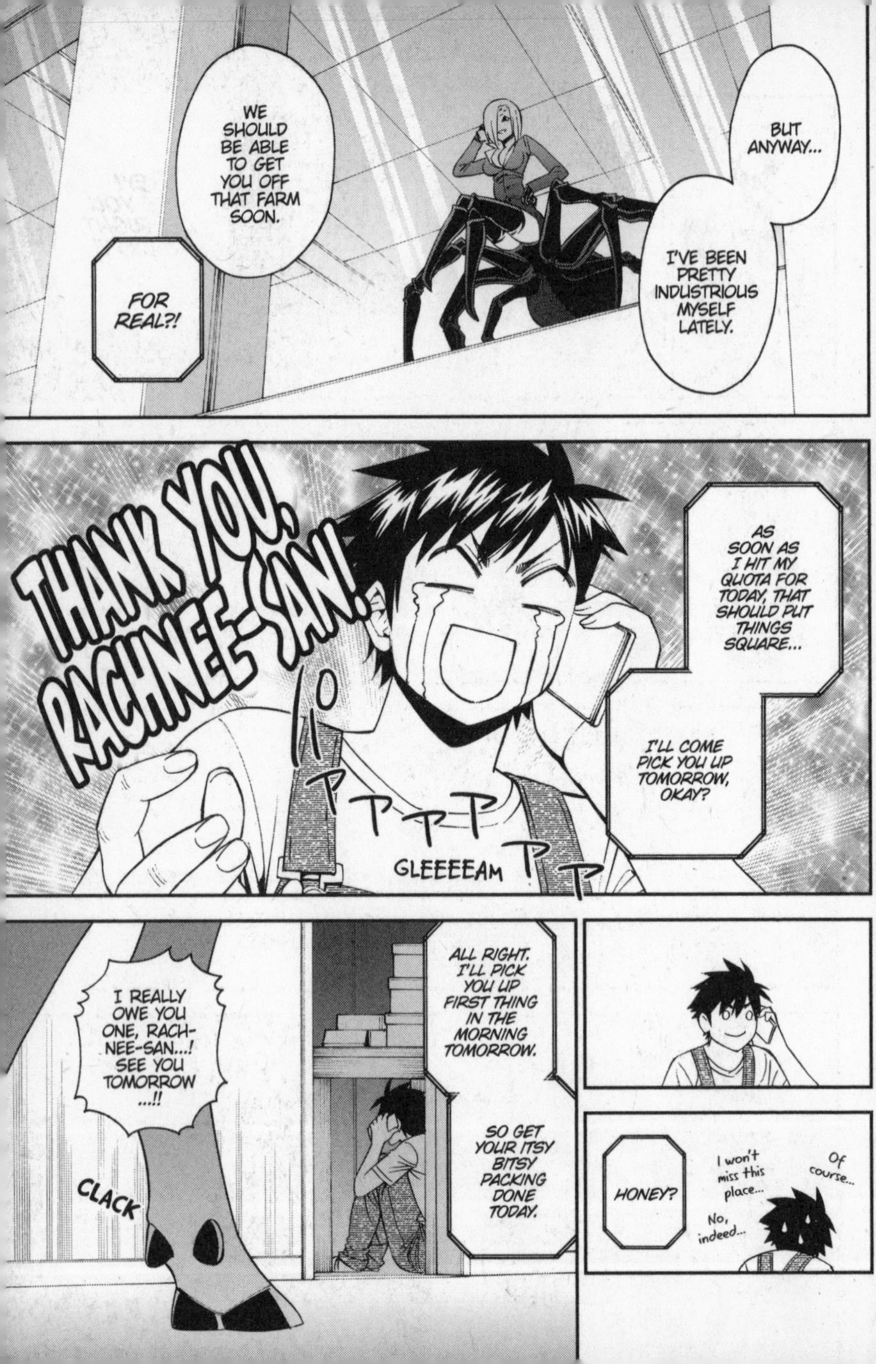

BUT ANYWAY...
I'VE BEEN PRETTY INDUSTRIOUS MYSELF LATELY.
WE SHOULD BE ABLE TO GET YOU OFF THAT FARM SOON.
FOR REAL?!
AS SOON AS I HIT MY QUOTA FOR TODAY, THAT SHOULD PUT THINGS SQUARE...
I'LL COME PICK YOU UP TOMORROW, OKAY?
THANK YOU, RACHNEE-SAN!
GLEEEEAM
Of course...
I won't miss this place...
HONEY?
No, indeed...
ALL RIGHT. I'LL PICK YOU UP FIRST THING IN THE MORNING TOMORROW.
SO GET YOUR ITSY BITSY PACKING DONE TODAY.
I REALLY OWE YOU ONE, RACH-NEE-SAN...! SEE YOU TOMORROW ...!!
CLACK

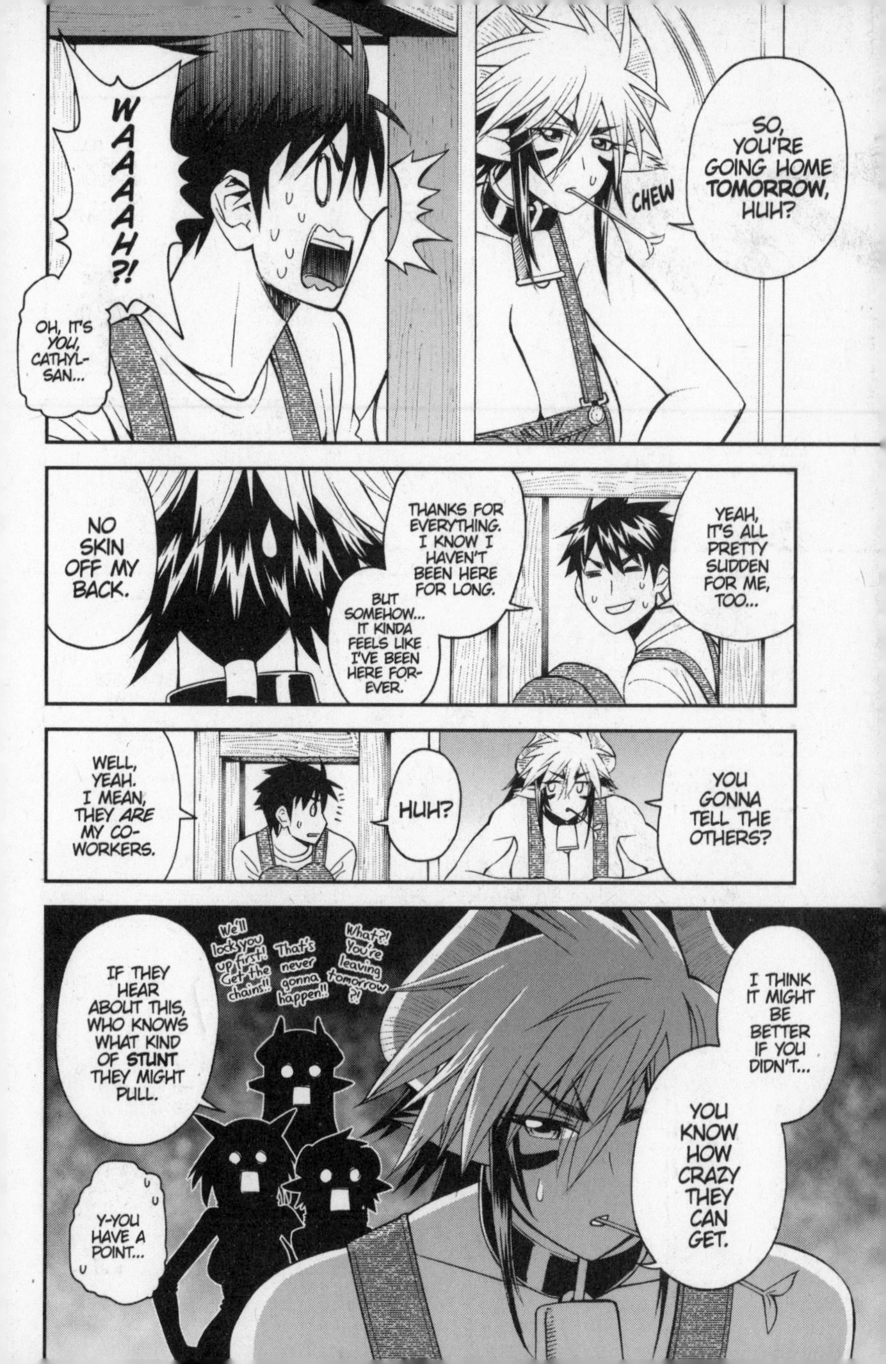
SO, YOU'RE GOING HOME TOMORROW, HUH?
CHEW
WAAAAAH?!
OH, IT'S *YOU*, CATHYL-SAN...
YEAH, IT'S ALL PRETTY SUDDEN FOR ME, TOO...
THANKS FOR EVERYTHING. I KNOW I HAVEN'T BEEN HERE FOR LONG.
BUT SOMEHOW... IT KINDA FEELS LIKE I'VE BEEN HERE FOR-EVER.
NO SKIN OFF MY BACK.
YOU GONNA TELL THE OTHERS?
HUH?
WELL, YEAH. I MEAN, THEY *ARE* MY CO-WORKERS.
I THINK IT MIGHT BE BETTER IF YOU DIDN'T...
YOU KNOW HOW CRAZY THEY CAN GET.
What?! You're leaving tomorrow ?!
That's never gonna happen!!
We'll lock you up first! Get the chains!!
IF THEY HEAR ABOUT THIS, WHO KNOWS WHAT KIND OF STUNT THEY MIGHT PULL.
Y-YOU HAVE A POINT...

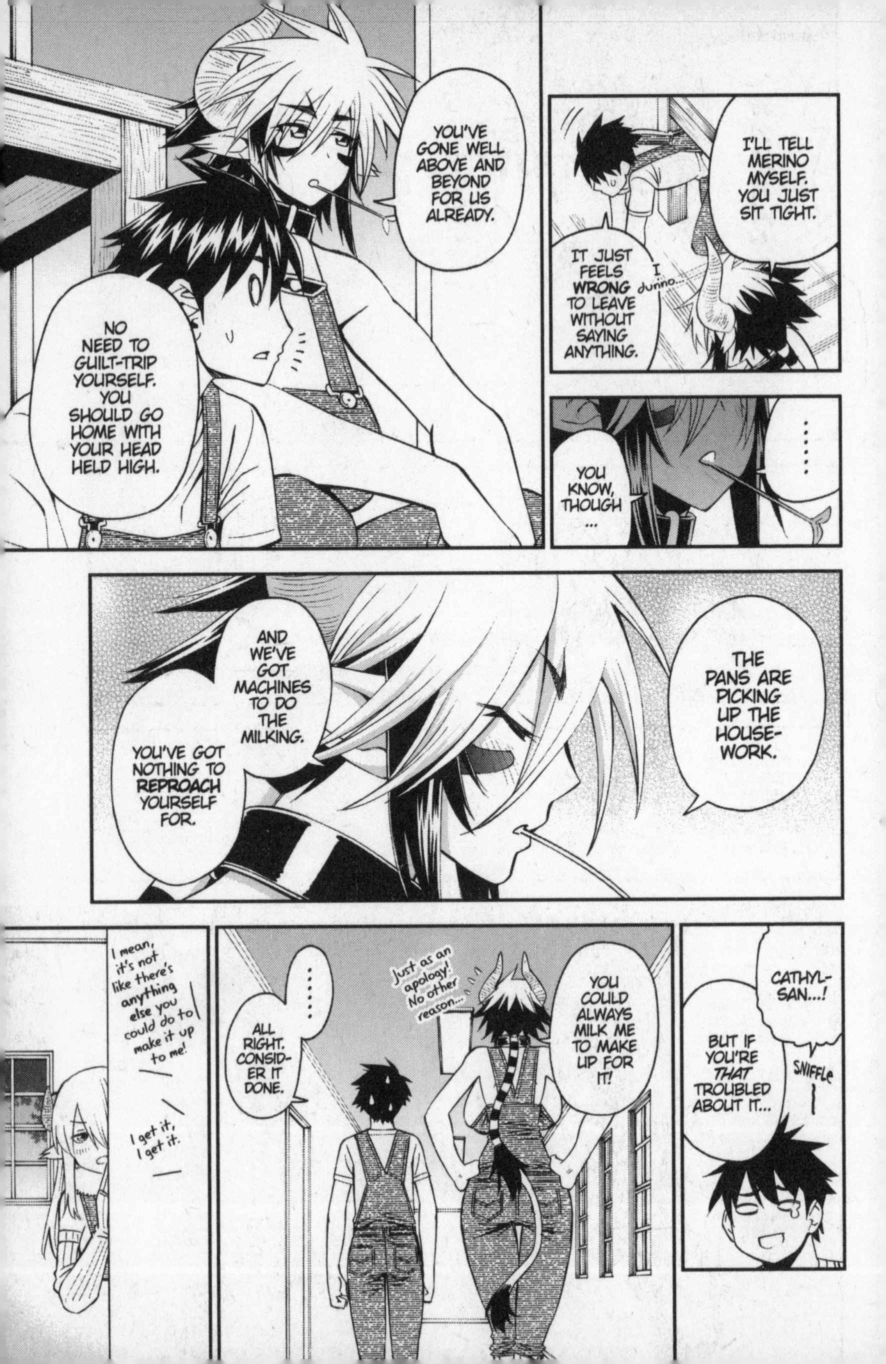
I'LL TELL MERINO MYSELF. YOU JUST SIT TIGHT.
IT JUST FEELS **WRONG** TO LEAVE WITHOUT SAYING ANYTHING.
I dunno...
......
YOU KNOW, THOUGH ...
YOU'VE GONE WELL ABOVE AND BEYOND FOR US ALREADY.
NO NEED TO GUILT-TRIP YOURSELF. YOU SHOULD GO HOME WITH YOUR HEAD HELD HIGH.
THE PANS ARE PICKING UP THE HOUSE-WORK.
AND WE'VE GOT MACHINES TO DO THE MILKING.
YOU'VE GOT NOTHING TO **REPROACH** YOURSELF FOR.
CATHYL-SAN...!
SNIFFLe
BUT IF YOU'RE *THAT* TROUBLED ABOUT IT...
YOU COULD ALWAYS MILK ME TO MAKE UP FOR IT!
Just as an apology! No other reason...
......
ALL RIGHT. CONSIDER IT DONE.
I mean, it's not like there's anything else you could do to make it up to me!
I get it, I get it.

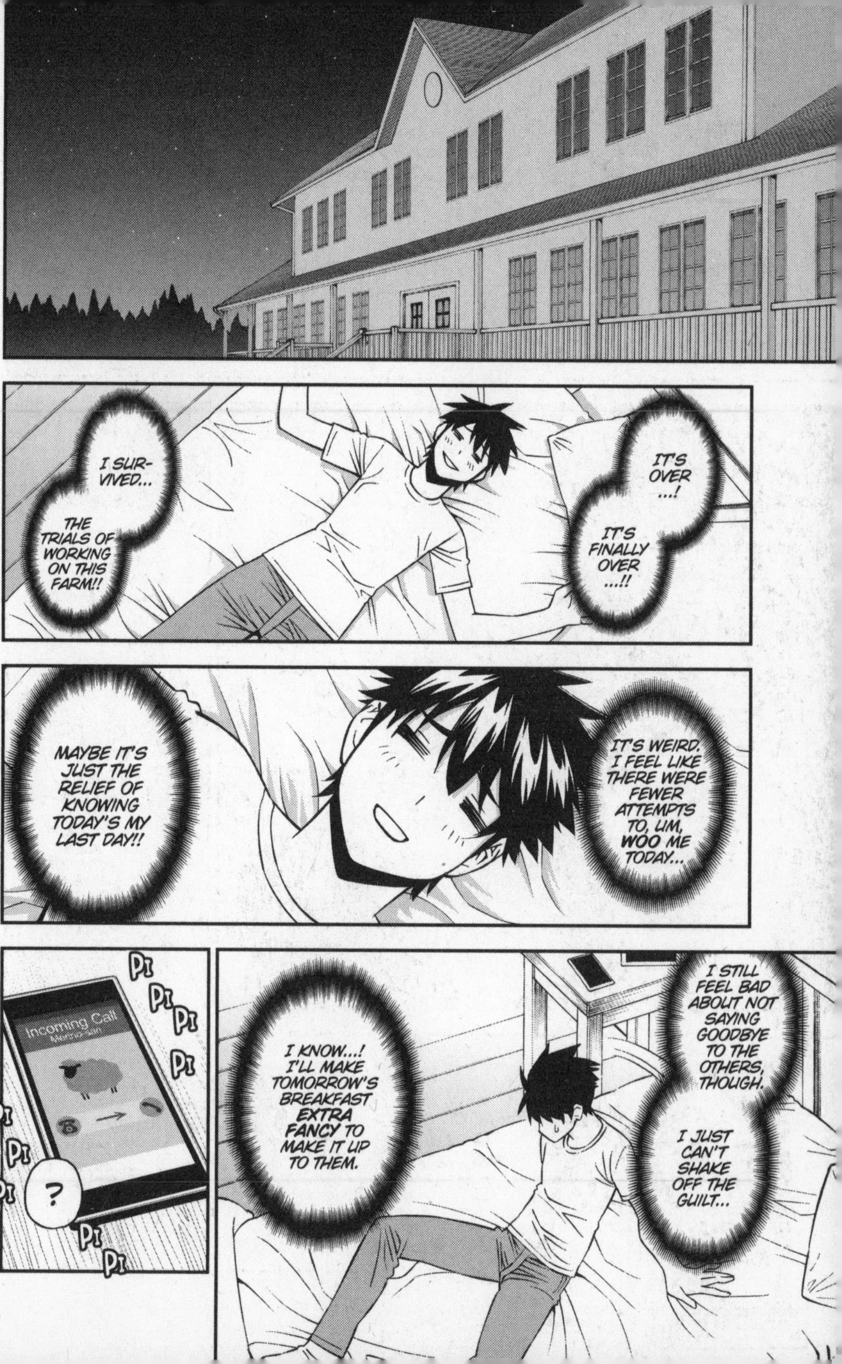
IT'S OVER ...!
IT'S FINALLY OVER ...!!
I SURVIVED...
THE TRIALS OF WORKING ON THIS FARM!!
IT'S WEIRD. I FEEL LIKE THERE WERE FEWER ATTEMPTS TO, UM, WOO ME TODAY...
MAYBE IT'S JUST THE RELIEF OF KNOWING TODAY'S MY LAST DAY!!
I STILL FEEL BAD ABOUT NOT SAYING GOODBYE TO THE OTHERS, THOUGH.
I JUST CAN'T SHAKE OFF THE GUILT...
I KNOW...! I'LL MAKE TOMORROW'S BREAKFAST EXTRA FANCY TO MAKE IT UP TO THEM.
PI PI PI PI
Incoming Call
PI PI PI
?
PI PI

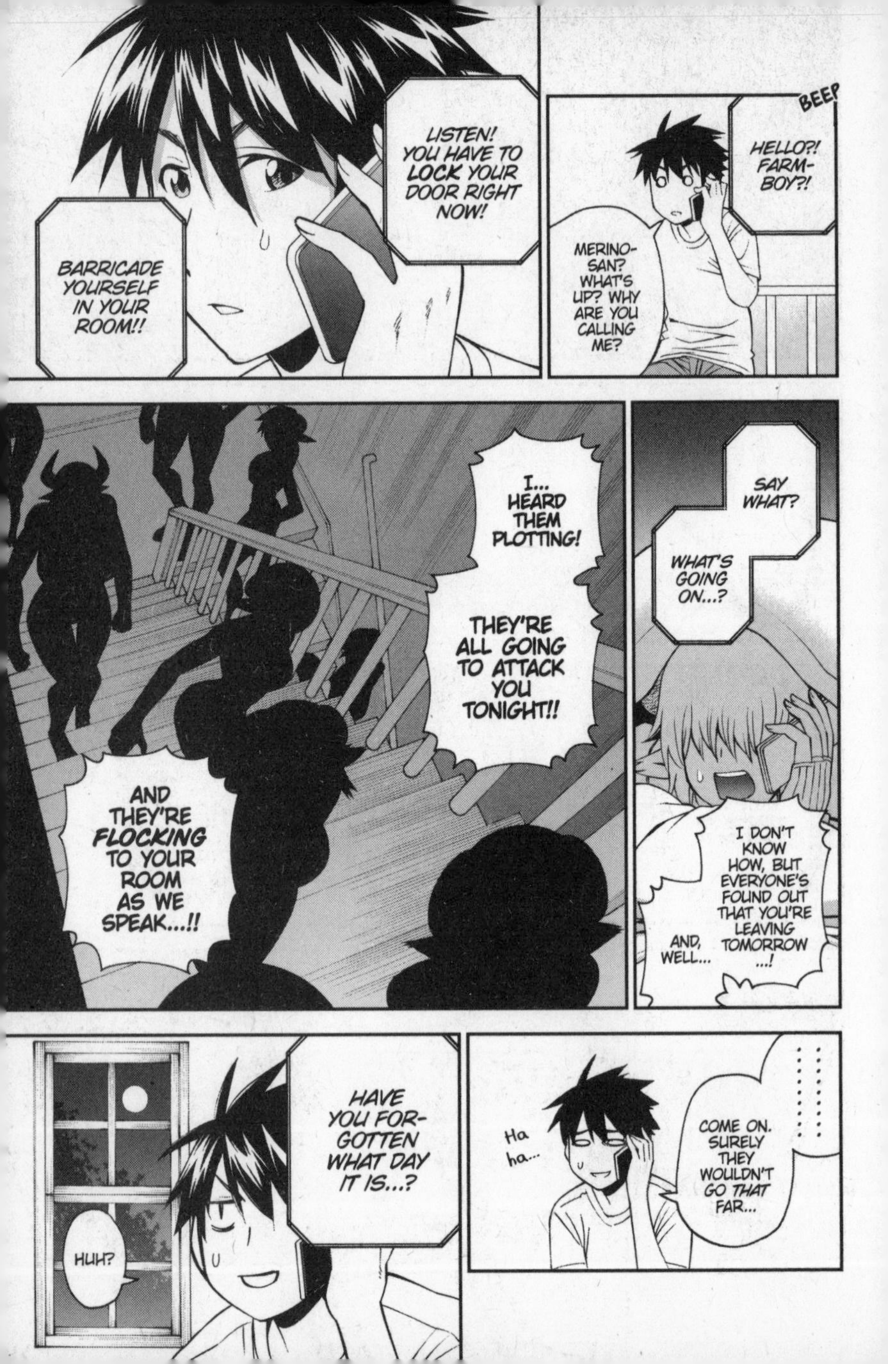
BEEP
HELLO?! FARM-BOY?!
MERINO-SAN? WHAT'S UP? WHY ARE YOU CALLING ME?
LISTEN! YOU HAVE TO LOCK YOUR DOOR RIGHT NOW!
BARRICADE YOURSELF IN YOUR ROOM!!
SAY WHAT?
WHAT'S GOING ON...?
I DON'T KNOW HOW, BUT EVERYONE'S FOUND OUT THAT YOU'RE LEAVING TOMORROW...!
AND, WELL...
I... HEARD THEM PLOTTING!
THEY'RE ALL GOING TO ATTACK YOU TONIGHT!!
AND THEY'RE FLOCKING TO YOUR ROOM AS WE SPEAK...!!
......
COME ON. SURELY THEY WOULDN'T GO THAT FAR...
Ha ha...
HAVE YOU FORGOTTEN WHAT DAY IT IS...?
HUH?

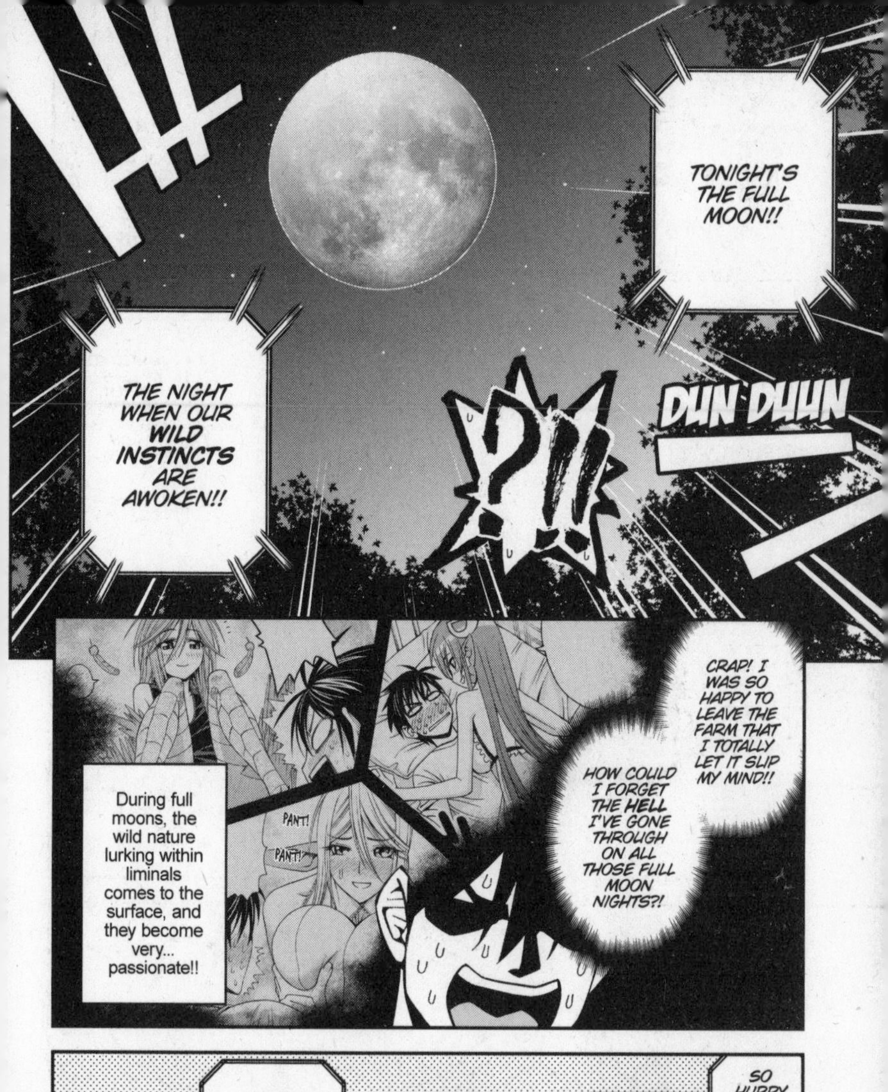
TONIGHT'S THE FULL MOON!!
DUN DUUN
?!!
THE NIGHT WHEN OUR WILD INSTINCTS ARE AWOKEN!!
CRAP! I WAS SO HAPPY TO LEAVE THE FARM THAT I TOTALLY LET IT SLIP MY MIND!!
HOW COULD I FORGET THE HELL I'VE GONE THROUGH ON ALL THOSE FULL MOON NIGHTS?!
PANT!
PANT!
During full moons, the wild nature lurking within liminals comes to the surface, and they become very... passionate!!
SO HURRY AND LOCK YOUR DOOR...
THEY'RE OUT OF CONTROL... THEY'RE PLANNING TO HAVE YOU GET THEM PREGNANT TO FORCE YOU TO STAY HE--
STAY HEEEE-AWWWW-WWWWW!
MERINO-SAN?!

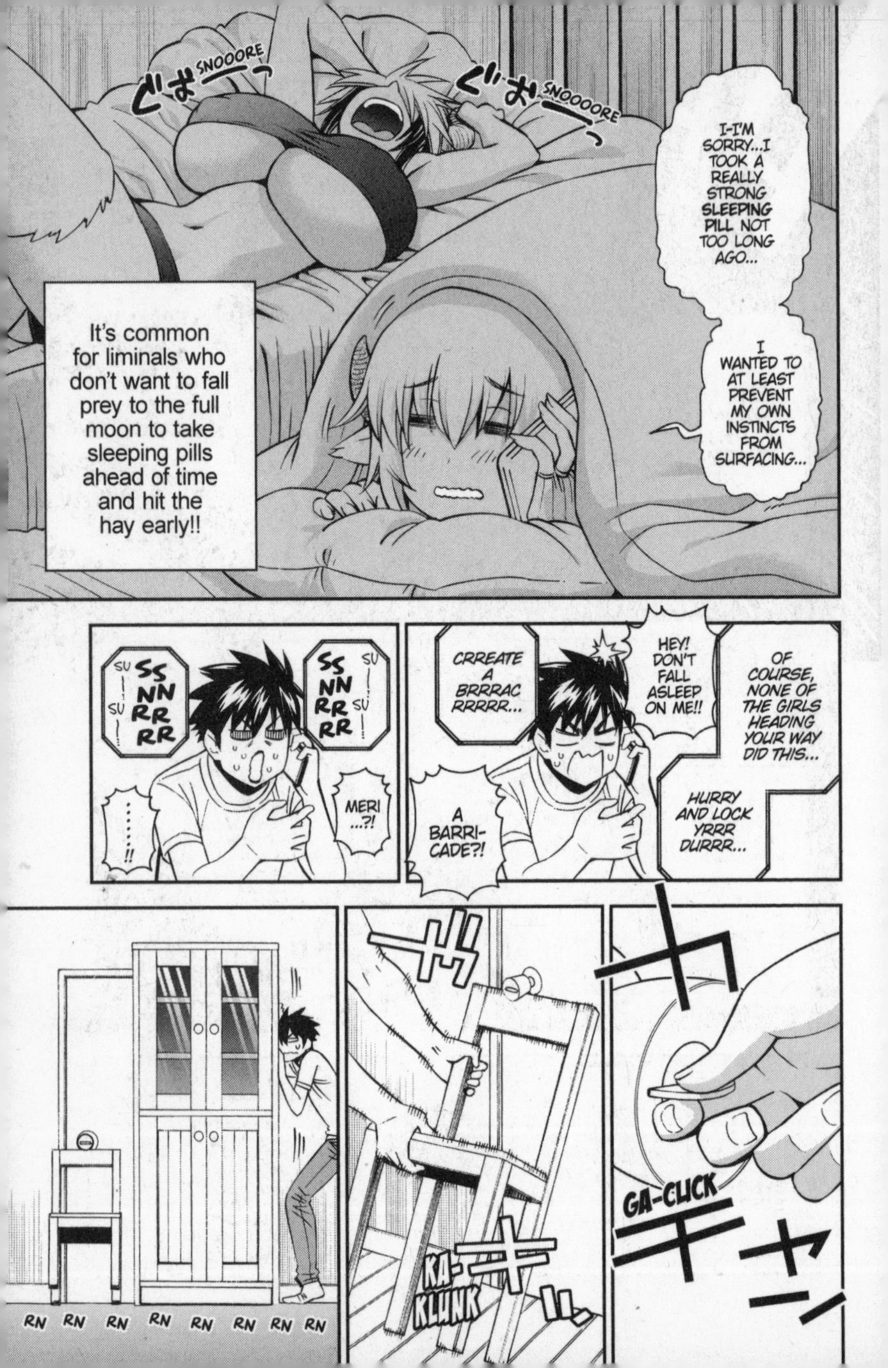
SNOOOORE
SNOOORE
I-I'M SORRY...I TOOK A REALLY STRONG SLEEPING PILL NOT TOO LONG AGO...
I WANTED TO AT LEAST PREVENT MY OWN INSTINCTS FROM SURFACING...
It's common for liminals who don't want to fall prey to the full moon to take sleeping pills ahead of time and hit the hay early!!
OF COURSE, NONE OF THE GIRLS HEADING YOUR WAY DID THIS...
HURRY AND LOCK YRRR DURRR...
HEY! DON'T FALL ASLEEP ON ME!!
CRREATE A BRRRAC RRRRR...
A BARRI-CADE?!
SS NN RR RR
SU- SU-
MERI ...?!
SS NN RR RR
SU- SU-
......!!
GA-CLICK
KA-KLUNK
RN RN RN RN RN RN RN RN

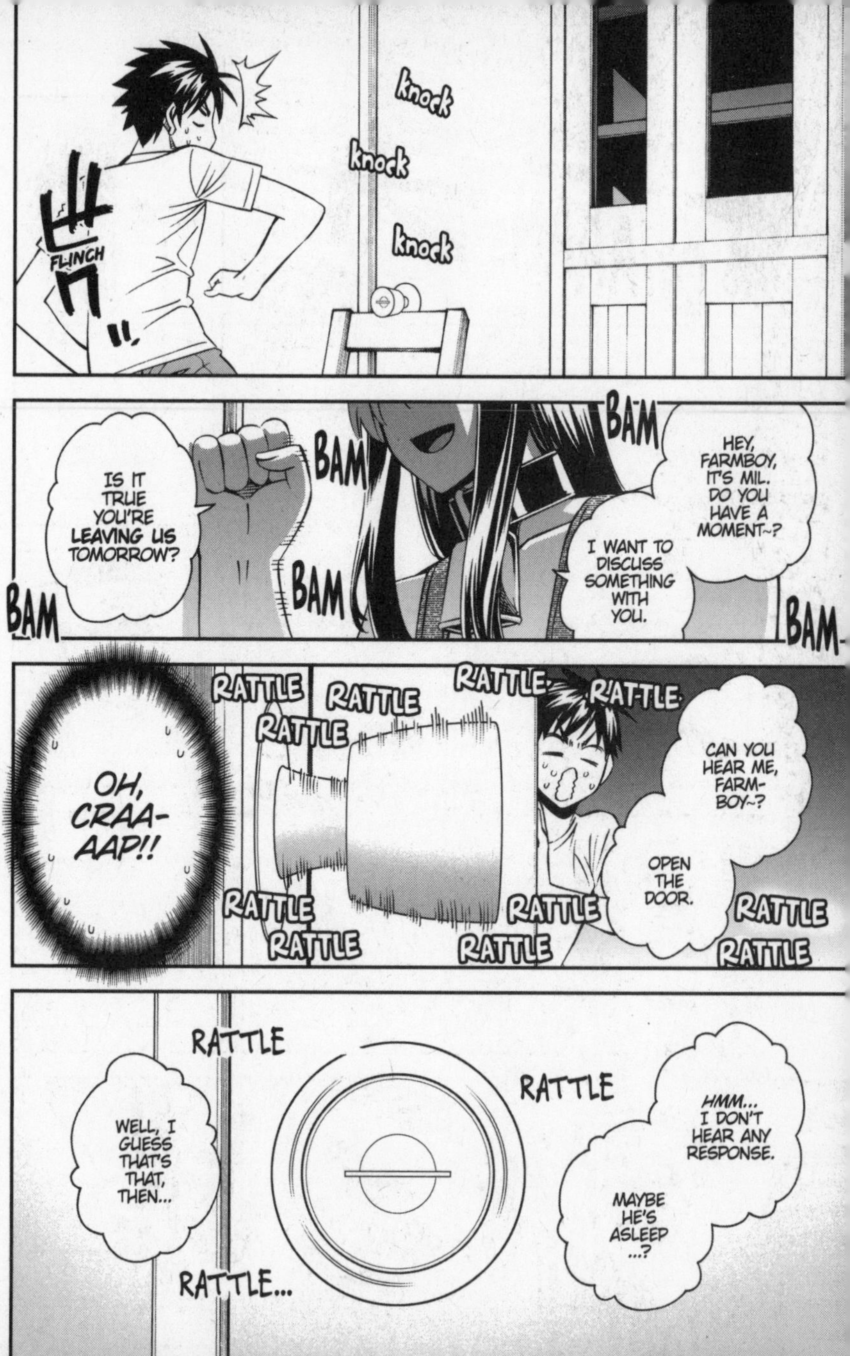
knock
knock
knock
FLINCH
!!
BAM
HEY, FARMBOY, IT'S MIL. DO YOU HAVE A MOMENT~?
I WANT TO DISCUSS SOMETHING WITH YOU.
BAM
BAM
IS IT TRUE YOU'RE LEAVING US TOMORROW?
BAM
BAM
RATTLE RATTLE
CAN YOU HEAR ME, FARMBOY~?
OPEN THE DOOR.
RATTLE RATTLE
RATTLE RATTLE
RATTLE RATTLE
RATTLE RATTLE
OH, CRAA-AAP!!
HMM... I DON'T HEAR ANY RESPONSE.
MAYBE HE'S ASLEEP ...?
RATTLE
RATTLE
WELL, I GUESS THAT'S THAT, THEN...
RATTLE...

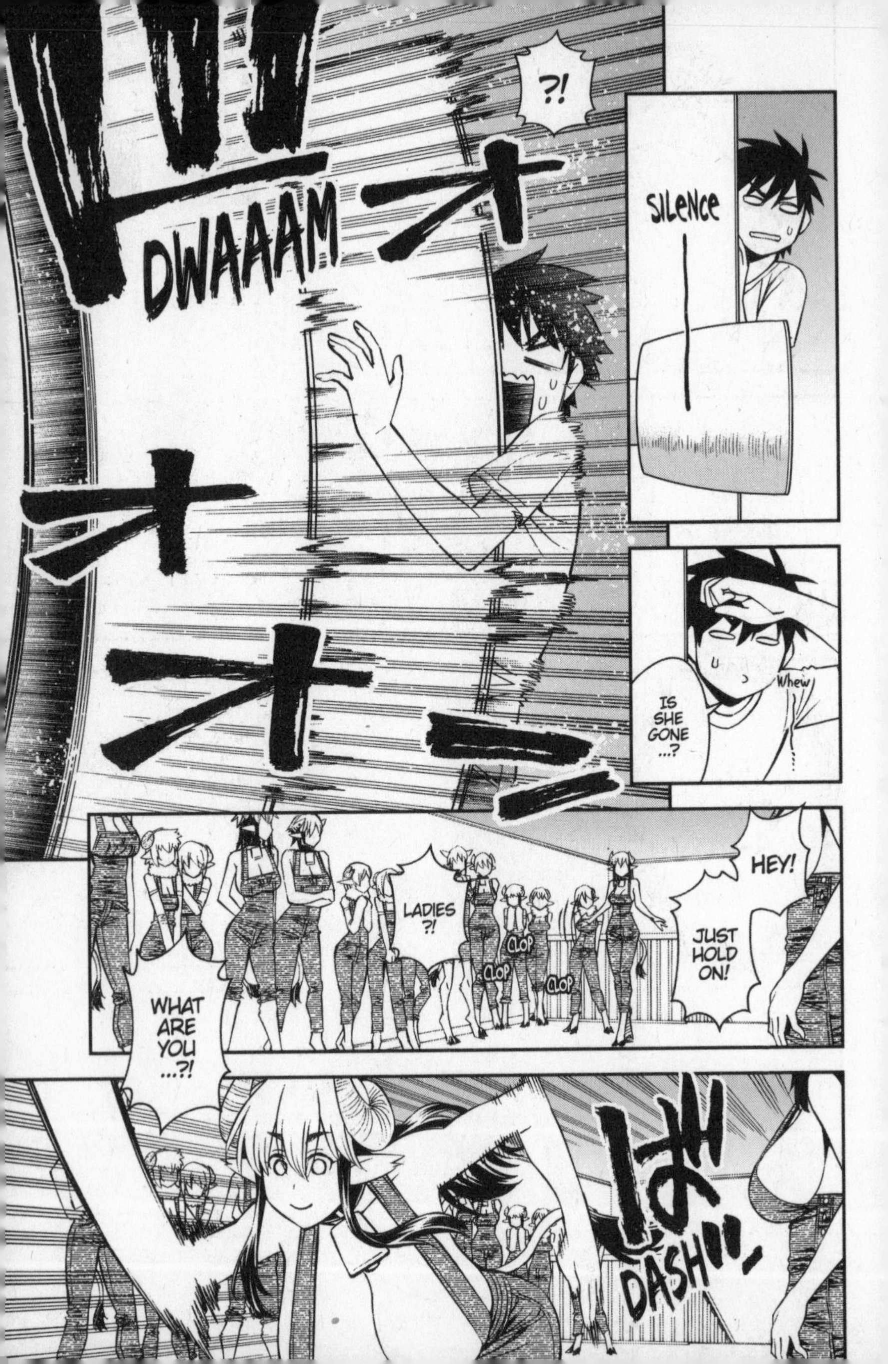
SILENCE
IS SHE GONE ...?
Whew
?!
DWAAAM
HEY!
JUST HOLD ON!
LADIES ?!
CLOP
CLOP
CLOP
WHAT ARE YOU ...?!
DASH

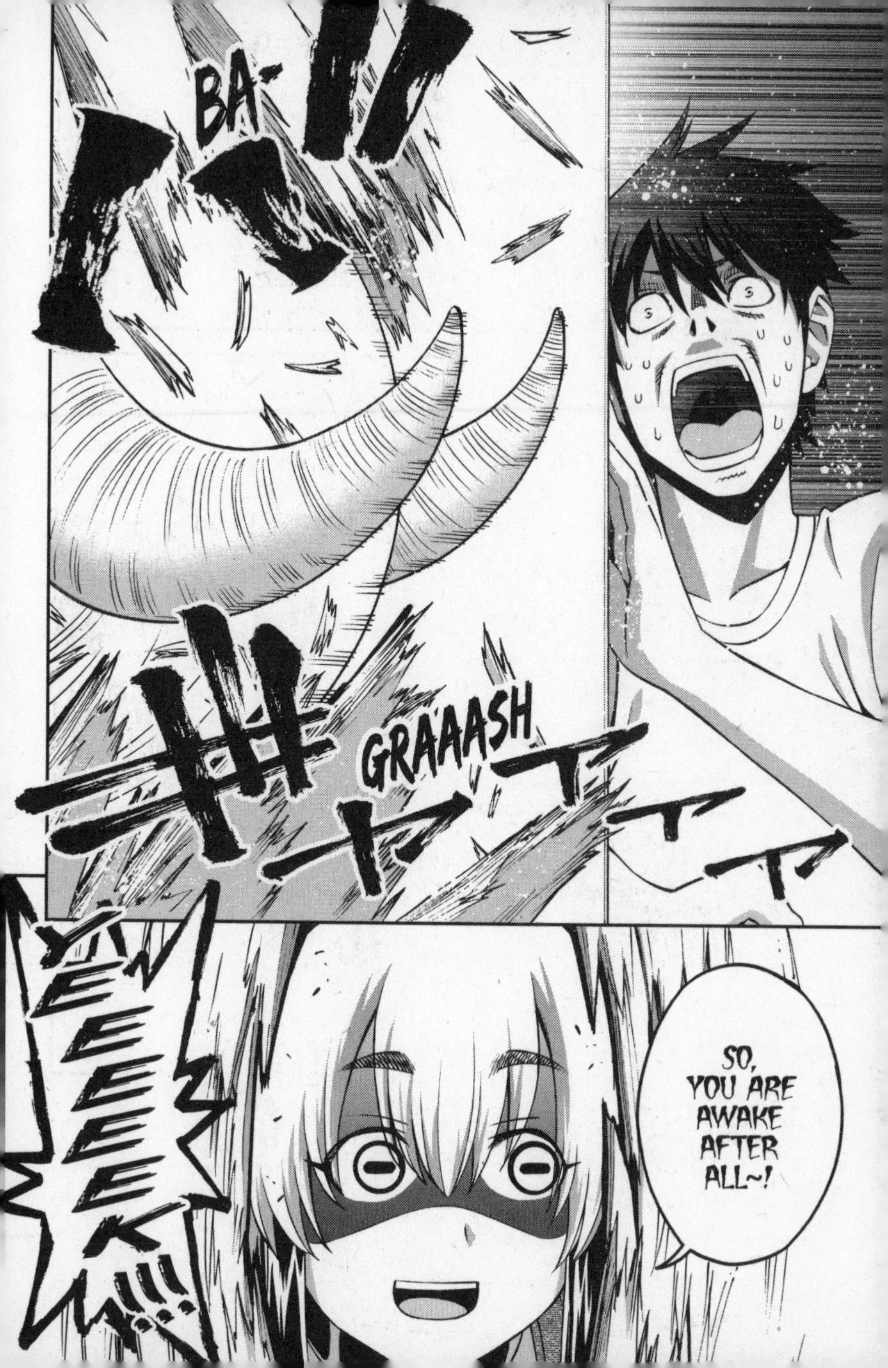

GRAAASH
BA-
SO, YOU ARE AWAKE AFTER ALL~!
YEEEEEEK!!!

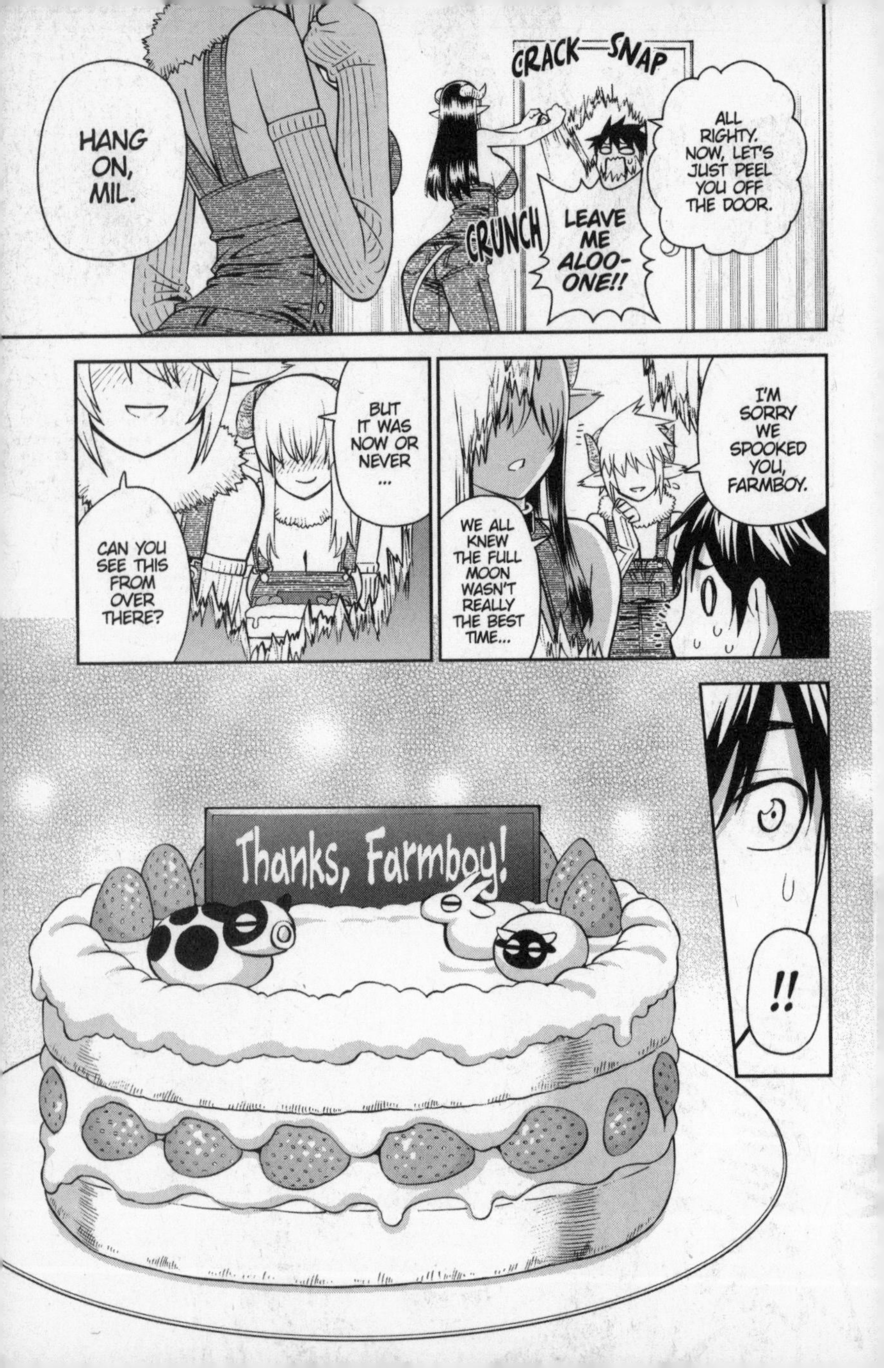

CRACK SNAP
ALL RIGHTY. NOW, LET'S JUST PEEL YOU OFF THE DOOR.
LEAVE ME ALOO-ONE!!
CRUNCH
HANG ON, MIL.
I'M SORRY WE SPOOKED YOU, FARMBOY.
WE ALL KNEW THE FULL MOON WASN'T REALLY THE BEST TIME...
BUT IT WAS NOW OR NEVER ...
CAN YOU SEE THIS FROM OVER THERE?
!!
Thanks, Farmboy!

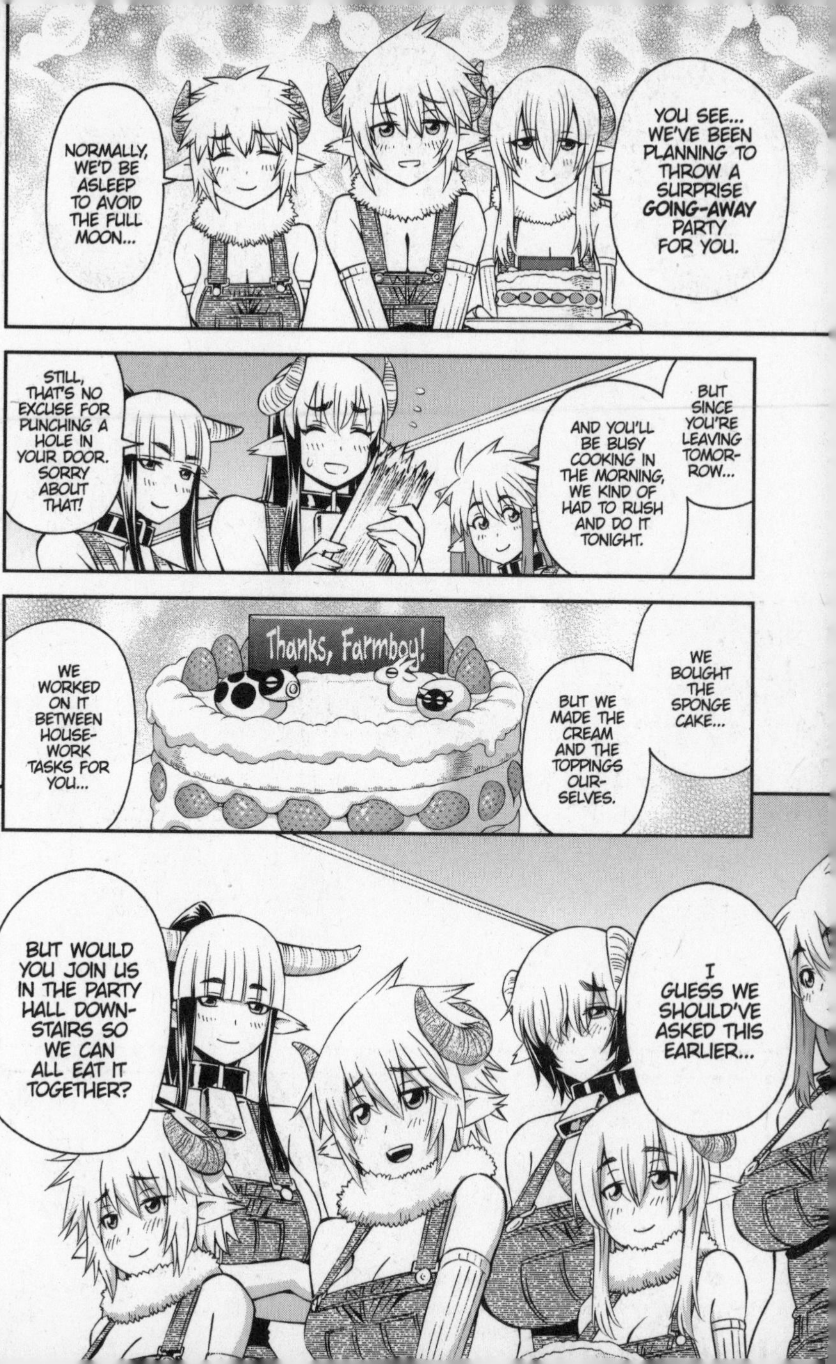
YOU SEE... WE'VE BEEN PLANNING TO THROW A SURPRISE **GOING-AWAY** PARTY FOR YOU.
NORMALLY, WE'D BE ASLEEP TO AVOID THE FULL MOON...
BUT SINCE YOU'RE LEAVING TOMOR-ROW...
AND YOU'LL BE BUSY COOKING IN THE MORNING, WE KIND OF HAD TO RUSH AND DO IT TONIGHT.
STILL, THAT'S NO EXCUSE FOR PUNCHING A HOLE IN YOUR DOOR. SORRY ABOUT THAT!
WE BOUGHT THE SPONGE CAKE...
BUT WE MADE THE CREAM AND THE TOPPINGS OUR-SELVES.
Thanks, Farmboy!
WE WORKED ON IT BETWEEN HOUSE-WORK TASKS FOR YOU...
I GUESS WE SHOULD'VE ASKED THIS EARLIER...
BUT WOULD YOU JOIN US IN THE PARTY HALL DOWN-STAIRS SO WE CAN ALL EAT IT TOGETHER?

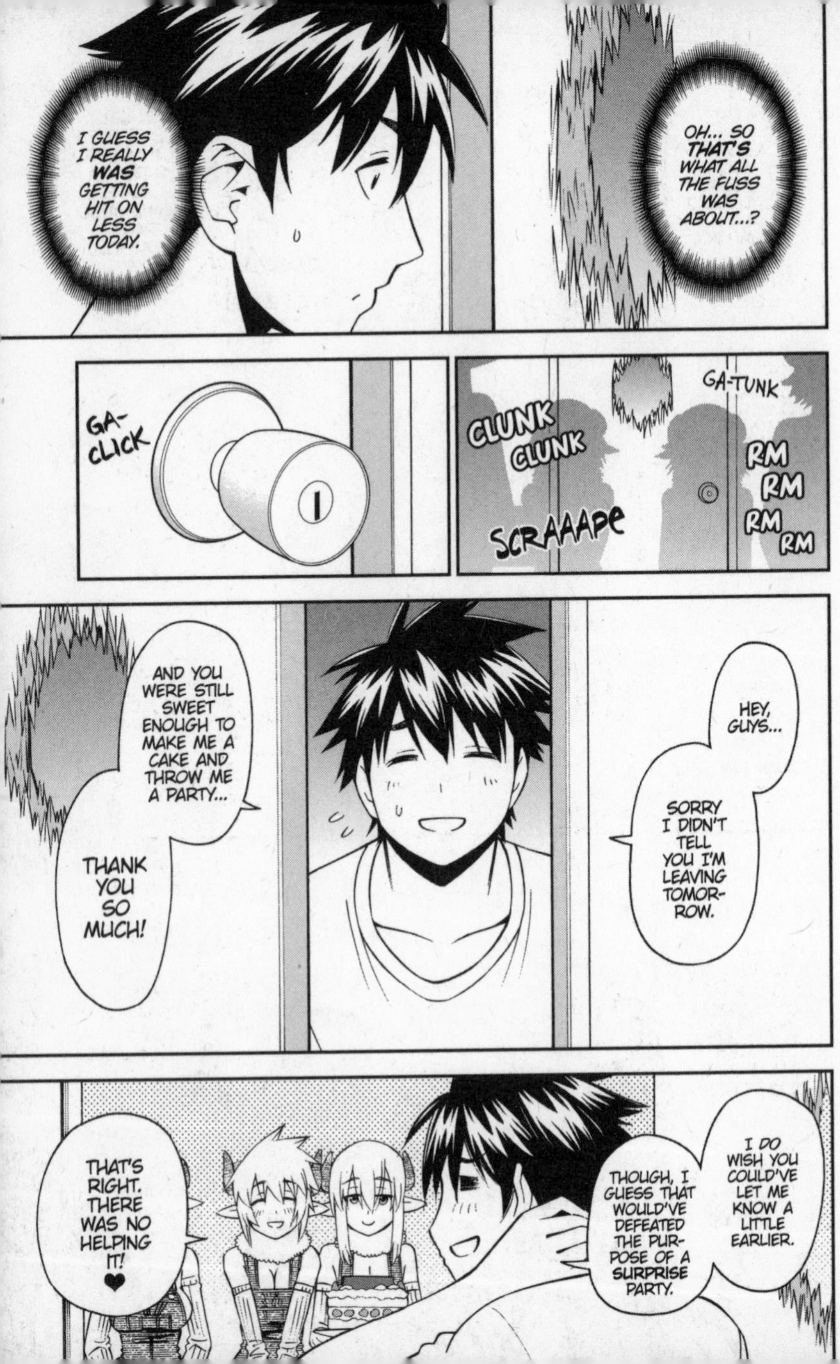

OH... SO THAT'S WHAT ALL THE FUSS WAS ABOUT...?
I GUESS I REALLY WAS GETTING HIT ON LESS TODAY.
GA-TUNK
CLUNK CLUNK
RM RM RM RM
SCRAAAPE
GA-CLICK
HEY, GUYS...
SORRY I DIDN'T TELL YOU I'M LEAVING TOMOR-ROW.
AND YOU WERE STILL SWEET ENOUGH TO MAKE ME A CAKE AND THROW ME A PARTY...
THANK YOU SO MUCH!
I DO WISH YOU COULD'VE LET ME KNOW A LITTLE EARLIER.
THOUGH, I GUESS THAT WOULD'VE DEFEATED THE PUR-POSE OF A SURPRISE PARTY.
THAT'S RIGHT. THERE WAS NO HELPING IT! ❤

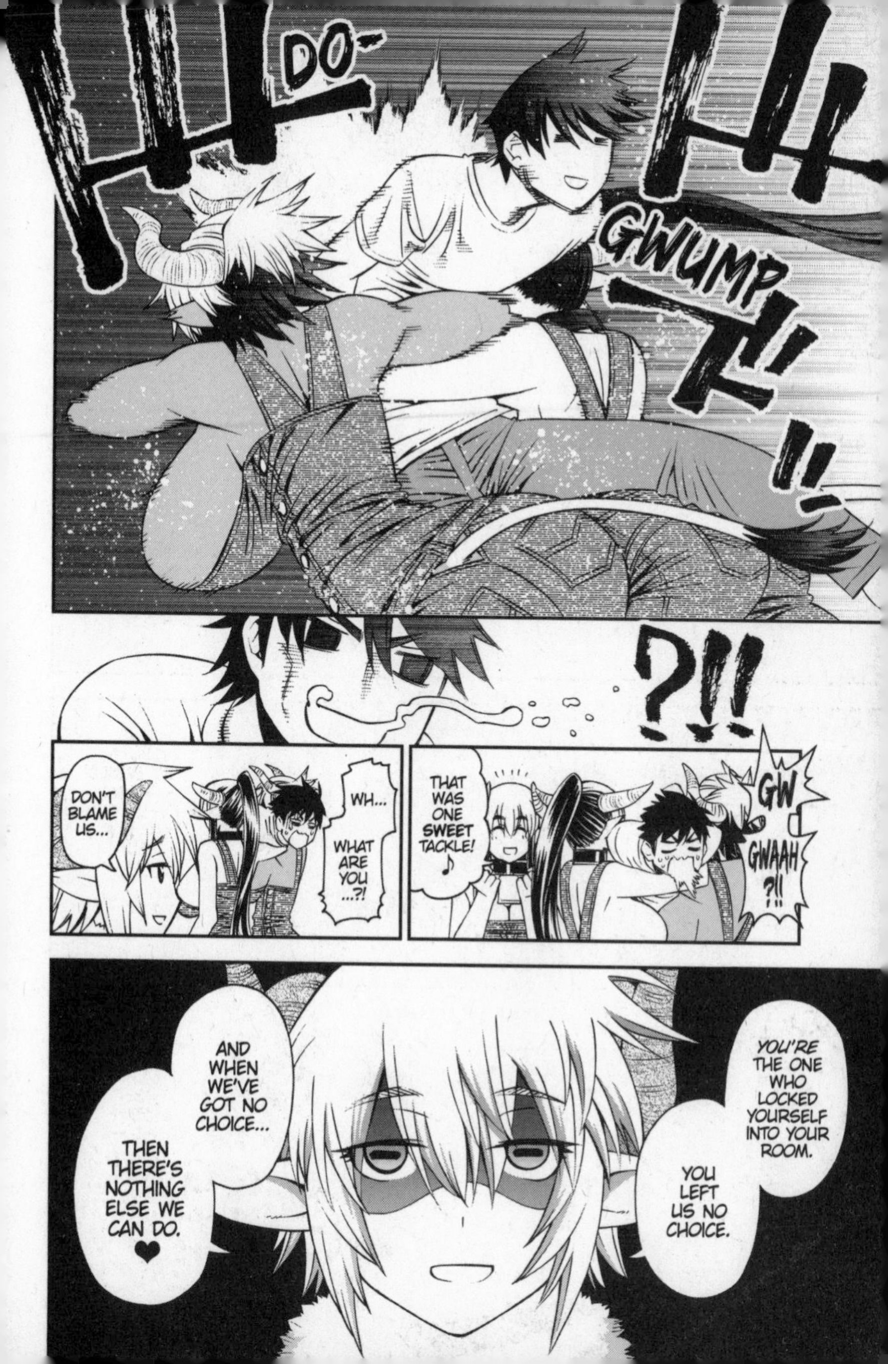
DO-
GWUMP
?!!
GW
GWAAH ?!!
THAT WAS ONE SWEET TACKLE! ♪
WH... WHAT ARE YOU ...?!
DON'T BLAME US...
YOU'RE THE ONE WHO LOCKED YOURSELF INTO YOUR ROOM.
YOU LEFT US NO CHOICE.
AND WHEN WE'VE GOT NO CHOICE...
THEN THERE'S NOTHING ELSE WE CAN DO. ❤

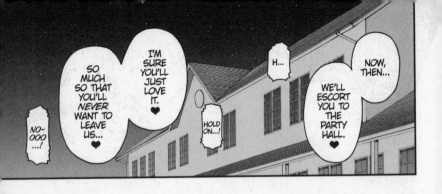

NOW, THEN...
WE'LL ESCORT YOU TO THE PARTY HALL. ❤
H...
HOLD ON...!
I'M SURE YOU'LL JUST LOVE IT. ❤
SO MUCH SO THAT YOU'LL *NEVER* WANT TO LEAVE US... ❤
NO-OOO...!
HERE YOU GO, FARMBOY. ❤
SAY, "AHHH!" ❤
THIS CAKE'S TOO SMALL FOR EACH OF US TO HAVE A PIECE. ❤
SO YOU CAN HAVE IT ALL TO YOURSELF, FARMBOY. ❤
OPEN WIDE~! ❤
WAIT A SEC! YOU CAN'T JUST KEEP FEEDING--
SHOVE
NGGGGH?!
DON'T STOP *NOW.* ❤
YOU HAVEN'T EVEN FINISHED HALF OF YOUR CAKE~! ❤

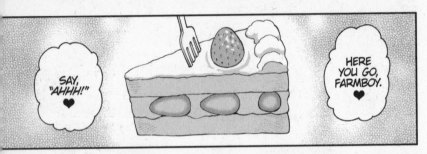

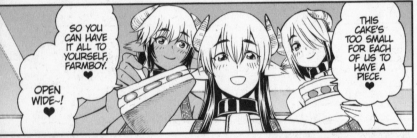

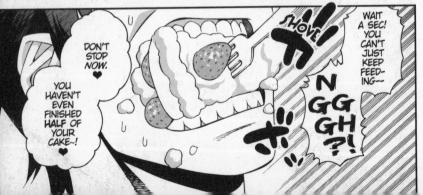

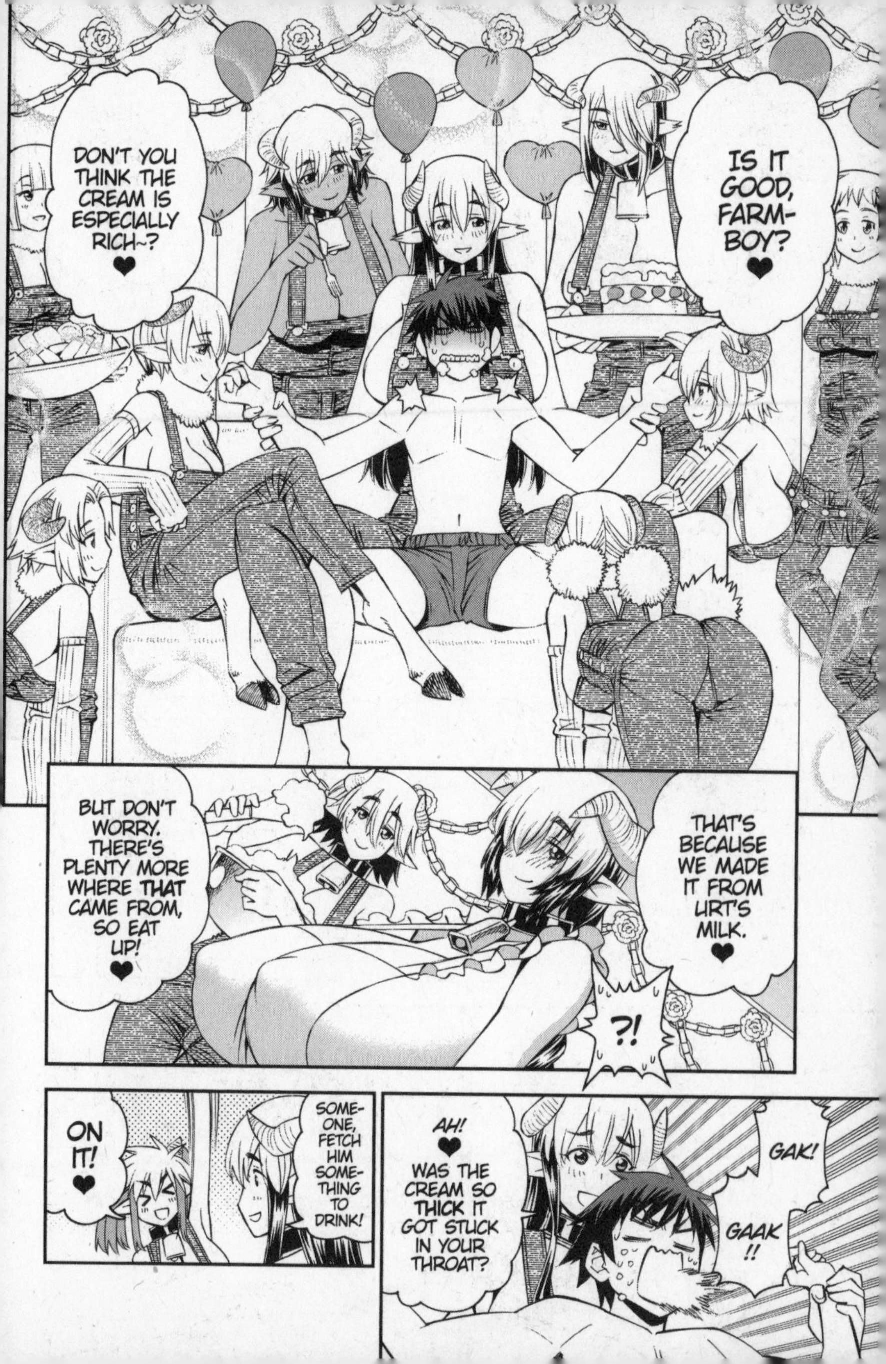
IS IT GOOD, FARM-BOY? ♥
DON'T YOU THINK THE CREAM IS ESPECIALLY RICH~? ♥
THAT'S BECAUSE WE MADE IT FROM URT'S MILK. ♥
?!
BUT DON'T WORRY. THERE'S PLENTY MORE WHERE THAT CAME FROM, SO EAT UP! ♥
GAK!
GAAK!!
AH! ♥ WAS THE CREAM SO THICK IT GOT STUCK IN YOUR THROAT?
SOME-ONE, FETCH HIM SOME-THING TO DRINK!
ON IT! ♥

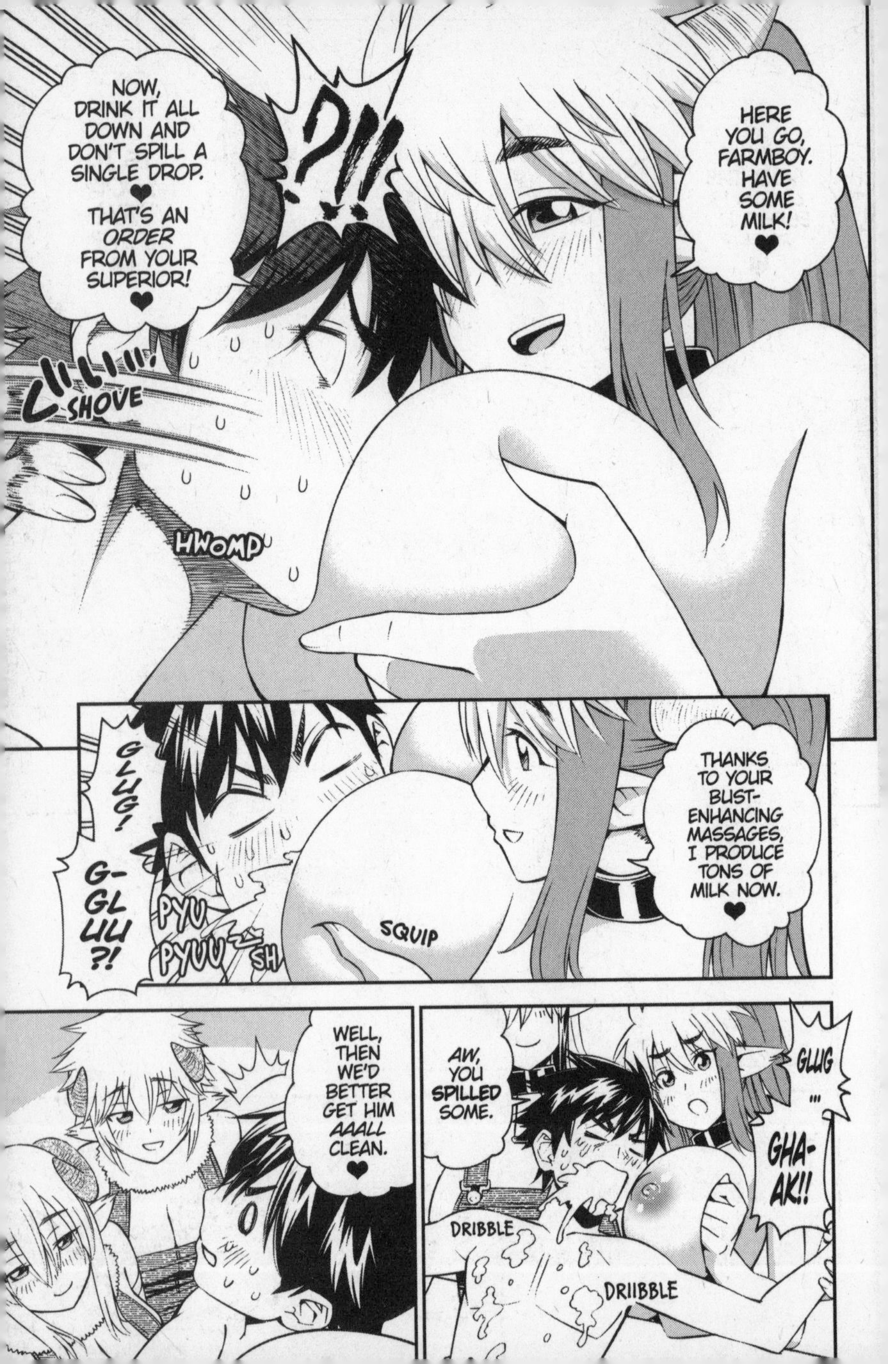
HERE YOU GO, FARMBOY. HAVE SOME MILK! ❤
?!!
NOW, DRINK IT ALL DOWN AND DON'T SPILL A SINGLE DROP. ❤
THAT'S AN *ORDER* FROM YOUR SUPERIOR! ❤
SHOVE
HWOMP
THANKS TO YOUR BUST-ENHANCING MASSAGES, I PRODUCE TONS OF MILK NOW. ❤
SQUIP
PYU PYUU SH
GLUG!
G-GLUU?!
GLUG ...
GHA-AK!!
AW, YOU SPILLED SOME.
DRIBBLE
DRIIBBLE
WELL, THEN WE'D BETTER GET HIM AAALL CLEAN. ❤

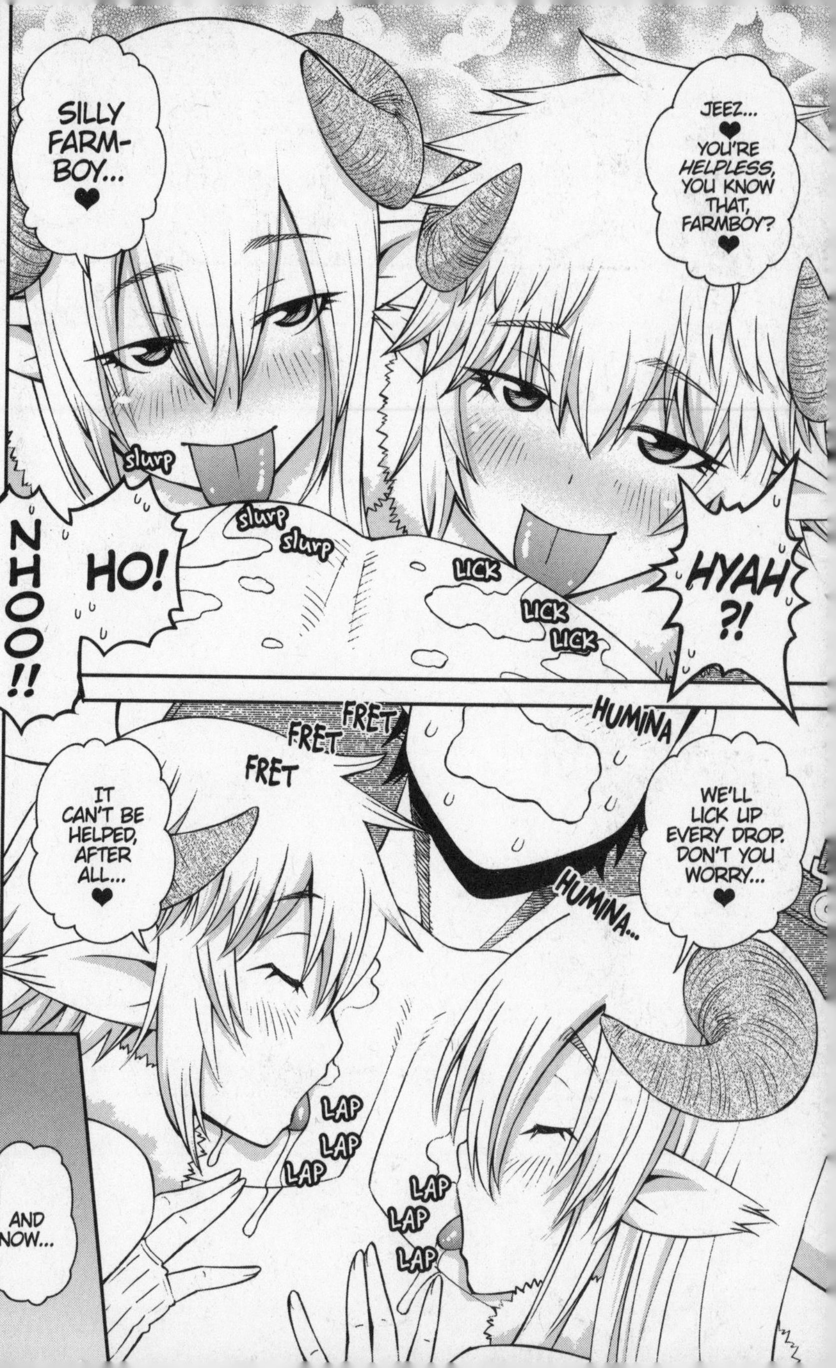
JEEZ... ♥ YOU'RE HELPLESS, YOU KNOW THAT, FARMBOY? ♥
SILLY FARM-BOY... ♥
HYAH?!
LICK LICK LICK
slurp
slurp slurp
HO!
NHOOO!!
HUMINA
WE'LL LICK UP EVERY DROP. DON'T YOU WORRY... ♥
HUMINA...
FRET FRET FRET
IT CAN'T BE HELPED, AFTER ALL... ♥
LAP LAP LAP
LAP LAP LAP
AND NOW...

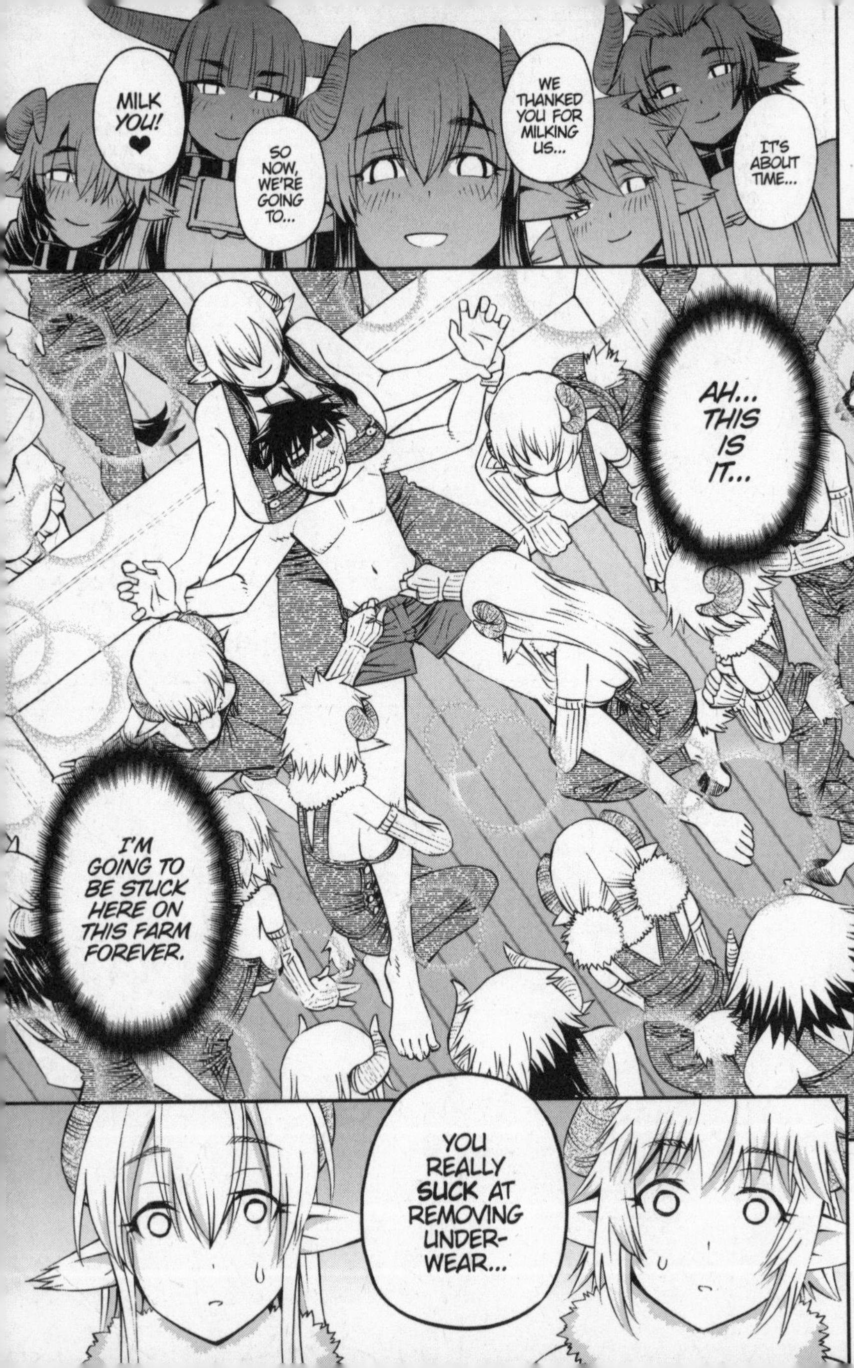
IT'S ABOUT TIME...
WE THANKED YOU FOR MILKING US...
SO NOW, WE'RE GOING TO...
MILK YOU! ❤
AH... THIS IS IT...
I'M GOING TO BE STUCK HERE ON THIS FARM FOREVER.
YOU REALLY SUCK AT REMOVING UNDER-WEAR...

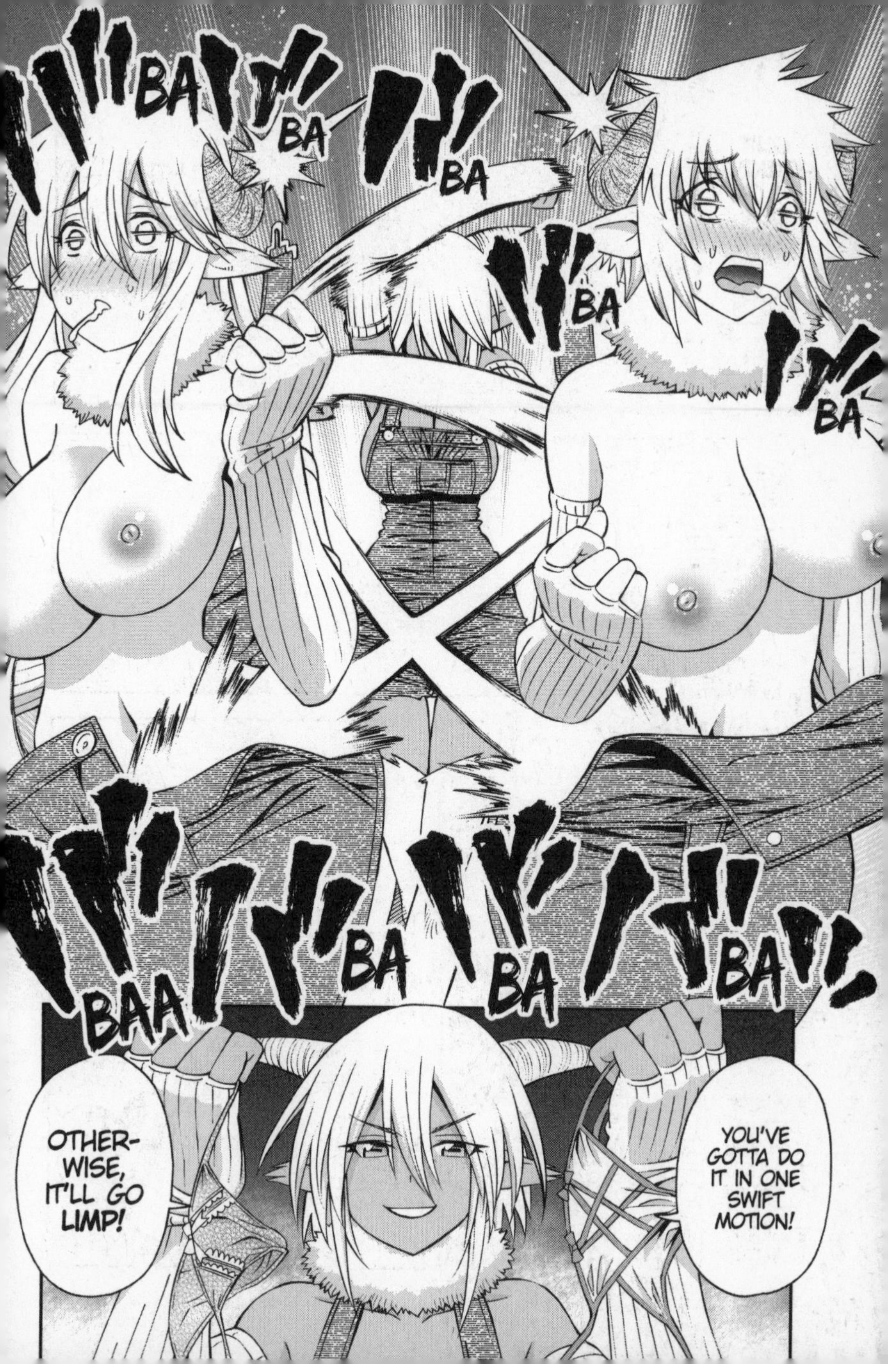
BA
BA
BA
BA
BA
BA
BAA BA BA BA
YOU'VE GOTTA DO IT IN ONE SWIFT MOTION!
OTHER-WISE, IT'LL GO LIMP!

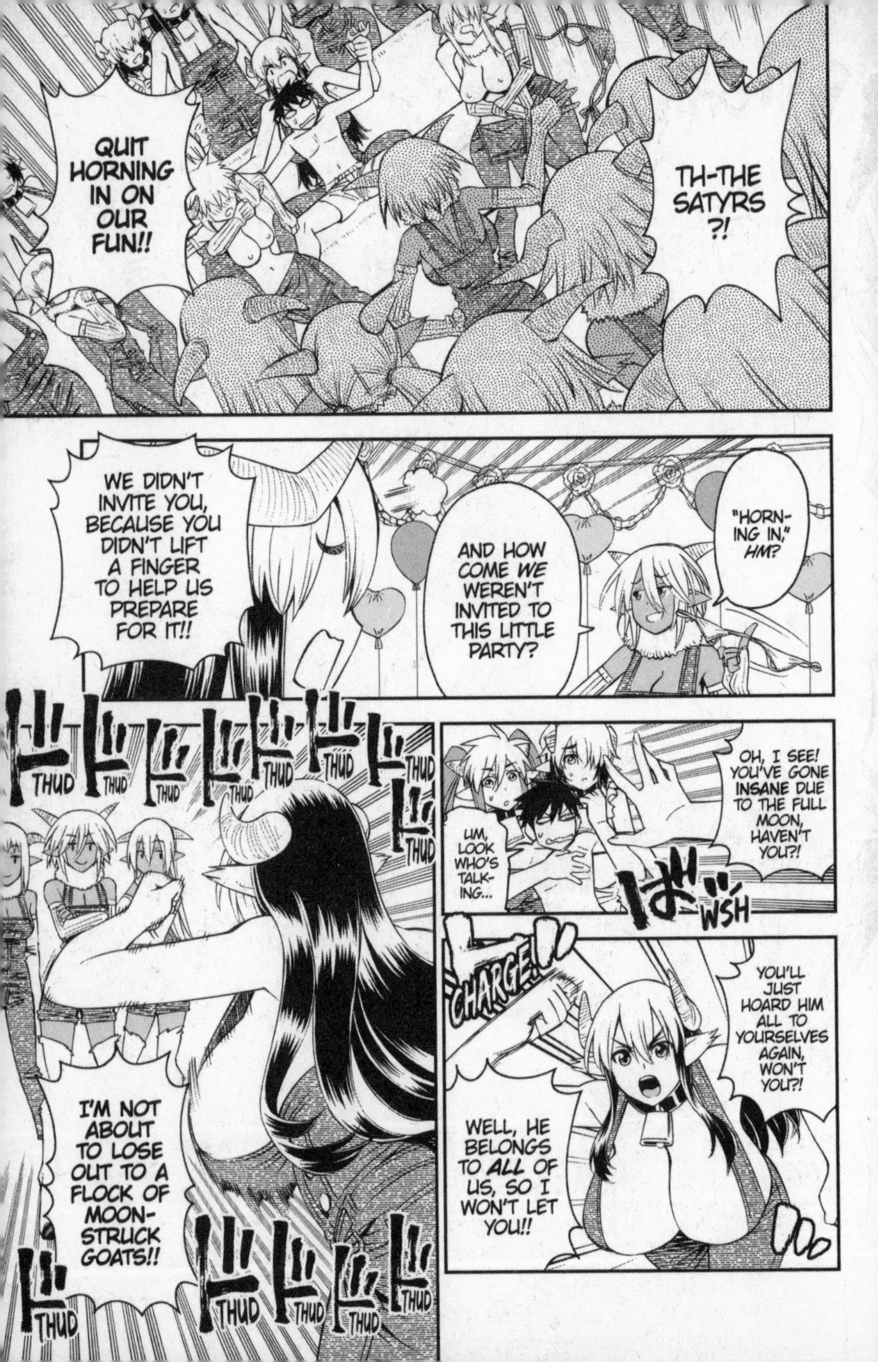
TH-THE SATYRS ?!
QUIT HORNING IN ON OUR FUN!!
"HORNING IN," HM?
AND HOW COME WE WEREN'T INVITED TO THIS LITTLE PARTY?
WE DIDN'T INVITE YOU, BECAUSE YOU DIDN'T LIFT A FINGER TO HELP US PREPARE FOR IT!!
OH, I SEE! YOU'VE GONE INSANE DUE TO THE FULL MOON, HAVEN'T YOU?!
UM, LOOK WHO'S TALKING...
WSH
CHARGE!
YOU'LL JUST HOARD HIM ALL TO YOURSELVES AGAIN, WON'T YOU?!
WELL, HE BELONGS TO ALL OF US, SO I WON'T LET YOU!!
THUD THUD THUD THUD THUD THUD THUD THUD
I'M NOT ABOUT TO LOSE OUT TO A FLOCK OF MOON-STRUCK GOATS!!
THUD THUD THUD THUD THUD

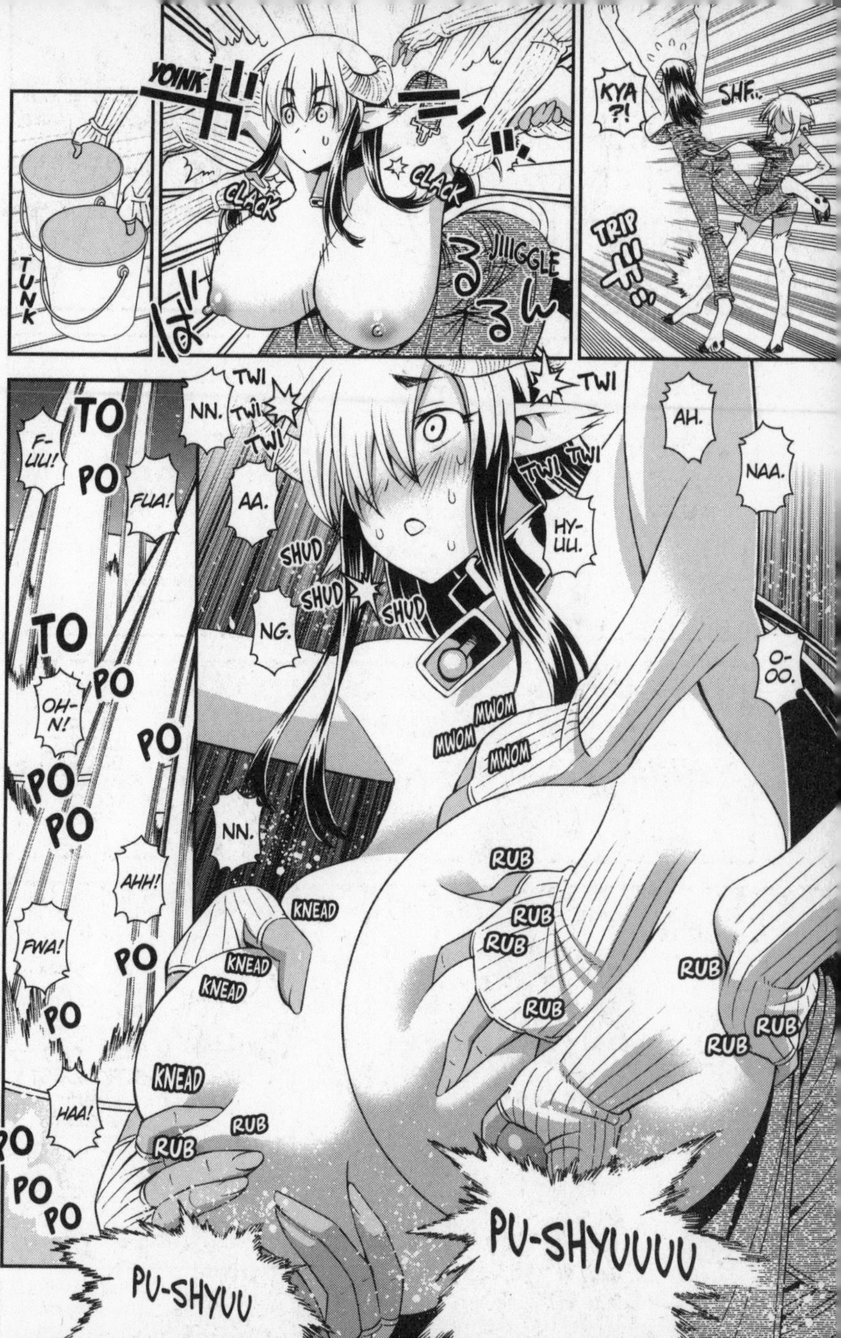

KYA ?!
SHF..
TRIP
YOINK
CLACK
CLACK
JIIGGLE
TUNK
TUNK
AH.
NAA.
TWI
O-OO.
HY-UU.
TWI TWI
TWI
TWI
TWI
NN.
AA.
SHUD
SHUD
SHUD
NG.
MWOM
MWOM
MWOM
FUA!
F-UU!
TO
PO
TO
PO
OH-N!
PO
PO
PO
NN.
RUB
RUB
RUB
RUB
RUB
RUB
RUB
KNEAD
KNEAD
KNEAD
KNEAD
AHH!
FWA!
PO
PO
HAA!
RUB
RUB
PO
PO
PO
PU-SHYUUUU
PU-SHYUU

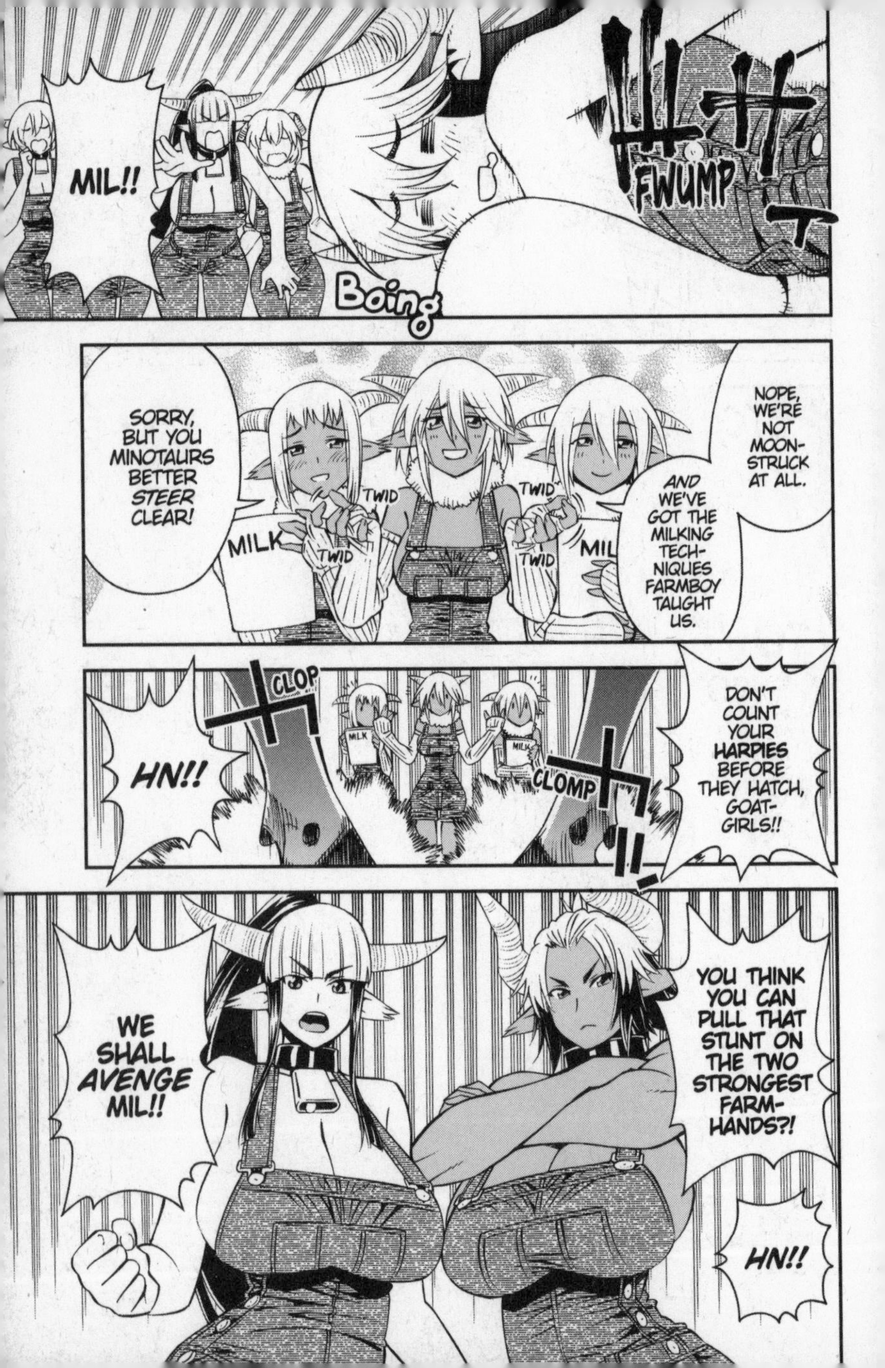
FWUMP
MIL!!
Boing
NOPE, WE'RE NOT MOONSTRUCK AT ALL.
AND WE'VE GOT THE MILKING TECHNIQUES FARMBOY TAUGHT US.
TWID
TWID
MIL
TWID
TWID
MILK
SORRY, BUT YOU MINOTAURS BETTER STEER CLEAR!
DON'T COUNT YOUR HARPIES BEFORE THEY HATCH, GOAT-GIRLS!!
CLOMP
MILK
MILK
CLOP
HN!!
YOU THINK YOU CAN PULL THAT STUNT ON THE TWO STRONGEST FARMHANDS?!
HN!!
WE SHALL AVENGE MIL!!

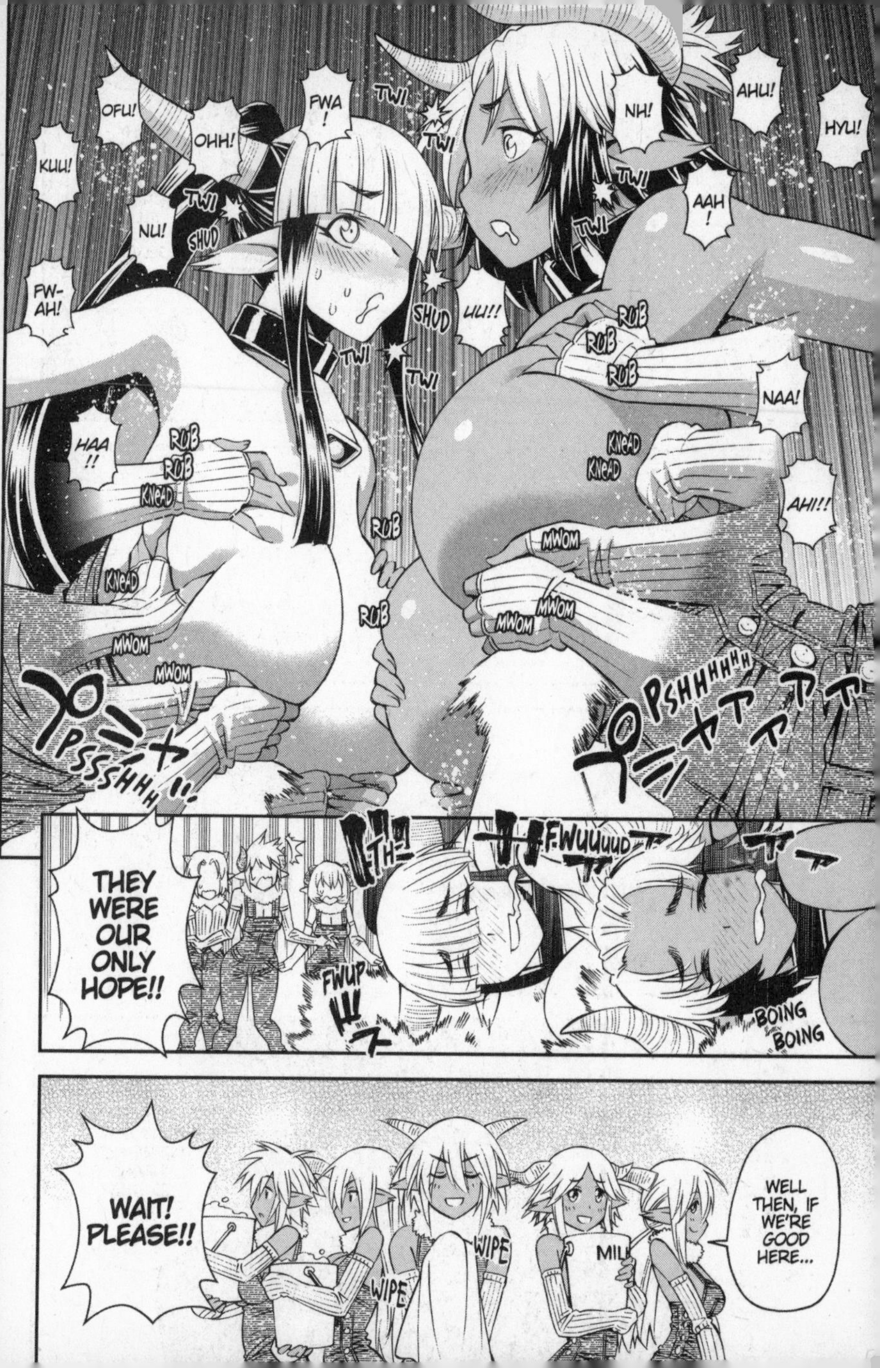

HYU!
AHU!
NH!
TWI
TWI
AAH!
TWI
TWI
FWA!
OFU!
OHH!
KUU!
TWI
NU!
SHUD
FW-AH!
RUB
RUB
RUB
NAA!
UU!!
SHUD
TWI
TWI
KNEAD
KNEAD
AHI!!
MWOM
MWOM
MWOM
HAA!!
RUB
RUB
KNEAD
RUB
KNEAD
RUB
MWOM
MWOM
PSHHHHHH
PSSSHHH!!
BOING
BOING
FWUUUUD
TH
FWUP
THEY WERE OUR ONLY HOPE!!
WELL THEN, IF WE'RE GOOD HERE...
MIL
WIPE
WIPE
WAIT! PLEASE!!

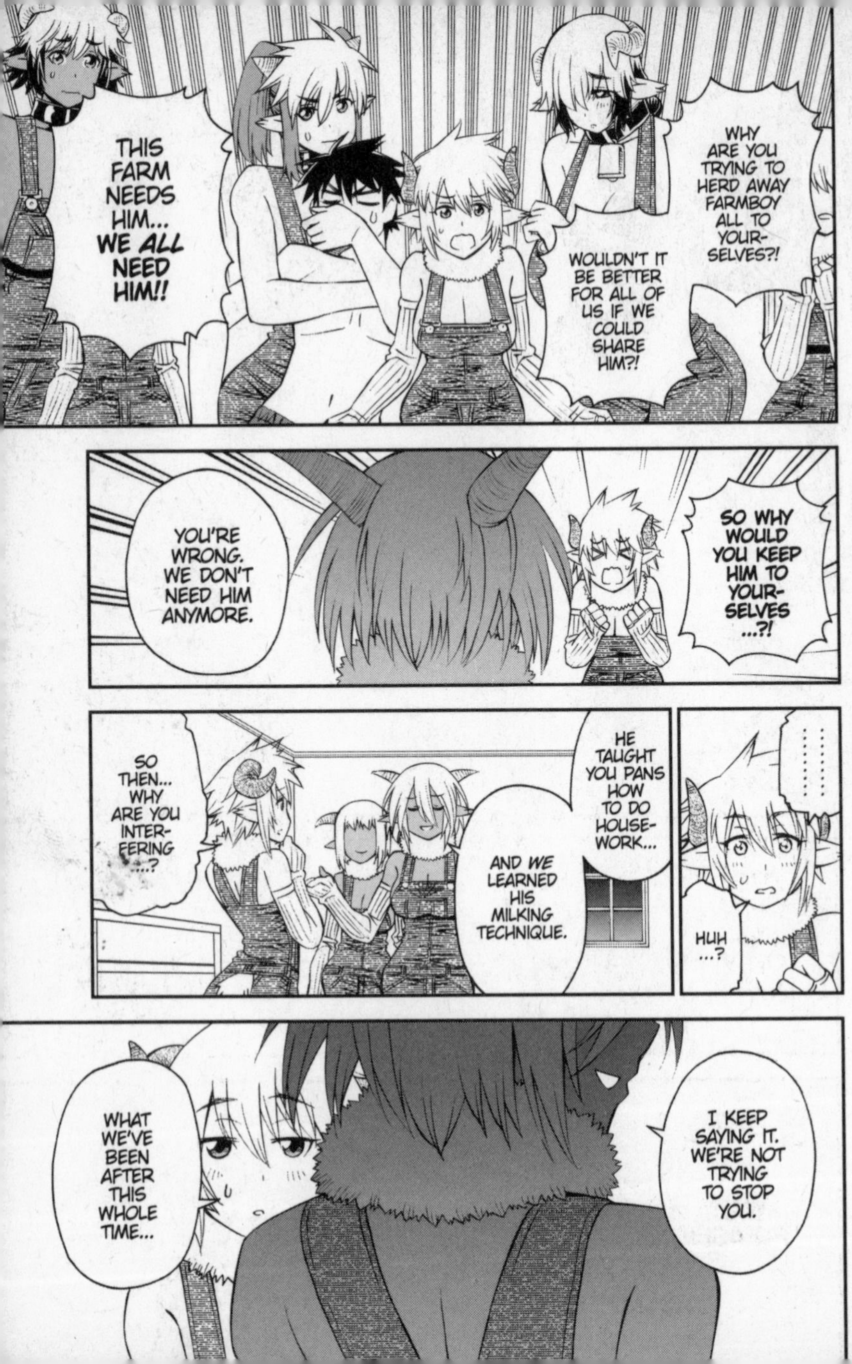
WHY ARE YOU TRYING TO HERD AWAY FARMBOY ALL TO YOUR-SELVES?!
WOULDN'T IT BE BETTER FOR ALL OF US IF WE COULD SHARE HIM?!
THIS FARM NEEDS HIM... *WE ALL* NEED HIM!!
SO WHY WOULD YOU KEEP HIM TO YOUR-SELVES ...?!
YOU'RE WRONG. WE DON'T NEED HIM ANYMORE.
......
HUH ...?
HE TAUGHT YOU PANS HOW TO DO HOUSE-WORK...
AND *WE* LEARNED HIS MILKING TECHNIQUE.
SO THEN... WHY ARE YOU INTER-FERING ...?
I KEEP SAYING IT. WE'RE NOT TRYING TO STOP YOU.
WHAT WE'VE BEEN AFTER THIS WHOLE TIME...

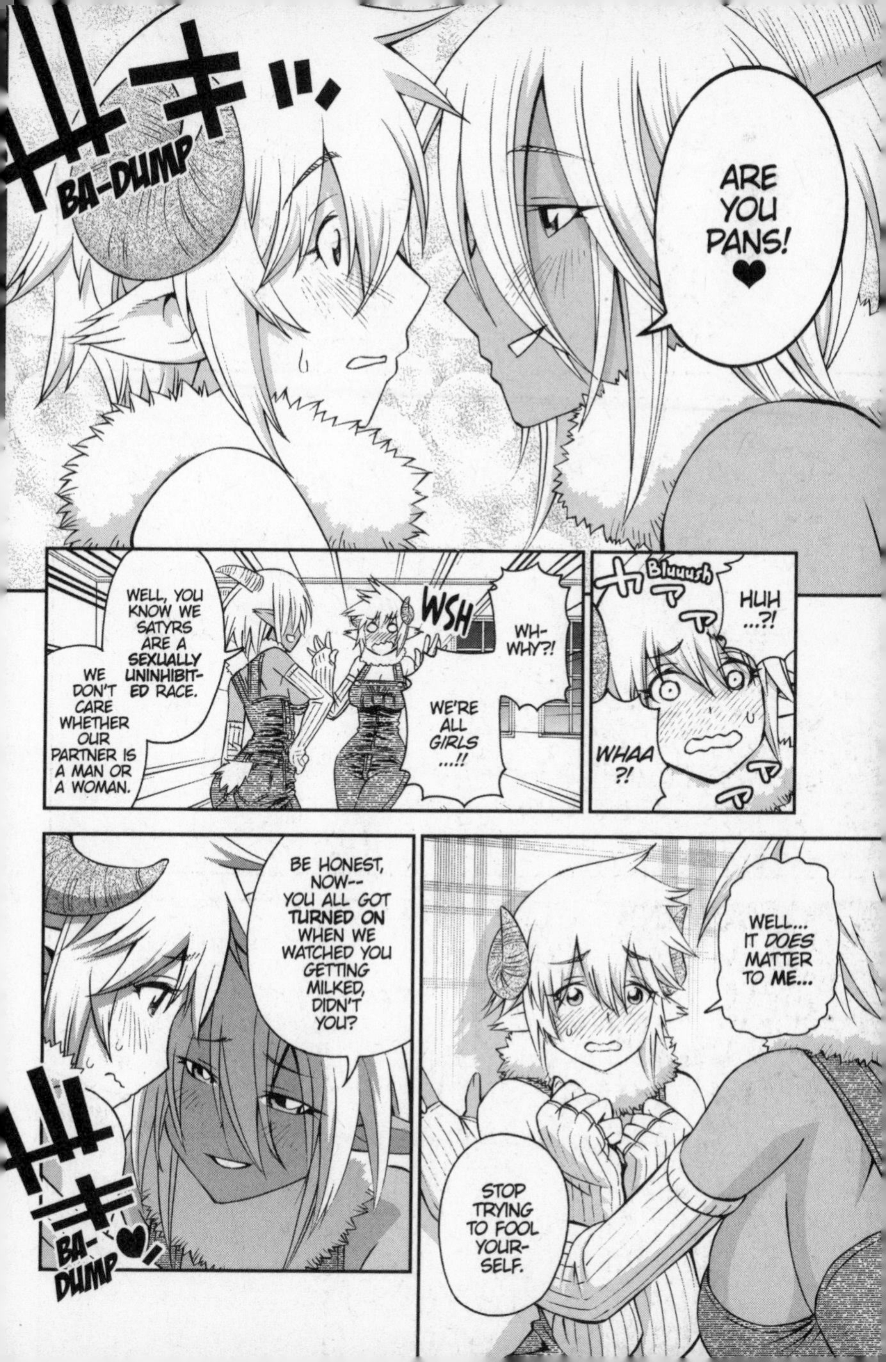
ARE YOU PANS! ❤
BA-DUMP
Bluuush
HUH ...?!
WHAA ?!
WH- WHY?!
WE'RE ALL GIRLS ...!!
WSH
WELL, YOU KNOW WE SATYRS ARE A SEXUALLY UNINHIBIT-ED RACE.
WE DON'T CARE WHETHER OUR PARTNER IS A MAN OR A WOMAN.
WELL... IT DOES MATTER TO ME...
STOP TRYING TO FOOL YOUR-SELF.
BE HONEST, NOW-- YOU ALL GOT TURNED ON WHEN WE WATCHED YOU GETTING MILKED, DIDN'T YOU?
BA-DUMP❤

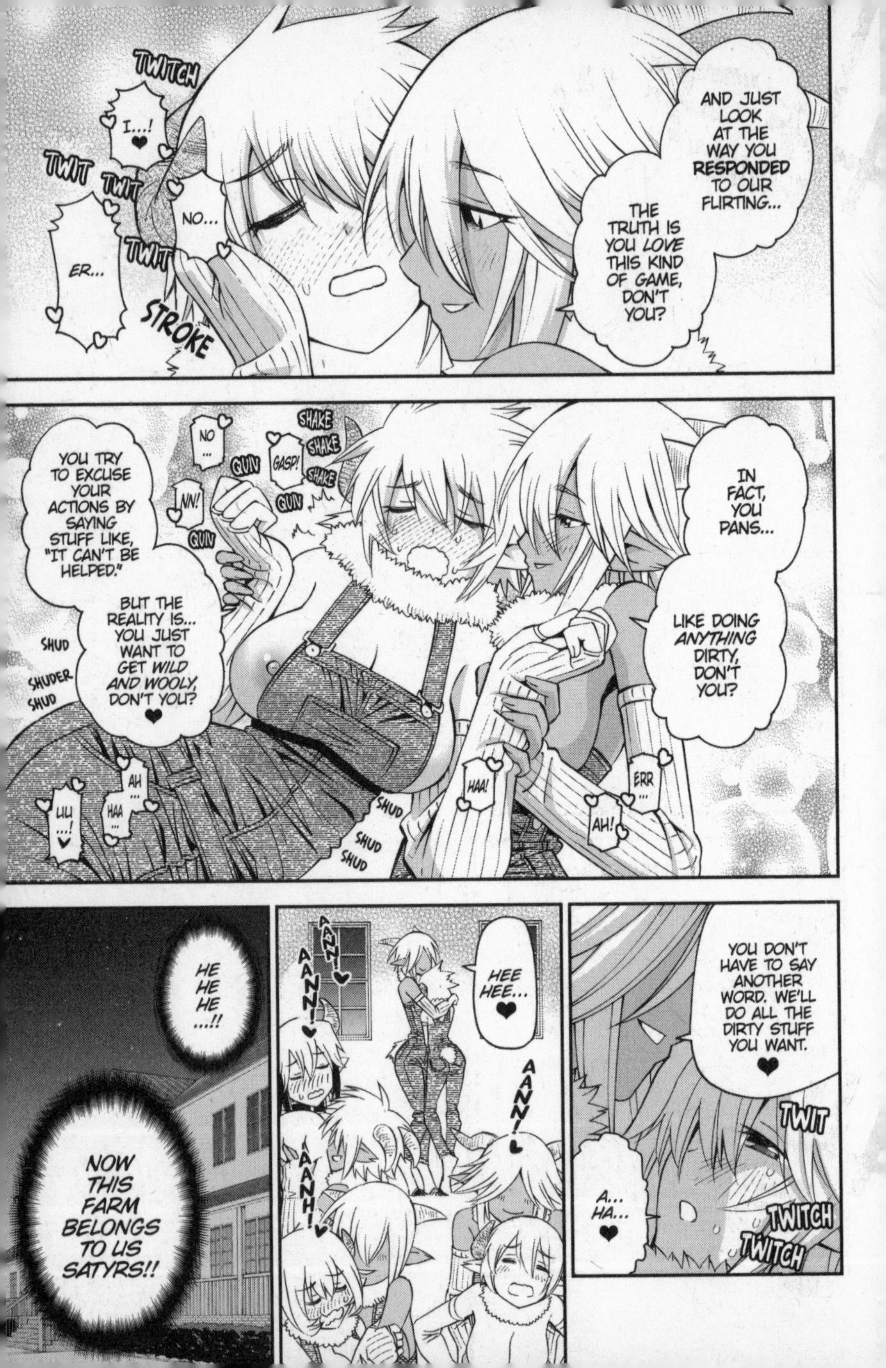
AND JUST LOOK AT THE WAY YOU RESPONDED TO OUR FLIRTING...
THE TRUTH IS YOU *LOVE* THIS KIND OF GAME, DON'T YOU?
TWITCH
I...!
NO...
TWIT
TWIT
TWIT
ER...
STROKE
IN FACT, YOU PANS...
LIKE DOING *ANYTHING* DIRTY, DON'T YOU?
SHAKE
SHAKE
SHAKE
GASP!
NO ...
QUIV
QUIV
NN!
QUIV
YOU TRY TO EXCUSE YOUR ACTIONS BY SAYING STUFF LIKE, "IT CAN'T BE HELPED."
BUT THE REALITY IS... YOU JUST WANT TO GET *WILD AND WOOLY*, DON'T YOU?
SHUD
SHUDER
SHUD
ERR ...
AH!
HAA!
SHUD
SHUD
SHUD
AH ...
HAA ...
UU ...!
YOU DON'T HAVE TO SAY ANOTHER WORD. WE'LL DO ALL THE DIRTY STUFF YOU WANT.
TWIT
A... HA...
TWITCH
TWITCH
HEE HEE...
AANN!
AANN!
AANN!
AANN!
AANN!
AANH!
HE HE HE ...!!
NOW THIS FARM BELONGS TO US SATYRS!!

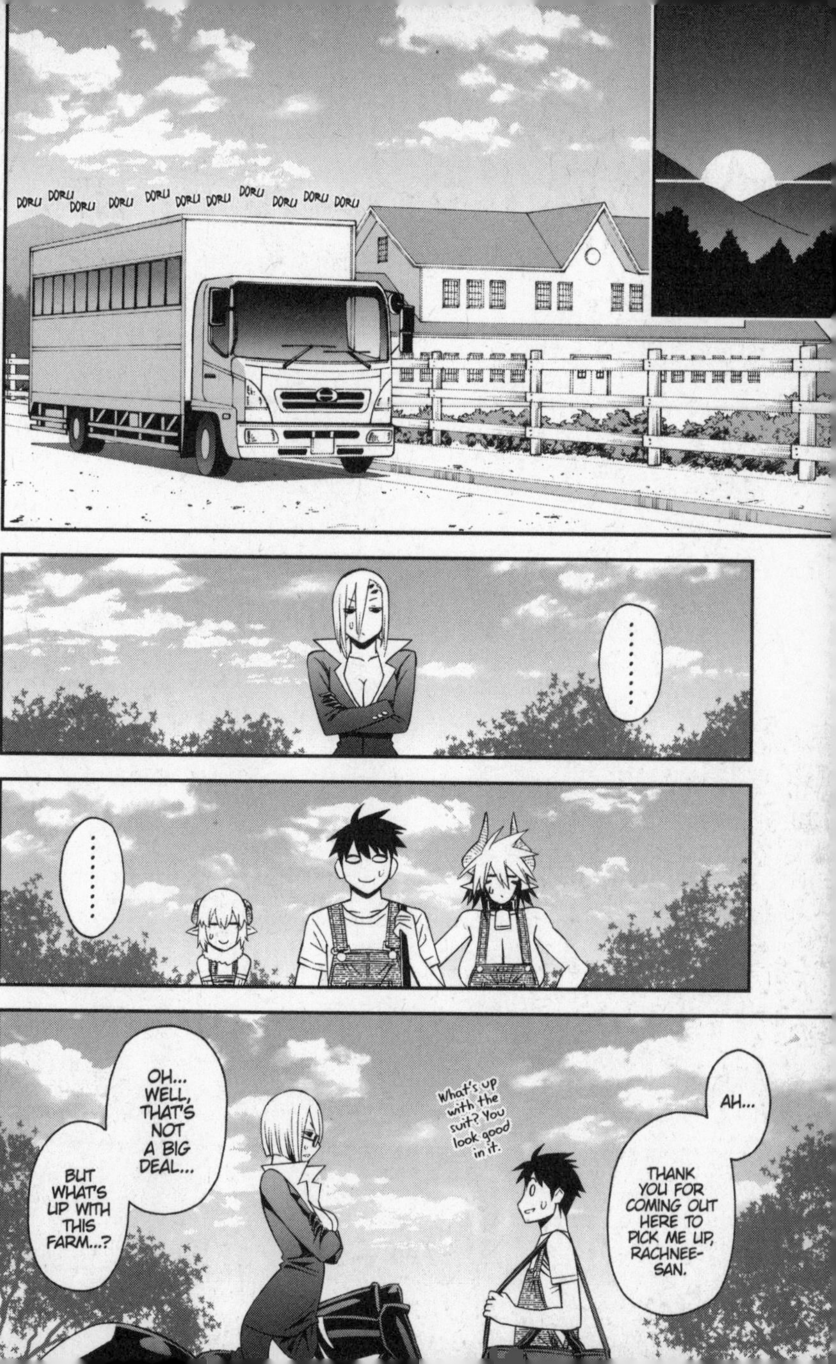
DORU DORU DORU DORU DORU DORU DORU DORU DORU DORU DORU
....
....
AH...
THANK YOU FOR COMING OUT HERE TO PICK ME UP, RACHNEE-SAN.
What's up with the suit? You look good in it.
OH... WELL, THAT'S NOT A BIG DEAL...
BUT WHAT'S UP WITH THIS FARM...?

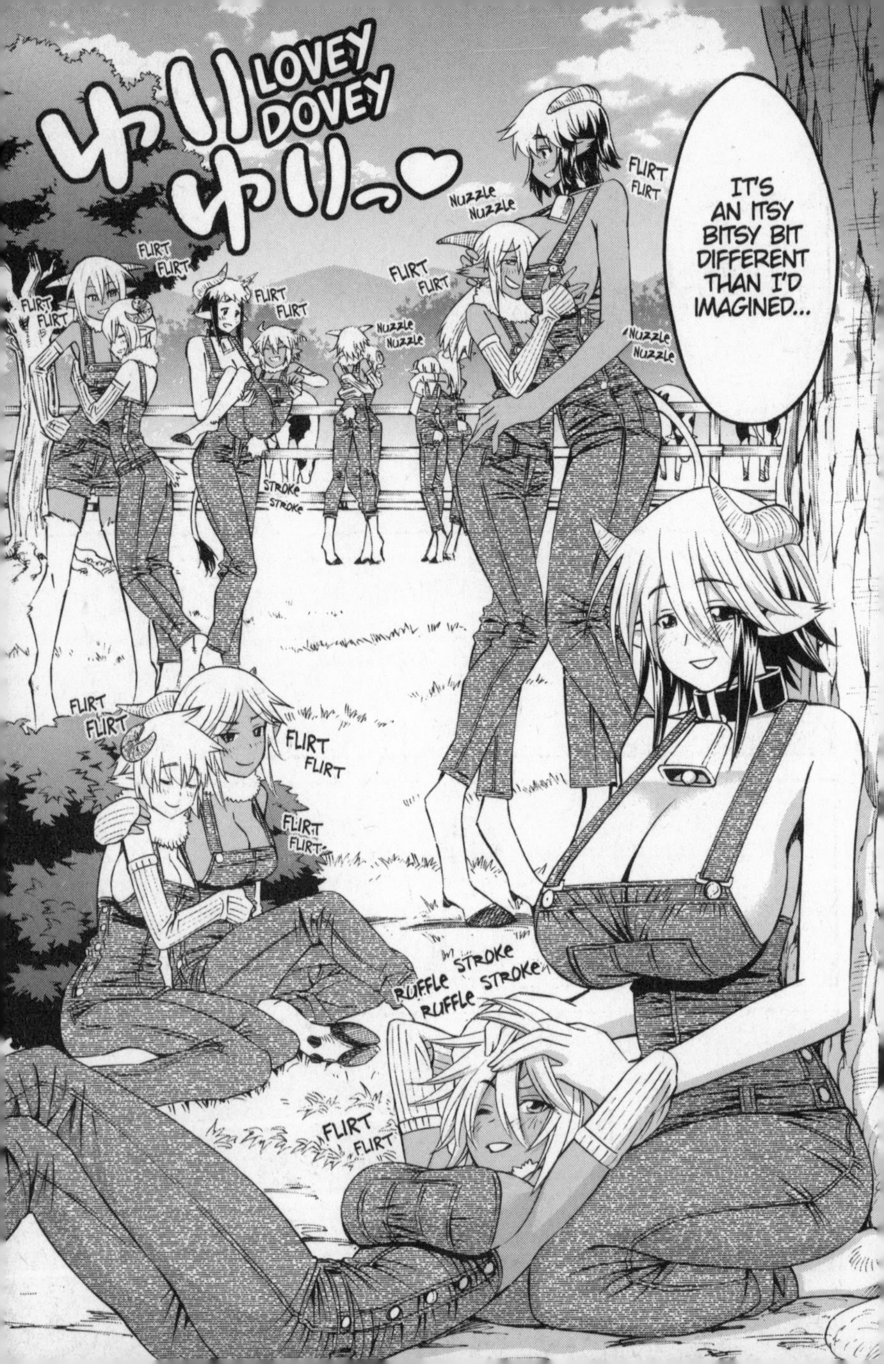
ゆりゆりっ♥
LOVEY DOVEY
IT'S AN ITSY BITSY BIT DIFFERENT THAN I'D IMAGINED...
FLIRT FLIRT
NUZZLE NUZZLE
FLIRT FLIRT
FLIRT FLIRT
FLIRT FLIRT
FLIRT FLIRT
NUZZLE NUZZLE
NUZZLE NUZZLE
STROKE STROKE
FLIRT FLIRT
FLIRT FLIRT
FLIRT FLIRT
STROKE STROKE
RUFFLE RUFFLE
FLIRT FLIRT

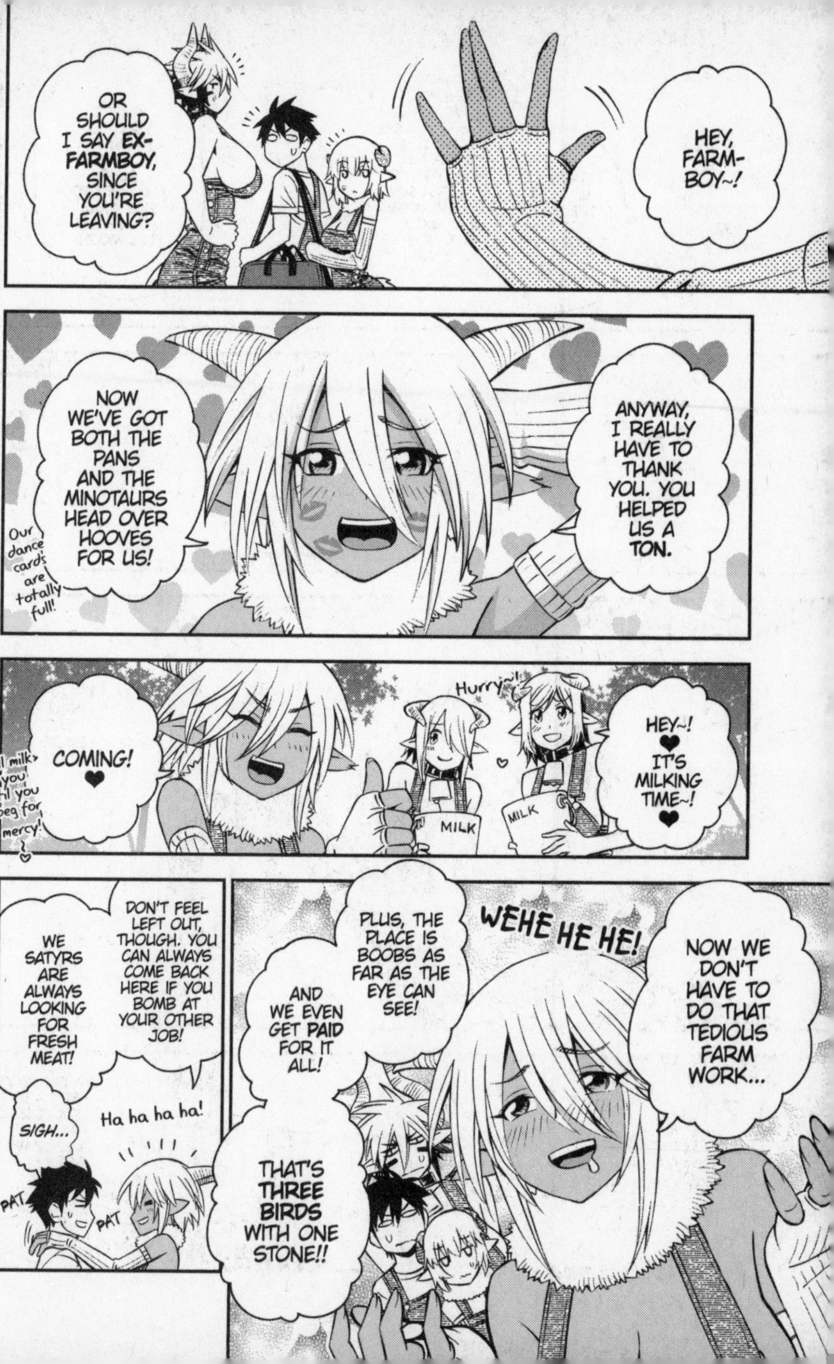
HEY, FARMBOY~!
OR SHOULD I SAY EX-FARMBOY, SINCE YOU'RE LEAVING?
ANYWAY, I REALLY HAVE TO THANK YOU. YOU HELPED US A TON.
NOW WE'VE GOT BOTH THE PANS AND THE MINOTAURS HEAD OVER HOOVES FOR US!
Our dance card's are totally full!
HEY~! ♥ IT'S MILKING TIME~! ♥
Hurry~!
MILK
MILK
COMING! ♥
I'll milk you 'til you beg for mercy! ~♥
NOW WE DON'T HAVE TO DO THAT TEDIOUS FARM WORK...
WEHE HE HE!
PLUS, THE PLACE IS BOOBS AS FAR AS THE EYE CAN SEE!
AND WE EVEN GET PAID FOR IT ALL!
THAT'S THREE BIRDS WITH ONE STONE!!
DON'T FEEL LEFT OUT, THOUGH. YOU CAN ALWAYS COME BACK HERE IF YOU BOMB AT YOUR OTHER JOB!
WE SATYRS ARE ALWAYS LOOKING FOR FRESH MEAT!
Ha ha ha ha!
SIGH...
PAT
PAT

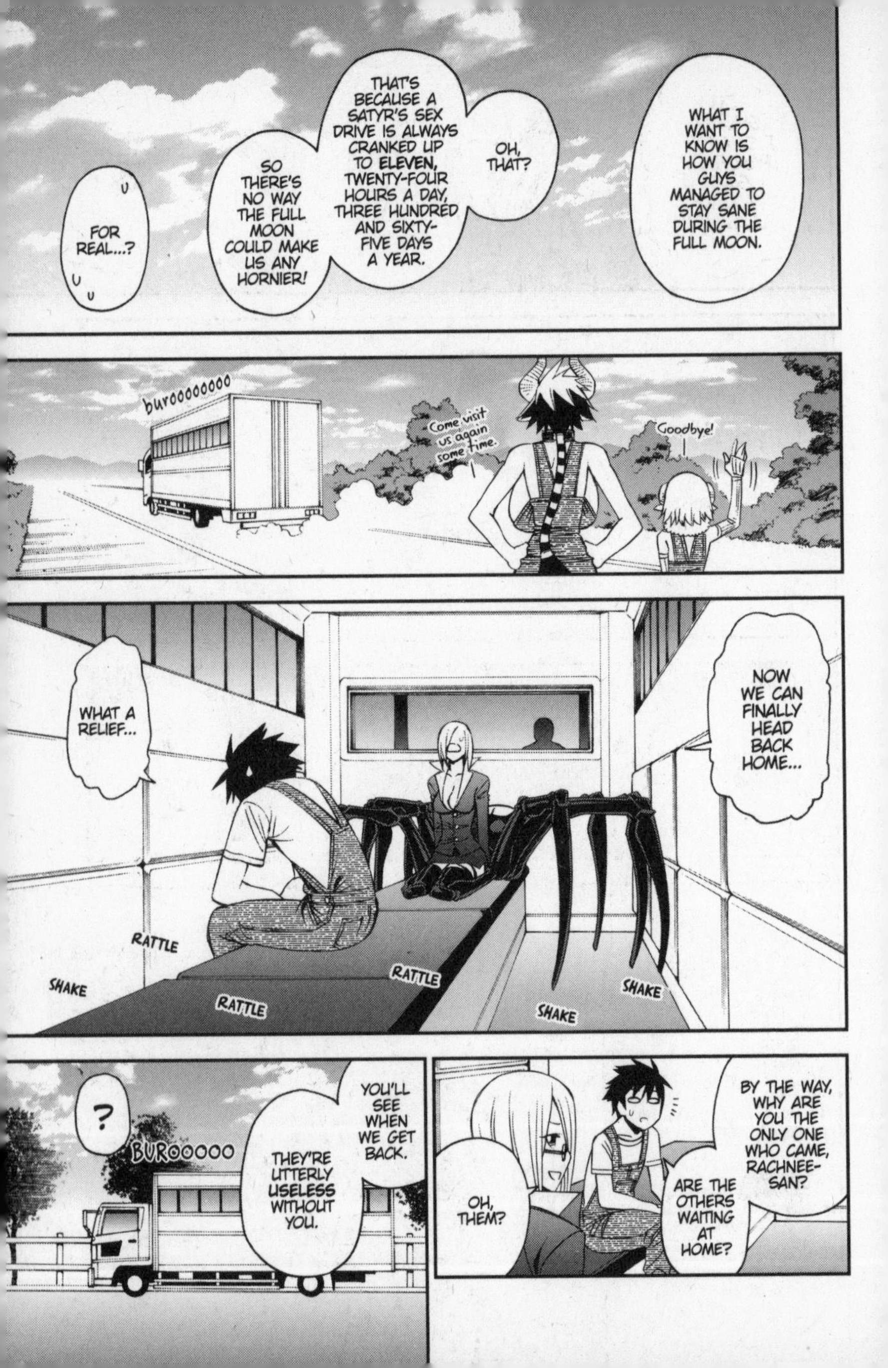
WHAT I WANT TO KNOW IS HOW YOU GUYS MANAGED TO STAY SANE DURING THE FULL MOON.
OH, THAT?
THAT'S BECAUSE A SATYR'S SEX DRIVE IS ALWAYS CRANKED UP TO ELEVEN, TWENTY-FOUR HOURS A DAY, THREE HUNDRED AND SIXTY-FIVE DAYS A YEAR.
SO THERE'S NO WAY THE FULL MOON COULD MAKE US ANY HORNIER!
FOR REAL...?
Goodbye!
Come visit us again some time.
buroooooooo
NOW WE CAN FINALLY HEAD BACK HOME...
WHAT A RELIEF...
SHAKE
SHAKE
RATTLE
RATTLE
RATTLE
SHAKE
BY THE WAY, WHY ARE YOU THE ONLY ONE WHO CAME, RACHNEE-SAN?
ARE THE OTHERS WAITING AT HOME?
OH, THEM?
YOU'LL SEE WHEN WE GET BACK.
THEY'RE UTTERLY USELESS WITHOUT YOU.
?
BUROOOOO

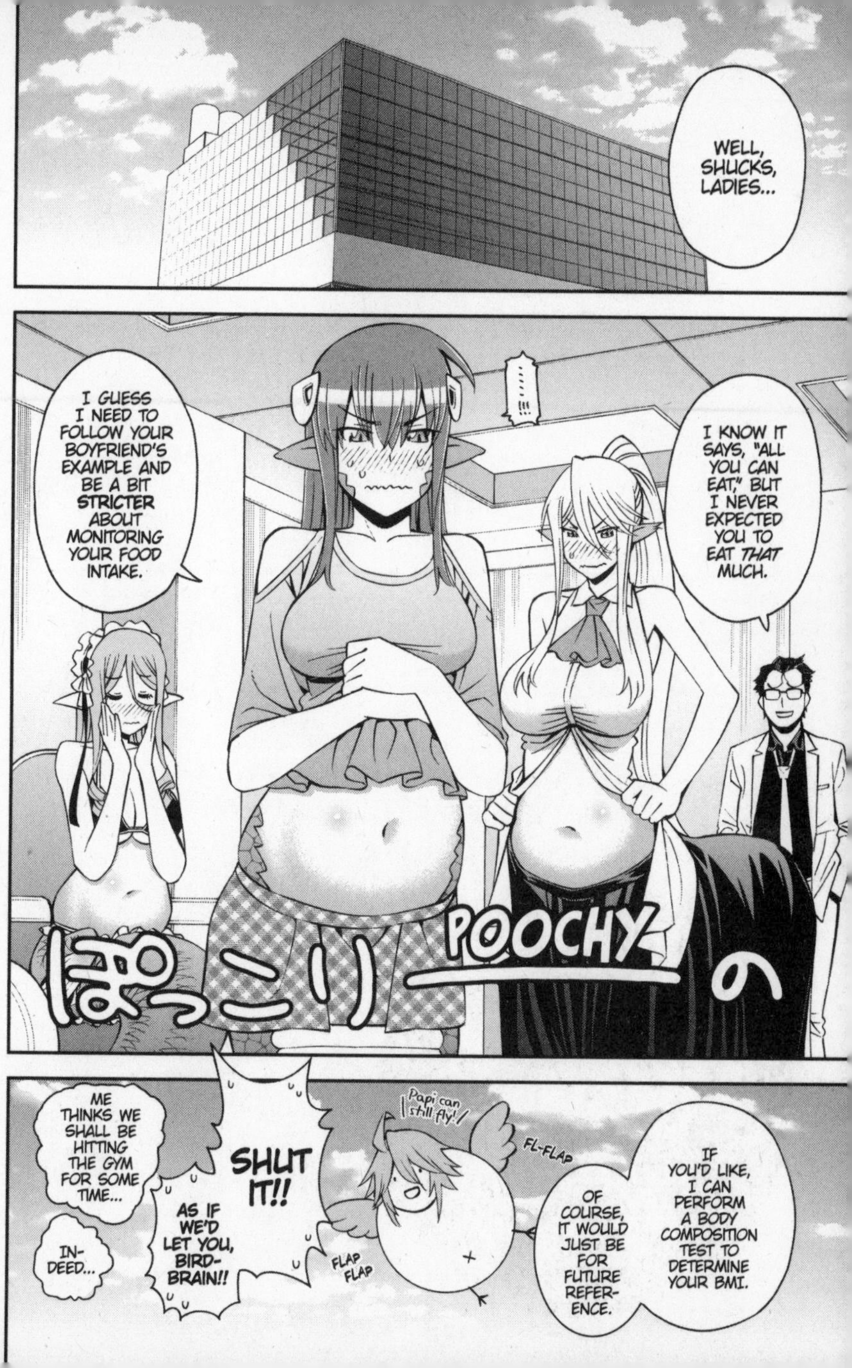

WELL, SHUCKS, LADIES...
I KNOW IT SAYS, "ALL YOU CAN EAT," BUT I NEVER EXPECTED YOU TO EAT *THAT* MUCH.
......!!!
I GUESS I NEED TO FOLLOW YOUR BOYFRIEND'S EXAMPLE AND BE A BIT **STRICTER** ABOUT MONITORING YOUR FOOD INTAKE.
POOCHY
ぽっこりーーの
IF YOU'D LIKE, I CAN PERFORM A BODY COMPOSITION TEST TO DETERMINE YOUR BMI.
OF COURSE, IT WOULD JUST BE FOR FUTURE REFERENCE.
Papi can still fly!
FL-FLAP
FLAP FLAP
SHUT IT!!
AS IF WE'D LET YOU, BIRD-BRAIN!!
ME THINKS WE SHALL BE HITTING THE GYM FOR SOME TIME...
IN-DEED...

Monster Musume

Everyday Life with Monster Girls

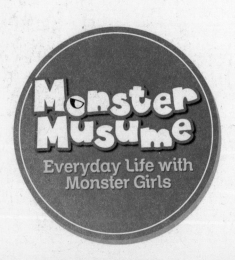

Farm Roster (Minotaurs)

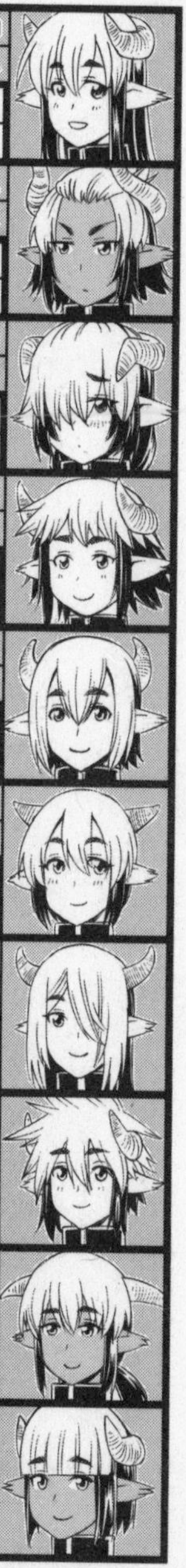

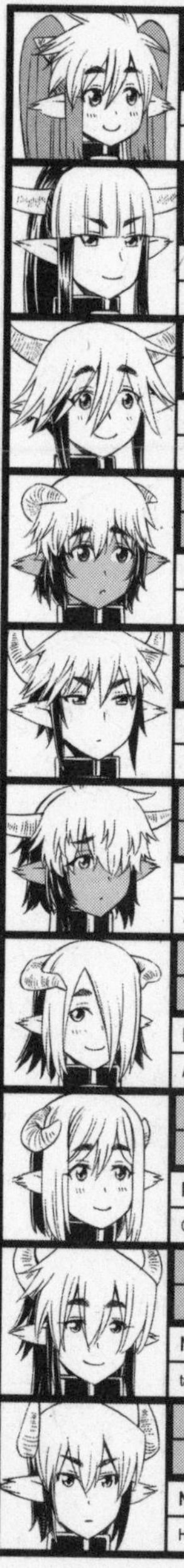

Name: Mil **Height:** 208cm **Measurements:** B134 W65 H96 **Cup Size:** N

A big sister to everyone. Looks over all the girls, and they look up to her. Scary when she gets mad.

Name: Cream **Height:** 185cm **Measurements:** B99 W59 H88 **Cup Size:** J

Drinks a liter of soy milk every day since she was told that it would make her breasts bigger.

Name: Cara **Height:** 220cm **Measurements:** B122 W69 H98 **Cup Size:** L

People think she's the strong, silent type, but in fact she has a communication disorder. Is fond of Urt.

Name: Chizu **Height:** 217cm **Measurements:** B127 W67 H95 **Cup Size:** M

Always straight to the point and has a somewhat outdated way of speaking due to watching a lot of period piece movies.

Name: Urt **Height:** 202cm **Measurements:** B150 W64 H94 **Cup Size:** Q

Has the largest breasts of anyone on the farm. Has recently noticed Cara watching her a lot and is a little freaked out.

Name: Cheda **Height:** 205cm **Measurements:** B129 W62 H97 **Cup Size:** N

Has a huge sweet tooth. Secretly planning a walking tour of the entire nation's dairy sweets.

Name: Camembert **Height:** 201cm **Measurements:** B105 W64 H95 **Cup Size:** K

Doesn't have much sense of taste, so she often snacks on corn intended for the livestock.

Name: Cotta **Height:** 208cm **Measurements:** B113 W66 H95 **Cup Size:** K

A member of the farm's tabletop RPG group, she often acts as DM but would prefer to play as a party member.

Name: Emmenta **Height:** 207cm **Measurements:** B113 W66 H95 **Cup Size:** K

A proud otaku, she often watches anime on the break room TV.

Name: Zola **Height:** 215cm **Measurements:** B126 W69 H108 **Cup Size:** M

Though she looks tough, she's surprisingly terrified of bugs. Cannot so much as approach a bug 3cm in size or larger.

Name: Ruyèr **Height:** 203cm **Measurements:** B124 W69 H108 **Cup Size:** M

Makes a lot of jerky as a hobby. Renowned for her ability to hold her liquor.

Name: Tilto **Height:** 203cm **Measurements:** B131 W62 H94 **Cup Size:** O

A closet otaku. She wants to talk to Emmenta about otaku things, but can't bring herself to do so.

Name: Raclette **Height:** 212cm **Measurements:** B113 W68 H98 **Cup Size:** K

A drinker, her favorite cocktail is the "Cowboy," which is a mix of whisky and cream.

Name: Zarella **Height:** 206cm **Measurements:** B107 W63 H97 **Cup Size:** K Cup

All about DIY, her motto is, "If you're gonna buy something, make it instead." Loves going to home supplies stores.

Name: Goda **Height:** 216cm **Measurements:** B123 W70 H103 **Cup Size:** M

A giant lush and troublemaker. Once she starts drinking, she keeps going until she throws up.

Name: Ricotta **Height:** 199cm **Measurements:** B109 W63 H95 **Cup Size:** K

Often plays video games in her free time. Her favorite games are farm simulators.

Name: Pone **Height:** 210cm **Measurements:** B115 W66 H99 **Cup Size:** L

Loves taking baths. Is sure to visit her favorite local bathing facility on days off.

Name: Parmino **Height:** 213cm **Measurements:** B120 W66 H100 **Cup Size:** L | A member of the tabletop RPG group. Focuses solely on actions that will please the whole party, making it hard for the story to progress.

Name: Quark **Height:** 200cm **Measurements:** B116 W64 H97 **Cup Size:** L | Hooked on online social network games, she can't stop playing gachas. She recently blew a lot of time trying to earn a high-rank prize, only to fail.

Name: Reggiano **Height:** 212cm **Measurements:** B117 W65 H99 **Cup Size:** L

Has a driver's license and acts as everyone's chauffer on days off. Parmino's elder sister.

Farm Roster (Pans & Satyrs)

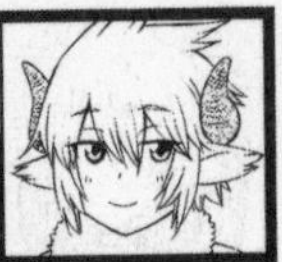

Name: Freesia **Height:** 163cm **Measurements:** B88 W56 H86 **Cup Size:** F

A late riser, she can't be bothered to groom herself. Her hairstyle is 100% bedhead.

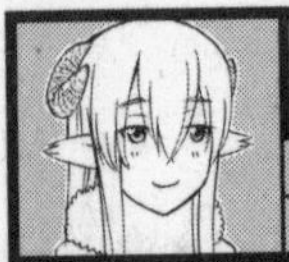

Name: Sappho **Height:** 165cm **Measurements:** B91 W59 H88 **Cup Size:** G

Gets her hair straightened once a month to maintain her beloved hairstyle.

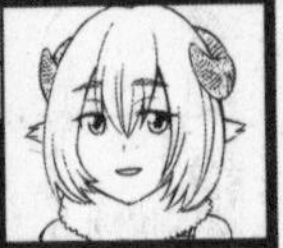

Name: Charolai **Height:** 160cm **Measurements:** B85 W54 H83 **Cup Size:** E

More interested in growing crops than raising livestock. Is having a hard time deciding what career she should pursue.

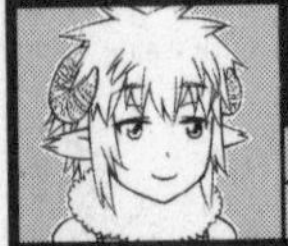

Name: Chevio **Height:** 157cm **Measurements:** B88 W60 H85 **Cup Size:** F

Sleeps an average of eleven hours per day. Often takes naps standing up even when she's working.

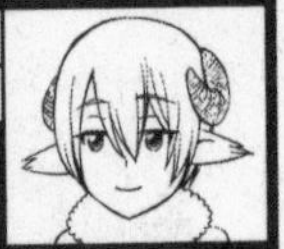

Name: Karak **Height:** 155cm **Measurements:** B84 W56 H84 **Cup Size:** E

Aspires to be an agricultural engineer. She's currently designing a new kind of milking machine in her spare time.

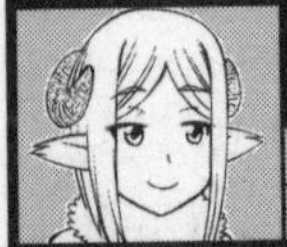

Name: Texl **Height:** 162cm **Measurements:** B89 W56 H87 **Cup Size:** F

A member of the tabletop RPG group. She's a newbie to role-playing and still isn't comfortable with it.

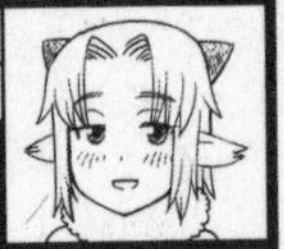

Name: Corriedal **Height:** 148cm **Measurements:** B80 W51 H84 **Cup Size:** D

The youngest on the farm. Everyone treats her like a beloved little sister.

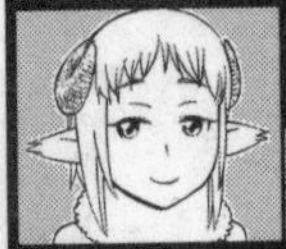

Name: Rom **Height:** 168cm **Measurements:** B93 W61 H90 **Cup Size:** G

Although she's skinny, she eats more than a minotaur. Her favorite food is potato salad.

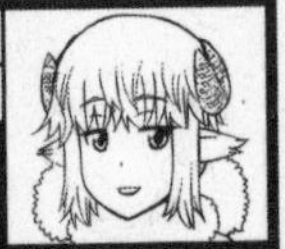

Name: Drys **Height:** 159cm **Measurements:** B88 W60 H86 **Cup Size:** F

Skilled at knitting, but recently she's become passionate about making wool felt dolls.

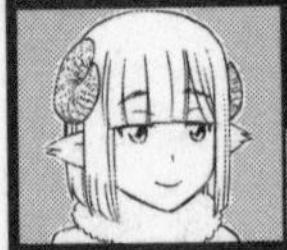

Name: Cacasia **Height:** 155cm **Measurements:** B89 W59 H91 **Cup Size:** G

Her hobby is watching movies, but there are no theaters nearby. Her favorite movie is *The Silence of the Lambs.*

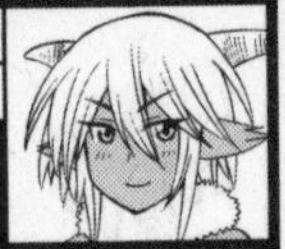

Name: Saane **Height:** 168cm **Measurements:** B94 W59 H85 **Cup Size:** H

The most sexual of any girl on the farm. She's perfectly happy with either boys or girls, but has a slight preference for boys.

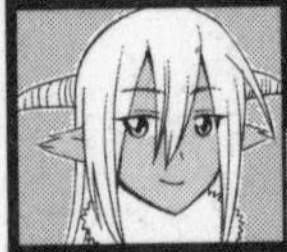

Name: Cashmere **Height:** 173cm **Measurements:** B91 W56 H87 **Cup Size:** G

Has beautiful platinum blonde hair. Believes the secret to hair care is increasing one's sex drive.

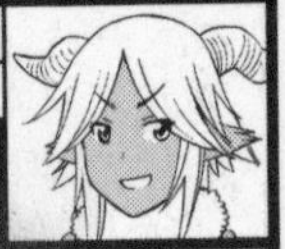

Name: Tokara **Height:** 163cm **Measurements:** B88 W58 H88 **Cup Size:** F

Has proven her stamina both at work and in bed. Focuses more on number of partners than on technique.

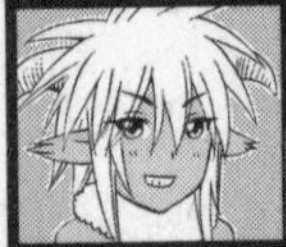

Name: Toggen **Height:** 171cm **Measurements:** B93 W56 H86 **Cup Size:** H | A master of all things technical, she can grasp the knack of just about anything. Focuses more on technique than on number of partners.

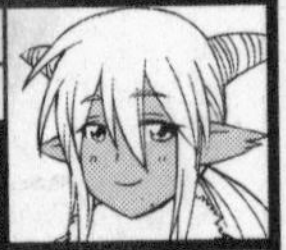

Name: Shiba **Height:** 166cm **Measurements:** B86 W56 H87 **Cup Size:** E

Naïve and retiring--for a satyr, but still very lusty.

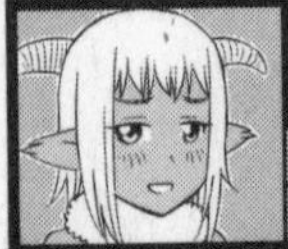

Name: Nubi **Height:** 169cm **Measurements:** B100 W60 H92 **Cup Size:** I

Has the largest breasts of any of the satyrs. Cream considers her a rival.

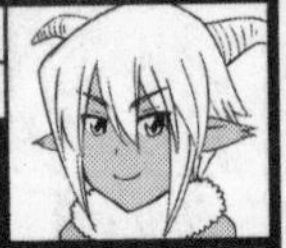

Name: Jamuna **Height:** 170cm **Measurements:** B95 W60 H89 **Cup Size:** H

A member of the tabletop RPG group. Loves to wank the rules and often upsets the DM.

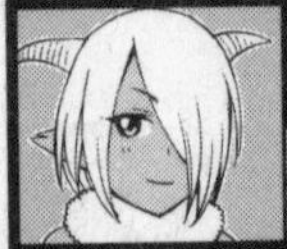

Name: Alba **Height:** 162cm **Measurements:** B88 W55 H87 **Cup Size:** F

A member of the tabletop RPG group. Very lucky with the dice, and frequently uses this to ruin the DM's plans.

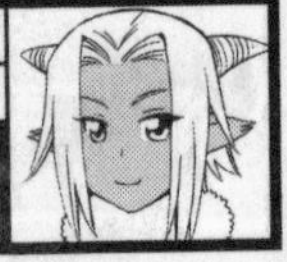

Name: Ankara **Height:** 169cm **Measurements:** B92 W59 H87 **Cup Size:** G

Came to Japan after being enraptured by the *Edo 48* (the Japanese *Kama Sutra*). Also reads the *Kama Sutra* religiously.

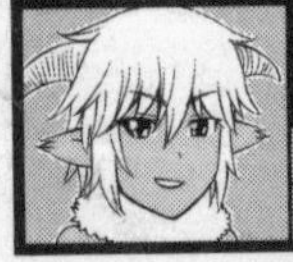

Name: Boer **Height:** 172cm **Measurements:** B90 W56 H89 **Cup Size:** F

Loves being up high and can't help climbing things. Gets excited when she's up high.

Milk Pudding

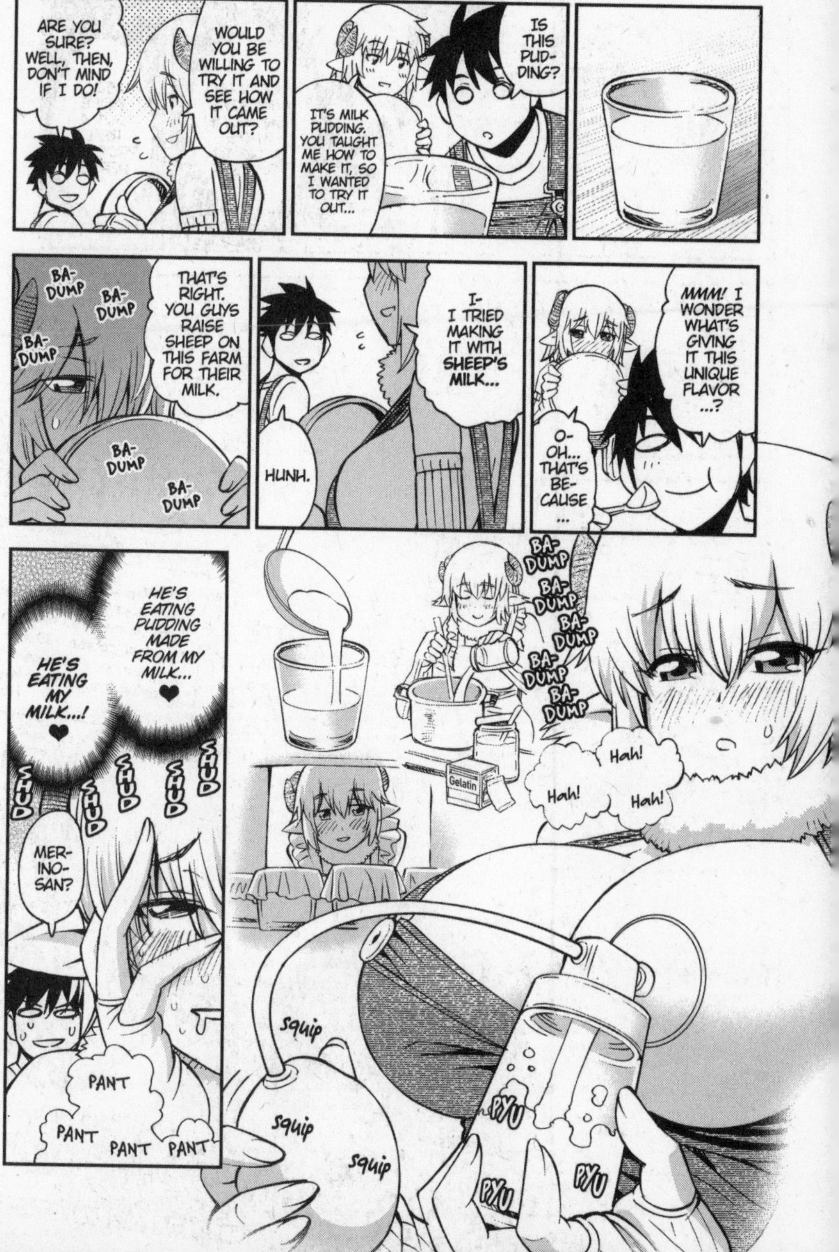
IS THIS PUD-DING?
IT'S MILK PUDDING. YOU TAUGHT ME HOW TO MAKE IT, SO I WANTED TO TRY IT OUT...
WOULD YOU BE WILLING TO TRY IT AND SEE HOW IT CAME OUT?
ARE YOU SURE? WELL, THEN, DON'T MIND IF I DO!
MMM! I WONDER WHAT'S GIVING IT THIS UNIQUE FLAVOR...?
O-OH... THAT'S BE-CAUSE...
I- I TRIED MAKING IT WITH SHEEP'S MILK...
HUNH.
THAT'S RIGHT. YOU GUYS RAISE SHEEP ON THIS FARM FOR THEIR MILK.
BA-DUMP BA-DUMP BA-DUMP BA-DUMP BA-DUMP
BA-DUMP BA-DUMP BA-DUMP BA-DUMP BA-DUMP
Gelatin
Hah! Hah! Hah!
squip squip squip
PYU PYU PYU
HE'S EATING PUDDING MADE FROM MY MILK... ❤
HE'S EATING MY MILK...! ❤
SHUD SHUD SHUD SHUD SHUD SHUD
MER-INO-SAN?
PANT PANT PANT PANT

Who's Milking Who?

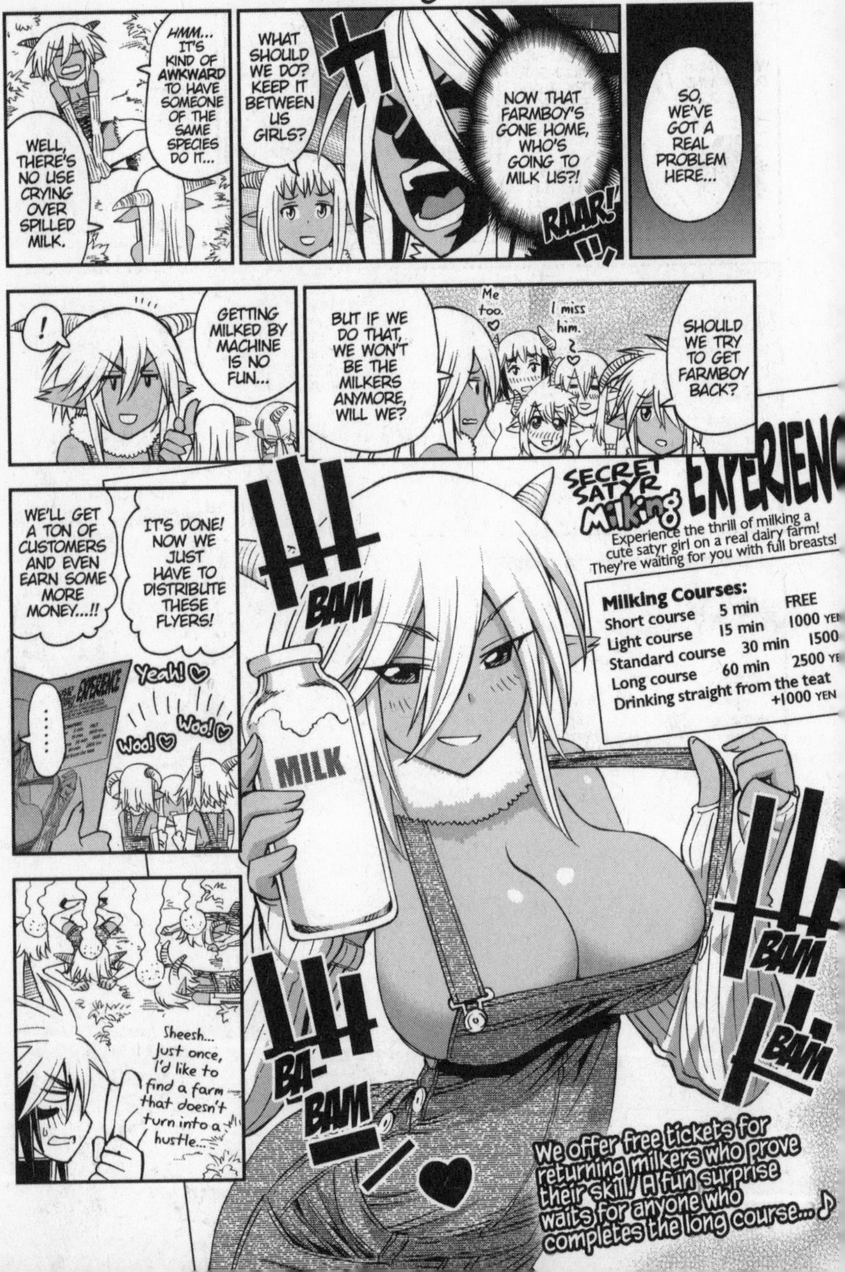

SO, WE'VE GOT A REAL PROBLEM HERE...
NOW THAT FARMBOY'S GONE HOME, WHO'S GOING TO MILK US?!
RAAR!!
WHAT SHOULD WE DO? KEEP IT BETWEEN US GIRLS?
HMM... IT'S KIND OF AWKWARD TO HAVE SOMEONE OF THE SAME SPECIES DO IT...
WELL, THERE'S NO USE CRYING OVER SPILLED MILK.
SHOULD WE TRY TO GET FARMBOY BACK?
I miss him.
Me too.
BUT IF WE DO THAT, WE WON'T BE THE MILKERS ANYMORE, WILL WE?
GETTING MILKED BY MACHINE IS NO FUN...
!
BAM
SECRET SATYR Milking EXPERIENC
Experience the thrill of milking a cute satyr girl on a real dairy farm! They're waiting for you with full breasts!
Milking Courses:
Short course 5 min FREE
Light course 15 min 1000 YEN
Standard course 30 min 1500
Long course 60 min 2500 YE
Drinking straight from the teat +1000 YEN
MILK
BAM
BAM
BA-BAM
We offer free tickets for returning milkers who prove their skill! A fun surprise waits for anyone who completes the long course...♪
IT'S DONE! NOW WE JUST HAVE TO DISTRIBUTE THESE FLYERS!
WE'LL GET A TON OF CUSTOMERS AND EVEN EARN SOME MORE MONEY...!!
Yeah!
Woo!
Woo!
......
Sheesh... Just once, I'd like to find a farm that doesn't turn into a hustle...

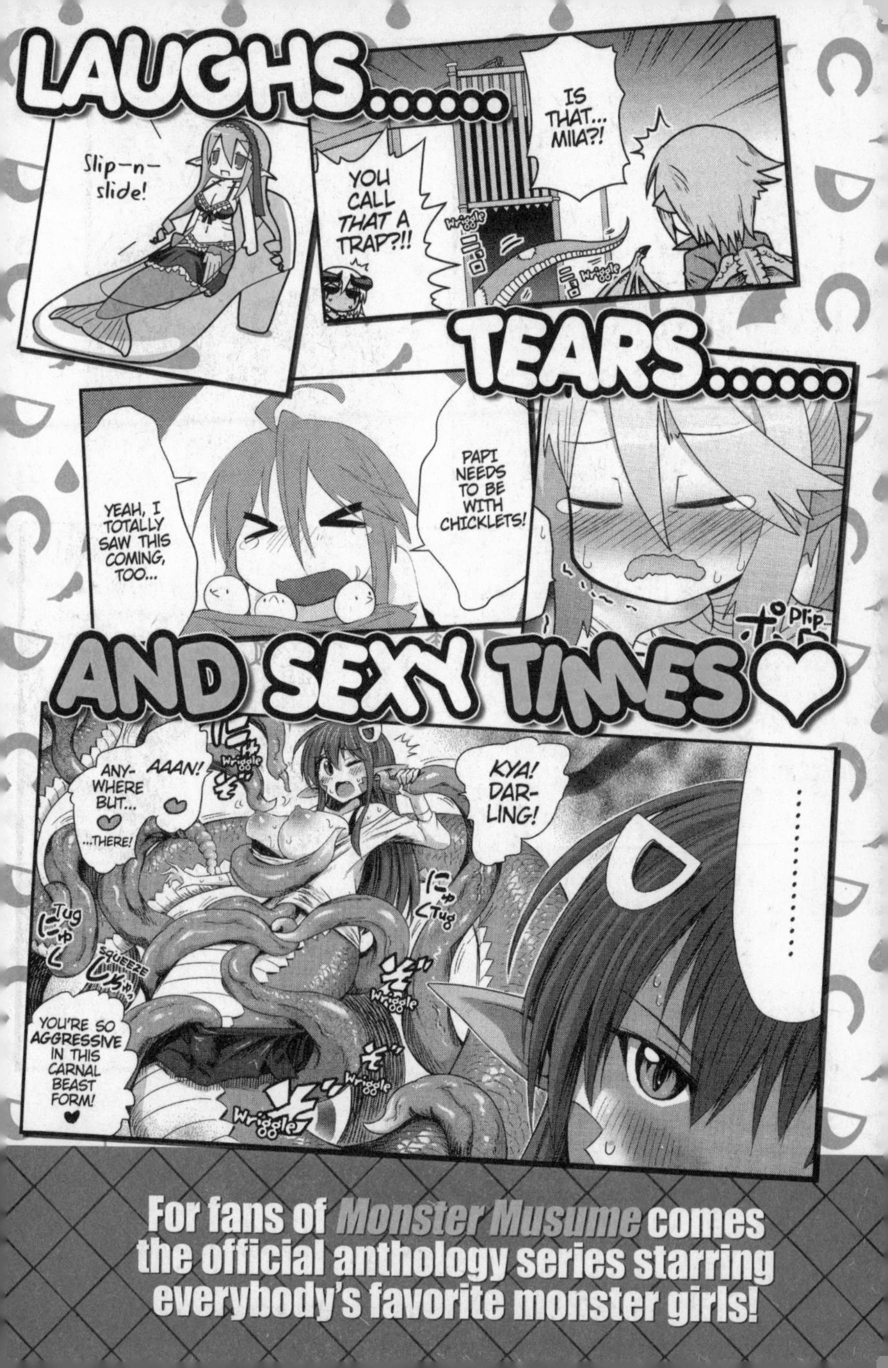
LAUGHS.......
IS THAT... MIIA?!
YOU CALL THAT A TRAP?!!
Wriggle
Wriggle
Slip-n-slide!
TEARS.......
Drip...
PAPI NEEDS TO BE WITH CHICKLETS!
YEAH, I TOTALLY SAW THIS COMING, TOO...
AND SEXY TIMES ♥
......
KYA! DARLING!
Tug
Wriggle
AAAN!
ANY-WHERE BUT... ♥ ...THERE!
Wriggle
Tug
Squeeze
Wriggle
Wriggle
YOU'RE SO AGGRESSIVE IN THIS CARNAL BEAST FORM! ♥

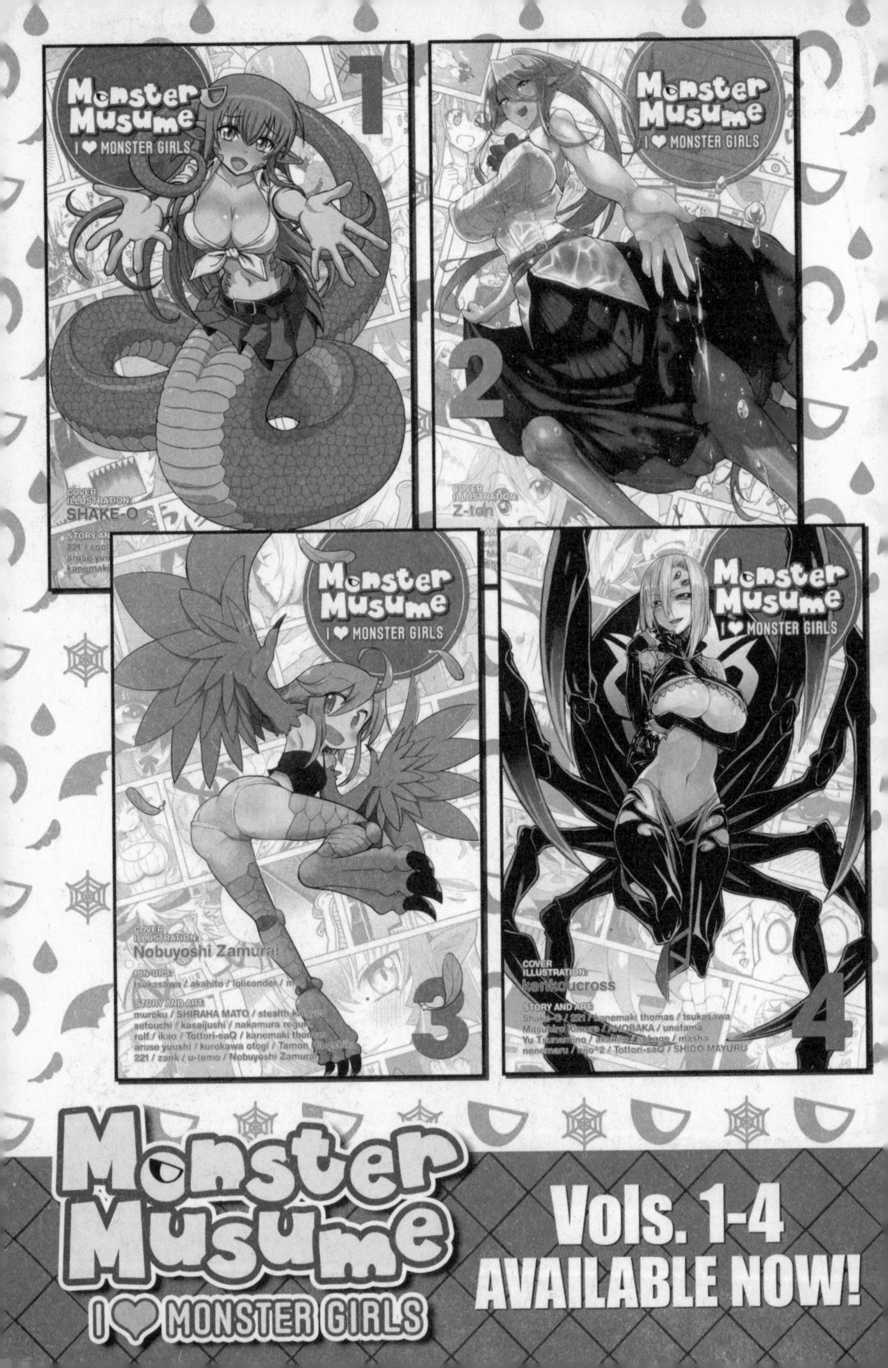
Monster Musume
I ♥ MONSTER GIRLS
1
COVER ILLUSTRATION:
SHAKE-O
Monster Musume
I ♥ MONSTER GIRLS
2
COVER ILLUSTRATION:
Z-ton
Monster Musume
I ♥ MONSTER GIRLS
3
COVER ILLUSTRATION:
Nobuyoshi Zamurai
Monster Musume
I ♥ MONSTER GIRLS
4
COVER ILLUSTRATION:
kenkoucross
Monster Musume
I ♥ MONSTER GIRLS
Vols. 1-4
AVAILABLE NOW!

Monster Musume

Everyday Life with Monster Girls

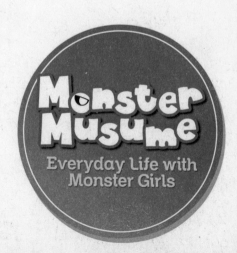

SEVEN SEAS ENTERTAIN

Monster M

story and art by **OKAYADO**

VOLUME 14

TRANSLATION
Ryan Peterson

ADAPTATION
Shanti Whitesides

LETTERING AND RETOUCH
Meaghan Tucker

LOGO DESIGN
Courtney Williams

COVER DESIGN
Nicky Lim

PROOFREADER
Janet Houck

EDITOR
Jenn Grunigen

PRODUCTION ASSISTANT
CK Russell

PRODUCTION MANAGER
Lissa Pattillo

EDITOR-IN-CHIEF
Adam Arnold

PUBLISHER
Jason DeAngelis

MONSTER MUSUME NO IRU NICHIJO VOLUME 14

Originally published in Japan in 2018 by TOKUMA SHOTEN PUBLISHING CO., LTD., Tokyo. English translation rights arranged with TOKUMA SHOTEN PUBLISHING CO., LTD., Tokyo, through TOHAN CORPORATION, Tokyo.

ISBN: 978-1-626928-31-2

Printed in Canada

First Printing: November 2018

10 9 8 7 6 5 4 3 2 1

FOLLOW US ONLINE: ***www.sevenseasentertainment.com***

READING DIRECTIONS

This book reads from ***right to left***, Japanese style. If this is your first time reading manga, you start reading from the top right panel on each page and take it from there. If you get lost, just follow the numbered diagram here. It may seem backwards at first, but you'll get the hang of it! Have fun!!

1
2
3
4
5
6
7
8
9

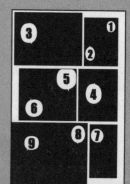